James Hunter

The Golden Treasury of the History,

topography, literature, science, art, and religion of the various countries of the globe, with biographies of their illustrious people

James Hunter

The Golden Treasury of the History,
topography, literature, science, art, and religion of the various countries of the globe, with biographies of their illustrious people

ISBN/EAN: 9783337427498

Printed in Europe, USA, Canada, Australia, Japan

Cover: Foto ©ninafisch / pixelio.de

More available books at **www.hansebooks.com**

QUEEN VICTORIA

THE

GOLDEN TREASURY

OF THE

HISTORY, TOPOGRAPHY, LITERATURE, SCIENCE, ART, AND RELIGION

OF THE

VARIOUS COUNTRIES OF THE GLOBE,

WITH

BIOGRAPHIES OF THEIR ILLUSTRIOUS PEOPLE.

BY

JAMES HUNTER, A.M.

SOLD ONLY BY SUBSCRIPTION.

PHILADELPHIA:
THAYER, MERRIAM & COMPANY, Limited.
1891.

INTRODUCTION.

THE study of History—including under this term not only a record of the great political events of different countries, but also of their customs, arts, sciences, literature, religion, and topography—has always had a special attraction for the well-constituted mind. Man is distinguished from the inferior animals as much by an intelligent curiosity as by any other endowment. It is this endowment, indeed, that prompts him to inquire into the unknown—to undertake perilous voyages of discovery, to push his researches into the secrets of nature, to make costly experiments in the domains of science and of art. But the poet has well said: "The proper study of mankind is man;" and in no way can this laudable spirit of inquiry be so legitimately gratified as by a study of the history of one's own and other countries, such as we now present.

If this be true generally, it applies with double force to our own time and country. The whole world is becoming knit together into one great family. Commerce and religion alike prompt us to regard all men as brethren. By means of the telegraphic wire and cable, information is now conveyed from clime to clime with the rapidity of thought, while the news from all lands is spread before the public daily by the periodical press. But these communications do not speak in the same way to all. To the man of culture all is intelligible and clear. He peruses them with pleasure, often with profit, and the information thus acquired takes its due place in his well-ordered mind, and, remaining fixed in his memory, is added to his store of knowledge. But there are many to whom such communications are all but valueless. They know little or nothing of the countries of which they read, and, as a consequence, news of them, or from them, is neither fully intelligible nor interesting to them. It does not amalgamate with anything previously in their minds, is imperfectly understood, and forgotten nearly as soon as read.

In America, especially, to which men flock from all parts of the world as to an asylum for the oppressed, no man can afford to be ignorant of the history and conditions of other lands. The uninformed man cannot take a proper position in an intelligent community; he feels afraid to express himself, and is humiliated and rendered unhappy by a sense of his inferiority.

It is with the view of putting it in the power of every inhabitant of this country to enroll himself in the former class that the following work has been compiled. The intelligent reader will perceive that it is not a mere bald record of dry details—a skeleton-history, in fact, as we sometimes find such publications to be—but that, while no fact of importance is omitted, it seizes more particularly on such salient events as are typical of the periods and countries described, and, by exhibiting these in fuller detail, endeavors to give the reader an insight into the life and modes of thought of the various peoples and times. With the object of enlivening the narrative and making it pleasing as well as instructive, appropriate illustrative poetical extracts are freely introduced, as well as interesting stories and legends. The topography of the different countries is fully exhibited and similarly treated. One feature well worthy of attention is the condensed reviews of the past and present state of the literature, religion, arts, and sciences of different countries, with brief biographies of the men who have most distinguished themselves in each department. The productions, industries, and resources of each land are fully shown, with its modes of government and present political situation. In short, the aim has been to overlook nothing that an intelligent reader will desire to learn concerning the countries treated. How that end has been attained it is for the generous American public to determine.

JAMES HUNTER.

ILLUSTRATIONS.

Title	PAGE
QUEEN VICTORIA	Frontispiece.
OXFORD, ENGLAND	11
CATHEDRAL OF YORK	13
WYCLIFFE	14
WESTMINSTER ABBEY	16
SUMMER SCENE IN ENGLAND	19
DRUIDICAL SACRIFICES	25
ALFRED THE GREAT IN HIS STUDY	31
BAPTISM OF CNUT	35
WILLIAM THE CONQUEROR	37
BURIAL OF WILLIAM THE CONQUEROR	40
WILLIAM II. (RUFUS)	41
HENRY I.	43
STEPHEN I.	44
HENRY II.	45
WARWICK CASTLE	46
MURDER OF THOMAS-A-BECKET	47
GATHERING OF CRUSADERS	50
RICHARD I. (CŒUR-DE-LION)	51
KING JOHN SWEARING VENGEANCE AGAINST THE BARONS	52
HENRY III.	54
EDWARD I. (LONGSHANKS)	56
A TOURNAMENT	57
EDWARD II.	59
THE TOWER OF LONDON	60
EDWARD III.	61
WINDSOR CASTLE FROM THE RIVER	64
CHAUCER: CHARACTERISTIC SCENES OF HIS TIME	65
RICHARD II.	68
COSTUMES OF RICHARD II.'s TIME	69
HENRY V.	73
HENRY VI.	74
MARGARET OF ANJOU AND THE ROBBER	76
EDWARD IV.	77
RICHARD III.	78
MURDER OF EDWARD IV.'s CHILDREN	79
EDWARD VI.	84
MARY I.	84
QUEEN ELIZABETH IN HER YOUTH	85
SIR FRANCIS DRAKE	86
SIR WALTER RALEIGH	87
SHAKESPEARE	88
CARRYING QUEEN ELIZABETH IN STATE	90
COSTUMES OF QUEEN ELIZABETH'S TIME	90
CHARLES I.	93
OLIVER CROMWELL	95
TRIAL OF CHARLES I.	96
EXECUTION OF CHARLES I.	97
MILTON DICTATING PARADISE LOST TO HIS DAUGHTER	101
CHARLES II.	102
WILLIAM III. (OF ORANGE)	104
COSTUMES, TIME OF WILLIAM AND MARY	105
QUEEN ANNE	106
COSTUMES OF ANNE'S TIME	107
LORD BYRON	113
PRINCE OF WALES	119
HOUSES OF PARLIAMENT, LONDON	123
PORTRAIT OF GLADSTONE	124
ST. PAUL'S CATHEDRAL, LONDON	127
IRISH JAUNTING-CAR	132
BESSBROOK LINEN MILLS AND VILLAGE, COUNTY ARMAGH, IRELAND	133
FATHER MATTHEW	135
ROSS CASTLE, KILLARNEY	136
MONUMENT TO DANIEL O'CONNELL	137
CHARLES STEWART PARNELL	138
BIRTHPLACE OF THOMAS MOORE	139
THE GIANT'S CAUSEWAY	140
OLIVER GOLDSMITH	142
CUSTOM HOUSE, DUBLIN	143
EDINBURGH	144
HOME OF ROBERT BURNS	145
ROBERT BURNS	150
JAMES WATT DISCOVERING THE POWER OF STEAM	151
"BRIGS O' AYR"	152
SIR WALTER SCOTT	153
THOMAS CARLYLE	154
SIR WILLIAM WALLACE	157
ROYAL REGALIA OF SCOTLAND	158
MARY STUART RECEIVING HER DEATH-SENTENCE	159
ST. AUGUSTINE, FLORIDA	161
SCENE IN CENTRAL AMERICA	163
PORTRAIT OF PIZARRO	165
SOUTH AMERICAN INDIANS	168
POPOCATEPETL	170
HIDALGO Y COSTELLO	172
BENITO JUAREZ, EX-PRESIDENT OF MEXICO	174
CYPRESS TREES AT CHAPULTEPEC	175
THE INCA HAUSCAR	176
BAY OF RIO DE JANEIRO	181
GALLERY OF DOM PEDRO I.	183
NIAGARA OF BRAZIL	187
TAIL-PIECE	188
HARBOR AND CITY OF QUEBEC	189
DEATH OF MONTCALM	192
THE THOUSAND ISLANDS	196
SCENE ON THE EASTERN COAST OF CANADA	198
THE CAPITOL AT WASHINGTON	200
PLYMOUTH ROCK	202
AN INDIAN ATTACK	203
PENN'S TREATY WITH THE INDIANS	205
PATRICK HENRY	211
LEXINGTON	212
DECLARATION OF INDEPENDENCE	215
ON THE WAR-PATH	217
GEORGE WASHINGTON	219
MOUNT VERNON	220
THE WHITE HOUSE; HOME OF THE PRESIDENTS	224
JOHN ADAMS	225
THOMAS JEFFERSON	226
JAMES MADISON	228
JAMES MONROE	229
JOHN QUINCY ADAMS	230
JOHN C. CALHOUN	231
A MORMON HOME	232
ANDREW JACKSON	232

3

ILLUSTRATIONS.

	PAGE		PAGE
Daniel Webster	233	Bismarck	351
Martin Van Buren	234	Von Moltke	353
General William H. Harrison	235	Crown Prince of Germany	356
John Tyler	236	Street in Vienna	357
James K. Polk	236	Napoleon and Louise	359
The Alamo, Mexico	237	Beethoven	360
Zachary Taylor	238	Glacier	362
Millard Fillmore	239	Novgorod	364
Franklin Pierce	240	Peter the Great	366
James Buchanan	241	Catherine the Great of Russia	368
Abraham Lincoln	242	Burning of Moscow	369
Vicksburg	243	Siege of Sebastopol	371
John Ericson	246	Alexander II.	372
Andrew Johnson	246	Reading Emancipation Proclamation	373
Indian Chief	248	Nihilist Printing Office	374
General Grant	249	Crossing the Steppes	375
Rutherford B. Hayes	250	Newsky Prospect	377
Samuel J. Tilden	251	Kremlin at Moscow	378
James A. Garfield	252	Cathedral at St. Basil	379
Chester A. Arthur	252	Odessa	380
General Hancock	253	Archimandrite	381
Stephen Grover Cleveland	255	Russian Nuns begging Alms	381
Giant Trees of California	256	Russian Family	382
Niagara Falls	256	Gold Mines, Siberia	383
Yosemite Valley	257	Siberian Dog-sledge	384
Switzerland of America	258	Constantinople	385
Point Chautauqua	259	Mosque	389
Tip-top House, Mount Washington	260	Alexander I. of Bulgaria	390
William Cullen Bryant	263	Dervishes	391
Henry Wadsworth Longfellow	264	Circassian	394
Birthplace of John Howard Payne	268	A Sultana's Room	395
Grand Canal, Venice	273	Remains of ruined Temple at Corinth	396
School of Vestal Virgins	277	Site of Troy	398
Statue of Julius Cæsar	281	Plato	402
Interior of St. Peter's, Rome	285	Aristotle	402
Raphael	287	King George I.	403
Galileo	289	View of Crete	404
Doge's Palace, Venice	290	Acropolis at Athens	405
Destruction of Pompeii	295	Tail-piece	406
Pope Pius IX.	296	The Pyramids	407
Guiseppe Garibaldi	297	Exterior of Temple of Isis	410
King Humbert IV.	298	Cairo	412
Angoulême	299	Doum Palms	416
Marie Antoinette	306	Moses' Well	417
Napoleon's Residence at St. Helena	307	Ferry of Kantara	418
Tomb of Napoleon I.	308	Egyptian Family	420
Blucher's March to Waterloo	309	A Street in Tunis	423
Porte St. Denis	310	Scenes in the Life of Dr. Livingstone	426
Column, Place Vendôme, Paris	311	Christmas at an African Station	427
Comte de Paris	312	Asiatic Types	429
General Boulanger	313	Birth of Christ	431
Royal Palace, Madrid	314	Church of the Holy Sepulchre	433
The Armada	317	Hillah, on the Euphrates	435
Spanish Priest	319	Avenue of Hindoo Temples	437
Bridge of Saragossa	320	Lucknow	440
King Alfonso XII.	322	Bombay	441
On the Coast of Norway	324	Hindoo Gods	443
The Vikings	325	Hindoo Musician	445
Queen Margaret awaiting the Attack of the Vitali	327	Hindoo Princess	447
		The Sacked Altar of Heaven, Pekin	449
Tycho Brahe	330	Chinese Hanging-Garden	451
Lake of Geneva	331	Interior of a Chinese Temple	452
Arnold von Winkelried at Sempach	335	Chinese Locomotion	454
John Calvin	336	Chinese Family	455
Belfry of Bruges	337	Chinese Children	457
Street in Ghent	338	Japanese Lady	458
Heidelberg Castle, from the Neckar	340	Japanese Family	460
Street in Berlin	342	Botanical Garden, Adelaide	462
Martin Luther	344	Ornithorhynchus	467
Mayence	346	Australian	468
First Printing-Press	347	Lake Rothe-Mahana	470
Copernicus	348	New Zealander	471
John Kepler	348	Dyaks of Borneo	474
Cologne Cathedral	350	A Volcanic Cone	475

CONTENTS.

INTRODUCTION . . . . .

ENGLAND.

ENGLAND TO THE TIME OF THE NORMAN CONQUEST.

Extent and physical aspect of England—Picturesque scenery—Homes of the poets—Agriculture, manufactures, and commerce—National debt—Army and navy—Religion of ancient Britain—Druidical sacrifices—Boadicea and her struggle with the Romans—Early British tribes and races—The story of Cædmon—Clothing and domestic habits of the earlier inhabitants of Great Britain—Scandinavian invasion—Alfred the Great—St. Dunstan and the Devil—Torture of Queen Elgiva—The Danes and Anglo-Saxons become one united people—King Cnut and "the pudding"—Godwin and his singular death 11

FROM THE NORMAN CONQUEST TO THE REIGN OF THE HOUSE OF LANCASTER.

Battle of Hastings and conquest of England—Norman law phrases in our American courts—Characteristic death of William the Conqueror—Assassination of William Rufus—Battle at Trenchbray—Wreck of the "White Ship"—Robin Hood, Little John, and Friar Tuck—Modes of trial by ordeal—Murder of Thomas-a-Becket, and penance of Henry II.—Poisoning of the fair Rosamond—Richard Cœur-de-Lion and his wars in Palestine—Saracenic terror of Richard—Romantic story associated with Richard's captivity in Austria—"The devil is loose"—Magna Charta—Murder at midnight of Arthur, heir to the throne of England—Eleanor of Castile sucking the poison from the wound of her husband—Roger Bacon and his great inventions and discoveries—His discovery of gunpowder—His persecution and imprisonment—The Welsh Bards—The first prince of Wales—Attempt to subjugate Scotland—Execution of Jews—Tournaments—Sports of the common people—Beheading of Gaveston—Terrible death of Edward II.—English and Scottish border warfare—Battles of Crecy and Poictiers in France—The "Most Noble Order of the Garter"—Wickliffe and the Reformation in England—Chaucer, "the Father of English Poetry"—Westminster Abbey—Insurrection of Wat Tyler and Jack Straw—The Battle of Chevychase—Whitington and his cat 37

FROM HENRY IV. TO THE EXECUTION OF CHARLES I.

Owen Glendower, Douglas, and Harry Hotspur—Battle of Agincourt—Rebellion of Jack Cade—The "Wars of the Roses"—Margaret of Anjou and the robber—Warwick, the "King-maker"—Introduction of printing into England—Witchcraft and astrology—Death of Richard III. at the battle of Bosworth—Impostures of Lambert Simnel and Perkin Warbeck—Battle of Flodden—Fall of Cardinal Wolsey—Tyrannical reign of Henry VIII.—"Bloody Mary"—Execution of Mary, Queen of Scots—Destruction of the Spanish Armada—Francis Drake and Sir Walter Raleigh—Shakespeare and the golden age of English literature—Lord Bacon—The translation of the Scriptures—The English Revolution under Cromwell, Hampden, Pym and others—Trial and execution of Charles I. 71

FROM THE COMMONWEALTH TO THE PRESENT.

The "Praise-God Barebones Parliament"—Milton and his poetry—The plague of London—Great fire of London—The "Rye-house Plot"—Bunyan and the "Pilgrim's Progress"—Battle of the Boyne—Newton and his discoveries—A brilliant age of literature—Rise and development of Methodism—Defeat of Charles Edward at Culloden—Founding of the British Empire in India—Conquest of Canada—The new style of reckoning time introduced—Hogarth and his pictures—English comedy—Victories over France and Spain on sea and land—Great poets of the eighteenth and nineteenth centuries—The steam-engine and other remarkable inventions and discoveries—English statesmanship and oratory—Catholic emancipation—Steam navigation—The Crystal Palace—Crimean war—Indian mutiny—The Zulu war and death of Prince Napoleon—The war in the Soudan and murder of General Gordon—Beaconsfield and Gladstone—Art, literature, science and philosophy in England at the present day 96

CONTENTS.

IRELAND.

Similarity of the aspect of the country and the character of the people—English rule in Ireland—Humorous Legends—St. Patrick and "The King of the Serpents"—Agriculture and manufactures in Ireland—Wit and humor of the beggars—The jaunting-car—Father Matthew and his temperance campaign—The Blarney Stone—The Lakes of Killarney and their beautiful legends—Legends of other lakes—Daniel O'Connell and Catholic emancipation—Charles Stewart Parnell and the Irish Home Rule Party—Irish statesmen, patriots, and orators—The poetry of Thomas Moore—The Giant's Causeway—Belfast and Dublin—The primitive inhabitants of Ireland—Irish civilization and scholarship at the period when other nations were sunk in darkness and barbarism—The great contributions of Ireland to English literature, science and art . . . 129

SCOTLAND.

A land rugged, but free and independent—The vast strides made in one century from obscurity and poverty to a foremost place in the civilization of the world—Geographical aspect of Scotland—The Highland and Lowland races—Their "fierce native daring" in warfare—Rob Roy—Agriculture and manufactures in Scotland—Scottish fisheries—The national religion—Scottish universities—Great names in literature science and art—Picturesque and beautiful scenery—Epochs of Scottish history—Wallace and Bruce—Mary, Queen of Scots—John Knox and the Scottish Reformation—Union of Scotland with England upon equal terms . . 144

CENTRAL AND SOUTH AMERICA.

A preliminary glance at the stupendous strides made every day by the United States—All climates within its territory—Its vast resources—Pre-Columbian discovery of America—Voyages of Columbus—Americus Vespucius—Search for the "Fountain of Youth"—The discovery of the Pacific ocean by Balboa—Invasion of Mexico by Cortez—Its conquest by Spain—Achievement of its independence—Capture of Mexico by the United States—Invasion of Mexico by the French, and the Austrian Prince Maximilian placed upon its throne—The Emperor Maximilian shot—Benito Juarez and Porfirio Diaz—Mexico described—Pizarro and the conquest of Peru—Wealth of ancient Peru—Peruvian war of independence under Bolivar—Peruvian silver mines—Railway traffic in Peru—Venezuela and her struggle for independence—Prosperous condition of Chili—The Argentine Confederation—Central America—The acquisition of Brazil by Portugal—Proclamation of independence—Extent, mineral wealth, and agricultural resources of Brazil—People of Brazil—The literary and scientific attainments of its present emperor 161

CANADA.

Discoveries of John and Sebastian Cabot—Jacques Cartier sails into and gives name to the "Gulf of St. Lawrence"—Founding of Quebec—Aboriginal inhabitants of Canada—The capture of Quebec and deaths of Generals Wolfe and the Marquis de Montcalm—Invasion of Canada and capitulation of General Hull—The fair dealing of the Dominion of Canada with her Indians—Louis Riel's rebellion—Murder of Scott—The Red River expedition under Sir Garnet Wolseley—The governmental constitution of Canada—Extent of territory—Progress in agriculture—Canadian fisheries—Navigation and railway travel—Vast resources of British Columbia 189

THE UNITED STATES.

THE UNITED STATES TO THE PERIOD OF THE REVOLUTION.

Settlement of the United States—John Smith and Pocahontas—Settlement of Maryland—The Pilgrims' voyage in the Mayflower—Colonization of New England—Penn's treaty with the Indians—James Oglethorpe and the settlement of Georgia 200

FROM THE AMERICAN REVOLUTION TO THE DEATH OF WASHINGTON.

Ignorance and folly of the English Government—The "Stamp Act" and its repeal—The tax on tea—Destruction of tea in Boston harbor—Eloquence of Patrick Henry—War declared between England and the Colonies—Lexington and Bunker Hill—Battles of Trenton, Princeton, and Bennington—Surrender of Burgoyne at Saratoga—Massacre in the valley of Wyoming—Treason of Arnold and execution of Major Andre—The siege of Yorktown—Surrender of Cornwallis—Treaty of peace between the English and United States—Life, character and appearance of George Washington—His death 208

CONTENTS.

LITERATURE AND GENERAL PROGRESS IN THE COLONIAL PERIOD.

First book written in America—Poetry, science and philosophy of Colonial authors—Jonathan Edwards—Benjamin Franklin, his writings, inventions and discoveries—The "Greatest Natural Botanist in the World" . 221

THE THIRTEEN STATES A NATION—ITS HISTORY TO THE WAR WITH MEXICO.

Convention at Philadelphia—Ability and energy of Alexander Hamilton—Duel between Hamilton and Aaron Burr—Hamilton's successful financial measures—Death of Washington—Adams' administration—Jefferson's administration—Trial of Aaron Burr for treason—Fulton's invention of the steamboat—War of 1812—The "Monroe Doctrine"—Visit of Marquis Lafayette—Eloquence of Henry Clay—Statesmanship of John C. Calhoun—Joseph Smith and the religion of the Mormons—Andrew Jackson's administration—His civil and military career—Daniel Webster and Robert Hayne—Panic of 1837—Invention of the telegraph by Morse—War declared against Mexico 223

FROM THE MEXICAN WAR TO THE PRESENT DAY.

Generals Taylor and Scott invade Mexico—Battle of Buena Vista—Capture of Mexico by General Winfield Scott—Zachary Taylor's victories—The Missouri Compromise—Stephen A. Douglas, "The Little Giant"—Election of Abraham Lincoln and outbreak of the Civil war—Defeat of the Southern Confederacy and surrender of General Lee to General Grant—Assassination of Abraham Lincoln—Reference to the sea-fight between the Monitor and Merrimac—Inventions of John Ericsson—Great fire in Chicago—Fire in Boston—Battle between General Custer and Sioux Indians—Death of Custer—Political contest between R. B. Hayes and S. J. Tilden—Assassination of President Garfield—Death of General Hancock—Career of Stephen Grover Cleveland 236

PHYSICAL FEATURES OF NORTH AMERICA.

Mountain systems of the United States—Giant trees of California—Falls of Niagara—The Yosemite Falls—The Switzerland of America—The "Switch-Back" railroad—Chautauqua—Mount Washington—United States Signal Service—Weather indications and cautionary signals 255

LITERATURE AND THE FINE ARTS.

Drake—Halleck—Bryant—Longfellow—Holmes, with extracts from his poetry—Poetry of Whittier—Sad life and death of Edgar Allan Poe—John Howard Payne, his dramatic works—Verses of "Home, Sweet Home" usually omitted—Remains of Payne brought from Africa to the United States—Living poets—Prose authors—Novelists—Historians and essayists—Progress in engraving and book-illustration—Chromolithography—American painters and sculptors—Musical compositions—American inventive talent 262

ITALY.

ROME.

Climate and physical aspect of Italy—Its wealth in art—Great achievements of the Italian people—Romulus and Remus and the she-wolf—The rape of the Sabines—The Horatii and the Curiatii—The rape of Lucretia and banishment of the Tarquins—Three Romans keep at bay a hostile army—War between Rome and Carthage—Stupendous victories gained by Hannibal over the Romans—Hannibal's defeat and death—Destruction of Carthage—Marius and Sulla—Caius Julius Cæsar, and anecdotes concerning him—His victories and reforms initiated by him—Assassination of Cæsar—Reign of Augustus, and golden age of Roman literature—Destruction of Jerusalem—Persecution of Christians and burning of Rome under Nero—Roman Catacombs—Career of Rienzi—The Colosseum—St. Peter's and the Vatican—Italian art—Michael Angelo and Raphael 273

PROMINENT CITIES OF ITALY.

Beauty of Florence—Dante and his "Divine Comedy"—Great men born in Florence—Its magnificent monuments and works of art—The city of Venice—Terrible government of the "Council of Ten"—The Bridge of Sighs—Grand Canal of Venice—Padua—Verona and the great men born there—Its manufactures and agricultural products—Interesting aspect of Milan—Magnificent cathedral in Milan—Beautiful situation of Naples—Life in Naples—Ruins of Pompeii and Herculaneum—A united Italy—Cavour, Mazzini and Garibaldi—Pope Pius IX.—Garibaldi's life in New York—Present government of Italy—Attempted assassination of King Humbert 288

FRANCE.

FRANCE FROM ITS EARLIEST HISTORY TO THE REVOLUTION.

Primitive inhabitants of France—Merovingian chiefs—Clovis, and founding of the French monarchy—Reign of Charlemagne—The Capet dynasty—The Crusades—Peter the Hermit—Capture of Jerusalem by Godfrey of Bouillon—Second crusade—Noble conduct of the Sultan Saladin—The Boy Crusade—Life in the middle ages—Tournaments—The Chevalier Bayard—Romantic literature—Richelieu, Mazarin, and Colbert—Rabelais and his humorous romances—Essays of Montaigne—Wits and literary men of France—Disgraceful reign of Louis XV.—Debauchery of the Court of France—Sufferings of the French people 299

THE REVOLUTION IN FRANCE.

Starvation amongst the French people—Storming of the Bastile—Insurrection of women—Mirabeau—Flight of Louis XIV.—"The Marseillaise" war-hymn—Trial and execution of King Louis—The assassination of Marat by Charlotte Corday—The "Reign of Terror"—Notable executions—The "Goddess of Reason" . . 304

FRANCE FROM THE OPENING OF THE CAREER OF NAPOLEON.

Character of Napoleon Bonaparte—Characteristic anecdotes—Personal appearance of Napoleon—His banishment and death at St. Helena—French Revolution of 1848, and flight of Louis Phillippe—French Republic and Empire under Louis Napoleon—Defeat of the Austrians by the French under Napoleon III.—The Franco-German war—Destruction of the Vendôme Column by the Communists—Magnificence of Paris—Its marvels of architecture—Museums, galleries and theatres—Present claimants to the throne of France—General Boulanger—French greatness in literature, science and art—France, the vineyard of the earth . . 306

SPAIN.

Geographical aspect of Spain—Earliest inhabitants of Spain—Sertorius and his tame fawn—Defeat of Roderic, "Last of the Goths"—Chronicle of the "Cid"—Defeat of the Moors by the Cid, after his death—Splendor of Granada—Palace of the Alhambra—Siege of Granada—"The Last Sigh of the Moor"—The Spanish Armada—Literature and art of Spain—Circumstances under which Cervantes wrote "Don Quixote"—Anecdote of Murillo—Anecdote of Marshal Soult—Madrid—Bull-fighting—Description of Seville and Valencia—The Virgin Mary and her portrait—Singular story concerning St. Vincent—Saragossa and its sieges—The maid of Saragossa—Revolution in Spain—Assassination of General Prim—Spain a republic—Alfonso becomes king—Spanish love for shows, games and festivals—Passion for dancing—Love of fighting—Various traits of the Spanish people 314

PORTUGAL.

Extent, climate, and resources of Portugal—Lisbon and its subjection to earthquakes—Camoens and his great poem, "The Lusiad"—Grotto of Camoens in China—Industry and commerce of the Portuguese . . 323

DENMARK, NORWAY AND SWEDEN.

The Scandinavian sea-kings—Charlemagne and the Norsemen—Mythology and war-songs of the Vikings—Norse settlements in England and France—Margaret, the "Semiramis of the North"—Victories of Gustavus Adolphus—The battle of Lutzen and death of Gustavus Adolphus—Career of Charles XII. of Sweden—Union of Norway and Sweden—Character of the Danes—Danish literature, art and science—Character of the Norwegians and the Swedes—Recreations and amusements 324

SWITZERLAND.

Early races of Switzerland—The House of Hapsburg—The vow of the Swiss patriots—Death of Gessler by William Tell—The battle of Morgarten—The Swiss Confederation—Battle of Sempach and heroic conduct of Arnold von Winkelried—Victory at Nefels and achievement of independence by the Swiss—The Sempach convention—Production and commerce—Exports of Geneva—Alpine ascents—Chamouni, Mont Blanc, and Lake of Geneva—Imprisonment of Bonnivard in the Castle of Chillon—Intellectual achievements of the Swiss 331

THE NETHERLANDS.

Religion of Holland and Belgium—City of Brussels—Character of the Belgians—Scenery of Holland—Dutch ancestry—Cleanliness—Legend of the Flying Dutchman 337

GERMANY.

United German Empire—House of Hohenzollern—Thirty Years' war—Peace of Westphalia—The Seven Years' war—Frederick the Great—Legends of the Rhine—Nibelungenlied—Life in Berlin—Luther and Melancthon—Luther throws the inkstand at the devil—Beautiful legend of St. Elizabeth—Anecdotes of Augustus II.—Dresden and Mayence—Invention of printing—Art, science and literature of Germany—Cologne cathedral—St. Ursula and the eleven thousand virgins—Franco-German war—Shrewdness and foresight of the Emperor William—Statesmanship of Bismarck—Generalship of Von Moltke—Surrender of the Emperor Napoleon III.—Proclamation of the German Empire in Versailles—Anecdote of Emperor William 340

AUSTRIA.

Area of Austria—Government and population of Austria—Defeat of the Turks under the walls of Vienna—Music and musicians—Palace of Schönbrunn—Bavaria—Bohemia—Curious relics in the cathedral of St. Vitus in Prague—Loretta chapel in Prague—Tyrol and the Tyrolese 357

RUSSIA.

Early history of Russia—Defeat of Peter the Great by Charles XII. of Sweden—Habits of Peter the Great—Palace of ice—Catherine the Great—Defeat of Kosciusko and ruin of Poland—French retreat from Moscow—War in the Crimea—Death of the Emperor Nicholas—Emancipation of the Serfs—Assassination of Alexander II.—The Nihilists—Alexander III.—Conquests of Russia in Central Asia—St. Petersburg—Moscow—The Kremlin—Novgorod—Religion of the Russians—Russian superstitions—Siberia—Siberian lack of hospitality 364

TURKEY.

Geographical position and population of Turkey—The Mahometan religion—Turkish history—Defeat of Bajazet by Tamerlane—Siege of Constantinople—Massacre of the Janizaries—War with Russia—Dancing Dervishes—Turkish shopkeepers—Women in Turkey—Legend of the Maiden's Tower 385

GREECE.

Remarkable physical features, climate and history of Greece—Supreme quality of its literature, philosophy, science and art—Lycurgus, Draco and Solon—Marathon—Thermopylæ—Plague at Athens—Epaminondas—Philip of Macedon—Defeat of Porus by Alexander the Great—Philosophers of Greece—Greek oratory and the drama—Modern history—Ruins of ancient cities and temples—Religion of the Greeks 396

EGYPT.

Early civilization of Egypt—Overflowing of the Nile—Pyramids and the Sphinx—Superstitions of the Egyptians—Rameses the Great—Statue of Memnon—Conquest of Egypt by Cambyses—Antony and Cleopatra—Invasion of Egypt by Napoleon—Assassination of General Kleber—Defeat of the French at Aboukir—Life in Cairo—Ruins of Egyptian temples and statues—Ruins of Thebes—Moses' Well—The Suez canal—Religion of ancient Egypt—Remarkable discovery of Mummies—The Soudan—Arabs of the Soudan—"Chinese Gordon"—Suakin 407

THE BARBARY STATES.

Morocco and the Moors—American resistance to slave-trading—Attack upon Tripoli by Commodore Preble—Capture of Algerine vessels by Commodore Decatur—Attack upon Algiers by an English fleet—Defeat of Abdel Kader by the French 422

CENTRAL AND SOUTH AFRICA.

Desert of Sahara—Wild animals of Africa—African Pigmies—Source of the Nile—The Congo and the Zambesi—African explorers and exploration—Livingstone's propositions in regard to Africa 424

SYRIA AND PALESTINE.

Syria and Palestine—The "Holy Places"—The Holy Sepulchre—Strange people in Jerusalem—Antioch and Damascus—Ruins of Tadmor—Ruins of Baalbec—Tyre and Sidon—Siege of Acre—Arabia and the Arabs—Nineveh—Hanging-gardens of Babylon—Fall of Babylon—Climate of Persia 429

INDIA.

Hindoo chronology—Hindoo literature—Invasion of India by Alexander the Great—British Empire in India—"Black Hole" of Calcutta—Lord Clive—Warren Hastings—Sepoy rebellion—Massacre at Cawnpore—

Storming of Delhi—Generals Havelock, Outram, and Sir Colin Campbell—Fall of the Mogul Empire—Physical geography of India—Hindoo architecture—Great cities of India—The Ganges—Hindoo Mythology—Juggernaut—The Thugs—Nautch or dancing girls—The Vale of Cashmere—Immolation of widows—Cashmerian character and language 437

CHINA.

Vast population of China—Great Wall of China—Invasion of China by Kubla Khan—Terrible earthquake in China—War between Great Britain and China—Humorous story of the American Minister to China—Insurrection in China—Chinese artificial lakes and hanging-gardens—Weird legends—Life in China—Chinese advertisements—Superstitions—Chinese locomotion—Dwarfing of the feet by females—Chinese government—Chinese in California 449

JAPAN.

Religion, manners and customs of the Japanese—United States treaty with Japan—The Tycoon and Mikado—Japanese love of Nature—Religion and mythology of the Japanese—Mechanical and artistic work—Physical features of the Japanese—Domestic habits of the Japanese—Female fashions—Modern civilization . . 458

AUSTRALIA.

Geographical position and history of Australia—Colonization of Australia—Van Diemen's Land—The Yarra-yarra—Sydney and Melbourne—New South Wales and Tasmania—The first Australian newspaper—Discovery of gold at Ballarat—Australian gold-diggings—Burke and Wills cross the Australian continent—Markets in Melbourne—" Paddy's Market "—" Sold again and got the sugar "—Chinese immigrants—Resources of Australia—Aboriginal inhabitants 462

NEW ZEALAND, POLYNESIA, AND THE MALAYSIAN ISLANDS.

Islands of New Zealand—Lake Rothe-Mahana—The Maoris—Gradual extinction of the Maoris—Sandwich islands—Decrease in their population—Society islands—Manners of the natives of Otaheite—Fertility of Java—Valley of poison—Upas tree—Character of the Malays 470

ENGLAND.

"O England, model to thy inward greatness,
Like little body with a mighty heart."

SUCH are the seemingly boastful words with which Shakespeare apostrophizes his native land. We say "seemingly boastful," for if ever any race had just cause to be proud of its record it is that noble race—Kelt, Anglo-Saxon, Dane, and Norman, blended and combined—which has given its "mighty heart" to this little realm of England, and which, as constituting the groundwork of that type of humanity now developing in our own country, is destined to carry America—mighty body harmonizing with mighty heart—to a point of eminence not hitherto reached by any nation.

England is, in extent, the smallest of all the great powers of Europe; yet in regard of territories and population dependent on her, as well as of manufactures, commerce, and wealth, she is far ahead of any of them. The area of England and Wales is 58,310 square miles, a little larger than the State of Illinois, yet her colonies and dependences extend into every clime of the world, while the roll-call of her drums beating *reveille* for her soldiers follows the sun through all the twenty-four hours of its daily course. Queen Victoria at this moment rules over one-seventh of the earth's surface and nearly one-fourth of its population, swaying the sceptre over a territory seventy times the extent of Great Britain and Ireland, and embracing a population of between three and four hundred millions of human beings. The white sails of her fleets gleam on every sea; her manufactures find their way into every land; while her Chaucer, her Shakespeare, her Bacon, and Newton, and Milton speak to the cultured intellects of all the world.

England constitutes the southern portion of the island of Great Britain, lying between 50° and 56° north latitude and 1° 46' east longitude and 5° 45' west. Its extreme length is 365 miles, and breadth 280. The total population is over 26,000,000.

England is a beautifully diversified, generally undulating country. Her mountains lie in four distinct groups—the Pennine range, stretching from the Cheviot hills on the Scotch border to the heart of England and forming a kind of back-bone to the country; the Cumbrian group in Cumberland and Westmoreland; the Welsh mountains; and the Highlands of Devon and Cornwall. The loftiest peak in England is Snowdon in the Welsh group, 3,570 feet above sea-level. Her hill and mountain ranges are generally separated from each other by rich and smiling valleys, each watered by its own stream, which not only lends life and beauty to the scene, but, in most cases, is utilized for some of the manifold purposes of industry. There are many fine tracts of uplands, mainly on the eastern slope or versant of the country. Generally these are productive, the north and south downs in Surrey, Kent, and Hampshire being especially remarkable for their fine breed of sheep. The York uplands, on the other hand, are bleak and solitary moors, almost destitute of verdure and foliage. A large proportion of England consists of extensive stretches of comparatively level land. One of the most fertile of these tracts is in the eastern and southeastern counties, comprising Norfolk, Suffolk, Essex, and Kent, noted for the splendid results attained by their scientific agriculturists. The largest level plain in England has an area of 1,300 miles, and is known as the Fenland—a district of low, marshy soil, traversed by canals and rivers well-nigh as sluggish. This marsh country has been much reduced within the memory of man by scientific draining.

Owing to the amount of rainfall and the undulating character of the ground no country has a more complete river-system than England, the greater rivers forming harbors and water-ways leading into the very heart of the kingdom. On the bosom of these short, but often broad and deep rivers, especially on the Thames, the Mersey, the Tyne, the Humber, and the Severn, float argosies more numerous and more richly-laden than sail on the surface of any

CATHEDRAL OF YORK.

other streams in the world. In addition to the rivers and their estuaries England enjoys many excellent natural harbors, formed by the indentations of its coast; the sea-line, by reason of its undulations, reaching a length of 2,000 miles.

No town in England is more than 120 miles from the sea, and almost every one of the important inland towns not reached by river water-ways is on a canal. Commencing from the northeast we shall enumerate the rivers, with the principal towns on them: The *Tyne*—Newcastle (capital of coal-district, large port), also Gateshead and South Shields (ship-building) at its mouth; the *Wear*—Sunderland (seaport, ship-building), farther up the river—Durham (fine cathedral). Two rivers, the *Ouse* and the *Trent*, unite to form the *Humber*—Hull (large port). The *Ouse* is formed of a congeries of small Yorkshire streams on whose banks stand many busy towns, notably Leeds (woollen) on the *Aire*, and Sheffield (cutlery) on the *Don*. Where the Ouse first becomes navigable stands York (seat of an archbishop, with noble cathedral); on the *Trent* is Nottingham (lace and hosiery). South of the *Humber* is the *Yare*—Yarmouth (seaport), and farther south is the *Thames*—London (capital of England, greatest seaport in the world) and Windsor (royal castle). On the south coast the streams are small,

WYCLIFFE.

but several important towns lie near their mouths or on bays, as Dover (town nearest France), Brighton (royal marine palace, fashionable watering-place), Portsmouth (principal naval station); on the *Itchen*—Southampton (famous port for ocean-going steamers) and Winchester (Anglo-Saxon capital, and cathedral); on the *Exe*—Exeter (cathedral); on the *Tamar*—Plymouth and Davenport (naval stations). On the estuary of the *Fal* or *Vale*, in Cornwall, and close to the Land's End, is Falmouth, with one of the best harbors in the kingdom, a chief rendezvous for fleets and mail-packets. Of this river and harbor the quaint old poet Drayton says:

> "Here Vale, a lively flood, her nobler name that gives
> To Falmouth, and by whom it famous ever lives,
> Whose entrance is from sea so intricately wound,
> Her haven angled so about her barbarous sound,
> That in her quiet bay a hundred ships may ride,
> Yet not the tallest mast be of the tall'st descried."

Turning up the west coast we come to the *Severn*, the largest river in England, on which stands Cardiff, largest town in Wales, the capital of South Wales coal-district; also the cities of Gloucester, Worcester, and Shrewsbury, all with cathedrals. The Severn has two tributaries, bearing the name of *Avon*, both famous. The Lower Avon is famed as having received the dust of Wickliffe, when his bones were dug up and cast into the stream:

> "The Avon to the Severn runs, the Severn to the sea,
> And Wickliffe's dust shall spread abroad, wide as thy waters be."

On it stand Bath (fashionable watering-place, hot springs), and Bristol, a large, busy town and harbor.

Still more famed is the Upper Avon, for upon it stands the town of Stratford, the birthplace of the immortal Shakespeare. Beautifully has it been sung by an anonymous poet, quoted by our own Longfellow:

> "Flow on, sweet river! like his verse
> Who lies beneath this marble hearse.
> Thy playmate once;—I see him now
> A boy with sunshine on his brow,
> And hear in Stratford's quiet street
> The patter of his little feet.
>
> "I see him by thy shallow edge
> Wading knee-deep amid the sedge;
> And lost in thought, as if thy stream
> Were the swift river of a dream.
>
> "He wonders whitherward it flows;
> And fain would follow where it goes,
> To the wide world, that shall ere long
> Be filled with his melodious song.
>
> "Flow on, fair stream! That dream is o'er,
> He stands upon another shore;
> A vaster river near him flows,
> And still he follows where it goes."

The *Wye*, another tributary of the Severn, is the most picturesque of the many crystal streams of Wales, vying in beauty with the English *Dove*. Beautifully does the poet, Charles Cotton, apostrophize the latter silver river:

> "O my beloved nymph! fair Dove!
> Princess of rivers! how I love
>   Upon thy flowery banks to lie,
> And view thy silver stream
> When gilded by a summer beam! . . .
> Such streams Rome's yellow Tiber cannot show
> The Iberian Tagus or Ligurian Po. . . .
> Nay, Thame and Isis when conjoined submit
> And lay their trophies at thy silver feet."

The *Eden*, one of England's fairest streams, flows close to the Scottish border:

> "Eden! till now thy beauty had I viewed
> By glimpses only. Nature gives thee flowers
> That have no rival among British bowers,
> And thy bold rocks are worthy of their fame."

WESTMINSTER.

On this stream, which Wordsworth celebrates in the above lines, stands the ancient city of Carlisle with its castle and cathedral. In the old days of the border wars between the English and Scots, Carlisle was the capital of the English side, and many a stirring tale, tradition, and ballad still commemorate these days of "sturt and strife." It was there the Scottish prisoners were imprisoned, and, in these iron times, too frequently "done to death." In particular many of the unfortunate Jacobites that followed "Prince Charlie" were executed here, and their heads set up on iron spikes over the city gates.

Other towns of note in England are Birmingham (centre of England; hardware manufacture); Bradford and Huddersfield, in Yorkshire (woollen factories), and Stafford, capital of Staffordshire, or the Black country as it is called from its numerous coal and iron works.

But the most romantic and beautiful region in England proper is the lake district of Cumberland and Westmoreland. The lakes lie in long, narrow valleys or dales among the vast mountains which constitute the Cumbrian group and render this region so grandly sublime. Helvellyn, the centre of the group, attains a height of 3,000 feet. Of these beautiful expanses of water we specify only a few of the most famed—Windermere, Ulleswater, Derwentwater, Wastwater, Coniston, and the lovely Grasmere, on whose banks stands Rydal Cottage, the home of the poet Wordsworth. As the chosen home of the poets of the lake school—Wordsworth, Coleridge, Southey, Wilson —no region has been so celebrated in song and poetry as this witchingly charming lake district. It would be easy to fill a volume with tributes to its charms. Space limits us, and we content ourselves with quoting the hymns of praise of two of the favorite "sweet singers" of England—Felicia Hemans and Robert Southey. It is thus that Mrs. Hemans sings of lovely, tranquil Grasmere:

> "O vale and lake, within your mountain urn
> Smiling so tranquilly, and yet so deep!
> Oft doth your dreamy loveliness return,
> Coloring the tender shadows of my sleep
> With light Elysian; for the hues that steep
> Your shores in melting lustre seem to float
> On golden clouds from spirit-lands remote,
> Isles of the blest and in our memory keep
> Their place with holiest harmonies. Fair scene
> Most loved by evening and her dewy star!
> O ne'er may man, with touch unhallowed, jar
> The perfect music of thy charm serene!
> Still, still unchanged, may one sweet region wear
> Smiles that subdue the soul to love, and tears, and prayer."

The principal towns in the lake district are Kendal and Keswick. We transcribe Southey's description of the view from his window in the latter town. The time is that "sober hour" when twilight spreads its mantle o'er the scene:

> "Pensive, though not in thought, I stood at the window, beholding
> Mountain, and lake, and vale; the valley disrobed of its verdure;
> Derwent retaining yet from eve a glassy reflexion,
> Where his expanded breast, then still and smooth as a mirror,
> Under the woods reposed: the hills that, calm and majestic,
> Lifted their heads in the silent sky, from far Glaramara,
> Bleacray and Maidenmour, to Grizedale and Western Withop

Dark and distinct they rose. . . .
In the West beyond was the last pale tint of the twilight,
Green as the stream in the glen with its pure and chrysolite waters. . . .
Earth was hushed and still; all motion and sound were suspended. . . .
Only the voice of the Greta, heard only when all is in stillness.
Pensive I stood and still: the hour and the scene had subdued me."

Wales is no less distinguished for its wild and picturesque scenery—the romantic beauty of its glens and hill-gorges, the profusion of its lonely lakelets and tarns, and of crystal streams meandering like silver threads among its mountain masses. It is thus that the poet addresses its sheltered and lovely Clwd, a river in North Wales, giving us, at the same time, a fine sketch of the scenery through which it flows:

"O Cambrian river, with slow music gliding
  By pastoral hills, old woods, and ruined towers;
Now midst thy reeds and golden willows hiding;
  Now gleaming forth by some rich bank of flowers.
. . . . Thou smooth stream
Art winding still thy sunny meads along,
Murmuring to cottage and grey hills thy song,
Low, sweet, unchanged.

What is likely to strike a stranger seeing England for the first time is its garden-like appearance—the almost total absence of brush and stronger weeds, the trim aspect of its fields and fences, the neatly dressed and cleanly-kept hedgerows of fragrant hawthorn, and the evident care that no nook shall escape cultivation. The density of the population demands that every rood of land be cultivated, while the tenant-farmer paying from $6 to $20 or $25 an acre of yearly rent cannot afford to let any of it lie unproductive. The magnificent mansions of its peers and other proprietors, embosomed amid the foliage of stately trees and surrounded by lawns of velvety smoothness, form a striking feature in the landscape; while the cozy, home-like dwellings of its farmers give an impression of competence and comfort; some of these brick structures, interlaced with strong wooden beams, have a peculiarly picturesque appearance. Any one who saw the English house in the Centennial grounds, Philadelphia, has a good idea of the homes of the minor squires and better class of farmers—that is, of the yeomen of England.

The principal cereal crops are wheat, barley, and oats. Of wheat large breadths are raised, the average yield being 30 to 35 or 40 bushels per acre. Oats are grown mainly for horses, barley for distilling. Notwithstanding the large yields won by her farmers, England cannot feed all her people, and has to import largely from this and other countries. She cannot even supply her children with the "roast beef of old England," and again the United States,

SUMMER SCENE IN ENGLAND.

Ireland, Scotland, etc., make up the deficiency. Much of the land of England is devoted to grazing, and dairy-farming is an important industry. For this industry her moist and mild climate is especially favorable, nourishing her pastures to a degree of fertility surpassed only by that of "The Emerald Isle."

The soil of the United Kingdom is in fewer hands than that of any country in the world, little over a quarter of a million proprietors owning 33,000,000 acres, or all the available land in England and Wales. Little more than 10,000 persons own over two-thirds of the country, while the twelve largest proprietors—all peers—own over a thirtieth. A million and a half of people are engaged in agriculture.

The condition of the yeomen of England used to be very enviable. An ancient rhyme expresses the contempt with which they looked down on the people of other lands:

> "A noble of Spain, a county of France,
> And a knight of the North Countrie,
> A yeoman of Kent, with his yearly rent,
> Would buy them out all three."

This rhyme begins to lose its force. The free importation of foreign produce has reduced the incomes of proprietors and farmers, so that the problem of the land has come to the front as one of the burning questions of the day. While the English yeoman was thus enviably situated it was far otherwise with his laborers. Poorly housed, poorly fed, poorly clad, poorly educated, their lot was hard and cheerless. Taking England all over, and allowing for loss by broken time, two and a half dollars a week, without board, is the average wage of the out-door laborer. But the little bird that whispered to Byron that "by-and-by the people would be stronger" was prescient of the future. The condition of the English agricultural laborer is on the eve of becoming the leading political problem which statesmen will have to face. The doctrine that the land is for the sole benefit of the few is fast becoming obsolete. The franchise is now conferred on poor as well as on rich, and the people are awakening to a sense of their rights and their power.

The fisheries are of great importance, yielding an annual product of $50,000,000, and employing 37,000 boats and 200,000 hands. The herring fishery takes the first place, but the salmon, mackerel, and oyster fisheries are also of great value. English statesmen look to the fisheries as the grand nursery for the navy.

But it is to her coal and iron that England is mainly indebted for her manufacturing supremacy. Her coal-fields are of large extent, and comprise extensive beds of bituminous coal from 30 to 40 feet thick. The principal deposits are in Northumberland and Durham, with New Castle as a centre;

in Staffordshire; and in Glamorganshire, South Wales, around Cardiff. In all, England has some 4,000 collieries. In 1883 17,000,000 tons of ore were extracted from her iron mines, while her puddling furnaces produced two and one-third million tons of manufactured iron. Nearly 600,000 persons are employed in mining, of whom 450,000 are under ground.

England's textile manufactures employ a yet larger number of hands. In all, in 1881, there were 6,189 factories, employing 777,703 actual operatives, representing 2,000,000 of persons dependent on this industry. Of these 2,579 were cotton factories, 1,412 woollen, and 630 worsted. Other textile factories are of flax, hemp, jute, silk, and hosiery. Her iron manufactories employ several hundred thousand hands, Birmingham and Sheffield being the great centres for the manufacture of hardware, agricultural implements, and cutlery.

In a great marine nation ship-building holds an important place. In 1883 there were built in Britain 365 sailing vessels and 806 steamers with a gross tonnage of 800,000. The principal yards are on the Clyde (Scotland), the Tyne, the Tees, the Mersey, and the Thames.

England is under a monarchy, limited by a Parliament consisting of two Houses—Lords and Commons. The sovereign has now little real influence, all power tending more and more to centre in the House of Commons, which is elected by nearly universal suffrage, and consists of 670 members. The House of Lords is a hereditary chamber, excepting that the two archbishops and twenty-four of the bishops have seats in virtue of their office. The hereditary peers number 402. The constitution of this chamber is now agitating the public mind, the more radical politicians advocating its abolition, the more moderate its reformation. The premier of the Cabinet is the most powerful man in Britain. Nominally he is selected by the sovereign; in reality he is the man recognized as the head of the party having the majority in the House of Commons. The Cabinet resigns whenever an important measure introduced by it is rejected by the Commons, and a dissolution of Parliament ensues. The nominal duration of each Parliament is seven years; the average duration is about four. The electoral districts are not absolutely equal numerically. Somewhat over 40,000 is the average population of a district. All the members of the Cabinet have seats in Parliament.

The chief universities of England are those of Oxford and Cambridge. In them the students live in colleges or halls, and their education is conducted principally by tutors, progress being tested by examinations. There are also university professors who lecture to all students. These colleges were founded at different periods from the thirteenth down to the eighteenth century; and many of them are very fine structures, as is evidenced by the engraving of St. John's College, Oxford, shown at beginning of this chapter. In Oxford there are, in all, twenty-four colleges; in Cambridge, seventeen.

Their endowments are large, those of the Oxford colleges for the year 1871 amounting to $2,065,000; those of Cambridge to $1,700,000. The students number about 5,000, and the clergy of the Established Church are largely trained at one or other of the universities. The towns themselves possess little independent importance. Besides these two universities, there are also those of London and Durham, where the teaching is more professorial.

Episcopacy is the established religion of England. The Archbishop of Canterbury is Primate of all England, the Archbishop of York being the next dignitary. There are in all thirty bishops. The question of maintaining a state church is now being much agitated, and from the progress that democratic ideas are making in England, there seems no reason to doubt that persons now living will see a dissolution of the union of Church and State. In England the Established Church still ministers to a majority—probably two-thirds—of the people. Next to it the Wesleyan Methodist Church has the most adherents, closely followed by the Baptists. In Wales the Methodists are in the majority, and in 1886 a bill was submitted to Parliament asking it to disendow and disestablish the English Church in that principality. Though rejected by a small majority, it will be offered again.

The national debt of England amounts (in 1886) to $3,782,000,000, and it has been proposed to increase it by $750,000,000 for the expropriation of Irish landlords. The annual income is $445,000,000. Of this nearly a third is required to pay the interest of the debt, and over a third for the army and navy.

The British army consists of 200,000 men, of whom 60,000 are for India exclusively. Her reserves, consisting of soldiers honorably discharged, amount to 47,000. Her militia amount to 140,000, and her volunteers—"for defence, not defiance"—number over a quarter of a million. England has thus a native force of 650,000 men. By the addition of the native army of India this is raised to 761,133.

But it is to

"The flag that braved a thousand years
The battle and the breeze"

that every Englishman looks with peculiar pride. The navy of England is the most powerful in the world. The total number of her war-ships is 480, of which 360 are steam-vessels, and 120 sailing. According to a return to Parliament in 1884, the actual number of fighting vessels ready for sea was 283, of which 41 were ironclads of the first and second class, ranging from over 3,000 to 8,000 tons each. The ambition of the typical English patriot is to have a navy "confident against the world in arms;" her statesmen, more modest, demand only that England should have a force of these mailed champions of the deep capable of coping with any combination likely to be formed against her. To man her fleet England has, of seamen and marines, 58,000 men, with a reserve of 21,000, to which may be added her coast-guard of 4,000.

We have thus endeavored to give our readers a bird's-eye view of the topography, constitution, religion, and resources (natural, industrial, and warlike) of this famed land. The question arises: Will England maintain herself in the high position she has attained? As mere narrators it is not our business to enter deeply into this question. One fact is evident. For over a century England has been pre-eminently the factory for the whole world. Her great wealth has been built up by her supplying wares to every land. This monopoly she is not to enjoy longer unchallenged. Countries—as our own—which, half a century ago or later, were her best customers, are now manufacturing for themselves, and striving to build up rival industries by protective tariffs. Already she has dangerous competitors on the continent of Europe. Whether the unquestioned energy, skill, and enterprise of her people will enable her to surmount the "breakers ahead," time alone can determine.

Montgomery closes his fine poem, "A Voyage Round the World," with the following eloquently patriotic stanzas. They make a fitting close to this branch of our subject:

> "Now to thee, to thee I fly,
> Fairest isle beneath the sky,
> To my heart as to my eye.
>
> "I have seen them, one by one,
> Every shore beneath the sun,
> And my voyage now is done.
>
> "While I bid them all be blest,
> Britain is my home, my rest;
> Mine own land, I love thee best."

We have no reliable account of the island of Britain anterior to that given us by the great Roman commander and historian, Julius Cæsar, who, at the head of two legions, invaded the country in the year 55 before Christ. He met with a people of the same race with the Kelts of Gaul, against whom he had been waging a war of conquest. The tribes that congregated on the cliffs of Dover to repel the Roman invasion were marked by the same reckless bravery and the same devotion to their leaders that continue to characterize their descendants. Cæsar, on seeing the white steeps crowned by these hordes of nearly naked, painted barbarians, directed his vessels to be rowed to Deal, where landing was easier. Though the Kelts, poorly armed with swords of soft metal and wicker shields covered with hides, were in no condition to contend on equal terms with the perfectly armed and trained legionaries of Rome, yet so determined was the resistance offered that Cæsar deemed it prudent to retire to Gaul, whence he returned next spring at the head of five legions, or thirty thousand infantry and two thousand horsemen. He defeated the Britons, crossed the Thames, took their chief town, and on receiving hostages and a promise of tribute (never paid) left Britain not to return. In his narration of the worthless conquest, Cæsar specifically mentions the extraordinary skill the Britons displayed in the management of their warchariots.

The condition of the natives of Britain at this time was that of barbarians. The land was covered with gloomy forests or spread into marshes, through which prowled the wolf, the wild boar, and other savage beasts. The natives were split up into numberless clans or tribes, and seem to have inhabited each its own village in the woods, surrounded by its defence of wicker-work, consisting of stakes driven into the ground interlaced with osiers. Tillage was all but unknown, the people subsisting on the flesh and milk of their herds of half-wild cattle, and on the produce of the chase and fishing. This last occupation they pursued in boats called coracles, consisting of a framework of wattle-work covered with raw hides.

Their religion was Druidism. All knowledge was confined to the Druids, who were at once the priests, judges, and bards of their tribes. Even the Vergobrets, or princes, quailed under the domination of these men. Their rites were cruel, human victims being offered to their deities. The mistletoe was regarded with especial veneration, and at their yearly festival in March the chief Druid, clothed in white robes, cut, with a golden knife, the sacred plant from the oak to which it clung.

For nearly a century the Romans seem to have forgotten the remote conquest, till, in A. D. 43, the Emperor Claudius resolved to reduce it to a Roman province. For eight years a brave chief, Caractacus, prolonged the defence, and even his defeat and capture did not terminate the struggle. At length, in 62, Suetonius, recognizing the fact that, so long as the sway of the Druids remained unbroken, conquest was impossible, determined to extirpate them in their chief seat, Mona (the isle of Anglesea), to which they had flocked as a last resort. For a moment, it is said, even the Roman soldiers faltered as they advanced to the massacre, appalled by the awful appearance and solemn words of the venerable chief Druid, and the frantic imprecations of the priests, priestesses, and other devotees gathered around him to protect him or die with him. The old man, verging on his hundredth year, his white hairs streaming over his shoulders and breast, and clad from head to foot in vestments white as his tresses, addressed the sacrilegious foe in words thus grandly voiced by Mrs. Hemans:

> "By the dread and viewless powers,
> Whom the storms and stars obey,
> From this dark isle's mystic bowers,
> Romans, o'er the deep away!

DRUIDICAL SACRIFICES.

> Know ye Mona's awful spells?
> She the mighty grave compels
> Back to yield its fetter'd prey.
> Fear ye not the lightning stroke?
> Mark ye not the fiery sky?
> Hence! Around our central oak
> Gods are gathering—Romans, fly!"

All was in vain. Their doom was sealed. The sands of Mona drank the blood of the last of the Druidical priesthood; the sacred groves and temples were levelled to the ground or committed to the flames.

But even the slaughter of the Druids did not terminate all resistance to the conquest of Britain. Boadicea, widow of the chief of the Iceni, suffered in her own person, as well as in those of her daughters, the grossest outrages from the brutal Roman soldiery. Stung to madness, she passed from tribe to tribe, rousing them to frenzy with the story of her wrongs. Under her personal leading London was captured and 70,000 Roman soldiers destroyed. Suetonius hurried back from Mona; a dreadful battle ensued near London; 80,000 British warriors were slaughtered, and Boadicea, in despair, put an end to her life.

Thus was accomplished the first conquest of Britain. It remained for the governor, Agricola (78 to 86), to consolidate it by wise administration. Under him heathenish rites were renounced, agriculture was introduced, roads were made, the metals began to be worked systematically, and the natives gradually adopted the usages of the Romans. Among other works executed by him were two chains of forts, erected with the view of restraining the barbarous Picts and Scots from harassing their more civilized and peace-loving brethren of South Britain. Rome continued in possession of Britain till 420, when her legions were recalled to defend the empire against the incursions of the flaxen-haired barbarians from the north of the Rhine. During her sway, not only had the Britons been taught the arts of peace, and introduced to a knowledge of Roman literature, but Christianity had become the dominant faith of the Romanized portion of the island.

No sooner were the Roman legions recalled than the Picts and Scots, swarming over the now undefended walls, renewed their inroads. In reply to a plaintive letter entitled "the groans of the Britons," craving aid from Rome, the afflicted people were informed that henceforth they must defend themselves. Weakened by long subjection, this they were unable to do, and in their extremity they had recourse to the hardy half-piratical tribes of Low Germans—Saxons and Angles—inhabiting the northern coast of Germany and the peninsula of Jutland. The first detachment of these warlike tribes landed at the mouth of the Thames in 449, and quickly compelled the northern marauders to retire to their native Highlands. But they themselves had no thought of returning to their own native shores. Attracted by the beauty and fertility of the country, they coveted possession of it for themselves, and made their first settlement on the isle of Thanet. Pretexts for quarrels were not difficult to find, and quickly they turned their arms against the people they had come to protect. The latter, compelled to fight for themselves, recovered their ancient valor, and for a century and a half the struggle for mastery went on, fresh hordes of Germans pouring in from time to time to succor, and share with their brethren.

A great battle fought near Chester in 607 decisively settled the supremacy of the Germans or English. As each of their chiefs took possession of what he conquered there arose seven different kingdoms, known as the Heptarchy, namely, Kent, Sussex, Wessex, Essex, East Anglia, Mercia, and Northumberland. The Saxons held the southern part of England, while the Angles or English tribes occupied all the north and east up to the Firth of Forth. The unfortunate Britons were driven to take refuge in the wilds of Cornwall and the mountains of Wales, in which latter principality their descendants maintain their native speech and cherish some of their native bardic usages till the present day.

Two circumstances evidence the thoroughness of this second conquest of Britain. Christianity, which, as it has been said, supplanted the native Druidism during the Roman occupation, disappeared; and the Low German dialects of the invading tribes (which eventually developed into our English speech) entirely superseded the Keltic language of the Britons. For a century and a half Britain remained under a paganism more debasing than that of the Druids.

In 597 Christianity was reintroduced into Saxon England by Augustine. Ethelbert, King of Kent, who had married a Christian princess from Paris, was the earliest convert, and his people followed his example. In the course of a century all England was re-won to the true faith, only the names of the days of the week, and a few scarcely understood customs, remaining to remind us that our English forefathers worshipped the Sun and Moon, as well as the personal gods Tiw, Woden, Thor, Frey, and Sæter.*

The Angles or Engles (Englise folk) acquired a taste for literature earlier than the Saxons, and to this are we to attribute the fact that they gave the name of Engleland (England) to the whole country. It is to a priest of this race— the venerable Bede—a monk of Jarrow, in Northumberland, in the eighth century, that we are indebted for our knowledge of early English history.

---

* The story of the motive for England's second conversion is thus told: The wars between the various tribes for supremacy filled the market-place of Rome with English slaves. Pope Gregory one day, seeing a number of fair-faced golden-haired children standing for sale in the forum, asked from what country they came. He was told they were Angles. "Not *Angles* but *Angels*," was his reply, "if only they were Christians." The result was the mission of Augustine and his brother monks, immediately on Gregory's learning of the marriage of Ethelbert with a Christian princess.

The Angles owed their superior culture to their being Christianized by missionaries from Ireland, who had settled in Iona. Aidan, a disciple of Columba (the founder of Iona), came south among the Angles, on the invitation of their king, and founded the monastery of Lindisfarne, whence light and truth rayed forth over all the district. In these early days Ireland was the most enlightened country in Europe.

The story of Cædmon, the earliest English writer, as told by Bede, illustrates the love of the Angles for music and poetry. Born in the seventh century he was originally cowherd of the monastery of Whitby, and noted only for ignorance. When the domestics used to assemble in the evening to recreate themselves with song and music, Cædmon was wont to steal out to the cowstable to hide his shame upon the harp being offered to him. One night when he had thus withdrawn he fell asleep in the stable-loft, when a stranger appeared and commanded him to sing. "I cannot sing," answered Cædmon; "for this cause I left the feast." "Be that as it may you shall sing to me." "What shall I sing?" "The song of the creation." In the morning Cædmon stood before the Abbess Hilda, and told his dream and recited his song. Abbess and brethren at once saw that a miracle had occurred and Cædmon had received the gift of song from heaven. A portion of Holy Writ was translated for him, and he was directed to put it into verse. Next morning he recited the additional verses. The abbess, now recognizing the divine grace in the man, bade him quit the secular habit and take on him the monastic life. Piece by piece the sacred story was worked into Cædmon's song, till it reached a bulk equal to nearly the half of *Paradise Lost*, to which some of it bears a striking resemblance.

There is one drawback to this strangely mysterious story. There is some evidence that "the song" was in existence before Cædmon was born. If so, pious fraud and an excellent memory raised the cowherd to what men call immortality as the author of the earliest English epic poem. Cædmon died in 680.

Many and bitter were the conflicts waged between the several petty kings of England, now the sovereign of one district striving for the overlordship of all the land; now, another. It was not till the English had been in the land for nearly 400 years that it became consolidated into one nation under Egbert, King of Wessex, who reigned from 827 to 837, his chief city, Winchester, becoming the capital of England.

No dweller in this land of freedom ought to forget that it is to these old English of North Germany and Jutland that we are indebted for the germs of these institutions which constitute the bulwark of our liberties—notably for trial by jury and our legislative assemblies, whether bearing the name of National Parliaments, Congresses, or State Legislatures. Jury trial had its origin in the Anglo-Saxon local courts for the settlement of disputes, consisting of twelve men presided over by a reeve, who had no voice in the decisions. Still more clearly, our constitutional deliberative assemblies have their root in the Witenagemote, or meeting of the wise men, whose function it was to assist the chief or king in the government of his people, and in the event of his death to elect a successor to him, taken from the royal family. When England became one nation, this assembly, composed of Ealdormen (Earls), Bishops, and Abbots, met regularly three times a year, as also on special occasions when summoned. In addition to their functions as counsellors of the sovereign these greater nobles or Earls were the judges of their respective districts, invested with the power of life and death. Below them were the Thanes, men who had risen to the ranks of the nobility by personal services to the king. Next to these came the Churls, freemen in whom we are to look for the prototypes of the famed yeomen of England. Last of all came the Serfs, a class bound to the soil on which they were born. This lowest class constituted two-thirds of the people of early England.

The Englishman used to wear a long woollen or hempen dress resembling the frock yet worn by English wagoners, and their legs were wound round by strips of cloth in lieu of stockings. Their houses were of wood, one story, and chimneyless, a hole in the ridge serving for the escape of the smoke from the fire that burned directly under it. The windows were unglazed, the first glass in the country being that brought from Italy for York Cathedral, or, as some say, for Hexham Abbey, and this the people flocked from far to see as a great marvel. In case of storm the windows were closed with shutters, in which occasionally a piece of thin, semi-translucent horn was inserted, affording just light enough to make darkness visible. At noon the lord and lady of the house took their place at the head of the dinner-table, seated on cross-legged stools, the family, dependents, and servants sitting along the table on benches. Square pieces of wood, called trenchers, served instead of plates, and the servants carried round the meat on spits, from which each one cut off his portion with his own knife, eating it without a fork. The bones or rejected pieces were thrown on the floor, which in the better class of houses was daily covered with fresh rushes, and for these waifs the great hunting-dogs struggled and fought. Mead or ale was quaffed freely, the lord and lady drinking from silver cups, and pledging the company with the words "*Wæs heal*" (wassail), or "Health to you," while the retainers responded by elevating their beakers of cow-horn and shouting "*Drinc heal.*" The Saxons, unlike their Norman successors, were gross feeders and stout drinkers, one of the chief delights in their heathen heaven or Walhalla being great feasts, with unstinted goblets of their favorite mead. But the Saxon was not insensible to the charm of poetry and music. The "gleeman" or wandering minstrel was often introduced at their feasts, joyously welcomed, and generously treated. Chroniclers say that even in time of war these ministers of pleasure were privileged to travel securely over the country at their discretion.

No sooner were the different kingdoms of England united into one than a new cloud darkened its horizon. Norway and its fellow Scandinavian kingdoms were at this time brought to order by a series of great sovereigns, and the bolder and more unruly spirits who would not submit to their rule were driven to the sea and embraced a life of piracy and war. These were the "Vikings" of the poet and chronicler, the "Danes" of English history. At first they contented themselves with landing on the eastern shores of England, filling their long ships with plunder and returning to their strongholds on the shores of the Baltic or North Sea for the winter. Tempted, like their Anglo-Saxon predecessors, by the richness and fertility of the country, they began to form settlements at various points, and to wage war with the English of the interior. And now began a struggle characterized by terrible ferocity. The Danes regarded the English as apostates from the ancient faith of their common ancestry, and religious hate embittered a conflict between races stern enough without such instigation. It was at the commencement of this gloomy period that "the bright, consummate flower" of Saxon manhood showed itself. Alfred, commonly known as Alfred the Great, grandson of Egbert, was born in 849. Though youngest of four sons, he was chosen to succeed his brother Ethelred on the throne, which he ascended at the age of twenty-three. Even before this he had given proof of his ability as a warrior in repelling the Danes, and on becoming king he redoubled his exertions. But the enemy poured fresh bands upon the coast, and in 878 the invaders had overrun all his ancestral kingdom of Wessex. Alfred, forced to take refuge in the woods and morasses, found shelter for a time in a cowherd's hut. There it is said he was set by the herdsman's wife to watch some cakes that were baking at the fire. Alfred, intent on repairing his bow, let the cakes burn, and was reproved by the indignant matron, with the remark that he was glad enough to eat them, though too careless to turn them. He did not cease to keep up communication with his friends, and building a stronghold on an elevation amid the marshes of Somersetshire, still known as Athelney or "the island of the nobles," he made frequent successful sallies against the enemy. On one occasion he introduced himself into their camp in the disguise of a minstrel, and, after amusing the unsuspicious Danes, disappeared as mysteriously as he came. Putting himself at the head of his followers, he fell upon the unguarded camp of the enemy and gained a great victory. Guthrum, their king, accepted baptism, and, withdrawing from Wessex, settled with his followers in the east of England, and ever after proved faithful in his allegiance. To meet his foes at sea he built England's first fleet, and on the arrival of Hastings, the great sea-king, he hurried to meet him, captured his fleet, routed his army, and compelled that robber-chief to flee to France. In 888 Alfred was recognized as king of all England. During the ensuing years of peace he rebuilt ruined cities, erected fortresses, trained his people to arms, encouraged husbandry and other useful arts, and inaugurated many wise laws and institutions which contributed to the future greatness of Britain. In an age of ignorance he was a scholar and patron of learning, himself translating several works from Latin into Anglo-Saxon. He died in 901 at the age of fifty-two, leaving his country in the enjoyment of peace and prosperity. It has been said that during his reign gold and jewels could be left unguarded by the wayside and would remain untouched by traveller or dweller.

It would carry us far beyond our bounds were we to enter into the details of the history of Alfred's successors. But it would be a sadly defective view of these early times did we omit reference to the church and the part it played in English history. Briefly it may be said that the monasteries and abbeys with which the country abounded were the depositories of all the learning of the time. The exquisitely illuminated missals and other manuscripts, still extant, testify to the devotion and diligence of the monks in multiplying and beautifying religious works. But there was another sphere in which the clergy played a great part. This was statesmanship, for which their superior learning and shrewdness especially qualified them. As illustrative of this phase of national life we shall briefly summarize the biography of St. Dunstan.

ALFRED THE GREAT IN HIS STUDY.
(By A. Maillart.)

Born of noble parents, in 925, and having an uncle Archbishop of Canterbury, Dunstan was carefully educated for the church; endowed with high talent, he became accomplished in many directions. He was not only a learned scholar, but he was also an excellent composer of music, a skilled performer on several instruments, a painter, a worker in design, a calligrapher, a jeweller, and a blacksmith. Being introduced by his uncle to the court of King Athelstan, the nobles, with true prescience of his character, from dread of his influence, procured his expulsion as a sorcerer.

He now assumed a new role. He constructed a cell, partly under ground, five feet long by two wide, so that he could not lie in it at full length, and this he made his bed-chamber, his workshop, and oratory. Asceticism of so pre-eminently pious character naturally stirred the devil to action, and he, putting his head in at the window one evening, when the saint was at work at his forge, attempted to allure him to his service by seductively immoral proposals. The temptation only roused the holy man to indignation, and parleying only till his tongs attained a white heat, he seized the foul fiend with this implement by the nose, and so held him till the neighborhood re-echoed with his yells.

It was impossible, in such an age, that sanctity of this proved character could pass unnoticed. On the accession of Edmund to the throne Dunstan was recalled to court. But in spite of his penances and exploits, in spite even of the odor of sanctity, he was still antagonized by the nobles, who knew his ambition and dreaded his talents and determination of character. A second time, therefore, he was dismissed, but on this occasion he was, in respect of his saintliness, created Abbot of Glastonbury. Edred, Edmund's successor, showed Dunstan great favor, and the vigorous policy of this reign is ascribed to the inspiration of the great monk. For the first time the Danes of Northumbria were reduced to a state of complete subjugation, while, on the other hand, the monkish orders were promoted to great pre-eminence and power. After a reign of nine years Edred died and was succeeded by Edwy. This prince had long suspected Dunstan of peculation, and knew him to be the bitter foe of his wife Edgiva, and one of the first acts of his reign was to degrade him from his office and banish him; while all his reforms in the church were frustrated, and the monks expelled from their monasteries. Dunstan fled to Flanders, narrowly escaping having his eyes put out by officers sent to seize him with this purpose. Almost immediately on his flight the Northumbrian Danes again rose, while, shortly thereafter, King Edwy's brother Edgar, a lad of fifteen, was chosen sovereign of the districts north of the Thames. Dunstan came home from his brief exile in triumph. The mysterious death of Edwy's beautiful wife Edgiva (whom Dunstan hated) broke that monarch's heart, and Edgar became King of all England. This boy-king was but a tool in the hands of the astute and determined churchman. Dunstan's opportunity had now come, and he quickly showed that the high estimate of his powers was in no respect exaggerated. All the districts of the country were consolidated into union more compact than had ever been known before; the Danes were again reduced to subjection and their kingdom broken up into earldoms; a navy was created to defend the coast against Norse invaders; the king was induced to visit every part of his dominions annually, holding courts of justice and granting audiences to his subjects; wild beasts were extirpated; the coinage reformed, and many other wise measures adopted which space forbids us to enumerate. Priestlike, Dunstan never forgot he was a churchman. Monasteries were founded in every part of the kingdom, and filled with celibate recluses and endowed till over a third part of the land of the country was in the hands of the church. The holy man himself accepted the highest dignity in the English church, namely, the Archbishopric of Canterbury.

On Edgar's death a struggle took place for the successorship. Like the war-horse of Scripture, Dunstan, smelling the battle from afar, again rushed into the arena of conflict. Partially foiled by a wicked and unscrupulous woman who murdered Edward, the successor preferred by Dunstan, the archbishop was compelled to place the crown on the head of Athelred, whose claims he had opposed. His credit and influence now declined; even his threats of divine vengeance were treated with indifference. Unable to bear up against the disgrace of discomfiture and contempt, Dunstan, in 988, retired to his archiepiscopal capital, where he died of grief.

The great blot on Dunstan's character is the suspicion (so strong as to be almost certainty) that he was an instigator of, or consenter to, the barbarities practised on Queen Edgiva, whose face was burned with red-hot irons to destroy her beauty, and who was subsequently hamstrung and tortured so that she died. The thoughtful reader of this story of Dunstan will not fail to gain from it large insight into the condition of England—intellectually, morally, and religiously—during the tenth century.

The bells that rung in the accession of Athelred, "The Redeless," sounded the knell of Anglo-Saxon supremacy. No sooner was the strong hand of Dunstan removed than the Danish settlers in the north renewed hostilities, aided by fresh bands of their countrymen who ravaged the coasts. The weak king had recourse to the fatal expedient of buying them off, and a tax, bearing the name of Danegelt, was imposed for the purpose of paying them an annual tribute. The Danes were at the same time permitted to settle where they chose, even in Wessex. To strengthen himself Athelred married Emma, daughter of the Duke of Normandy, and it was soon seen that the so-called peace was only a screen for treachery. Urged by secret orders from the king the men of Wessex rose on St. Brice's day, 1002, and pitilessly massacred the Danes. Among others killed were Gunhild, sister of Swegn, King of Norway, as well as her husband and child. Swegn vowed vengeance, and kept his vow ruthlessly. Through and through Wessex he marched at the head of his terrible "Berserkers," "lighting his war-beacons as he went, leaving behind him only corpses and the smoke of burning dwellings." In ten years Swegn was master of all England, but died just on the eve of his coronation. Athelred at once returned from the court of his brother-in-law, where he had taken refuge, and inspired by the example and counsels of the chivalric Normans conducted himself with such resolution that he compelled the young Norse king, Cnut, to withdraw to his native land. Athelred died in 1016, leaving it to his son Edmund, called, from his hardihood, "Ironsides," to continue the struggle with Cnut, who had returned at the head of fresh forces. Well did the young Englishman vindicate his surname. He fought five pitched battles with the Danes, and peace was restored by an arrangement by which Cnut became sovereign of North England, while Edmund was king of all the rest. In 1017 Edmund was murdered by his nobles at Oxford, and the Danish or Norse king, Cnut, was sovereign of all England.

Cnut was not only a brave warrior, but he was a wise and thoughtful man. He married the Norman Emma, widow of Athelred, and strove, with success, to weld the Danes and the Anglo-Saxons into one united English people. One main distinction is to be noted between the conquest of England by the Danes and the conquest of Britain by the Anglo-Saxons. The British Kelts and the Teutonic Saxons and Angles were peoples totally dissimilar in race, speech, and religion. The Danes and Anglo-Saxons were nearly allied branches of the same stock. So soon as the stumbling-block of religion was removed by the conversion of the Danes, the two races naturally and easily coalesced. Cnut proved his title to be regarded among the wisest and best of England's kings by his treatment of the Christian church. His Danish predecessors had been merciless, when they had the power, in their destruction of religious houses, and the massacre of their inmates. Cnut, whether from policy or conviction, encouraged his people to unity of faith with the Christian Anglo-Saxons, founded and endowed religious houses, and even protected pious Christians on their pilgrimages to Rome against the robbers of the Alps. Thus did Angles, Saxons, and Danes become fused into one people.

There is no king of whom more pleasant stories are told than of Cnut. One cold Candlemas-day he set out on foot to attend mass at Ely Abbey. The abbey stood on high ground in the midst of a morass, which was frozen over. Cnut's attendants hesitated to venture on the ice and dissuaded the king from attempting to cross. At length a jolly countryman, who from his plumpness bore the sobriquet of "The Pudding," stepped forward: "What!" said he, "are you Christians, and afraid to go to God's house or to let your king go? Lo, I will go before him, and we shall pass in safety." "Where this good fellow goes, I will follow," said Cnut, "so help me the Christians' God." The passage was made in safety, and "The Pudding" was rewarded by being made proprietor of a piece of land. Whether there was politic arrangement in the matter we cannot know. In any case in these days of credulity it had its influence in reconciling the Danes to acceptance of the Christian faith. The pleasing song which he composed while rowing, on one occasion, on the vast fen waters surrounding the abbey and listening to the monks' even-song, goes to prove that his regard for these holy men was sincere. "Merrily sang the monks of Ely when Cnut the king rowed by. Row, boatmen, near the land, and hear we these monks sing." The story of Cnut's rebuke to his fawning courtiers, who professed to believe he could control the winds and the tides, is too well known to require recital.

BAPTISM OF CNUT BY AUGUSTINE.

Cnut died, lamented, in 1036, and was succeeded first by a son, Harold, and on Harold's death by another son, Harthacnut. Both of the great man's sons so disgusted the people by their cruelties and excesses that, on Harthacnut's death, in 1041, they called Edward the Confessor, son of Cnut's wife Emma by her former husband, Athelred, to the throne, and the Anglo-Saxons greatly rejoiced to see a king of their own stock once more sovereign of England. Edward was, after all, only half-English, and he had been brought up among his mother's relations in Normandy. To the displeasure of his people he surrounded himself too much with Norman counsellors and courtiers. He had, however, the wisdom to select as his principal adviser the great Earl of Wessex, Godwin, son-in-law of Cnut, and the ablest statesman in the kingdom. Godwin by his skill and influence was able to maintain peace between the jealous English and the haughty Normans. An interesting story is told regarding the manner in which Godwin first rose to distinction. Ulf, a Danish *jarl*, who had received in marriage a sister of Cnut, after one of the battles with Edmund Ironsides, was separated from the rest of the army. He wandered all one dark, inclement night, and in the morning met a youth driving out some cattle. Ulf asked his name, and the reply was: "I am Godwin, son of Ulfnoth, and you are, I think, a Dane." Ulf confessed that he was, and begged the young man to show him the way to the Severn, where he expected to find the Danish fleet. "The Dane would be a fool who trusted a Saxon for his guide," said the youth: "how know you I will not betray you?" "I can trust *you*." "Ah, but you cannot trust the Serfs, who, if they find you, and me guiding you, will slay both of us." Ulf offered the young man a golden ring and redoubled his entreaties. "I will take nothing from you, but I will lead you to my father's house, and there you shall lie hid till night, when I will guide you." At night, when the two were setting out, Ulfnoth told Ulf that his son would never be able to return, and begged him to keep him among his people and present him to King Cnut. This was the foundation of Godwin's greatness. He married Gydu, sister of Ulf, and thus was brought into near connection with Cnut.

The story of Godwin's death as given by the Norman chroniclers is no less interesting. One of King Edward's brothers had been slain, and there was suspicion that Godwin was privy to it. One day, when the king and Godwin were feasting, one of the cup-bearers chanced to make a false step, but saved himself from falling by laying hold of a brother who ran to help him. "See," said Godwin, "how one brother helps another." "Yes," said the king, "so would my brother have helped me, had he lived." "I know you suspect me of his death," replied Godwin, "but may God cause this morsel of bread to choke me if I am guilty of his murder." Scarcely had he uttered the words when he fell back, struck by the hand of Heaven, his soul going straight into the presence of his Maker for judgment.

Edward himself was a pious man and a just ruler. Such was his sanctity that his touch was believed to cure scrofula or the "king's evil," a belief that continued to attach itself to the royal family till the days of Queen Anne. A hundred years after his death he was canonized as a saint.

On Edward's death, in 1066, Harold, son of the great Saxon Earl Godwin, was chosen by the Witenagemote to ascend the throne.

Scarcely had Harold begun to reign ere a terrible rival appeared to dispute his claim.

NORMAN CONQUEST.

WILLIAM THE CONQUEROR. 1066—1087.

A hundred years before the date of which we now write a great band of these same Norse Vikings who had so long harassed England appeared in their long ships in the Seine, under a leader, Rolf or Rollo, and speedily overran that district of France known then as Neustria, but later as Normandy. The spirit of these people may be judged of by their conduct when the French king consented to give up this fairest portion of his domain to the daring invaders, on condition that their chief would kiss his foot in token of vassalage. This Rolf absolutely refused to do, and was persuaded with difficulty to permit one of his followers to kiss the foot in his stead. The proxy, as proud as his master, refused to kneel, but seizing the king's foot whilst he himself stood upright, after performing the meaningless act, tossed it from him right up, thus overturning both monarch and throne, amid the rude laughter of his companions. Charles and his courtiers were in such dread of their new vassals that they did not dare to resent the insult.

WILLIAM I. (THE CONQUEROR).

William, Duke of Normandy, claimed the English throne on terms of an alleged will made in his favor by Edward the Confessor, and landed at the head of a great army of Normans in October, 1066, to maintain his claim. Harold, fresh from a victory over the Danes, who had renewed their incursions, hurried south to meet him. The result was a great battle at Hastings, wherein Harold was slain, and William gained a decisive victory, which established him on the English throne.

William brought with him his bard Taillefer, to celebrate the assured victory, and he rode in front of the Norman knighthood, as they charged on the English footmen standing around their king on the height of Senlac, tossing his sword in the air and catching it again, as he chanted the song of Roland. We are unable to reproduce the strain he sung after the battle and which was chanted for long years after at the great feasts in the royal and baronial halls. We give in place the lay of one of England's greatest martial poets—Thomas Campbell:

"I climbed to yon heights where the Norman encamped him of old,
With his bowmen and knights, and his banner all burnished with gold,
At the conqueror's side there his minstrelsy sat harp in hand
In pavilion wide; and they chanted the deeds of Roland.
Still the ramparted ground with a vision my fancy inspires,
And I hear the trump sound, as it marshalled our chivalry's sires.
On each turf of that mead stood the captors of England's domains,
That ennobled her breed and high-mettled the blood in her veins.
Over hauberk and helm as the sun's setting splendor was thrown,
Thence they looked o'er a realm—and to-morrow beheld it their own."

These French Normans were no longer the rude sea-rovers and swordsmen—the terror of all the sea-coasts of Europe—that their ancestors had been. During their hundred years of intercourse with the more cultured Franks they had adopted their speech, religion, and manners, inspiring everything they borrowed with their own splendid vitality. They were indeed the very pink of medieval chivalry, the most warlike, vigorous, and brilliant race in Europe. They looked on the plainer English people with contempt and spoiled them without mercy. The land was wrested from the Anglo-Saxon earls, and thanes, and churls, and conferred by William on his nobles and other followers. In this we see the origin of the great estates, held in some cases by the heirs and descendants of these fortunate favorites, at the present day. Normans were put into all places of dignity and power; and the feudal system was introduced, by which the great nobles were granted almost unlimited power over all their tenants, on condition of their coming to the aid of the king in case of war, along with all their retainers. The larger properties were divided into smaller holdings, the possessor of each of which was bound by the same oath to his over-lord as he to the crown. "Hear, my lord," swore the vassal, as kneeling bareheaded and without arms he placed his hands within those of his superior, "I become liegeman of yours for life and limb and earthly regard; and I will keep faith and loyalty to you for life and death, God help me."

The English—a solid German people—had little feeling for elegance or art. The few remains of their buildings show these to have been strong, indeed, but tasteless. Their domestic buildings were all but exclusively of wood. The Normans had acquired not only refinement of taste but a good knowledge of architecture. Immediately after the conquest the land began to be covered with castellated fortresses, fortified with moat and drawbridge, portcullis, barbican, and bastion, and having narrow slit-like windows whence arrows could be poured on an enemy. In the single reign of Stephen no fewer than 1,115 of such castles were built. Their lords were petty tyrants; while their retainers sallied forth from these robber-holds armed cap-a-pie, swords by their sides and lances in their hands, to plunder the English yeomen and burgesses at pleasure. No company of travellers, no caravan of goods, was safe from their attacks. The poor natives, who constituted the entire trading and industrial community, had no redress. These protected bravoes retired with their booty into the strongholds of their chiefs and laughed their victims to scorn.

It is thus that Crabbe, "Nature's sternest painter but the best," celebrates Belvoir Castle, one of the most ancient in Britain. On its site a mighty chief of the Britons built his hold; afterward a Saxon lord erected on it a castle; and last came the Norman baron. Here we allow the poet to speak for himself.

> "A Norman baron, in succeeding time,
> Here, while the minstrel sang heroic rhyme,
> In feudal pomp appeared. It was his praise
> A loftier dome with happier skill to raise;
> His halls, still gloomy, yet with grandeur rose;
> Here friends were feasted, here confined were foes.
> No softening arts in those fierce times were found,
> But rival barons spread their terrors round;
> Each in the fortress of his power secure,
> Of foes was fearless and of soldiers sure;
> And here the chieftain, for his prowess praised,
> Long held the castle that his might had raised."

Hunting by hawk and hound, or shooting the deer with arrows, were favorite pastimes. Near William's castle of Winchester, Hampshire, lay a great stretch of heathy ground, nearly 60,000 acres in extent, interspersed with frequent copses of beech and oak and verdant glades between, a favorite haunt of deer, wild boars, and other game. But for one drawback this constituted a noble hunting-ground. It was peopled by many a village and hamlet, by many a plain Saxon churl's homestead and many a serf's cottage. Without a scruple the wretched natives were driven forth and their homes burned. The entire tract was converted into hunting-ground under the name of the New Forest—a name which at an interval of 800 years it yet bears. Sixty-five such forests were thus created in England, with what misery to the people our readers can judge. The forest laws were of terrible severity, the penalty for killing a stag or wild boar being loss of the eyes. The very dogs of the dwellers on the borders of the forest were mutilated by having the balls of their feet cut out so that they could not follow the chase. "William," says the Saxon chronicle, "loved the great deer as if he had been their father."

Every effort was made to suppress the native speech. Norman-French was the language of the court, of law, of the church, of literature, and of the schools. To teach English at school was a punishable offence. Even to this day Norman-French law phrases linger in our law-courts. When the crier of an American court calls out on its opening each morning, "O yes! O yes! O yes! I declare this honorable court now open," he is but repeating the old Norman Oyez! Oyez! Oyez! hear ye! hear ye! hear ye!

Nor must we forget to speak of the curfew. Precisely at sundown on every summer evening, and at 8 o'clock in winter, there rang out a peal from every church tower and monastery steeple in England, commanding the people to cover their fires, extinguish every light, and retire to rest.

We have spoken of the castles of the nobles that now studded the land. In these the prime object was strength, combined with which there was

BURIAL OF WILLIAM THE CONQUEROR.

some degree of grandeur. It was different with the noble Gothic ecclesiastical structures that now began to "arise like exhalations" over all the country. The remains of these creations of genius (especially of those of centuries somewhat later, whose ornamentation has been likened to "frosted lace-work") testify that with all his sternness the Norman had a true sense of the beautiful.

William's death was characteristic. On one occasion, when he was sick, the King of France made a silly jest on his corpulence. "Our brother in England," he said, "is a long time lying in! There will be great doings at his churching." "When I get up," William said grimly, "I will go to mass in Philip's land, and will bring a rich offering for my churching. I will offer a thousand candles for my fee: flaming brands shall they be, and steel shall glitter over the fire they make." In fulfilment of this stern vow William traversed France, devastating it with fire and sword. In passing through the town of Mantes, while it was in flames, his horse stumbled on a burning brand, and William was sorely injured by being thrown heavily against the pommel of his saddle. He was borne home to Rouen, the capital of his paternal Duchy of Normandy, to die.

WILLIAM RUFUS. 1087—1100.

William had conquered England by his sword, and he disposed of the succession according to his pleasure. He left his hereditary Duchy of Normandy to his eldest son Robert, surnamed Curthose; but England he gave to his second and favorite son William, called, from the color of his hair, William Rufus, or red head.

WILLIAM II. (RUFUS).

With the Normans came the romance of war. But for them the Crusades, the first of which commenced during William's reign, would have had few English representatives. The holy land had fallen under the sway of the Saracens, who submitted the pious pilgrims to the sites of our Lord's passion and resurrection to manifold indignities and injuries. At length a returned pilgrim, Peter the Hermit, received authority from the pope to call on the princes and nobles of Christendom to proceed to Palestine, and rescue the holy places from Saracen rule. Forthwith, from every Christian land, there issued men whose high purpose it was

> "To chase those pagans in these blessed fields
> Over whose acres walked those blessed feet,
> Which fourteen hundred years ago were nailed
> For our advantage on the blessed cross."

One of the foremost to listen to the summons was Robert Curthose, a much less calculating man than his brother William. His weak point was want of money, and he offered to give his Duchy in pledge to the Red King, provided he would advance the needed gold. The terms were gladly accepted and a transaction carried through, that for centuries gave the English sovereigns a colorable claim to dominion over French territory.

It is not our province to enter into the details of the expedition on which Robert now set out. It is only needful to state that after the loss of incalculable lives, Jerusalem was taken and the kingship offered to Robert. This proffer he declined, purposing to return and look after his interests in Europe.

Here we may pause for a moment to note, that, comparatively fruitless as this and all succeeding crusades were in direct results, indirectly they contributed largely to the civilization and culture of the nations participating in them. They broadened the minds of men by opening up to them new fields of observation; they brought nationalities into contact with each other and taught them to act in harmony, or at least in concert; they familiarized Europe to some extent with the learning of the East; they promoted navigation and ship-building and extended the knowledge of astronomy. Above all, they may be said to have originated and fostered that spirit of chivalry which for centuries was the main humanizing influence in these otherwise dark and fierce ages.

During Robert's absence in Palestine the Red King met his death. His end, like his father's, was tragical. While hunting in the New Forest he was shot by an arrow sped from a bow discharged by his friend and companion, Sir Walter Tyrrell, to whom he had given "three long arrows." Whether the shot was designed will never be known. This, at least, is certain, that, in expiation, Sir Walter set off to join the crusade. Men were not slack to see in William's fate an act of divine retribution for the depopulation of the New Forest. His corpse lay uncared for, where he fell at the foot of an oak tree, till one Purkiss, a charcoal-burner, belonging to the forest-hamlet of Minestead, came by and lifted it up, and carried it in his rude cart, which dripped with the blood flowing from the wound, to Winchester. Purkiss' descendants still dwell at Minestead, and the way by which he travelled is still called the King's Lane. The oak under which William fell stood till 1745, and a stone now marks the place.

> "A Minestead churl, whose wonted trade
> Was burning charcoal in the glade,
>   Outstretched amid the gorse
> The monarch found; and in his wain
> He raised, and to St. Swithin's fane
>   Conveyed the bleeding corse.
>
> "And still—so runs our forest creed—
> Flourish the pious woodman's seed,
>   Even on the self-same spot:
> One horse and cart, their little store,
> Like their forefathers, neither more
>   Nor less, their children's lot.
>
> "Thus in those fields the Red King died
> His father wasted in his pride,

> For it is God's command,
> Who doth another's birthright rive,
> The curse unto his blood shall cleave,
> And God's own word shall stand."

Taking advantage of Robert's absence, Henry, the youngest son of the Conqueror, now mounted the throne.

HENRY I. (BEAUCLERC).   1100—1135.

Judging from the character of the successive kings of England one is forced to the conclusion that a really good man is one of the rarest things in nature. Henry (surnamed from his learning Beauclerc), the youngest son of the Conqueror, was one of England's ablest kings. He shielded the people against the exactions of the nobles, gave them a charter of liberties, renounced the right to plunder the church, and conciliated his people by marrying the Scotch princess, Maud, great-granddaughter of Edmund Ironsides, thus uniting the Norman and Saxon lines. Yet he was a grasping, heartless, cold-blooded man. His brother Robert, on his return from Palestine, made an attempt on the throne, but finding the people devoted to Henry he recrossed to France without a battle. Several of the greater nobles, fretting at the restrictions Henry laid upon them, had favored Robert. Their estates were confiscated and parcelled out among a lesser nobility of the king's creation, while their owners pined eyeless in noisome dungeons.

HENRY I.

Robert managed badly in Normandy. It is said he was so poor that he had sometimes to lie in bed because he had no clothes to wear. Some of his nobles, disgusted, invited Henry over to take the duchy. Henry appeared in France at the head of an army, mainly composed of native English. The two brothers met in battle at Trenchbray, and once more English bows and bills confronted, as at Hastings, the swords and lances of Norman chivalry. The English gained the victory, and they gloried over it as a set-off for Hastings. Robert was captured, and lingered twenty-eight years a prisoner in Cardiff Castle. Having once attempted to escape, his heartless brother caused his eyes to be burned out with red-hot irons.

Henry's death was sadder than that of either his father or brother William. His son, William the Atheling, with a crowd of nobles, prepared to accompany him on his return to England. There was unbounded festivity on board the "White Ship," on which the young prince had embarked. Scarcely had she cleared the harbor till she struck a rock. One terrible cry rung through the silence of the night and reached the ears of the king. When morning came only the top-mast was visible, with two men clinging to it. One dropped off before he was rescued, and the only survivor of all that jovial crew was a poor butcher of Rouen. When Henry was made aware of the fatal truth he dropt senseless to the ground, and rose never to smile again. He died in 1135.

Henry named his daughter, Maude, married to Geoffrey Plantagenet, Earl of Anjou, as his successor. But in these iron days men did not take readily to a female sovereign, so Stephen of Blois, grandson of the Conqueror, seized the throne.

STEPHEN I.

The condition of England during Stephen's sway was appalling. The great nobles, knowing the weakness of his claim, thought they could do as they wished. Baron made war on baron; travellers were waylaid, and wealthy burgesses were immured in dungeons and tortured till they yielded up their wealth. When Stephen attempted to check these atrocities, they turned round and told him that not he, but Maude Plantagenet, was their sovereign. On their invitation, Maude came over, and a civil war ensued, which resulted in the division of the kingdom between Stephen and Maude's son, Henry. During the war "confusion became worse confounded." The land was a prey to disorderly soldiery. The woods were filled with outlaws, mainly English, who killed

STEPHEN I.

the king's deer, preyed on the Normans and wealthy priests and burgesses, but spared their poor countrymen, and were generous to the peasantry, often bestowing on them a portion of their spoils. These were the dwellers in the "merrie green-wood," whom the old ballad-makers delighted to celebrate. Robin Hood, the bandit-hero of Sherwood Forest, "the English ballad-singer's joy," with his jovial companions, Little John, Friar Tuck, and their sylvan mistress, Maid Marion, belong, indeed, to a subsequent reign, but they were the accepted types of the class.

Stephen lived but a year after the division of the kingdom, and Henry Plantagenet assumed the crown without opposition.

HENRY II. (PLANTAGENET).   1154—1189.

The second Henry was only in his twenty-first year when he mounted the throne of England in circumstances so perplexing. But he was of the stuff of which rulers are made—an active, vigorous man with much of the ability, and many of the accomplishments, of his grandfather Henry I. He set to work to educe order out of confusion, moving from place to place unweariedly.

HENRY II.

He cleared the country of foreign soldiery, dismantled or demolished many of the robber holds of the nobility, confirmed a charter of privileges to his people, and, in the words of a historian, "no one in so short a time had done so much good, and gained so much love, since Alfred." He established trial by jury on a more satisfactory basis than formerly, and reformed the judiciary system. Here it is interesting to note some of the old modes of trying suspected or accused persons. One was by ordeal, or submitting the case to the judgment of God. If the prisoner could plunge his hand into boiling water, or carry a red-hot bar of iron a certain distance, without exhibiting any scar, he was pronounced innocent. Sometimes he was bound hand and foot and thrown into water. If he sank he was innocent; if he swam, guilty. This was a favorite and effectual way of disposing of witches. Another mode was trial by wager of battle. This mode was introduced by the Conqueror and continued in legal force till the reign of George III.

The two grand events in Henry's reign was his conflict with the church and the conquest of Ireland.

Hitherto clerics (that is, all educated persons, whether in holy orders or not) were subject only to ecclesiastical courts, which could not inflict capital punishment. This was called benefit of clergy. Henry was resolved to amend this. More than 100 murders were committed in the early years of his reign by clergy who suffered no adequate punishment. A parliament of nobles and prelates was convened at Clarendon, which enacted certain " constitutions " or laws, the most important of which were those limiting and defining the power of the pope, and making clergy amenable to the regular secular courts.

At this time the ablest subject in the kingdom was Thomas-a-Becket. He rose to be Henry's high chancellor and most trusted minister. A strangely romantic tradition associates itself with Thomas-a-Becket's birth. It is told that in the reign of Henry I. the citizens of London were amazed by the sight of a maiden in eastern dress, who wandered the streets, plaintively uttering the word "Gilbert." Certain seafaring men told how she had prevailed on them to take her on board their ship in a port of the Holy Land by constantly repeating the word "London." The rude mob pursued her till she came to the front of a house occupied by Gilbert-a-Becket, who, with his servant, Richard, had just returned from a pilgrimage to Palestine. Richard went out to the

WARWICK CASTLE.

hunted maiden, who fainted on seeing him. He carried her to the house of an honorable widow, desiring her to take care of her for his master's sake.

Meanwhile Gilbert-a-Becket betook himself to the Bishop of London and told his story. He related how he and Richard had been captured and made slaves to a wealthy emir. He attracted the notice and gained the love of the chief's daughter, who offered to contrive his escape if he would make her his wife. Gilbert did escape, but he left the generous maiden behind. She left home, riches, and father, and with only these two words—his name and that of his city—reached his door. Five other prelates were present when Gilbert told his story. One, the Bishop of Chichester, exclaimed that Heaven itself

MURDER OF THOMAS-A-BECKET.

must have conducted the damsel. All united in urging immediate marriage. The next day she was brought to St. Paul's Cathedral and was there baptized and married. Next year she gave birth to her distinguished son Thomas.

Even on the supposition that the story is entirely accurate, Thomas-a-Becket was, at any rate, a true-born Englishman on the father's side, who was of pure Saxon blood. Being the first of his race who had risen to high office since the conquest, the people were proud of him, and reverenced him. He himself assumed a state and dignity almost regal. In 1162 he was made Archbishop of Canterbury, whereupon, at once renouncing his luxurious habits, he assumed an austere and saintly character. He became the champion of the church and antagonized Henry's endeavors to subordinate it to law. Henry's rage was terrible, and Becket fled to France, visiting Rome to confer with the pope! Both the pope and the King of France took part with the archbishop. At length, after two years, reconciliation was effected, and Becket returned to England, entering Canterbury amid the plaudits of the people. Emboldened, he began to act with the greatest insolence, and seemed inclined to renew the war with the king. The Archbishop of York, and others whom Becket had excommunicated, repaired to the king, who was in Normandy. Henry on hearing their detail of grievances exclaimed, "How miserably am I reduced that I cannot have rest by reason of one single priest! Is there no one to relieve me?" Four ardent knights at once set out for Canterbury, and ordered Becket to absolve the excommunicated persons or quit the kingdom. Becket defied them, despising their threats. They retired and armed themselves, and when the time of evening service was come, backed by their followers, murdered Becket before the altar. A cry of horror went up from all Christendom. Henry bent before the storm. Becket was canonized under the title of St. Thomas of Canterbury, and numerous miracles were worked at his tomb, which for centuries was a favorite shrine of pious pilgrims. Thus the fine old poet Chaucer says:

> "And chiefely from every shire's end
> Of Engleland to Canterbury they wend
> The holy blissful martyr for to seek,
> Who them hath holpen when that they were sick."

Dearly had Henry to aby the zeal of his knights. Humbling himself, he made a pilgrimage to the saint's tomb, alighting from his horse and approaching it barefoot. The livelong night he passed on his knees at the shrine, and, in the morning, placing a scourge in the willing hands of the monks, he submitted his back to their bitter discipline. This humiliation gained him absolution, and as, on the very day he thus prostrated himself, his army gained a victory over the Scots, his people knew he was reconciled to Heaven, while the sanctity of St. Thomas shone out clearer than ever.

But a yet more far-reaching event of Henry's reign was the conquest of Ireland, a conquest whose full consequences have scarcely been realized at the present day. So soon as Henry ascended the throne he looked with cupidity toward Ireland, and, so early as 1156, he received from Pope Adrian a bull authorizing him to reduce it. Henry bided his time. Ireland was then divided into five kingdoms, Roderic, King of Connaught, being Lord-Paramount. Dermot, King of Leinster, thinking himself wronged by the Lord-Paramount, had recourse to Henry for redress. This was just the pretext Henry desired, but, not willing to appear personally, he gave Dermot permission to apply to his subjects. He appealed to Strongbow, Earl of Pembroke, who, on the promise of Eva, Dermot's only daughter, in marriage and the succession to his kingdom, set out with a body of men to Dermot's assistance. His trained men easily routed the undisciplined Kernes of Ireland, and Strongbow espoused Eva, and on Dermot's death became sovereign of Leinster, as also of large portions of the adjoining kingdoms, with Henry as his superior. When Roderic, at the head of 50,000 men, besieged Pembroke in Dublin, the latter put the untrained rabble to flight with great slaughter. In 1172 Henry himself came over and held his Christmas in Dublin, where, in a huge palace of wicker-work, he entertained the Irish princes who acknowledged themselves his vassals. Ineffably better would it have been for England had the "Wild Irishry" driven Pembroke and his crew of adventurers into the Irish Sea. No such Pandora's box, replete with woes, was ever presented to man as this gift of Ireland by the English pope, Adrian Breakspear, to England's king, Henry Plantagenet.

Henry could rule a kingdom; he could not rule his own family. He had five sons, and these unnatural children repeatedly rose against their father. In one attempt, in 1173, they were abetted by William, King of Scotland, who invaded England. It was just when Henry was doing penance at Becket's tomb. King William was captured and not released till he owned himself vassal to the English crown. It was on this acknowledgment that Edward I. afterwards based his claim to the sovereignty of Scotland.

Worn out by the continued ingratitude and turbulence of his boys, Henry retired to the castle of Chinon, France. There, after a treaty of peace on account of their last rising had been signed, the king, who was sick in bed, asked to see a list of the rebels he had pardoned. The first name that met his eyes was that of John, his favorite child. Heart-broken he turned his face to the wall with these words: "Now let the world go as it will, I am done with it." Thus he died in 1189. "Uneasy lies the head that wears a crown."

Henry was not a faithful husband. He had a mistress, Rosamond Clifford, named from her beauty "The Fair Rosamond." To save her from his queen, Eleanor, he placed her in a bower in the centre of a maze at Woodstock, to which access could be gained only by following a clue of thread. Eleanor got possession of the clue, and, threading the mazes of the labyrinth, came on poor Rosamond, and compelled her to drink a bowl of poison. The desire to avenge the wrongs of their mother no doubt instigated Henry's boys to rebel against their father.

RICHARD CŒUR DE LION. 1189—1199.

Henry was succeeded by his son, Richard of the Lion Heart, the hero of the romance of English history.

The result of the first crusade had been the capture of Jerusalem. But the Saracens, under their great leader Saladin, had lately recaptured the Holy City and all the rest of Palestine, save a few towns on the coast. A grand crusade was organized, and Richard of England and Philip of France agreed to unite their forces and fight in company. The place of rendezvous was Messina, in Sicily, and while there, Richard espoused the daughter of the King of Navarre. The other participants in the crusade were already in the Holy

GATHERING OF CRUSADERS.

Land. Richard's advent was the signal for renewed effort. He knew no fear himself and taught others to despise it. He found a numerous Christian army, among which were the French troops, besieging Acre, while Saladin was at hand with a great force to relieve it. Richard captured Acre, and defeated Saladin at Ascalon, performing miracles of valor, and was pressing on to the Holy City, when dissensions, instigated by Philip, so sickened Richard, that, after making a peace with Saladin, by which free access to the Holy Places was guaranteed to Christian pilgrims, he reluctantly turned his face homeward.

The terror of his name endured for centuries in Palestine. The Arab chiefs used to chide their starting horses with the question, "Dost thou think that yonder is the Malek Rik (King Richard)?" The Saracen mother was wont to still her crying child by threats that Malek Rik would take it, or to hush it to sleep with a lullaby assuring it that the terrible Richard would not get it.

Richard had made many enemies in Palestine by his arrogance, plain-speaking, and roughness. Among these was Leopold, Duke of Austria, whose banner he had thrown down and trampled in the dirt. Sailing homeward, Richard was shipwrecked in the Adriatic, and became a captive of this very duke. The Emperor of Germany caused Cœur-de-Lion to be given up to him and held him prisoner, transferring him from one imperial castle to another, the object being to secure a great ransom. There is a romantic story associated with Richard's captivity. All tidings of their beloved king were lost to the English. One Blondel, a musician and a favorite of Richard's, went from city to city and castle to castle in search of him, long in vain. He came one evening to a castle in which there lay an unknown prisoner of note. Blondel played and sang the first verse of a song which he and Richard, in happier days, had composed together. Forthwith the second verse sounded out from the castle's grated window. Blondel's mission was accomplished: he had found him whom he came to seek. He hurried home to England, and reported the vast ransom required for the king's delivery.

RICHARD I. (CŒUR DE-LION)

The people grudged no sacrifice. Ladies gave up their jewels, the churches melted down their plate. Richard approached London amid a nation's plaudits. On entering the city the citizens in their joy made such profuse display of wealth that a German noble, who accompanied him home, half bitterly said: "My King, had our master but dreamed of the riches of England, thy ransom would have been four times greater."

When Philip of France heard that the Lion-heart was again free, he wrote Richard's traitorous brother John, who had tried to steal the kingdom from him: "Take care of yourself, for the devil is loose." John prepared to flee; but, at his brother's command, remained, and on meeting him threw himself at his feet. When Richard was asked by his mother to pardon John: "I forgive him," he said, "and hope I shall as easily forget his injuries as he will my pardon."

The death of Richard was valiant and romantic as his life. His vassal, the Viscount of Limoges, had found a treasure and sent Richard a part. He demanded the whole, and on his demand being refused, besieged the viscount's castle. One day, while he was viewing the castle, Bertrand de Gourdon shot at him with his cross-bow and wounded him mortally. The castle was taken and all in it put to death, save Gourdon. The king summoned him into his presence and asked what he had done that he should desire to slay him. "You killed my father and my two brothers, I have revenged them; do with me as you will." Struck by the undaunted reply, the king ordered him a sum of money and his liberty.

KING JOHN LACKLAND. (1199—1216.)

One grand event marks the reign of this mean monarch. This was the wringing from him of Magna Charta, the charter of the English people's liberties. Thus does God out of seeming evil educe good. We shall briefly recite how this was effected.

The heir to the crown of England was Arthur, son of Richard's next brother Geoffrey. The boy being only twelve years old, Richard left the crown to John. But when Arthur was fifteen, he was encouraged by Philip of France to make war in support of his claim. Being defeated he was confined in a castle on the banks of the Seine in Normandy. There, one night, he was awakened at midnight, and ordered to enter a boat in which sat the king and one attendant. Arthur's presaging heart foretold him his fate. He threw himself on his knees and begged pitifully for his life. In the words of the old ballad, it is vain "to beg for grace from a graceless face." He was seized by the hair and a dagger buried in his heart. John had even brought a large stone with him into the boat, and weighting the body with that, sunk it in the Seine.

JOHN SWEARING VENGEANCE AGAINST THE BARONS.

This deed of barbarity cost John Normandy and most of his French dominions. Philip summoned him to answer for the murder. He refused to appear, and in his absence was condemned to death, and all his territories declared forfeited. Such was the horror felt at his crime that, on Philip entering John's hereditary territory, every place was surrendered without a blow, and naught of France was left to him save Guienne.

We of the present day cannot appreciate what it was in the dark ages for a sovereign to strive with the pope. Into such a strife John fell over the appointment of an archbishop of Canterbury. The pope wisely nominated a native Englishman, Stephen Langton, for the office. John, Norman at heart and loving none of the English race, resisted obstinately. The result was that the land was laid under papal interdict. The comforts of religion were withdrawn; the churches were closed: "no knell was tolled for the dead, for the dead lay unburied; no merry peals welcomed the bridal procession, for no couple could be joined in wedlock." John retaliated on the church, and excommunication followed, and finally a papal bull of deposition. No man owed the king duty; any man might slay him. Philip of France was commissioned to execute the pope's decrees. John, craven-like, succumbed, for his people had fallen from him, and on his knees before the papal legate acknowledged himself the pope's vassal and his kingdom a fief of Rome.

Black hate lay in John's heart towards the barons who had failed him and used his extremity to restrain the too enormous power of the crown. Three years of outrage on his part brought matters to a crisis. The English Archbishop of Canterbury read to the barons the charter of Henry I., and they swore on the altar to make war on John till he had granted them one yet fuller. John found himself face to face with a people in arms. He was in a deadly plight.

> "The color of the king did come and go
> Between his purpose and his conscience."

But the barons were inexorable. A meeting was agreed on; the time, 15th June, 1215; the place, the broad, smooth, green meadow of Runnymede, on the banks of the Thames, spreading out fair and fertile beneath the heights of Windsor, crowned by its ancient castle. There the Magna Charta was spread forth and signed—the great charter of the liberties of the English people; in which the serfs, who still constituted the bulk of the people, were for the first time recognized as having rights. The original charter is still to be seen, bearing John's great seal, in the British Museum.

Next year John died, after a wicked reign of eighteen years.

HENRY III. 1216—1272.

Henry, John's son, was only ten years of age at the death of his father. The early years of his reign present few points of interest. He grew up devoid of the grosser vices of his father, but he had more of the southern

HENRY III.

troubadour than the stern northern warrior in his composition. He thought little of affairs, and recked not of extortions, but loved to indulge extravagant tastes for splendor and gayety, in which his youthful queen encouraged him. He loved music, poetry, romance, sculpture, and painting. In his palace fun, frolic, songs, pageants, and dancing were the order of the day. A babel of languages—Italian, Provençal, Gascon, Latin, French, English—says the "Cameos of History" from which we quote—were spoken at his court. Minstrels were there of all nationalities. There was Richard, the king's harper, who had forty shillings a year and a tun of wine. There was Henry of Avranches, the arch-poet, who wrote a song on the rusticity of Cornishmen, to which a Cornishman, Michael Blampayne, replied by describing him as having "the legs of a sparrow, the mouth of a hare, the nose of a dog, the teeth of a mule, the brow of a calf, the head of a bull." There was Ribault, the troubadour, who in a fit of madness imagined himself rightful king, and nearly killed Henry when cutting the royal bed to pieces with his sword, till secured by the action of Margaret Bisset, one of the queen's ladies. There was the half-witted jester, with whom the king and his brother Aymer might be seen playing like boys, and pelting each other with turf. His palace was gorgeously decorated with tapestry, paintings, and sculpture. One piece of jewelry is specially mentioned—a silver ewer for perfumes, in the shape of a peacock, the tail set with precious stones.

There was soon an end to Henry's treasures, and he had recourse to unconstitutional exactions. Like several other weak kings, James I. for example, he had extravagant notions about the divine right of kings, believing that

"Not all the water in the rough rude sea
Can wash the balm from an anointed king."

Had he been allowed his will he would have been tyrannous. One of his attempts was to subordinate the charter to royal prerogative. As from the oppression of John sprang the Magna Charta, so from Henry's faithlessness sprang the English House of Commons. Upon the occasion of Henry demanding a supply of money the clergy deputed the primate and certain bishops to remonstrate with him. At the conference, the charter was read aloud, all the prelates standing with lighted tapers in their hands. At the close of the reading, sentence of excommunication was pronounced against whoever should violate it, the tapers being at the same moment cast on the ground and extinguished, the primate solemnly saying: "May the soul of him who incurs this sentence stink in hell." The king, laying his hand on his heart, replied: "So help me God, I shall observe and keep these things as I am a Christian man, a knight, and a king crowned and anointed." Yet no sooner was the ceremony over than the promise was gone from his mind.

It was now apparent that stronger measures were needed, and a confederacy of nobles was formed, with Simon de Montfort, Earl of Leicester, at the head. After sundry negotiations an action took place between the forces of the king and those under Leicester at Lewes, Sussex, in which the royalists were defeated and Prince Edward, Henry's son, taken prisoner.

Leicester was now in effect sovereign of England, carrying the king about with him, and making what regulations he chose in his name. In 1265 he directed the sheriffs "to elect and return two knights for each county, two citizens for each city, and two burgesses for each burgh in the county." This is interesting to every student as exhibiting the origin of the House of Commons.

Prince Edward at length escaped, and raised an army which met that of Leicester at Evesham, in Worcestershire, defeating it with terrible slaughter. Of all the barons and knights in Leicester's army only ten remained alive, the great baron being struck down after demanding quarter.

After the defeat and death of Leicester all opposition to royal authority was at an end. Prince Edward, whose nature was essentially warlike, took advantage of the calm to head a crusade in the east, where he renewed the fame of Richard the lion-hearted. A romantic story is told in connection with this crusade. The Prince of Jaffa professed a desire to embrace Christianity, and sent one day an envoy to Edward, who was reclining in his tent during the heat of the day. Springing suddenly on the prince the Saracen attempted to plunge a dagger in his heart. Edward received the blow on his arm, and then killed the ruffian with his own weapon. But the dagger was poisoned, and Edward must die unless the venom was extracted, and who would risk a life to save that of the heroic prince? Eleanor of Castile, the prince's spouse, with true wifely devotion, periled her own life to save that of her husband. Kneeling by the side of his couch she sucked the poison from the wound. Both were spared; he to be a loving husband, she to be an honored wife.

Henry III. died after a reign of fifty-five years. There have been but three English sovereigns who reigned over fifty years—Henry III., Edward III., George III. Queen Victoria approaches this term.

We have already indicated the dawn of English literature in connection with Cædmon, Alfred, and the venerable Bede. We have now to record the dawn of English science. Roger Bacon, a monk of Oxford, and the most enlightened man of his age, flourished during the reign of Henry III. He applied his learning chiefly to making useful discoveries, and invented the telescope, microscope, and many other mathematical and astronomical instruments; discovered the errors in the calendar and gave data for rectifying them that come very near truth. His most famed discovery is that of gunpowder, but he did not contemplate it as an instrument of destruction. Like Galileo, and other pioneers of science, he suffered persecution, having been twice imprisoned by the church, the last imprisonment lasting ten years. On account of his extraordinary knowledge he received the name of the "Doctor Mirabilis."

EDWARD LONGSHANKS. 1272—1307.

Edward, son of a weak father, was one of England's great kings, eminent alike in war and statesmanship.

The Welsh still regarded themselves as the rightful owners of all England, and their native bards sung of the glories of the days of Arthur and his round table and kept alive the national spirit. Llewellyn, their prince, refused to do homage to Edward, who, marching into Wales, compelled him to submit. But their bards recalled a prediction of their national prophet, Merlin, and in 1282 inspired the people to rise against their rulers. Edward, a second time, led a host into the mountains, and, Llewellyn having been slain, finally annexed Wales to England. His good queen had accompanied him on the campaign, and at Caernarvon Castle gave birth to a son, called, from his birthplace, Prince of Wales. Edward told the chiefs that, if they would come to Caernarvon, he would give them a prince who never spoke a word of any language but their own. They came, and the king descended to them bearing his baby in his arms. A Welsh nurse was given the infant, so that the first words he spoke were Welsh. Thus was Wales reconciled to English rule. Ever since, the heir to the English crown bears the title of Prince of Wales.

EDWARD I. (LONGSHANKS).

A TOURNAMENT.

Far different was the task Edward set himself when he endeavored to subjugate Scotland, and fortunate was it for England that he failed. This episode, however, falls more under Scotch than English history and is relegated thither accordingly.

While occupied with the attempt to conquer Scotland, Edward lost his hereditary duchy of Guienne in France. Some dispute having arisen about the ceremony of doing homage, Edward surrendered the duchy into the hands of Philip, on the promise of receiving it back. Philip once having got it into his hands would not restore it, and Edward was too busy with his Scottish war to reclaim it.

One of the worst traits in Edward's character was his relentless severity to such enemies as fell into his power, and his harshness to the Jews. The cruel death inflicted on Wallace, the Scottish patriot-hero, and the execution of 300 Jews, and the banishment of 16,000 from the country, with only money enough to carry them abroad (Edward seizing all the rest of their property) are stains on his memory.

Never did the martial spirit of England rise to a higher pitch than under this king. Every castle had its tilting-yard, where the young men practised all the exercises and manœuvres of war and chivalry. Riding at the ring and mock combats were of daily occurrence. But the tournament, in which fair ladies looked on, while knights rode against each other with sharpened lances, was the crowning spectacle. A smile and a scarf bestowed by the Queen of Beauty was held ample guerdon for risk of life and limb. These meetings were usually proclaimed for a long time beforehand that knights from a distance might be able to attend. Kings and princes, queens, and the wives and daughters of the nobles were among the spectators. Sometimes the combat was "a l'outrance," or to the death of one of the combatants. The yeomen and common people had their sports also, among which may be specified archery, foot-ball, leaping, vaulting, and the like athletic exercises. About Christmas time mummers used to go about in quaint disguises dancing and capering to the sound of pipe and tabor. Bull-baiting and bear-baiting were later enjoyments.

EDWARD II. 1307—1327.

The reign of this sovereign is little more than a detail of follies on the part of the king and violence on that of his nobles. He was much under the influence of favorites. In the beginning of his reign a worthless person, named Gaveston, occupied this position. Twice was he expelled the kingdom by the nobles, whom his insolence and sneers had irritated. On making his reappearance a third time he was seized and carried to Warwick Castle. There it was debated what should be done with him. A single remark by a noble sealed his doom: "You have caught the fox: if you let him go, you will have to hunt him again." He was forthwith carried to a height by the banks of the pleasant Avon and beheaded.

While Edward and his nobles were wasting time in fruitless strife, Robert Bruce, now King of Scotland, was capturing one strong place after another. Finally, on the 24th day of June, 1314, was fought the decisive battle of Bannockburn, in which the English were utterly routed. This battle secured the independence of Scotland.

The remaining days of Edward were miserable indeed. He fell under the influence of new favorites (father and son, named Spenser), who ultimately shared the fate of Gaveston. His wife deserted him and went with her son, Edward, to the court of her brother Charles, King of France. There she formed an attachment for Roger Mortimer, who had fled to France to escape punishment for his enmity to the Spensers. She arranged a marriage between her son, Edward, and Philippa, daughter of William, Count of Hainault—one of the few redeeming events of this dismal reign. Furnished with troops by William, she returned to England and raised the standard of revolt, with the object of gaining supremacy for herself and Mortimer. The king fled, but being shipwrecked near Swansea, surrendered and was hurried to a felon's prison in Berkeley Castle.

EDWARD II.

In 1327 Parliament declared the crown vacant, and young Edward was crowned, with the title of Edward III.

One autumn night shrieks of anguish rang out from the gloomy walls of Berkeley Castle. Next morning the citizens of Bristol were invited to come and behold the body of the unhappy second Edward. No outward marks of violence were seen, but the features were distorted as if with agony. No one doubted that Mortimer was the author of his death, and that it was produced by introducing a red-hot iron, through a tube, into his intestines.

This reign is notable as being the first in which Parliament asserted its right to depose an unworthy king.

EDWARD III. (OF WINDSOR). 1327—1377.

Edward was fourteen years of age when he ascended the throne, and had one of the longest and most brilliant reigns in the history of England. The various characters of the English sovereigns constitute a strange comment on the doctrine of heredity. Some of her worst kings were sons of worthy sires; some of her greatest the offsprings of weak and worthless fathers. Of the latter class was the third Edward.

A council of nobles was appointed to administer the government during the king's minority. Practically the queen and her favorite, Mortimer, held the government in their hands. Mortimer's insolence exceeded that of the

THE TOWER OF LONDON.

Gavestons and Spensers and drew on him the hate of the nobles. The Scots, under the powerful Earl of Douglas, began that system of border warfare which harassed England down till the union. The young king raised an army and went to meet the marauders, but his heavy-armed soldiers were little fit to cope with the light-armed and well-mounted Scottish moss-troopers. Edward was forced to retire from lack of supplies, and the result was the treaty of Northampton, signed in 1328, in which the independence of Scotland was fully acknowledged.

Already galled by Mortimer's arrogance, the proud barons, ill able to stomach this new humiliation which they ascribed to him, determined to rid themselves of him. The king readily entered into their schemes, and, being now eighteen years of age, took the government into his own hands. A Parliament was summoned at Nottingham, and Mortimer and the queen took up their abode in the castle. One night the king and a party of friends gained entrance into Mortimer's chamber by a secret passage. The queen heard the door burst open, and called out from her bed in an adjoining apartment:

EDWARD III.

"Sweet son! Fair son! Spare my noble Mortimer." In vain. He was made prisoner, tried by Parliament, condemned for the murder of the late king, and hanged at Tyburn.

As Edward I. was called "Hammer of the Scots," the third Edward might, with equal justice, be termed the "Hammer of the French."

Believing himself to be rightful heir to the French throne on grounds which will be better shown under the history of France, and irritated at the French king on account of the countenance he showed to his enemies of Scotland, Edward determined to enforce his claim, and his people supported him with enthusiasm. Thus began the hundred years of war with France, which, glorious as it was to England's courage and prowess, ended in her losing all her dominions in France save the single city of Calais.

England won her first great sea-fight off Sluys (1340), King Edward sitting on board his ship in a black velvet dress, while his hardy sailors showed the mettle which was in the future to characterize the Jack Tars of Britannia. It was probably here that warlike use was first made of Roger Bacon's discovery.

This defeat was so unexpected that no one durst tell King Philip of it. At last the court jester was prevailed on to break the news to him in his own way. "Ah, what dastardly cowards these English are!" said the fool, in Philip's hearing. "How so?" asked the king. "Because at Sluys they dared not jump into the sea, as our brave men have done." The king demanded an explanation, and learned from his courtiers the disastrous story.

The earliest conflict in this great war was Crecy (August, 1346), where Edward, called, from the color of his armor, the Black Prince, won his spurs, at the age of sixteen. The grand distinction between the armies of England

and France was that the English army was composed mainly of yeomen—men athletic, well fed, drilled to warlike exercises, enthusiastically loyal, and the finest archers in the world; while the armies of France were still those of the Middle Ages, made up of mailed knights and hordes of ill-fed, despised, and untrained serfs. It is thus we are to account for the facility with which small English armies put to flight great French hosts. At Crecy the English were but thirty thousand strong, while the French were four times as numerous, yet young Edward did not hesitate to offer it battle. Here, for the first time, the famed Genoese cross-bowmen and the English archers encountered each other, to the total discomfiture of the former. The battle is thus graphically described in "Cameos of the History of England," a work we have already acknowledged our obligations to. After telling us that the English, after partaking of dinner, sat down in order, sheltering themselves from the rain that was falling, with their bows beside them carefully protected, while the Genoese, who had marched eighteen miles, were ordered, on arriving on the ground, at once to begin the battle, it goes on to say that, on the approach of the latter, "the English yeomen quietly rose up, each man in his place, so that as they stood their battalions took the form of a harrow, in squares like a chess-board. Each donned his steel cap, and drew his bowstring from the case where it had been kept dry. The Genoese 'leapt forward with a fell cry,' hoping to frighten their enemies; finding the English stood still, they hooted again and came forward; then with a third cry discharged such of their cross-bows as were not too wet to use. Then came the arrows from the 2,000 long bows, piercing heads, arms, and through cuirasses; and, mingled with these, came large balls of iron, propelled from the hill above with sounds like the retreating thunder of the storm, doing deadly execution, and terrifying men and horses. The Genoese gave back, but behind them were the brilliant and impatient knights of France 'who burned to be down upon the English.' But when they came within the flight of these deadly shafts they brooked them as little as did the Genoese; their horses capered and curveted and became unmanageable, and the wild Welshmen rushing down with their knives killed them in great number." On their flight the first English line-of-battle, led by the prince, was charged by a large body of cavalry under the French king, who broke through the archers, and the Earl of Warwick, trembling for the boy, despatched a knight to the king—who was watching the fight from the top of a windmill—to solicit him to send aid to his son. "Is my son hurt?" asked the hardy veteran. "No, sire, but hard-pressed." "Tell him he shall have no aid from me: let the boy win his spurs." The result was the total overthrow of the French. John, the blind King of Bohemia, who fought on the French side, was slain, and his coat of arms (crest three ostrich feathers, motto *Ich dien*) has ever since been borne by the heir apparent to the English throne.

The subsequent events of this struggle belong rather to French than

English history. Immediately after the victory of Crecy Edward captured Calais, which remained English for more than two hundred years. The noble devotion of its six burghers, who offered their own lives in ransom for those of the garrison and citizens, and the generous intervention of Queen Philippa, who on her knees supplicated their lives from the king, will be detailed in its proper place. After Crecy the young prince conquered nearly the whole of the south of France, where he spent the greater part of his life. During the siege of Calais, England was invaded by David, King of Scots, who, being defeated at Neville's Cross, was taken prisoner. In 1356 took place the famous fight at Poictiers, between the Black Prince and King John of France, wherein the disparity of numbers was still greater than at Crecy, and the victory yet more decisive, the French king being captured. Thus two kings were prisoners in England at the same time. The treatment of both captives was generous and chivalric. Both were magnificently entertained at the newly-built castle of Windsor, and a grand tournament was held in their honor, in which both exhibited their knightly attainments. After a captivity of eleven years, David of Scotland was ransomed. Terms had been previously arranged for the ransom of John, but on his returning to France his nobles made difficulties about raising the money, whereupon the king, saying, "If honor were banished from the rest of the world, she should find an abode in the heart of kings," turned his face from them and went back to his captivity in England, where he died eight years after Poictiers.

The gallant Black Prince was induced to enter Spain on behalf of Peter the Cruel of Castile, against whom his subjects had revolted. He fought bravely as ever, but Peter shamelessly broke his engagements. The prince returned to France in deep decline and bankrupt, and shortly died. The English provinces being left without a defender, were speedily, one after another, recovered by the French. His father survived the prince but a few months.

The reign of Edward was notable for many things besides feats of war.

The stately palace of Windsor was built, every county being required to furnish a rated number of masons, carpenters, etc. The noble Order of the Garter was instituted. At a ball the garter chanced to drop from the stocking of the Countess of Salisbury. The king courteously picked it up and gallantly bound it on his own leg. Seeing the courtiers smile, he uttered the words which became the motto of the order: "Honi soit qui mal y pense" (Shame be to him who thinks ill thereof)—a terse commentary on the text: "To the pure all things are pure." This seemingly trivial circumstance was the occasion of founding the noblest of all England's orders of knighthood. The first institution of twenty-six knights, consisting of nobles of the highest rank in England, was celebrated at Windsor in 1344, on the day sacred to St. George, the patron saint of England, and within St. George's chapel at Windsor Castle, then rising into glory and beauty under the hands of the skilful architect, William of Wykeham, Bishop of Winchester. Three hundred ladies, attired in blue velvet mantles and the crimson kirtle of the order, graced the imposing ceremony. Every knight had a historic name. At the head stood the king himself, and next him the gallant Black Prince; the remaining twenty-four knights following in order. Each wore the silken garter at his knee, the " robe of heavenly blue," a kirtle of crimson, and on the left shoulder the cross of St. George; each as admitted swore to fight for God, St. George, and the king; and each hung his banner, rich with armorial bearings, over the stall in the chapel where he knelt and joined in the prayers day by day offered up for the " Most Noble Order of the Garter." The number of knights was after-

WINDSOR CASTLE FROM THE RIVER.

wards raised to forty, and the order is still the highest honor in the power of the English crown to bestow. One decoration alone contends with " the Garter" for pre-eminence in the eyes of England's bravest warriors. This is the simple Victoria cross, conferred for personal prowess on great commanders and simple privates alike. Ever since the conquest Latin had been the language of literature and the church, French that of the court and of law, while the yeomen and peasantry held to the English tongue of their fathers. Now all the people—Britons, Anglo-Saxons, Anglo-Danes, and Normans—were becoming amalgamated and blended into one English people, and English was becoming, accordingly, the national speech. By the end of the reign i

CHAUCER: CHARACTERISTIC SCENES OF HIS TIME.

was taught in the schools, and in 1375 a statute was passed enacting its use in courts of law. The methods of war were changed. Hitherto the main reliance had been on knights armed cap-a-pie. Wallace and Bruce had taught England the value of foot-soldiers, and Crecy and Poictiers were won by small armies mainly composed of her unrivalled yeomen-archers. Roger Bacon's new explosive, gunpowder, was first used for artillery purposes in this reign. Hitherto Parliament had consisted of but one house. It was now divided into two, the peers and prelates constituting the House of Lords, and the representatives of the people, the House of Commons, where they could deliberate and resolve unawed by barons and church dignitaries. We have here, then, the origin of that branch of Parliament which really sways the destinies of England. This reign saw the rising of the "Morning Star of the Reformation," John Wickliffe, whose influence on the future of England, intellectually, socially, and spiritually cannot be overestimated. Although much of his work falls under a subsequent reign, for the sake of connection we give a very brief view of it as a whole here. Born in Yorkshire, in 1324, he studied in Oxford for the priesthood. Taking his degree in 1363, he began forthwith to read lectures on divinity in which anti-popish views were first expounded. Appointed parish priest of Lutterworth, Leicestershire, in 1374, he continued his life-work of opposition to the papacy. In the struggle maintained by Edward and his Parliament against papal aggression, he supported the king powerfully with his pen, denouncing the pope as "Antichrist." Persecution followed, but all hostile proceedings only served to make him a more thorough reformer. In 1378 he entered on his great work of translating the Scriptures into English, and circulating them among the people, with the result of not only enlightening them spiritually, but also of powerfully advancing the spread of the English language. The seed he sowed soon brought forth fruit. The Lollards, as his disciples were called, were found not only among the poor but in the church, the castle, and even on the throne. His work done, he died, worn out with toil and harassment, in 1384. "Being dead, he yet speaketh."

To this and the succeeding reign belongs also Geoffrey Chaucer, the "Father of English poetry." Born in 1324, evidently of gentle blood, he is said to have studied both at Oxford and Cambridge. He was attached to the court, and in 1359 was with the army of invasion in France, where he was captured. Ransomed by the king, he married one of the ladies of the chamber of the queen. Later he held several appointments of honor and profit, and in 1386 sat in Parliament as one of the knights of the shire of Kent. He was author of numerous poetical works, but the "Canterbury Tales," wherein are seen "all that stirring and gaily apparelled time, as in some magic mirror," form the durable monument to his memory. "He was buried in Westminster Abbey, the first of the illustrious file of poets whose ashes rest in that great national sanctuary."

In this reign the wages of a workingman was but three pence a day, yet in some respects he was better off than his modern representative, for this sum would purchase as much meat as four shillings or a dollar now. His cottage presented a degree of plenty and cheerfulness not met with at present among the agricultural laborers. Performances, called Mysteries and Miracle plays, in which the subjects were taken from the legends of the saints, Scripture history, and the passion of our Lord, were often given, generally by travelling actors. The court-yards of most great houses had galleries round them, for convenience in witnessing these exhibitions. Of tournaments and other amusements we have already spoken. The best houses of the towns-people were rough wooden buildings with latticed windows, and their bedsteads were closed like a child's crib. The shops or stores were stalls or booths covered, and ranged in rows along the streets, like the stalls in some of our older markets. The principal manufacture was woollen, England being famous for the abundance and excellence of its wool. Bakers, brewers, dyers, and weavers were almost all women. Learning had as yet made little progress beyond the church and the cloister, for Edward was long dead ere Wickliffe's translation appeared to arouse the people with a thirst for reading.

We have been thus comparatively minute in regard to the leading events and characteristics of this reign as we regard it as the transition period between the Middle Ages and modern times. New institutions were inaugurated; new modes of thought and new ideas were born and disseminated. Medievalism is behind us: the England of to-day begins to take shape.

RICHARD II. 1377—1399.

Richard was son of the Black Prince and no sovereign ever ascended the throne of whom greater things were expected. He verified the remark we have already made, that some of the weakest kings were sons of great fathers.

But great events often distinguish weak reigns. Richard's reign is memorable for the fact that in it commenced, in overt form, that struggle which in one shape or another has continued unabated to the present day—the struggle, namely, of poverty against wealth, of natural right against privilege, of the oppressed against the oppressor; in short, of labor against capital.

> "Freedom's battle once begun,
> Bequeathed from bleeding sire to son,
> Though baffled oft is ever won."

A poll-tax of a shilling a head (equal to sixteen times that amount now) was imposed on every person over fifteen. The insolence of a collector to a girl under age, the daughter of a tiler named Wat, so irritated the father that he struck the villain dead. He did more: he roused the common people of his county, Kent, and led them, armed with scythes, flails, and sticks, towards London, people flocking to them in thousands by the way. By the time they reached London it is said they numbered 300,000. At Blackheath, a priest, John Ball, preached to them, taking for his text a popular rhyme:

> "When Adam delved, and Eve span,
> Who was then the gentleman?"

He taught them that all men were naturally equal, and advocated the doing away with nobles, bishops, judges, and lawyers. One bad feature of a mob is that worthless characters always associate themselves with it with evil intent. This mob was no exception. The houses of the gentry were plundered and many people killed. Yet in London itself the great mass—the real villagers—seem to have acted with wonderful moderation. As evidence of this it is told that a man who tried to secrete a silver cup he had stolen was thrown into the river. Their great desire was to see the king and lay their grievances before him. Richard, who was but sixteen years of age, acted with more spirit and discretion than he ever again manifested. With a few unarmed men he went in his barge to Mile-end, where 60,000 were assembled, and gently asked what they wanted. The answer was," Freedom for ourselves and our children."

RICHARD II.

He granted their prayer, and thirty clerks were set to work to write charters of freedom, which, being given to all who came forward to claim them, the better part of the mob quietly dispersed. But Wat Tyler, with Jack Straw and the more desperate of the party, instead of going to Mile-end to meet the king, had broken open the tower, murdered the Archbishop of Canterbury, and committed other atrocities. Next day Wat at the head of 20,000 rioters met the king and the Mayor of London in Smithfield, and riding up to the king behaved with such audacity that Walworth drew his sword and killed him with one blow. "My friends," said Richard, "you have lost your leader. Follow me: I will take his place." Turning his horse, he rode gallantly at the head of the multitude into the open fields. Meantime a cry had gone forth in London that the king was in the hands of the rebels and the citizens rose as one man and flew to the rescue. The mob, seized with a panic, fell on their knees imploring pardon. This was granted them on condition of their instantly returning to their homes, which they gladly did, and the insurrection was at an end.

We have written thus in detail of this struggle because it has its own interest and its own lesson for us of the present day. The king prevailed by reason of his justice, reasonableness, and manliness.

Scotland had now firmly established its independence, but there was a chronic state of feud and conflict between the English and Scottish knights and barons along the border. Of these the Percies of Northumberland were the most distinguished on the English side: the Douglases, on the Scotch. The battle of Otterburn, so famous under its ballad-name of Chevychase and which Shakespeare thought not unworthy of his muse, falls under this reign.

On attaining the age of twenty-two, Richard assumed entire control of the government, dispensing altogether with Parliament, and relying for support on a standing army of 10,000 men—the first levied in England. His despotic courses led to conflict with his nobles. One day the Dukes of Hereford and Norfolk—both of royal blood—while riding in company fell into discourse regarding Richard's character. Norfolk declared him to be unworthy of credit, and Hereford denounced Norfolk as a traitor. Norfolk brought a counter-charge of disloyalty against Hereford. A court of chivalry decided that the matter should

COSTUMES OF RICHARD II.'S TIME.

be left to the judgment of God, by wager of battle. On the day appointed the combatants appeared in the lists. They sat with lances in rest, awaiting the signal for onset, when Richard threw down his truncheon and forbade the fight, passing sentence of banishment on both—on Norfolk, for life; on Hereford, for ten years.

Hereford went to France, and while he was there his father, John of Gaunt, Duke of Lancaster, the king's uncle and the most powerful man in all England, died. Hereford (now Duke of Lancaster) claimed his estates; but the king, on the pretext that an exile could hold no land, seized them for himself. Lancaster knowing that discontent was all but universal resolved to assert his rights. He landed in England during the king's absence in Ireland. Nobles and people flocked to his standard, and he reached London at the head of 60,000 men. His uncle, the Duke of York, had raised 40,000 to oppose him, but, on discovering the inclination of his own army, made common cause with Lancaster. Richard on his arrival in England found himself all but deserted and retired to the castle of Conway in Wales. The Earl of Northumberland was sent out with a force to try to obtain possession of his person. Fearing that if the king saw the force he would make off by sea, Northumberland concealed his troops in a hollow place behind rocks between Flint and Conway and went to the castle with but five attendants. Terms were easily arranged with the king. Both were insincere; the king never meant to keep the terms, Northumberland wanted only to entrap his person. Yet mass was solemnly performed and both swore on the sacrament to observe the conditions faithfully. They dined together, and set off for Flint. On reaching the declivity and seeing pennons, Richard exclaimed: "God of Paradise aid me! I am betrayed," and turned his horse's head to return. Northumberland, laying his hand on the bridle, said: "I have promised to convey you to Henry of Lancaster, and thither must thou go." The poor king submitted with the words: "May the God on whose body you laid your hand to-day reward you for this at the last day." Richard was taken to London and lodged in the tower, where he was forced to sign his abdication. The instrument being read in Parliament and his deposition unanimously voted, Lancaster, who was present, claimed the crown, and his claim was at once admitted. Richard died, a prisoner, in Pontefract Castle, not without the suspicion that he was starved to death.

With Richard ended the Plantagenet kings—an able but hard and tyrannical race. But there is a soul of goodness even in things evil. Out of tyranny comes rebellion; out of rebellion, often, liberty.

The events calling for special notice in this reign are—(1.) The emancipation of the serfs. This had been progressing gradually in previous reigns; notably, the desire of many barons for money to enable them to go on the crusades had led them to sell their freedom to many in this degraded condition. Now Wat Tyler's rebellion in great manner consummated their emancipation. (2.) The first appearance of a standing army, levied as we have seen, not against a foreign foe, but in support of despotism. (3.) The settlement of a colony of Flemings as weavers in the west of England: west-of-England cloth is still ranked among the best. (4.) Richard Whittington (famed, with his cat, in nursery literature) was mayor of London in this reign. The real Whittington was a knight's son and a great coal-merchant. The cat is a myth. (4.) The production of Chaucer's Canterbury Tales, the earliest really great English epic poem; and the founding of the oldest of England's great public schools, namely, that of Winchester.

HOUSE OF LANCASTER.

HENRY IV. (BOLINGBROKE). 1399—1413.

Henry was not nearest heir to the throne, and conscious of the weakness of his claim he tried to propitiate all parties. The nobles, with the glories of Crecy and Poictiers fresh in their memories, fretted over the loss of the English possessions in France. To them he held out the glory and the gains of another French war. The growth of reformed ideas began to alarm the church: to it he held out the promise of persecution. Domestic troubles prevented him from immediately fulfilling his first promise; there was naught to hinder him implementing his second.

At the king's instigation a statute was enacted dooming every heretic to death by burning at the stake. When the Commons House of Parliament prayed the barbarous edict might be at least mitigated, Henry replied that he wished it had been more severe. A London preacher, by name William Salter, was the first to suffer the dread penalty, and Henry enforced his reply to the appeal of the Commons by at once signing the death-doom of another martyr.

Wales was a conquered country, but the spirit of the people, inspired by their patriot bards who sung the glories of their early heroes, was unsubdued. Owen Glendower, a Welsh gentleman, having suffered wrong at the hands of an English noble and been refused redress by Parliament, put himself at the head of his countrymen and raised the standard of revolt. The belief that he was the lineal descendant of their own prince Llewellyn, and that he possessed supernatural power, added to his influence. Thrice did Henry lead an army into Wales. Thrice he came back baffled.

> "Three times hath Henry Bolingbroke made head
> Against my power; thrice from the banks of Wye
> And sandy-bottom'd Severn have I sent him
> Bootless home and weather-beaten back."

The belief in Glendower's supernatural powers was based on the fact that he had studied at Oxford and had acquired a knowledge of the science of that age. He seems to have utilized this belief for his own purposes. Thus tersely and vividly does a Welsh bard celebrate his country's favorite hero, and proclaim his hate of the Saxon.

> "Cambria's princely eagle, hail! of Grwffwd Vychan's noble blood,
> Thy high renown shall never fail, Owen Glendower, great and good.
> Lord of Dwrdws fertile vale, warlike, high-born Owen, hail!
> Loud fame has told thy gallant deeds; in every word a Saxon bleeds;
> Terror and flight together came, obedient to thy mighty name;
> Death in the van with ample stride, hewed thee a passage deep and wide."

Douglas, at the head of 10,000 Scots, had made an inroad into England, and been defeated at Homildon by Harry Hotspur and himself taken prisoner. The king despatched orders that the captives should not be ransomed. The hot-blooded Percies resented the command, liberated the Douglas, and entered into alliance with him and Glendower to depose the ungrateful king and crown the rightful heir, Edward Mortimer, Earl of March. Douglas and Hotspur set out at the head of their forces to join Glendower, but ere effecting a junction were met by the king with an equal force at Shrewsbury. It was on this day that Prince Henry, the king's son, commenced his career of glory. Young Hotspur and Douglas performed prodigies of valor, plunging into the fight in search of the king. He had caused several knights to wear armor similar to his own, and one after another of these Douglas slew.

>   "Another king! they grow like Hydra's heads:
>   I am the Douglas, fatal to all those
>   That wear those colors on them."

The royal forces were victorious. Hotspur was slain and Douglas made prisoner.

>   "Go to the Douglas, and deliver him
>   Up to his pleasure, ransomless and free:
>   His valor shown upon our crests to-day
>   Hath taught us how to cherish such high deed
>   Even in the bosom of our adversaries."

Such was the spirit of the young prince, with whom remained the honors of the day.

The elder Percy perished in a subsequent revolt.

Every reader of Shakespeare is familiar with the youthful escapades of the madcap Prince Henry, who afterwards became one of England's greatest kings. His wild pranks brought him and one of his companions before the chief-justice. Henry demanded his friend's release, and on refusal drew his sword. The justice instantly ordered him to prison, and the prince meekly submitted. "Happy the monarch," said the king, "who has a judge so resolute, and a son so willing to obey the laws!"

King Henry expired in the forty-sixth year of his age and fourteenth of his reign. The great stain on his rule was the burning of Lollards for heresy.

HENRY V. 1413—1422.

One of the best proofs of this prince's wisdom was his requiring Chief-Justice Gascoigne, who had condemned him to prison, to continue in office. In the same spirit he dismissed the companions of his youthful follies; restored the long-imprisoned Earl of March (the true heir to the throne) to liberty; conciliated the powerful family of the Percies by restitution of their forfeited estates; and gave to the bones of Richard II. a royal burial in Westminster Abbey.

In this reign the persecution of the Lollards or followers of Wickliffe, whose chief "heresy" was the denial of transubstantiation, was intensified. Sir John Oldcastle, their leader, and many others perished at the stake. The new doctrines began to be associated with those of abolition of social distinctions and the equalization of property—in short, with ideas akin to modern communism. Such was the intensity of the hate to such notions that, thirty years after Wickliffe's death, his bones were disinterred, burned, and cast into a brook running into the Avon. In the following lines Wordsworth makes this act the emblem of the diffusion of his doctrines:

> "As thou these ashes, little brook, wilt bear
> Into the Avon—Avon to the tide
> Of Severn—Severn to the narrow seas—
> Into main ocean they—this deed accurst
> As emblem yields to friends and enemies,
> How the bold teacher's doctrine, sanctified
> By truth, shall spread throughout the world dispersed."

Henry burned to recover the English possessions in France, and yet more to recover the honor lost by England having had so many fair provinces wrested from her. When one is resolved to fight, pretexts are not far to seek. Of course there was the old claim of the English kings to the throne of France. Henry crossed the channel with 10,000 men, and, at Agincourt, on St. Crispin's day, 1415, in three hours converted a French army of ten times their number into a disorderly, rushing rabble. On his return to England, exulting people rushed into the water and bore him ashore on their shoulders. The road towards London was strewed with flowers, and his entry into the city was like a Roman triumph.

HENRY V.

Next year he reduced Rouen, married Catherine, the daughter of the insane King of France, was appointed regent of France, and received a promise of the crown on the death of the king. In the following year he reduced all France to the north of the Loire. In the midst of his career, death removed him in 1422, in the thirty-fourth year of his age, leaving an infant son to succeed him.

The most notable advance made towards constitutional liberty during Henry's rule was the step gained by the House of Commons that no law should be valid without receiving its assent. The famous navy of England, also, had its commencement in this reign, the first ship ever owned by government having been built during it. Before that the seaport towns furnished all the ships needed for maritime purposes. Henry's widow, Catherine, married Owen Tudor, a Welsh gentleman, their grandson becoming Henry VII., and founder of the Tudor dynasty.

HENRY VI.   1422—1461.

This sovereign was crowned at the age of nine months. A regency was formed of which the Duke of Bedford was head. Instantly war was renewed between France and England, memorable for the active part taken in it by the Maid of Orleans, to whom the French king (Charles VII.) was indebted for his restoration. The events of this war belong to the history of France, and all that needs to be said of it here is that, during the minority of Henry VI., all the territories conquered by his father were regained by France, save the solitary town of Calais. Such was the end of the 100 years' war.

HENRY VI.

The English were not a people to bear such a loss of territory and of honor patiently. Discontent was universal, and, when the Duke of Bedford died, discord and strife broke out over the successorship.

Henry was not of the stuff to control the discordant elements in such a period of discontent and disorder. He was a mild, pious man, of feeble, almost imbecile intellect, and ductile temper. At the age of twenty-three he married Margaret, daughter of the Duke of Anjou, a bold, masculine woman, in whose hands he was little more than a puppet. This was no age for such a ruler. A new rebellion broke out in Kent, headed by a turbulent fellow named Jack Cade. The statement of their grievances shows how far the people had advanced on the road to liberty since the days of Wat Tyler. In their "complaint" submitted to government there is no mention of serfage; only of bad counsellors; undue interference by the nobles in elections; extortions by tax-gatherers, and such like. Cade marched on London at the head of 20,000 men, having encountered and scattered the royal forces at Sevenoaks. Poor Henry fled affrighted to Kenilworth Castle. For three days Cade held London, before he was put down. On a promise of pardon and redress of grievances the body of the insurgents retired to their homes. Cade with a few followers fled southwards. Being pursued and caught he was slain by the sheriff of the county, at Iden, Sussex.

We come now to one of the most disastrous epochs in English history. It will be remembered that Henry IV. was not the rightful heir to the throne. His father, John of Gaunt, was third son of Edward III., while Lionel, second son of that monarch, had issue now represented by Richard, Duke of York. On the other hand Henry had obtained the crown by choice of the people, and it had now been in his family, unchallenged, for sixty years. It is probable, therefore, if Henry VI. had been a man like his father his right would never have been questioned. Unfortunately he rather took after his maternal grandfather, the insane King of France, and Richard of York was by Parliament appointed Protector of the kingdom. The king's imbecility and the insolent arrogance of the queen seemed to invite York to press his claim for the crown. On the king's partial recovery he refused to give up his power, and levied an army to maintain himself in his position. This opened the civil war between the houses of York and Lancaster, called the "Wars of the Roses," from a white rose being the cognizance of the house of York, and a red rose that of the house of Lancaster. Tradition and Shakespeare have attributed these badges to a dispute between the two leaders in the Temple Gardens, when York exclaims:

> "Let him that is a true-born gentleman,
> And stands upon the honor of his birth,
> If he suppose that I have pleaded truth,
> From off this briar pluck a white rose with me."

And Somerset, relative and defender of the reigning house of Lancaster, replies:

> "Let him that is no coward nor no flatterer,
> But dare maintain the party of the truth,
> Pluck a red rose from off this thorn with me."

The first encounter was at St. Albans, May, 1455, and the Yorkists were victorious. Other engagements followed with various success, till a compromise was arrived at by which York was to have the crown on the king's death.

But Margaret had borne a son to the king, who, by this arrangement, was disinherited, and to this his high-spirited mother would not submit. She raised an army, overthrew the Yorkists at Wakefield, December, 1460, and, the duke having fallen, she caused his head to be encircled with a paper crown and set up on the walls of York. The gleam of success was transient, for York's son, Edward, after routing the queen's forces at Mortimer's Cross, entered London in triumph, February, 1461, and his claim being now admitted by Parliament, he mounted the throne, amid the acclamations of the people, as Edward IV. The unhappy king passed the last seven years of his life a prisoner in the tower, save the brief period he was taken out, and set on the throne, by Warwick.

Never did any royal lady experience so many vicissitudes as Margaret of

MARGARET AND THE ROBBER.

Anjou. After the disastrous battle of Hexham she fled with her young son to a forest, where she wandered about amid the darkness of night, without protection, and exhausted with fatigue, terror, and hunger. In this wretched condition a robber approached her with a drawn sword. She, rendered fearless by desperation, met him without sign of alarm, and placing her little boy in his arms said, "My friend, this is the son of your king, and I, his mother, confide him to your protection." He, nobly responding to the trust placed in him, conducted mother and child to a place of concealment, and assisted them to escape from the country. She, latterly, escaped to Flanders, where she placed herself and son under the protection of Philip, Duke of Burgundy.

Of all the great men who took share in this quarrel of the rival houses none was so distinguished as the Earl of Warwick, called the "King-maker," who favored the house of York. Tradition says he entertained every day at table in his different castles, 30,000 persons, and at his palace, Warwick Lane, London, six oxen were eaten every morning at breakfast by his retainers.

From the beginning of the "Wars of the Roses," by the first battle at St. Albans, to its close at Bosworth field in the reign of Richard III., thirty years elapsed, during which twelve pitched battles were fought, no less than eighty princes were slain, while the ancient nobility was almost annihilated.

The best thing to note in the reign of the unfortunate Henry is the founding of Eton College, the second of the great schools to be founded, Winchester being the first. His reign, also, saw Chaucer in his bloom.

EDWARD IV.

For the first three years of his reign Edward had to struggle to keep his position. Within a month of his accession he obtained a victory over his enemies at Towton, Yorkshire, March, 1461, and finally, after the decisive battle of Hexham, May, 1464, King Henry fell into his hands, and the unfortunate Margaret and her son escaped, as has been already told, to Flanders. This closed the war for a time.

Edward though of a generous disposition was impetuous and imprudent. By his desire Warwick went to France to solicit for him the hand of a sister-in-law of Louis, King of France. While the king-maker was on his mission, the king as he was hunting met with Elizabeth Woodville, a knight's daughter, and married her secretly. This insult to himself the king-maker resolved to revenge by restoring the poor imbecile, Henry VI., to the throne. Thousands at his bidding abandoned the white rose for the red, and in 1469

EDWARD IV.

Edward fled to Holland, while Henry was released from prison and set on the throne. But in 1471 Edward returned to England, gave battle to Warwick, on Easter Sunday, at Barnet, where the great earl was slain. The undaunted Margaret had meantime come over from France, hoping to find her husband king, but in the next month Edward routed the Lancasterians at Tewkesbury, capturing both Queen Margaret and her son, Prince Edward. The latter was murdered the day after the battle; the queen, after an imprisonment of four years, was ransomed by the King of France; while poor Henry died one of those deaths so common in the tower, he was murdered. Edward died in 1483, the latter years of his life presenting few political incidents of importance.

This reign is remarkable for the introduction of printing into England. William Caxton, a London merchant, was sent by Edward to transact some business in the Netherlands, and during his stay visited Cologne, where he acquired a knowledge of the art, and on his return set up a press in Westminster. The first book printed in England was a "Treatise on the Game of Chess." Caxton printed a great many religious works, some histories, and the poems of Chaucer. Learning began to be appreciated, and people began to give their money for the founding of schools, rather than of monasteries. Many new colleges were built in Oxford and Cambridge. Nevertheless many superstitions still continued. Even among the most enlightened there existed a belief in witchcraft, alchemy, and astrology. Poor old women were still scored on the forehead or burned or drowned as witches; the alchemist was unwearied in his researches after the *elixir vitæ*, which was to cure all diseases, and give to age the vigor and bloom of youth, and after the philosopher's stone, which was to convert all metals into gold. The astrologer still told people their future, by a study of the planets which dominated at their birth. Of medicine and surgery little was known, the former being practised by monks, the latter by barbers.

RICHARD III. 1483—1485.

This sovereign, brother to the last king, is probably more generally known

RICHARD III.

through Shakespeare's delineation of him than from works of plain history. His brother, Edward IV., left two sons, one about thirteen, the other nine. Immediately on his brother's death he assumed the title of Protector, and getting the poor boys into his power sent both to the tower. They were never again seen, and were believed to have been smothered by hired assassins. Having thus cleared the way, he caused himself to be proclaimed king by the citizens of London. Soon after his coronation he passed several laws for the encouragement and protection of home trade, with the view of conciliating the guilds and corporations in towns in his favor. He also established English consuls in the trading towns on the Mediterranean.

MURDER OF EDWARD IV.'S CHILDREN. (By ⟨?⟩ Sain.)

Possibly the most important of the institutions established by him was the post-office, in imitation of the couriers instituted by Louis II. of France. But nothing could reconcile the great body of the people to his cruelties. He had caused several nobles to be beheaded without a trial on a charge of treason. A conspiracy was the result, headed by the Duke of Buckingham, to restore the line of Lancaster, and after a battle at Bosworth, where Richard was slain, Henry, Earl of Richmond, a descendant of John of Gaunt, Duke of Lancaster, was hailed king on the field of battle under the title of Henry VII.

HENRY VII.   1485—1509.

Henry's first act, after ascending the throne, was a wise one. He married the eldest daughter of Edward IV., and thus terminated a long-standing quarrel by the union of the white rose with the red.

Henry's claim to the throne was by no means clear, and the leading political events of his reign were insurrections arising from claims made by persons professing to be nearer heirs. There lay in the tower a young prince, the Earl of Warwick, nephew of Edward IV., whose title many thought better than Henry's. Suddenly a report spread that Warwick had escaped, and a young man appeared in Dublin—where the Duke of Clarence, Warwick's father, had been esteemed as governor of Ireland—and was there, amid popular acclaim, crowned King of England. As soon, however, as he ventured into England his party was routed at Stoke, 1487, and he himself turned into the royal kitchen to serve as a scullion by Henry, who had a talent for turning everything to the best account. He was really the son of a carpenter, and his true name was Lambert Simnel. After him appeared Perkin Warbeck, who professed to be the younger son of the late king, spared by the assassin who had murdered his brother. This claimant was patronized by the Duchess of Burgundy, sister of Edward IV., and supported by James IV. of Scotland, and to this day many believe he was the genuine heir. He married a beautiful Scotch lady, Catherine Gordon, daughter of the Earl of Huntly, afterwards known as the "White Rose of England," who proved her faith in him by remaining true to him through all his misfortunes. After many adventures he fell into Henry's hands and was sent to the tower. In 1499 Henry, pestered by a third claimant, in order to free himself from further trouble, had both young Warwick (who was still in the tower) and Warbeck convicted of a plot and beheaded.

Henry died in 1509 and was buried by the side of his wife in the beautiful chapel adjoining Westminster Abbey, which he had built for himself.

Margaret, eldest daughter of Henry, was married to James IV., King of Scotland, and it was in consequence of this marriage that James VI. of Scotland, her great-grandson, inherited the throne of England on the death of Elizabeth.

Bacon wrote a history of Henry's reign and says "justice was well administered, save when the king was partei." Hume reckons it "the dawn of civility and science in England."

To the intelligent reader the following account of the daily life in the house of a great nobleman in the reign of Henry VII. will have more interest than the bald recital of political incidents. In the castle of the Earl of Northumberland everybody rose at six, when mass was said, all the knights, squires, and servants being present. After mass came breakfast, when there was set on the earl's table, for himself and lady, a quart of beer, a quart of wine, salt fish, red herrings, and sprats in season. This was the ordinary fare on fish days; on flesh days a chine of mutton or piece of boiled beef was substituted for the fish. At ten o'clock the whole family dined in the great hall; supper was served at four, and at nine the gates were closed, after which no one was allowed to pass in or out. The earl reckoned on dining from thirty to sixty strangers every day. The expense of each person for meat, drink, and firing was calculated at two-pence half-penny a day, equivalent to about sixty cents of our money.

Maps and charts were first brought to England in this reign by Bartholomew Columbus, who came to make proposals respecting the projected voyage of his brother. Henry was willing to support Christopher, but before Bartholomew got back to Spain he had sailed in the service of Ferdinand and Isabella, and the Spaniards became masters of the New World.

Artillery was first largely used in this reign. It was artillery gave Henry his easy victory over the Cornishmen who supported Warbeck. Throughout the Middle Ages the call of a baron had been enough to raise a formidable revolt. Yeomen and retainers took down their bow from the chimney-corner, knights buckled on their armor, and forthwith an army threatened the throne. Without artillery, such an army was now helpless, and the one train of artillery lay at the disposal of the king. Gunpowder had ruined feudalism.

HENRY VIII. 1509—1547.

We now come to the time when the old customs founded on the Roman Catholic faith were abolished, monasteries and convents shut up and abolished, and the religious orders which had formerly played so prominent a part, alike in Anglo-Saxon and Norman times, disappear. Such a change could not have been effected by a sovereign less absolute than Henry VIII.

Henry was second son of Henry VII., and ascended the throne at the age of eighteen. His elder brother was dead, and had left a widow, Catherine of Arragon, a daughter of the illustrious sovereigns of Spain, Ferdinand and Isabella. Soon after his accession she became the wife of Henry VIII., and this was the immediate cause of the great revolution in the English church and English faith. Catherine was his senior by a few years.

The first twenty years of Henry's reign were quiet enough. In the beginning of it (1513) were two short wars, one with France and one with Scotland, in which latter war the victory of Flodden was won. Cardinal Wolsey, Archbishop of York, was minister from 1515 till his fall in 1529, and this was the best governed portion of Henry's reign. Henry was an eager student of theology, and in 1521 produced a book in defence of the seven sacraments against Luther, which earned him the title of "Defender of the Faith," a title still borne by the English sovereigns. But as Catherine aged, Henry became dissatisfied and wished a younger wife. He professed to be troubled in conscience on account of his marriage with his brother's widow and prayed the pope to divorce the union. But Catherine was the sister of Charles V. of Spain, probably the most powerful monarch in Christendom, and the pope hesitated and temporized. Ever since the days of Wickliffe the new ideas had been operating like yeast in the English mind, and many were eager to see a check put upon the power and influence of the church. The pope had named a commission, of which Wolsey was a member, to try the divorce, but on the king declaring his intention of marrying Anne Boleyn, a young lady who had been about the court, Wolsey declined to act, and the commission was withdrawn. The revocation of the commission was virtually the end of the papal power in England, the steps that followed being the working out of the inevitable results. Wolsey was deprived of power in 1529 and a ministry appointed, in which for the first time laymen held the highest places. The king's chief adviser was Wolsey's old servant, Cromwell, while Sir Thomas More was appointed chancellor.

Wolsey whose fall we have thus noted was a churchman and statesman of the school of Dunstan and Thomas-a-Becket. He rose from the lowest ranks to be prime minister of England, archbishop, and cardinal, and, except the king himself, was the richest and most powerful man in the kingdom. He built the fine palace of Hampton Court, and presented it to the king. He was one of the ablest and most faithful ministers that ever a sovereign had. The words in which Shakespeare makes him address his servant Cromwell after his fall are among the noblest, and, at the same time, the most pathetic in literature:

> "Be just and fear not:
> Let all the ends thou aim'st at be thy country's,
> Thy God's, and truth's; then, if thou fall'st, O Cromwell,
> Thou fall'st a blessed martyr.

> O Cromwell, Cromwell!
> Had I but served my God with half the zeal
> I served my king, he would not in mine age
> Have left me naked to mine enemies."

Henry now appealed to Parliament and measure after measure was passed limiting clerical power and papal influence. Henry was declared head of the church in England, the tax of Peter's pence was abolished, and the pope's claim for the annats or first year's revenue of every benefice declared invalid. In 1533 the king married Anne Boleyn, and Cranmer, Archbishop of Canterbury, held a court and pronounced a sentence of divorce between Henry and Catherine, declaring the marriage to have been null from the beginning. Parliament also settled the succession on the issue of Anne Boleyn to the exclusion of that of Catherine. Scarcely had these measures passed when news came from Rome that the pope had pronounced a judgment finding Henry's marriage with Catherine valid. On the day following Henry called into operation the act abolishing the pope's authority.

The ruthlessness of Henry's character now manifested itself. He mercilessly sacrificed every one who stood in his way. Minor victims fell unheeded, but all Europe was shocked when Sir Thomas More and Fisher, Bishop of Rochester, were put to death for refusing to acknowledge the new succession, and to admit the king's right to the headship of the church. Cromwell also fell a victim. Within a short time after the birth of the Princess (afterwards queen) Elizabeth, Henry's love for Anne Boleyn ceased, and he had her executed. On the day after the execution he married Jane Seymour, who died in giving birth to Edward VI. From his next wife, Anne of Cleves, he procured a divorce. His fifth wife, Catherine Howard, was within a few months of her marriage divorced and executed for adultery, and his sixth wife, Catherine Parr, survived him, and so the catalogue ends. Henry himself died in 1547, in the fifty-sixth year of his age and thirty-eighth of his reign.

Not the least painful feature associated with the reformation was the suppression of religious houses and the appropriation, by this tyrant, of their revenues, plate, jewels, and other valuables for his own use. All the fine old abbeys were dismantled of their beautiful paintings and magnificent decorations, and the books and manuscripts that had been the work of so many ages given up to destruction. The inhabitants were expelled, many to starve or beg, while the higher orders were compelled to resign their property to the crown. The suppression of these houses was a serious misfortune to the poor, who had been accustomed to look to them for succor in all their distresses.

In the last will of King Henry it was set down that his son Edward, born by Jane Seymour, should succeed him; but in the event of Edward dying without children the crown should devolve on the Princess Mary, daughter of Catherine of Arragon, and after her on Elizabeth, daughter of Anne Boleyn. It so happened that all three did reign in succession.

EDWARD VI.   1547—1553.

This reign is chiefly noticeable for the completion and consolidation of the work of reformation. Images were removed from churches, Roman Catholic bishops imprisoned, the cup extended to the laity in communion, the celibacy of the clergy made no longer obligatory, and a new service-book was drawn up by Bishops Cranmer and Ridley, assisted by other divines. The most meritorious work done by the king himself was the founding of a large number of grammar schools, known as King Edward's schools. On account of the Scottish government refusing to let their Queen (Mary) marry Edward, in accordance with a contract, war broke out with that country, and the Scotch were completely defeated at Pinkie, in September, 1547. Edward died in July, 1553.

EDWARD VI.

MARY.   1553—1558.

Mary, who succeeded on the death of her brother Edward, could not be expected to feel favorably towards the reformation, for it arose from the desire of King Henry to get rid of her mother. Still, although a warm friend of the Catholic church, she was not at first disposed to be severe, but rather interfered to mitigate the cruelties of Bishops Gardiner and Bonner. After her marriage with Philip of Spain—a stern, coarse bigot—those bloody persecutions began which have stained her name. Among other victims was Cranmer, Archbishop of Canterbury, who had pronounced sentence of divorce against her mother. In an unnecessary war with France, provoked

MARY I.

QUEEN ELIZABETH IN HER YOUTH.

by Philip. Calais, the last English possession, was lost, and the queen was so much grieved that the loss is supposed to have hastened her death.

ELIZABETH. 1558—1603.

Elizabeth was in her third year when her mother, Anne Boleyn, was beheaded. She ascended the throne at the age of twenty-five, and one of the first acts of her reign was to call to her counsels Cecil, to whose courteous judgment and clear intellect she had the good sense, to the very last, to subordinate her own capricious temper. Like her sister Mary, Elizabeth on her accession, had promised to allow all her subjects the enjoyment of their religious opinions undisturbed. No sooner, however, was she established on the throne than she adopted measures to repress Catholicism and re-establish the Protestant religion. Catholics were fined and imprisoned, or even executed, who refused to attend the Protestant churches. At the same time it must be acknowledged that she took every means to extend the commerce and increase the opulence of her country, which, under her, reached a degree of prosperity it had never hitherto attained. The progress of navigation, under Drake, Frobisher and others, was unparalleled. Two great political events distinguish this reign—the captivity and execution of Mary, Queen of Scots, and the defeat and dispersion of the famous Spanish Armada. The former is the one great blot on Elizabeth's name; her conduct on the occasion of the threatened invasion by the latter constitutes her chief claim on the world's respect. Mary, fleeing from her rebellious subjects in Scotland, appealed to her cousin for succor and shelter. For eighteen melancholy years she was kept a prisoner, and at length, on the pretext that she was the centre of Catholic plots, she was beheaded in Fotheringay Castle, Feb. 7th, 1587.

SIR FRANCIS DRAKE

Beautifully and pathetically does the poet Burns make the unfortunate Mary apostrophize the coldly, calculating, callous Elizabeth:

"But as for thee, thou false woman,
  My sister and my fae!
Grim vengeance yet shall whet the sword
  That through thy heart shall gae.

> "The weeping blood in woman's breasts
>   Was never known to thee,
> Nor the balm that drops on wounds of woe
>   Frae woman's pitying e'e."

Philip of Spain had several causes for hating Elizabeth. She had refused to marry him, for though he had been her sister's husband he had proposed marriage to her. Then she befriended the Huguenots of France and the Netherlands, who struggled against his authority; and, finally, her navigators, Drake and others, had seized and plundered several of his American settlements. On July 19th, 1588, the formidable Spanish fleet came in sight of Plymouth, whereupon Elizabeth's admiral, Lord Howard of Effingham, ordered eight of his lightest ships, stowed with combustibles, to be set afire in the middle of the night and sent adrift among the ships of the enemy. The result was such consternation and confusion that the destruction or dispersion of the armada was effected by the small, but ably handled fleet of England.

SIR WALTER RALEIGH.

The weakest point in Elizabeth's character was her fondness for favorites. Chief among these was the Earl of Essex. Sent to Ireland to quell Tyrone's rebellion, he conducted matters so improvidently that his troops melted away by death and desertion. He returned to England only to face the accusations and persecution of enemies bent on his destruction. Galled to desperation, he proceeded from folly to folly, till he was seized, arraigned for high treason, convicted and executed. It cost Elizabeth a sore struggle ere she could sign the warrant for his execution. A story is told that in happier days the queen had taken a ring from her finger and given it to Essex with an injunction to send it to her whenever he should be in danger. This ring, after his condemnation, he gave to the Countess of Nottingham to convey to the queen. The hard-hearted woman, counselled by Cecil, Essex's great enemy, withheld the token, and the queen, indignant at Essex's not appealing to her, signed the warrant of his doom. The countess, when on her death-bed, sent for the queen and confessed what she had done, imploring forgiveness. Wild with rage and grief, the queen seized the dying woman by the shoulder and shook her violently, exclaiming, "God forgive you; I never will!"

Another of the queen's favorites was Sir Walter Raleigh. Distinguished in many ways, he was a famous navigator and sailed on voyages of discovery to America. He was the first to take possession of the oldest of all the States, to which he gave the name of Virginia, in honor of the "Virgin Queen." A vessel sent out by Raleigh left a number of settlers on an island on the American coast, where they would all have perished had they not been discovered and carried home by Drake. They brought tobacco with them, and smoking soon became one of the accomplishments of the fashionable youth of England. Whether the weed brought was a boon or the reverse, we leave our readers to determine. A less dubious gift of his to England was that of potatoes.

SHAKESPEARE.

The Elizabethan is the golden age of English literature. The single name of Shakespeare elevates it above the competing epoch in the world's history. William Shakespeare was born April 23d, 1564, at Stratford-on-Avon, Warwickshire, the third of eight children born to John Shakespeare and Mary Arden, who had brought her husband a dowry of fifty-four acres of land. John Shakespeare rose to be high bailiff and chief-alderman of Stratford, but falling later into poverty, William, at the age of fourteen, had to be taken from the free grammar-school of the burgh, and set to work. Ben Jonson (himself a ripe scholar) says of him, "he had little Latin and less Greek." At the age of nineteen he married Anne Hathaway, who in six months presented him with a daughter. In 1586, falling into a poaching scrape, he left Stratford and came to London and became associated with Blackfriars' theatre, where he rose to be actor, dramatist, and shareholder. By 1611 the whole of his immortal plays, thirty-seven in number, were produced. A year after the completion of the last he retired to Stratford, where he had by purchase acquired considerable property. There he died in his fifty-second year, leaving two daughters. No lineal representative of the great dramatist remains. Besides plays, he produced in his twenty-ninth year a poem, "Venus and Adonis," and, next year, the "Rape of Lucrece." His sonnets, fifty-four in number, were first printed in 1609.

Only second to Shakespeare was Edmund Spenser, author of the "Faerie Queen." He was born of good family in London in 1553, and was educated as a sizar at Cambridge. In 1579 was published his "Shepherd's Calendar," dedicated to Sir Philip Sidney, through whose influence he received the appointment of secretary to Lord Grey, queen's deputy in Ireland, where, for his services, he received a grant of the estate of Kilcolman, Cork, covering some 3,000 acres, where he chiefly resided. Here he wrote his "Faerie Queen," and, with his friend Raleigh, read the manuscript while sitting

"Amongst the cooly shade
Of the green alders, by the Milla's shore."

By Raleigh he was taken to England and introduced to Queen Elizabeth. In Tyrone's rebellion his house or castle at Kilcolman was burned, he and his wife escaping with difficulty, whilst their youngest child perished in the flames. He died, Ben Jonson says, for "lack of bread" in London, January, 1599, and was buried near Chaucer in Westminster Abbey. Spenser's other works are his "Complaints," "Mother Hubbard Tale," "The Tears of the Muses," etc., with a prose work entitled a "View of Ireland." Another great name in this reign is that of Lord Bacon, author of "Novum Organon," "Advancement of Learning," "Essays," etc., and recognized as father of the inductive philosophy. All his works are irradiated by the light of an intellect, at once one of the most capacious and profound that ever appeared before men. Alas, that his moral nature was as grovelling as his intellectual towered above that of other men. Appointed keeper of the Great Seal, and in 1619, Lord Chancellor, with the title of Lord Verulam, he polluted the stream of justice by truckling to the sovereign and powerful favorites, as well as by directly accepting bribes for unjust judgments. Well has Pope said of him:

"If parts allure thee, think how Bacon shined
The wisest, brightest, meanest of mankind."

We have space to mention further, as lights of this reign, only the names of the dramatists Ben Jonson, Beaumont and Fletcher, and Marlowe, and of Sir Walter Raleigh and Sir Philip Sidney, each great as statesman, warrior and writer.

Elizabeth did not long survive her favorite Essex. When her end approached her ministers urged her to name her successor. Some one named Lord Beauchamp, heir to the Suffolk claim. "I will have no rogue's son," she cried hoarsely, "in my seat." At the mention of the name of the King of Scotland she raised her hand feebly to her head, which her ministers took as a sign of consent. She expired March 24th, 1603, in the seventieth year of her age and the forty-fifth of her reign.

One of the remarkable features in this reign was the appearance of the

Puritans. Many who had been exiled by Mary took refuge in Geneva, and there learned the doctrine of Calvin, the founder of Presbyterianism. These persons, when they returned on the accession of Elizabeth, were horrified to

CARRYING QUEEN ELIZABETH IN STATE.

find that she retained many of the prayers and observances of the Catholic Church. Though discountenanced by the queen, their public preaching, exhortations and way of living had a visible effect on the manners of the age. In particular, Sunday, or Sabbath as they named it, began now to be observed with seriousness, instead of being regarded as a day of pastime and excess.

COSTUMES OF QUEEN ELIZABETH'S TIME.

In this reign was enacted the first compulsory law for the relief of the poor, which is the foundation of the present poor-laws of England; coaches were first introduced, and a German set up the first manufactory of needles. In

1588 the first paper-mill was established, and the art of weaving stockings was invented by a Cambridge student. Neither coffee nor tea were known. But ladies, even of the highest rank, were wont to regale themselves at a seven o'clock breakfast with hot mead and ale. May Day was a great festival, when the rustics used to repair to the woods, where they sang and danced till daylight, carrying home with them wild flowers, branches of trees, and, above all, the May-pole, drawn by oxen. This May-pole was set up on the village green, and a queen of the May chosen from among the village lasses. Every reader will recall Tennyson's lines :

> " You must wake and call me early, call me early, mother dear ;
> To-morrow 'll be the happiest time of all the glad New Year,
> Of all the glad New Year, mother, the maddest, merriest day ;
> For I'm to be queen o' the May, mother I'm to be queen o' the May."

JAMES I.   1603—1625.

By the accession of James VI. of Scotland to the English throne, the whole of the three kingdoms were united, under one monarch, in the united kingdom of Great Britain and Ireland. As many of the events of the following reigns have reference to Scotland and Ireland as well as England, we will, with the view of economizing space, treat all such under one or other of these countries.

The leading characteristic of the monarchs of the Stuart race was their conviction that they ruled by " right divine," which unfortunately was often interpreted by its members to mean " right divine to govern wrong," and so was the cause of the misfortunes which seemed to dog the name. James was a weak, timid, vain man—" the most learned fool in Europe "—and full of the conviction that he was above and independent of all ministers, Parliaments, or other restraining agencies. Both he and his male successors thought they could raise what money they wished by their own uncontrolled edict, and that they could prescribe to their subjects what form of religion they should follow, and what faith they should hold.

The most notable event in King James' reign was the gunpowder-plot. Scarcely had he been a year on the throne till some fanatical Roman Catholics formed a plot to blow up the parliament house when the King, royal family, and all the peers should be assembled. A Yorkshire gentleman, Guy Fawkes, who had run through his patrimony, was hired to execute the plot, with sufficient assistants. A mine was run under Parliament, and a cellar also under the house hired, and twenty barrels of gunpowder placed in it. Parliament was to assemble November 5th, when Fawkes was to fire the mine by means of a slow match. On October 26th, Lord Monteagle, a Catholic nobleman, received an anonymous letter warning him to stay away from Parliament. The letter was laid before the secretary of state and the king. The cellar was searched, the gunpowder found, and a man discovered with a dark lantern in his hand and matches in his pocket. This was Fawkes. He and most of the conspirators were apprehended and put to death. For over two centuries the escape of the king was commemorated in the English Church as a day of thanksgiving.

Another plot had been laid before to deprive James of the sovereignty, which would not be referred to here, were it not that it cost England the life of one of her illustrious sons, Sir Walter Raleigh. He was a party to the plot, and was in consequence confined in the Tower for thirteen years, during which time he wrote his "History of the World." At length, pretending that he knew of a gold mine in South America, he was permitted to levy a band of adventurous companions and go forth with them as their guide to the mine. The expedition proved a failure, and when he returned home he was beheaded for his old treason.

A plan was afoot for a marriage between the King's eldest son, Prince Charles, and the daughter of Philip, King of Spain. The prince, however, was averse to marrying a woman he had never seen. Being fond of adventures, he and the Duke of Buckingham, the king's favorite, persuaded James to allow them to travel to Spain in disguise. They set off on the romantic mission, with a single attendant each, under the names of John and Thomas Smith. On their way Charles saw at Paris the Princess Henrietta of France. Arrived at Madrid, the knights-errant made themselves known, and the prince was magnificently entertained. But the end of it all was that the Infanta and prince did not take to each other. The match was broken off, and in the end Charles subsequently married Henrietta of France.

James had been brought up in the Presbyterian Church, but discovering after some time's sojourn in England that Presbyterianism was not "a religion for a gentleman," he sent, in 1617, commissioners to Scotland to force the people into the English Church. The people, either not agreeing with the king in his notion, or not desiring to be converted so summarily into "gentlemen," declined to conform ; and this step of James was the cause of great future trouble in that country.

James died in 1625.

London streets were first paved in this reign, each householder paving the portion opposite his house, and the fronts of all new houses were ordered to be of brick or stone.

The great literary undertaking in this reign was the translation of the Scriptures into the form we had them until the recent revision. Besides Wickliffe's translation, there were others, as Tyndale's, in existence, but their language was becoming obsolete. No such work was ever so successfully executed. This and the works of Shakespeare had the effect of crystallizing the English language in the form in which it was spoken three hundred years ago.

CHARLES I.   1625—1629.

Charles was twenty-five years of age when he ascended the throne, and one of his first acts was to marry Henrietta of France, whom he had seen when on his Quixotic expedition to Madrid. He was a decorous, earnest man, of irreproachable character in private life, a good husband and fond father; but, on the other hand, in political affairs he was unscrupulous, and resorted to dissimulation and fraud for the accomplishment of his ends. He had, besides, inherited the most extreme notions of kingly prerogative—the divine right of kings, as it was called—and he imbibed from his father the fixed notion that a national Episcopal Church, to which everyone must be compelled to conform, was alone consistent with regal authority. The Parliaments in the commencement of his reign, instead of complacently granting supplies in accordance with his demands, showed themselves rather disposed to vindicate the people's rights and liberties. This was not at all what he

CHARLES I.

desired, and after causing several members to be imprisoned, he dissolved the Houses and governed the country eleven years without either Parliament or a responsible ministry. He took, in place, Laud (Archbishop of Canterbury) and Strafford (of Star-Chamber notoriety) as his advisers. The two great questions of his reign were freedom of conscience and the right of the people to have a voice in taxing themselves. Both of these claims Charles denied. The Puritans (as the non-conformists were called) were treated by the half-popish Laud with merciless severity. Many who refused to conform to what they regarded as unscriptural and idolatrous usages, were dragged before a secret and irresponsible court, called the Star-Chamber, and punished by imprisonment, whipping, the pillory, and by having their ears cut off, their nostrils slit, and their cheeks branded by red-hot irons. In consequence, many fled overseas to New England, where they could worship God in accordance with their conscience, none daring to make them afraid. The Scots he roused to open revolt by forcing Episcopacy upon them.

All this time Charles was in desperation for money. He now fell on a device to raise it, which, with Laud's persecutions, and Strafford's Star-Chamber secret tribunals, roused the spirit of the people of England also to active opposition. From Anglo-Saxon times the maritime towns of the kingdom had been required to furnish shipping in seasons of danger. Charles' subservient lawyers now held that an equal obligation lay on the whole kingdom, and accordingly writs for "ship-money" were issued to the sheriffs of every county, requiring them to levy it on the people. Many refused to pay the unconstitutional tax, and prominent among these was John Hampden, who both as a private man and a member of subsequent Parliaments with "dauntless breast" withstood the despotic impost.

Charles was now so distressed for money that he summoned a Parliament in hopes of being relieved from his difficulties. But the people sent many Puritan representatives to the House of Commons, and this body—now the stronger—led by Hampden, Pym and others, instead of granting him immediate relief, demanded numerous concessions which he resolutely refused to grant. He saw, in fact, he must surrender every prerogative he claimed—spiritual despotism, unchecked power of taxation, etc.—or go to war. He chose the latter alternative and set up the royal standard at Nottingham. He was supported by many of the nobility and gentry—cavaliers as they were called—but the townspeople and yeomen, in general, joined the parliament. Such was the commencement of the civil war, in which Oliver Cromwell, a country gentleman and brewer of great military talent, rose to be commander. For three years Charles struggled against his Parliament, and many battles were fought, till at length his forces were utterly routed at Naseby, and he himself fled in disguise to the Scottish army. The Scots gave him up and from that time forth he was, although not in actual confinement, virtually a prisoner. Weary of the situation he attempted to escape. Being captured, he was ultimately conducted to London, tried in Westminster Hall, condemned to death, and executed at Whitehall, January 30th, 1649.

Newspapers began to be first regularly published, and banking had its origin in this reign. The Puritans began to be called "Roundheads" from the fashion of wearing their hair closely cropped. They wore a dress of coarse gray, black, or brown cloth made in the plainest fashion, and the old-fashioned high-crowned hat. The cavaliers or court party, on the other hand, wore long ringlets, silk or satin doublets, with slashed sleeves, lace collars, and flat beaver hat with feathers.

Charles was a liberal patron of the fine arts. Van Dyck, the famous

OLIVER CROMWELL.

TRIAL OF CHARLES I.

Flemish painter, settled in England at his request, and was by him pensioned and raised to knighthood. Many of the finest portraits in the royal palaces, the mansions of the nobility and the national gallery are by him. Had Charles lived in a more peaceful time, he would, like Louis XIV. of France, have founded a national school of art.

COMMONWEALTH.

England was now without a king or House of Lords. The entire government was vested in the Commons. The Scots had, indeed, proclaimed Charles II., but Cromwell hurrying from Ireland met the Scots and defeated them first at Dunbar and then, decisively, at Worcester. It was in these

EXECUTION OF CHARLES I.

battles, and that of Marston Moor, that Cromwell's famed "Ironsides" earned their fame.

The following poem conceived in the true spirit that inspired Cromwell's "Ironsides" reveals to us the secret of their success. They fought in faith, and with perfect confidence in themselves and their cause·

THE BATTLE OF MARSTON MOOR.

"Hot Rupert came spurring to Marston Moor;
    Praise we the Lord!
Came spurring hard with thousands a score.
    Praise we the Lord! . . .
He bade us flee, that they might pursue;
So from trench and leaguer straight off we drew,
But we halted on Marston Moor anew;
    To the Lord our God be glory! . . .

"Then the shot of their guns through our stilled ranks tore;
    Praise we the Lord!
Then a pause and a hush fell on the war;
    Praise we the Lord!
Then their squadrons thickened, and down once more
Came Rupert and Hell with a rush and a roar,
More fierce and fell than they came before;
    To the Lord our God be glory!

"Not so, O Lord, was it with thine own;
    Praise we the Lord!
To us were thy truth and mercy shown;
    Praise we the Lord!
Through our closed-up ranks were our trumpets blown:
Then no shout, but a deep psalm rose alone,
And we knew that our God would his might make known.
    To his holy name be glory!

"And Cromwell, his servant, spoke the word;
    Praise we the Lord!
'On! smite for the Lord! spare not!' we heard;
    Praise we the Lord!
Hotly our spirits within us stirred;
Reins were loosened and flanks were spurred,
And the heathen went down before God and his word.
    To his name alone be glory!"

Many stories are related of the adventures of Charles after Worcester. For some days he stayed disguised as a laborer at a farm-house and cut faggots in the wood. On a subsequent day, seeing a party of horsemen approaching, he climbed amongst the dense foliage of an old oak, and lay hid till they passed, listening to their talk about capturing him. The oak is still known as the "Royal Oak," and is to this day a popular sign for public houses. Amid all his distresses Charles was gay and played many a prank among his friends. He escaped to Féchamp in Normandy. Though upwards of forty persons, many in humble circumstances, had been privy to his escape, and though Parliament had offered £1,000 for his capture, not one was base enough to betray him.

Cromwell, whose ambition was as boundless as that of the great Napoleon, and whose influence over his soldiery was equally unlimited, now resolved to vindicate his authority by the support of a military force, and get rid of Parliament. With this view he persuaded his officers to present a petition to the Commons, asking for the arrears of pay due them, and, next, and more especially, that it should dissolve itself. As Cromwell foresaw, Parliament treated the petition with scorn. This was what he wanted. He repaired at once to the House with 300 soldiers, whom he posted outside. Entering, he listened for a time to the debate, then stamped with his foot as a signal for his men to enter. Seizing the mace, the emblem of royal authority, with the words, "Take away that bauble," he ordered the members to disband themselves and give place to honester men; then locking the door, and putting the key in his pocket, he returned to his officers at Whitehall.

Such was the dissolution of the Long Parliament, a deed regarded in history as one of the most daring and unconstitutional ever performed. Cromwell's next object was to have a Parliament in name, which should be entirely under his authority. The mode of election was novel. The ministers through the country were directed to take the sense of their congregations respecting persons "faithful and fearing God," and to send up their names. From these Cromwell selected one hundred and thirty-nine, to whom he gave authority for fifteen months. The members were largely fanatical enthusiasts. One of them was called Praise-God Barebones, and from him the Parliament got the name of the "Barebones Parliament." By it Cromwell was named "Protector of the Commonwealth." In reality he was an unlimited monarch, and probably the ablest that ever ruled England. He sustained the national honor abroad in a manner such as had not been known from the days of Elizabeth. After defeating the Dutch twice at sea, he made an honorable peace with them; from the Spaniards he captured Jamaica, and his fleet, under Blake, seized many of their treasure-ships on their homeward voyages from America. France and Spain and all the continental powers sought his favor.

Cromwell died in 1658, and was succeeded by his son Richard, a quiet, inoffensive man, who discovering he could not be happy in a lofty position, resigned his dignities and retired to private life.

During Cromwell's time Puritanism was dominant in England. All kinds of amusement were forbidden; even Christmas pastimes were prohibited. Bear-baiting was put down, not, says Macaulay, because it hurt the bear, but because it was pleasing to the people. Coffee and sugar were introduced, and the general post office and regular banking-houses established in London.

John Milton, the "Prince of British Poets," lived and wrote during the time of the Commonwealth. Milton was born in London in 1608, his father being a scrivener and a man of "plentiful estate." He was educated at Cambridge, and on completing his studies retired to a country house of his father, where he spent five years, reading classic authors and composing "Comus," "Lycidas," "Arcades," "L'Allegro," and "Il Penseroso." In 1641 he engaged in the political and religious controversies of the times, on the side of the Commonwealth, and his pen is said to have been as terrible as Oliver's sword. Unceasing study affected his sight, and in 1654 he became totally blind. After the restoration of Charles II. he retired from public view and produced his immortal works, "Paradise Lost" and "Paradise Regained." "Paradise Lost" was published in 1667. He received five pounds from the publishers for the copyright, and a promise of five pounds more when 1,300 copies should have been sold. He died in 1674, leaving property of the value of £1,500. Wordsworth says of him: "Thy soul was like a star, and dwelt apart." Dryden, in associating him with Homer and Virgil, says:

> "Three poets, in three distant ages born,
> Greece, Italy, and England did adorn;
> The first in loftiness of thought surpassed,
> The next in majesty, in both the last.
> The force of nature could not further go,
> To make a third she joined the other two."

CHARLES II. 1660—1685.

Man is a creature of extremes. During the Commonwealth England was under the somewhat gloomy rule of Puritanical fanaticism; now she rebounded under Charles to the opposite extreme of unbounded license. Unfortunately, in her sovereign she found an example to justify her in the wildest indulgences. Gay, jovial, unprincipled, witty, denying himself no pleasure, his character is thus summed up in the elegiac quatrain written by the witty Rochester on the door of his bed-chamber:

> "Here lies our Sovereign Lord the King,
> Whose word no man relies on;
> He never says a foolish thing,
> Nor ever does a wise one."

MILTON DICTATING PARADISE LOST TO HIS DAUGHTER.

More tersely yet he describes him as "a merry monarch; scandalous, but poor."

Never was monarch more enthusiastically received than Charles on his return from exile to London. Looking at the exulting masses the king quaintly remarked that he could not conceive why he had stayed away from them so long.

One of the first acts of Charles and his Parliament was to bring to trial all concerned in the execution of his father. Several were executed, others imprisoned or fined, and many fled. This settled, he looked out for a wife, thinking much more of the dowry than the disposition or person of the lady. He selected the richest princess in Europe, Catherine of Portugal, married her, and forthwith neglected her, and proceeded to surround her with mistresses and dissipate her fortune. A great naval war with Holland resulted only in several desperate conflicts at sea, neither party deriving advantage from the contests. Two great domestic calamities mark this reign—the plague and the great fire in London. It was in 1665 that the plague broke out in the month of April among the poor of St. Giles. All precautions to check it were ineffectual. It did its work with fearful rapidity. When a person was found to be seized, the door was fastened up, marked with a red cross with the words "God have mercy on us," and no one was allowed to go in or out. Food was set down outside the door, and carts came round to take away the dead, who were all buried in long trenches. The court and all who were able left the city, the grass growing green in the streets. The effect on different minds was remarkable; some employed their time in religious exercises, others plunged into the wildest dissipation, the solemn stillness being occasionally broken by sounds of unhallowed merriment from taverns and haunts of vice. Over a hundred thousand persons died in London alone, and similar ravages occurred in the other large towns of the kingdom.

CHARLES II.

Next year the great fire occurred, which burnt down whole streets and even destroyed St. Paul's Cathedral. It probably did good by clearing away many dirty streets and narrow alleys, where plague might have lingered; not the less it was a fearful misfortune. The king and his brother gained much favor by their presence at the fire and doing their utmost to stay it. It was checked at last by blowing up large areas with gunpowder. The monument on Fish-street Hill was erected (1671–1677) to commemorate the fire.

Like his father and Laud, Charles tried to force Episcopacy on Scotland, and the poor people who resisted were subjected to cruel persecution, the details of which will be given under the history of that country.

The king had no children, and a story was circulated that Charles was to be murdered, and his brother, a Roman Catholic, set on the throne. Charles laughed at it and said, "No one would kill me to make you king, James." Not the less, when public clamor demanded the lives of the suspected persons, Charles in his easy, selfish way, did not put out a hand to save them.

A real plot, called the Rye-house Plot was formed to compel the king to make his illegitimate son, the Duke of Monmouth, his heir. Lord Russell and others joined it from their hatred to Catholicism. The plot was discovered and its leaders executed. When Lord Russell was tried, his wife, Lady Rachel, sat beside him all the time and was his great comfort. Monmouth was pardoned, but fled to Holland.

Charles is said to have spent the last Sunday of his life in playing cards and listening to idle songs. Struck with apoplexy, he sent for a Catholic priest and was received into the church which he had believed in without daring to acknowledge the fact, for fear of losing his crown.

"Paradise Lost," Milton's grand work, was really written in this reign. A scarcely less famed literary production was the "Pilgrim's Progress," by John Bunyan. Originally a travelling tinker of loose habits, Bunyan on being converted became a member of the Baptist Church, of which he was chosen to be the preacher. Being convicted for holding conventicles, he spent twelve years in Bedford Jail, where he laid all posterity under obligations by writing this marvellous allegory.

A standing army was established by Charles in times of peace as well as of war. Tea was brought to England by the Dutch East India Company. The best law passed was the Habeas Corpus Act. The Quakers appeared as a new sect in this reign, and were shamefully persecuted, which drove William Penn with many followers to seek refuge in America, that refuge of the oppressed.

JAMES II. 1685—1688.

James was really a better man than his brother. He was, at least, open and honest in joining the church in which he believed; but he was a grave, sad, stern man, and people disliked him because he had not the graces of his light-hearted, gay, unprincipled brother.

The Duke of Monmouth attempted a rising, but his friends being routed at Sedgemoor, he was taken prisoner and executed. The royal vengeance was now let loose on the adherents of Monmouth. Sir George Jeffreys, the chief-justice, was sent to try all who had been concerned, from Winchester to Exeter, and he hung so many, and treated all so savagely, that his progress was called the "bloody assize." James now issued an edict that a person might be chosen to any office in the state whether he were a member of the established church or no, and ordered it to be read in the churches. Archbishop Sancroft objected, and he and six bishops presented a petition praying the king that they should not be forced to read it. With the hereditary absolutism of the Stuarts, James committed all the seven bishops to the tower, and had them tried for libel. England was deeply stirred, and there was general exultation when an honest jury gave a verdict of "not guilty."

James was twice married. His first wife was an English woman and a Protestant, and the two daughters she bore him were brought up as Protestants. The eldest, Mary, married her cousin, Prince of Orange, Stadtholder of Holland; Ann's husband, Prince George of Denmark, was also a Protestant. James' second wife was an Italian princess and a Catholic. So long as James had no son, the people bore with him, as he was growing old, in the hope of getting a Protestant sovereign in William at his death. But at length a son was born of the second marriage. Forthwith correspondence was opened with the Prince of Orange, who, on December 5th, 1688, landed at Torbay, Devonshire. People of all classes flocked to him. It was but three years from the bloody assize, and people had not forgotten it in those parts. James fled to France, and the English Revolution was accomplished.

WILLIAM (AND MARY). 1689—1702.

On the day of James' departure the Dutch sovereign entered the palace as if he were hereditary king. It was proposed to crown both Mary and her husband, but William refused to accept the crown unless he were sole monarch. The people, however, conditioned that he should sign a bill of rights securing them against further encroachments by the sovereign. This "Bill of Rights" was, in fact, a new and more complete Magna Charta. Toleration was proclaimed, as also the liberty of the press.

But James had still many friends in

WILLIAM III. (OF ORANGE).

Ireland, known by the title of Jacobites. All Roman Catholics were, of course, of this party, but there were many Protestants, especially of the aristocracy, also well-affected towards him. It was, therefore, judged that if James appeared in Ireland, that country would rise in his behalf. Louis XIV. furnished him with a small army, which on his landing was largely reinforced by Irishmen. William hurried over to meet him with both English and Dutch troops, and on July 12th, 1690, James was totally defeated by the Prince of Orange at the Battle of the Boyne. To this day the extreme Protestants of Ireland call themselves Orangemen, and parade on the anniversary of the battle, wearing bouquets of orange-lilies.

A rising of the Scots under Dundee was brought to nought by that leader's death at Killiecrankie.

COSTUMES, TIME OF WILLIAM AND MARY.

Towards the end of William's reign a European war broke out on the subject of the succession to the crown of Spain, whose king had died childless. The King of France had married a sister, and claimed the crown for his grandson. William was prepared to take part against France. Just as the war broke out, in riding near Hampton Court, he had his collar-bone broken by a fall from his horse, which trod on a mole-hill, in consequence of which he died. A favorite toast with the Jacobites, for well nigh a century after, was, "the little gentleman with the velvet coat."

QUEEN ANNE.   1702—1714.

Of course James, son of James II., was the legitimate heir to the throne. But it was now the law of England that none but a Protestant should inherit the throne, and James was Catholic. Anne, married to Prince George of Denmark, therefore succeeded. The war of the Spanish succession was now raging, and England was deeply engaged in it. The Duke of Marlborough won many victories over the French in Germany, among which those at Blenheim and Ramilies were most famed. Gibraltar was taken in 1704, by a combined Dutch and English fleet, and has remained in the possession of England ever since.

A yet more important occurrence was the union of England and Scotland. Since the succession of James I. they had been ruled by one sovereign, but they had still separate legislative assemblies. The English thought it best that there should be but one Parliament in London, to which the Scotch should send representatives. They send now seventy-two. The Scotch, however, were to retain many of their old laws, have their own national church, and, in short, enjoy practical independence in local affairs. This union, though at first unpopular in Scotland, has conferred unquestioned benefits on, and proved a blessing to, both countries. Well had it been for England, had its union with Ireland been accomplished under similar conditions. The union with Scotland was completed on May 1st, 1707. Queen Anne died in 1714.

QUEEN ANNE.

Anne's reign was rendered illustrious by some of the greatest names, both in literature and science, which England has produced. Foremost among these is that of the great mathematician and philosopher, Sir Isaac Newton. Born at Woolsthorpe, Lincolnshire, in 1640, he studied at Cambridge University, where he distinguished himself by his profound mathematical learning.

Returning home to Woolsthorpe he pursued original investigations, and one day, sitting in his garden there, the fall of an apple suggested to him the most magnificent discovery of science—the law of universal gravitation. He also investigated the laws of light, and much improved the telescope. The principal results of his labors are embodied in a great work entitled "Principia." He died in 1727, and his remains received a resting-place in Westminster Abbey. Well has Pope said of him:

> "Nature and nature's laws lay hid in night;
> God said, 'Let Newton be!' and there was light."

COSTUMES OF ANNE'S TIME.

Space permits us to enumerate only a few more of the illustrious names of this brilliant era. Eminent among these were John Dryden and Alexander Pope. Dryden was born of good family in 1631. He studied at Cambridge, and there he laid the foundation of that learning which enabled him to enrich his prefaces with unrivalled discussions on literary methods. The most dishonorable part in Dryden's character was his political tergiversation. He wrote his "Heroic Stanzas" in honor of Cromwell, and hailed the return of Charles II. with his "Astræa Redux." He was distinguished alike as a heroic, didactic and satirical poet, and as a dramatist. His verses on "Alexander's Feast" have won universal fame. He died in 1700.

Alexander Pope was born in London in 1688, of Roman Catholic parents, to which faith he adhered. His father, a linen merchant, left considerable means, and the poet acquired a delightful abode at Twickenham, where he continued till his death in 1744. He was a poet almost from infancy, "lisping in numbers, for the numbers came," and surpassed all his contemporaries in metrical harmony and correctness. Among his earlier pieces we note his "Essay on Criticism," "Rape of the Lock," "Windsor Forest," "Epistle to Eloisa" and "Elegy on an Unfortunate Lady." His famous translation of Homer's Iliad and Odyssey netted for him the hitherto unexampled sum of upwards of £8,000. The poet expressed his gratitude in the well-known couplet:

> "And thanks to Homer, since I live and thrive,
> Indebted to no prince or peer alive."

In 1735 appeared his "Essay on Man," full of splendid passages of mingled sweetness and dignity, as seen in the following:

> "Hope springs eternal in the human breast;
> Man never is, but always to be blessed.
> The soul uneasy and confined from home,
> Rests and expatiates in a life to come."

His "Dunciad" exhibits his powers as a satirist.

Other great luminaries of this reign were: Joseph Addison, editor of the *Spectator*, the most elegantly correct of all England's prose writers; Daniel Defoe, author of "Robinson Crusoe," the most realistic describer of scenes real or imaginary; and the unrivalled satirist, Dean Swift, whose most popular work, "Gulliver's Travels," has amused and delighted generations of children, young and old.

GEORGE I. 1714—1727.

Anne was the last of the Stuart dynasty to sit on the British throne. Her unfortunate brother, James III. (the child born to James II. from his second marriage), still wandered an exile in France and Italy. He had married a princess belonging to the Polish house of Sobieski, and had a son Charles Edward. By an act, called the "Act of Settlement," the succession was limited to the Princess Sophia (grand daughter of James I,) and her heirs, being Protestants. The son of this princess was George, Duke of Brunswick and Elector of Hanover, and he, accordingly, on Anne's death, was called to the throne, to the exclusion of the Stuarts, father and son. George was a heavy, dull man, ignorant of English, whose heart never warmed to his new subjects, nor theirs to him. To the last he preferred his native Germany to England. There still existed many Jacobites (as the adherents of the exiled Stuarts were called) in the kingdom, particularly in Ireland, in the north of England, where many great families were Catholic, and in the Highlands of Scotland, where devotion to a hereditary chief was the cardinal virtue. In 1715 the Earl of Mar raised the standard of rebellion at Bræmar, close to Balmoral, where Queen Victoria has her Highland home, and the clansmen flocked to him in thousands. Forthwith he marched southward and was met by the Duke of Argyll, at the head of a royalist army, at Sheriffmuir, near Dunblane. There was fought an indecisive battle, in which the left wing of either host fled in headlong flight, while the right wings were victorious. This fight has been graphically portrayed in a well-known half-humorous, half satirical Scottish song:

> "Some say that we ran, and some say that they ran,
> And some say that nane ran ava', man ;
> But of a'e thing I'm sure, that at Sheriffmuir
> A battle there was that I saw, man.
> And we wan and they ran, and they wan and we ran,
> And we ran and they ran awa', man."

This checked Mar's southward progress, and his army disbanded itself.

At the same time a number of noblemen and gentlemen of the south of Scotland and north of England—at the head of whom were the Earl of Derwentwater, the Lords Nithsdale, Kenmare and Carnwath—proclaimed James as King of England and, joined by 2,000 Highlanders, marched south as far as Preston, where, being cooped up, they surrendered at discretion on the very day of Mar's ineffective battle at Sheriffmuir. The leaders paid for their treason with their lives.

The remainder of George's life was passed in tranquillity. He died at Osnalrack, on his way towards his beloved Hanover, in 1727, and was succeeded by a son of the same name.

This reign saw the rise and development of Methodism. At the beginning of the eighteenth century England was spiritually moribund. The revival of religion began with a small group of Oxford students, among whom three figures detach themselves from the group. Whitfield, whose preaching produced an excitement such as England had never seen before ; Charles Wesley, who came to add sweetness to this sudden and startling light, and John Wesley, who embodied in himself not this or that side of the vast movement, but was the movement itself. In power as a preacher he stood next to Whitfield ; as a hymn-writer he was second only to his brother Charles, while he possessed qualities in which both were deficient—an indefatigable industry, cool judgment, and a faculty for organization. He had, besides, a learning and skill in writing which no other of the Methodists (as he and his party were called) could lay claim to. His life, from 1703 to 1791, almost covers the century, and the Methodist body had passed through every phase of its history ere he sank into the grave at the age of eighty-eight. The influence of this body of earnest Christians on the spiritual life of the middle and lower classes in England cannot be overestimated. Hitherto they had been all but ignored by the aristocratic church. No man cared for their souls. When they found men who spoke to them like brethren and sisters, with true earnestness, power, and love, they "received the word gladly." In Wales, especially, these evangelical men swept all before them.

GEORGE II. 1727—1760.

This king, like his father, pretended to no accomplishments beyond those of a soldier. In his own words he had neither knowledge of nor taste for either poetry or painting. A war having broken out in Germany, over the succession to the Empire, France and England, as usual, took different sides. George was present at the battle of Dellingen, and, with the aid of the Earl of Stair, won it. This was the last fight in which a king of England took personal part. His son, the Duke of Cumberland, was shortly thereafter defeated with great loss by the French at Fontenoy, in 1745. This defeat encouraged Charles Edward, son of (the so-called) James III., to make another attempt to win back the throne of his fathers. He landed in the West Highlands and the chieftains, followed by their clans, flocked to his standard, so that he shortly found himself at the head of some thousands of mountaineers. His exploits and adventures belong as much to the history of Scotland as that of England, and will be there narrated. Suffice it to say, his Highlanders were utterly defeated at Culloden, near Inverness, in April, 1746. The subsequent barbarities of Cumberland have caused his name to be execrated in Scotland to the present day.

In the reign of this George the foundation of England's great Indian Empire was laid by a brave officer named Clive, who rose to be a peer and governor-general of India. The most striking episode in this war is that of the Black Hole of Calcutta. A native Indian prince, at the head of a large army, suddenly came down on this city, the capital of the English possessions. Most of the English escaped by getting on board ships in the Hooghly. Those who could not—146 in number—were seized and, in the hottest season of the year, thrust into a room twenty feet square, with only two small grated windows, named the "Black Hole." The heat and want of pure air speedily deprived some of existence; others died raving mad, their entreaties for water being mocked at, and in the morning only twenty-three were found alive.

The vast territory of Canada, belonging to France, was also added to the British dominions. The final and decisive battle in this war was fought out between French and English troops under the walls of Quebec, September 12th, 1759, the gallant English General Wolfe falling at the very moment of victory. As he lay on the ground he heard the officers, who stood sorrowing around him, exclaim, "They run, they run!" "Who run?" asked the expiring hero.

"The French." "Then I die happy." In this American war with the French, General Washington, then a young officer, first signalized himself, fighting on the side of England.

George II. died in October, 1760.

In this reign the British Museum was formed, turnpikes established, and canal-making begun. One of the most remarkable changes was the introduction of the new style of reckoning time. Julius Cæsar fixed the Julian year as consisting of 365 days, 6 hours. The true year consists of 365 days, 5 hours, 49 minutes. Hence, in the eighteen hundred years which had elapsed from the time of Cæsar, an error of eleven days had crept in. This was now rectified by causing the second day of January, 1752, to be called the 13th. At the same time the year was made to begin on the 1st of January, and not, as formerly, on the 25th of March.

In art, Hogarth, the celebrated painter and engraver, was pre-eminently distinguished for representing in pictures engraved by himself the follies and vices of his time. In 1733 appeared his six pictures of "The Harlot's Progress," and these were followed by similar representations of dissipation and folly, such as "The Rake's Progress," "Enraged Musicians," "Marriage à la Mode," "The Election." He died in 1764, and was interred at Chiswick. His monument bears an inscription by his friend Garrick. Garrick ranks as one of the greatest—probably the very greatest—of English actors. He exhibited what has been called a Shakespearean universality, being equally at home in the highest flights of tragedy, and the lowest depths of farce. He wrote also forty plays, some original, some adaptations of old plays. Samuel Johnson, the lexicographer, distinguished both as a poet and prose-writer, and yet more distinguished as a conversationalist, as he is depicted to us in the pages of Boswell; and Goldsmith, one of England's most pleasing poets, novelists and dramatists—witness his "Deserted Village," "Vicar of Wakefield" and "She Stoops to Conquer"—are also to be reckoned among the lights of this reign. Other great names are Hume, the historian; Fielding and Smollet, novelists; and Sir Joshua Reynolds, president of the Royal Academy, and prince of English portrait painters.

GEORGE III. 1760—1820.

Personally, the most remarkable things about this monarch—a respectable, dull, obstinate man—were the facts that he reigned longer than any other British sovereign, and that for the last ten years of his life he suffered from mental derangement, so that he could take no part in public affairs. The most distinguished political character in this reign was William Pitt, probably the ablest prime-minister that ruled England from the days of Wolsey. He was by nature a liberal man, and but for the obstinacy of the king would have emancipated the Catholics and introduced other measures tending to extend the boundaries of human freedom, for his was too clear an intellect not to see whither the world was trending. Had his counsels been followed it is doubtful whether even our War of Independence would have found a place in history; certainly it would have been fought out on some other issue than that of taxation without representation. But the history of this war belongs to American history and will be dealt with there. Suffice it to say that George's pig-headed obstinacy lost England the brightest jewel in her diadem. Of this loss the honest poet Burns speaks thus, in his birthday address to this monarch:

> " 'Tis very true, my sovereign king,
> My skill may well be doubted;
> But facts are chiels that winna ding,
> And downa be disputed.
>
> " Your royal nest beneath your wing
> Is e'en right reft an 'clouted,
> And now the third part of the string,
> And less, will gang about it
> Than did a'e day."

France and Spain had aided the United States, and this provoked war with them, in which these countries suffered greatly at sea by the gallantry of the British fleet under Byron, Hood, and Rodney; but the most brilliant exploit was the defence of Gibraltar by Elliot against the combined fleets of these two powers. Peace was concluded in 1783, when American independence was conclusively acknowledged.

For ten years Britain had peace, when the outbreak of the French Revolution, and the terrible scenes that followed thereon, especially the execution of the king and queen, brought on the longest and most formidable war in which Britain was ever engaged. It was by the statesmanship displayed in this war that Pitt earned for himself the titles of "the Heaven-sent minister" and "the pilot that weathered the storm." The details of this war will better appear elsewhere. Several British commanders, military and naval, won glory in the struggle, as Abercrombie, Moore, St. Vincent, and Hyde Parker, but the two names that stand out above all others are those of Nelson and Wellington. The crowning sea-fight of Trafalgar, won by the former, shattered the navies of France and Spain; Waterloo, won by the latter, sent the Emperor Napoleon to St. Helena, and closed the war.

The great Irish Rebellion of 1798 will find its place in our history of Ireland. Suffice it to say here that in 1801 the Irish Parliament in Stephen's Green, Dublin, came to an end and Ireland was reunited to Britain.

As already indicated, George III. was laid aside during the last ten years

LORD BYRON.

of his reign by mental derangement, during which the government was carried on by a regency under the Prince of Wales, afterwards George IV.

To specify with any degree of adequacy the progress made in science, the mechanical inventions, the development of manufactures, the spread of trade and commerce, and the manifold improvements in social life during this reign, would demand a large volume. Chief among these advances was the practical discovery of the steam-engine by James Watt. This mechanician, engineer and man of science was born at Greenock, Scotland, in 1736, his father being a respectable merchant and magistrate of the burgh. He early manifested a turn for mathematics and a great interest in machines, and in 1757 was appointed mathematical instrument-maker to the University of Glasgow. Living in the college in close intercourse with the professors, with access to books, he became a diligent experimenter in the application of science to the arts. In 1763 a Newcomen air-engine for pumping water out of mines was sent to him for repair, and this set him thinking of how steam could be applied for turning machinery in mills. In 1769 he took out a patent for an invention for this purpose, and in subsequent years, down to 1785, obtained patents for a series of inventions perfecting his idea. In 1774 he had become partner with Matthew Bolton, of Soho, near Birmingham, and in this work his first engine was constructed. His discoveries revolutionized the manufacturing industries of the world. Acquiring a competency he retired from business in 1800, and died at Heathfield, Staffordshire, in 1819. Mr. Arkwright, afterwards Sir Richard Arkwright, made great improvements in cotton manufacture by the invention of new machinery, while Mr. Wedgewood made no less important improvements in the manufacture of china and porcelain. Geographical science was advanced by Captain Cook, who made three voyages around the world.

The most original and vigorous thought of this period found its expression in poetry, and amongst its great poets the most noteworthy are Byron, Coleridge, Wordsworth, Scott, the last of whom is at the head of all the writers of prose fiction. Byron was born in London, 1788, his father being a profligate officer of the guards, his mother of the family of the Gordons of Gight, Aberdeenshire. His granduncle, whom he succeeded in the title, killed a man in a drunken brawl, was tried before the House of Lords and acquitted, but was of such a character that till his death he was known as "wicked Lord Byron." Byron's father dissipated his wife's fortune and deserted her, whereupon she retired, with her little lame boy, to Aberdeen, to bring him up on her reduced income of £130 a year. Upon succeeding to the title in his eleventh year, he was sent to Harrow School and thence to Cambridge. In early youth he published a collection of poems under the title of "Hours of Idleness," which were savagely handled by the *Edinburgh Review*. By way of retort Byron wrote his scorching satire, "English Bards and Scotch Reviewers." To use his own phrase, he rose one morning and found himself famous. With the wreath of triumph on his brow he wandered, for two years, over Spain, Albania, Greece, Turkey and Asia Minor, and on his return gave to the world the two first cantos of his great poem, "Childe Harold." Every one saw the "Childe" was himself. In rapid succession followed the "Giaour," "Bride of Abydos," "Manfred," "Mazeppa," "Don Juan," and numerous other pieces. He returned to Greece, was appointed commander-in-chief of an expedition to Lepanto, but sickened and died in 1824, aged thirty-six years.

Samuel Taylor Coleridge was born at Ottery, Devonshire, in 1772, his father being a clergyman of the English church. He studied at Cambridge, but growing tired of college life enlisted as a private soldier in a dragoon regiment. Here he was miserable, and one of the officers, a scholar, going into the stables one morning, found chalked up the following sentence in Latin:

"Eheu! quam infortunii miserrimum est fuisse beatum!"

Through this officer's influence he was discharged. Afterwards he formed an intimate friendship with Southey and Wordsworth, and settling near each other they formed the school of the "Lake Poets." The use of opium shattered his system physically and mentally, and he entered the family of a Mr. Gillem, Highgate, where he was cared for till his death. His prose works are admirable alike for originality, power of thought, and felicity of diction, but it is on his "Christabel" and "Rime of the Ancient Mariner" that his fame now mainly rests. As a conversationalist he was second only to Samuel Johnson. He died in 1834.

William Wordsworth was born at Cockermouth, Cumberland, 1770, his father being law-agent for the Earl of Lonsdale. The poet studied at Hawksworth School and Cambridge University. He visited France in 1791, and hailed the French Revolution with enthusiasm:

"Bliss was it in that dawn to be alive,
But to be young was very heaven."

Receiving two small legacies he devoted himself to study and seclusion, forming a close friendship with Coleridge and Southey. He is regarded as the head of the "Lake School." At Rydal Mount, on the beautiful lake of Grasmere, he lived for thirty-one placid, happy years. Of this period he says:

"Long have I loved what I behold,
The night that calms, the day that cheers,
The common growth of mother-earth
Suffices me—her tears, her mirth,
Her humblest mirth and tears.

> "The dragon's wing, the magic ring
> I shall not covet for my dower,
> If I along that lowly way
> With sympathetic heart may stray
> And with a soul of power."

Even more beautifully he elsewhere expresses his sympathy with all the shows of nature:

> "To me the meanest flower that grows can give
> Thoughts that do often lie too deep for tears."

Being appointed distributer of stamps for the county of Westmoreland, he was placed beyond the frowns of Fortune, and on the death of his friend Southey was made poet-laureate of England, with an income of £300 a year. He passed away peacefully in 1850, in his eightieth year. His poems were mostly written in the open air amid the scenes he loved so well, and which he has so tenderly depicted. His greatest work is "The Excursion," a philosophical poem in blank verse. His other pieces are numerous, among which we may specify: "The White Doe of Rylstone," "Sonnets on the River Duddon," "The Waggoner," "Peter Bell," "Yarrow Revisited."

Sir Walter Scott, being a Scotchman, we refer to Scotland.

We cannot close this reign without referring to Chatham, Fox and Burke, three of the greatest orators of all time. Burke, had he not been a politician, would have been one of the lights of literature, as is evidenced by his grand "Essay on the Sublime and Beautiful," and many other papers. Goldsmith says of him, he

> "Gave up for party what was meant for mankind."

GEORGE IV. 1820—1830.

Happy is the reign that has no history. The fourth George's reign merits this benediction so far as wars and outward complications were concerned. Otherwise it was marked by the same fertility of mechanical invention, the same advance in material prosperity that characterized that of his father. The grand political feature in this reign was Catholic emancipation, gained for his Catholic fellow-countrymen by Daniel O'Connell, the Emancipator of Ireland. This measure passed both houses of Parliament and received the royal assent in 1829. George had considerable ability and address, and from his personal attractions and his position, it was the habit to style him "The first gentleman of Europe." Allowing for the difference in the customs and modes of thought of the ages in which they lived, George IV. and the second Charles were very closely akin in character. His treatment of his wife at and after his coronation exposed him to considerable obloquy. He died in 1830.

This reign was notable for the spread of education among the working classes and the establishment of societies for the diffusion of useful knowledge, as well as for the mitigation of the severity of the laws. The first steam-boats that worked for hire in Britain appeared on the Clyde, Scotland, in 1811; in 1822 an iron steam-boat was launched on the Thames to run between England and France, and four years later a voyage was performed by steam to the West Indies. Atlantic steam navigation came later. Railways were begun in this reign, but there was little passenger travel on them till after George's death. Emigration to the United States, Canada, Australia and South Africa was largely developed. George made two journeys—one to Scotland and the other to Ireland—he being the first of the House of Brunswick who ever visited either of these two kingdoms.

WILLIAM IV. 1830—1837.

George IV. left no child, and was succeeded by his next surviving brother, William, Duke of Clarence. He had been a sailor and was an elderly man ere he mounted the throne. He was a slow, good-natured man, inclined to befriend the people. The leading political measure in his days was the Reform Bill. The English House of Commons is composed of members representing burghs and members representing counties, with a few representatives of universities. Hitherto the right of electing members had been restricted to a few burgesses in each burgh and to free-holders in counties. Some ancient burghs sending members to Parliament had become so much depopulated that the owners of the soil nominated the persons to represent them. These were called "pocket burghs" or "rotten burghs." Old Sarum, for example, sent two members and had not one inhabitant. On the other hand several great modern cities, as Manchester and Birmingham, were not represented at all. The Reform Bill of 1832 conferred the right of voting on every person paying £10 of yearly rent in burghs, and £50 in counties. At the same time fifty-six burghs in England and Wales were entirely disfranchised, and forty-two new ones created. Since then new reform measures have extended the franchise, so that it is now practically universal. Another great measure of this reign was the liberation of the West Indian slaves, at an expense to the mother country of £20,000,000 paid to the slave-owners. William died in 1837. He was the last English king who reigned over the State of Hanover. The Salic law prevails there, so that it cannot be ruled by a woman.

The earliest great railway for passenger traffic as well as freight, that, namely, between Liverpool and Manchester, was formally opened September 15th, 1830. The London and Birmingham Railway, the first that had a metropolitan terminus, was opened in 1838.

VICTORIA.   1837.

Queen Victoria is daughter of Edward, Duke of Kent, fourth son of George III. In 1818 he married the Princess of Laningen, and on May 24th, 1819, was born his daughter, Alexandrina Victoria, who on the death of William, in 1837, succeeded to the throne, her father being dead. She was crowned, amid general rejoicing, in Westminster Abbey, June 28th, 1838. In February, 1840, she married Albert, Prince of Saxe-Coburg and Gotha, and no woman had ever a more faithful husband. The queen's eldest daughter, the Princess Royal, was born November 21st, 1840, and her eldest son, Albert Edward, Prince of Wales, November 9th, 1841. She had seven other children, three sons and four daughters, the youngest, the Princess Beatrice, being born April 14th, 1857. In January, 1858, the princess royal was married to the crown-prince of Prussia, and in March, 1863, the Prince of Wales married the Princess Alexandra of Denmark. The Queen was left a widow by the sudden death of her husband, the Prince-Consort, on December 14th, 1861. The only child of the queen who married a subject is the Princess Louise, her fourth daughter, who in March, 1871, became the wife of the Marquis of Lorne, eldest son of the Duke of Argyll.

The queen had been trained with admirable care and solicitude by her widowed mother, and on reaching the throne in her eighteenth year, she was found not only to be mistress of many accomplishments, but to be possessed of a sound judgment, an excellent heart, and a real desire to promote the well-being of her subjects. In all her laudable efforts she was not only encouraged, but more generally guided by her consort, than whom England never had a more intelligent ruler. He devoted himself specially to schemes for enlightening the people and advancing the arts of peace. In May, 1857, there was opened, under his auspices, in a magnificent structure of glass and iron (called the "Crystal Palace"), in Hyde Park, London, the first of those great international industrial exhibitions or "world's fairs," which has had so many imitators. His object was not only to promote the material welfare of the different peoples of the world, but to unite mankind, more and more, into one great family.

Only two years after this broke out the great Crimean War. Turkey had long been in a decaying state; and one day the Emperor of Russia asked the English ambassador if he did not think the Turkish power a very sick man that would soon be dead. The ambassador gave the emperor to understand that the sick man, if die he must, was to be allowed to die in peace. In reality neither England nor France could bear that Russia should gain a great accession to its power on the Mediterranean. In consequence when Russia attacked Turkey, English and French (and latterly Italian) armies were sent to defend

PRINCE OF WALES.

her. It was judged best to carry the war into Russia itself, and the result was the landing in the Crimea of the English and French armies, under Lord Raglan and Marshal St. Arnaud, in the autumn of 1854. A great victory was gained at the landing, in the storming of the heights of Alma. Sebastopol was besieged, and obstinately defended for a year. During the winter the English soldiers suffered horribly through the ineptness of the commissariat and other departments, and the rascality of contractors. Florence Nightingale came to their aid as a ministering angel, and by her deeds of mercy to the sick and wounded earned a name that will never die. There were two more famous battles. One was that of Balaklava, in which six hundred English horsemen charged, by a blunder of some commander, a whole battery of Russian cannon. This is the Charge of the Light Brigade, celebrated by Tennyson:

"Half a league, half a league,
Half a league onward,
All in the Valley of Death
    Rode the six hundred.
"Forward the Light Brigade,
Charge for the guns,' he said;
Into the Valley of Death
    Rode the six hundred.

"Forward, the Light Brigade!'
Was there a man dismay'd?
Not, tho' the soldier knew
    Some one had blunder'd:
Their's not to make reply,
Their's not to reason why,
Their's but to do or die;
Into the Valley of Death
    Rode the six hundred.

"Flash'd all their sabres bare,
Flashed as they turn'd in air
Sabring the gunners there,
Charging an army, while
    All the world wonder'd:
Plunged in the battery smoke,
Right through the line they broke;
Cossack and Russian
Reel'd from the sabre stroke
    Shatter'd and sunder'd.

"Then they rode back, but not—
    Not the six hundred. . . .
When can their glory fade?
O! the wild charge they made!

> All the world wonder'd.
> Honor the charge they made!
> Honor the Light Brigade,
>   Noble six hundred!"

The other fight was that of Inkerman, wherein by sheer obstinacy the English gained a decisive victory. The capture of the forts defending the city, September 8th, 1855, forced the Russians to evacuate it, and a peace was soon thereafter made, the Russians agreeing to leave Turkey at peace.

Scarcely had the rejoicings for the successful issue of the Crimean War come to an end, when news reached England of the mutiny of the native soldiers (sepoys) in the British army in India. The story of this terrible outbreak will find place in our account of Hindostan. In the meantime England carried on a successful war with China, and acquired full possession of Hong-Kong, and a strip of coast territory on the mainland opposite. In 1868 took place a war with Theodore, Emperor of Abyssinia, who had shut up some missionaries and skilled workmen, invited by him to his capital, Magdala. Magdala was taken, the prisoners released, and the war closed with scarce the loss of a man. In 1873-74 a war with the Ashantees was brought to a successful close. In 1878, at the end of a sharp war between Russia and Turkey, the Island of Cyprus was ceded to England by the Turks, on account of the good offices of Mr. Disraeli, the English premier, at the Berlin convention. In the same year England went to war with the Afghans, and also with the Zulus (a Caffir people of South Africa), ultimately bringing both contests to a successful issue. One incident of the last war cast a gloom over England. The young Prince Napoleon had obtained leave to go out with the English army and take part in the campaign. One day, when out surveying the country, a party of natives sprang out of the reeds and long grass upon him, and ere he could take horse, slew him.

Immediately on the cessation of the Zulu campaign, the Boers, the descendants of Dutch settlers in South Africa, demanded independence, and after a short war, this was granted them by Mr. Gladstone, who was then in power. Egypt had been for long in a desperate financial position and unable to pay the interest due English and French bondholders. A system of "dual control" was therefore established, in accordance with which its finances were managed by two commissioners—one French, the other English—named by the respective governments. The Egyptians ill-brooked to see the affairs of their country controlled, and many of its offices filled, by foreigners. Troubles arose, culminating in a massacre of English and French residents in Alexandria. This city was cannonaded and captured by the English fleet. The Khedive of Egypt professed to be content that his country should remain subordinate, but his minister, Arabi Pasha, putting himself at the head of the army, took the field against an English land force, which had been despatched to quell disturbances. He was utterly routed by General Wolseley (created Lord Wolseley) at Tel-el-Kebir, and a British force now holds Lower Egypt. But in the Soudan a fanatic appeared claiming inspiration, to whom the Arab tribes flocked with enthusiasm. He threatened lower Egypt. British troops were sent to check him. His followers fought with the desperation of devotees, and although his death has brought a lull, the struggle is not yet over. The murder of the brave General Gordon, who volunteered to go to Assouan, with the view of pacifying the Arab tribes, brought much obloquy on Mr. Gladstone and his ministry, who encouraged him to undertake the mission, and then left him to his fate.

Two men—neither, in the strict sense of the term, an Englishman—have had more to do with shaping the policy of England for the last forty years than all others combined. These are the late Earl of Beaconsfield and Mr. Gladstone, both distinguished in the literary as well as in the political world.

Benjamin Disraeli (Lord Beaconsfield) was born in 1804, at Bradenham, Bucks, England; son of Isaac Disraeli, author of "Curiosities of Literature," etc., a landed proprietor, and a strict Jew of Spanish origin. When but a boy of eleven, young Disraeli, with that gift of prescience which distinguished him above all men, professed the Christian faith, was baptized, and received into the English Church. At the age when most youths go to the University, he entered a solicitor's office to qualify himself for a government appointment. In 1825 he took the world by surprise by his novel, "Vivian Grey," and this was followed at intervals by other brilliant works of fiction, "The Young Duke," "Coningsby," "Sybil," "Lothair," etc., etc.

In 1837 he entered Parliament as a Conservative. His maiden speech, conceived in a tone of high-flown eloquence, was received with shouts of laughter. Stopping, he for a moment looked calmly around on his derisive audience, and then, uttering these remarkable prophetic words, "You will not hear me now, but the time will come when you will hear me," took his seat. Mr. Disraeli adhered to Sir Robert Peel till that minister adopted the policy of free trade, when his unrivalled powers of brilliant invective and polished sarcasm raised him to the leadership of the Conservative party. He rose to be three times Chancellor of Exchequer in Lord Derby's administrations, and in 1860 was named by the queen Prime Minister of England, and alternated with Mr. Gladstone in that high office till his death. In 1877 he was raised to the House of Lords, with the title of Earl Beaconsfield.

Disraeli's influence over his party, in political matters, may be said to have been supreme. In 1866 he prevailed on them to pass a reform bill admitting a large body of the working classes to the franchise. Among other measures due to him we may note the Congress of Berlin (1878) on the Eastern Question, the acquisition of the island of Cyprus by England, and of a paramount influence in the Suez Canal. The tact, intellect and genius displayed by him at

HOUSE OF PARLIAMENT, LONDON.

the congress of plenipotentiaries at Berlin led Prince Bismarck to pronounce him the ablest statesman in Europe. On his return, bringing "peace with honor," he was created a Knight of the Garter, a D. C. L. of Oxford and Edinburgh, and had many other honors conferred on him. He died at Hughenden Manor, his hereditary estate in Bucks county, in 1881.

Since the days of Pitt and Fox, England had never seen two such great competing statesmen as Disraeli and Gladstone.

"Brethren in arms, yet rivals in renown."

As the former was unchallenged leader of the Conservative party, so Gladstone has been followed with scarcely less unquestioning obedience by the Liberals.

The Right Hon. William Gladstone, scholar, statesman and orator, son of Sir John Gladstone, Bart. of Fasque, Kinardineshire, Scotland, was born, 1809, at Liverpool, where his father, originally from Leith, had won wealth

GLADSTONE.

and eminence as a West India merchant. He was educated at Eton and Oxford, closing a brilliant career with a double first degree in 1831. In 1832 he entered Parliament as a Conservative, and rendered Sir Robert Peel eloquent and effective aid in passing his free trade measures through the Commons. Mr. Gladstone has held several offices in many successive administrations from 1834 downwards; as Chancellor of the Exchequer under Lord Palmerston, he manifested such mastery of finance that ever since he has been regarded as unrivalled in his management of this intricate subject. Though Mr. Gladstone's early sympathies bound him strongly to the High Church and Tory party, the gradually expanding liberalism of his ideas brought him frequently into opposition to his former friends, and eventually, in 1857, he separated himself from the Conservative party, but continued to represent Oxford University, till his defeat by a Tory candidate in 1865. After the death of Lord Palmerston he became leader of the Liberal party in the Commons, and, since then, he has been at the head of each Liberal administration. As an orator Mr. Gladstone has no rival in Parliament, and in debate it is questionable if any one since the days of Burke has equalled him. In 1869 Mr. Gladstone passed a measure disestablishing the Episcopal Church of Ireland; in 1870 he passed his first Land Bill for Ireland; in 1871 he abolished the army purchase system, and in 1872 carried the Ballot Bill. In 1875 he announced his intention of retiring from public life, but some proposals of the Disraeli ministry led him again, in 1880, to precipitate himself into the political arena, when he made his marvellous "Midlothian Campaign."

The reign of Victoria has been a time of great literary activity, and books have multiplied to an unprecedented degree. At the same time it must be admitted that the first quarter of the century is richer in names of the highest eminence than any subsequent portion of it. No poet approaches the heights attained by Scott, Byron, Shelley, Keats, Campbell, Southey, with the single exception of Tennyson. This is essentially an age of novels, reviews and periodicals. Great names in fiction are Dickens, Thackeray, Bulwer Lytton, Miss Brontë and Miss Evans (George Eliot). As historians we quote Hallam, Macaulay, Carlyle. Ruskin is eminent as a writer on art. In poetry, in addition to Tennyson, there are Mr. and Mrs. Browning, Matthew and Edwin Arnold. A notice of Carlyle will appear under Scotland.

Charles Dickens was born at Portsea, February, 1812. His father was a comparatively poor man, a clerk in the navy pay-office, and Charles was set to work in a blacking warehouse at six shillings a week. Undoubtedly much of his subsequent success was due to his severe experience and training here. He learned the many varieties of life, pitiful and laughter-moving, that swarmed in the streets of London. His father's circumstances improving, he entered an attorney's office, and having mastered short-hand, he spent two years in reporting law cases in Doctor's Commons and other courts. At nineteen he entered the gallery of the House of Commons as parliamentary reporter for the newspapers. His life as an author commenced in 1834. In 1836 appeared his "Sketches by Boz" and the "Pickwick Papers." From that moment his fame was established. These were followed by "Oliver Twist," "Nicholas Nickleby," "Master Humphrey's Clock," "Martin Chuzzlewit," etc. In 1867-68 he visited the United States, and returned to England with £10,000 as the result of thirty-four readings. He died in June, 1870, and received the honor of interment in Westminster Abbey.

William Makepeace Thackeray was born of a good old English family at Calcutta, in 1811, his father being in the Indian civil service. He left his son a fortune of £20,000. When seven years of age the boy was sent home to be educated in the Charterhouse School, London. His ambition was to become an artist, and his drawings were quaint, picturesque, truthfull, yet they missed the touches of a master-hand. Under the pseudonym of Michael Angelo Titmarsh he became a contributor to the magazines and published his "Sketch-books." His "Snob Papers" and "Jeames' Diary," in *Punch*, first gave him reputation, which was heightened and established by the appearance of "Vanity Fair." His remaining leading works are known to all readers—"Pendennis," "The Newcomes," "The Virginians," "Esmond," etc. He was cut off in the fullness of his powers on the 24th of December, 1863.

Alfred, Lord Tennyson, poet-laureate of Britain, is son of the Rev. G. C. Tennyson, born at his father's parsonage of Somersby, Lincolnshire, in 1810. He was educated by his father and at Cambridge University, where as an undergraduate he gained the chancellor's medal for a poem, the subject being "Timbuctoo." In 1830 appeared a volume of "Poems, Chiefly Lyrical," but it was not till 1842, when a new edition appeared, with several important poems added, that his true merit was generally recognized. The author of such pieces as the "Mort d'Arthur," "Locksley Hall," the "May Queen" and "The Two Voices," was seen to be entitled to the first rank among the English poets, and this estimate was more than sustained by the works that followed. In 1850 appeared his "In Memoriam," and on the death of Wordsworth, in 1851, the laureateship fell to him as a matter of course. "In Memoriam" was followed in subsequent years by "Maud," "The Idyls of the King," "Enoch Arden," "The Holy Grail," etc. He has also produced some dramas. He was raised to the peerage and now enjoys the serene evening of his days with "honor, love, obedience, troops of friends," in his pleasant residence of Somersby, Isle of Wight. He has also an estate and residence in Surrey.

Not only has there been remarkable progress in the sciences during the last three reigns, but many novel theories have been put forth in accord with the explanation of natural phenomena. One of the new theories that have startled the world is that so ably propounded by Darwin, and accepted by many scientists of highest name, foreign as well as British, regarding the origin of species. Darwin holds that the various species of plants and animals, instead of being each especially created and immutable, have all sprung from the lowest form of life, and by continual adaptation, natural selection, and survival of the fittest, have gone on developing and improving, and are still going on indefinitely, passing from lower forms to higher. Thus, taking the highest animal—man—he began as a mass of formless jelly, became developed into a mollusc, from that into a fish, a reptile, a quadruped, a monkey, and at last, after myriads of years of development, he attained his present state. This is the doctrine of evolution. Scarcely less novel is the doctrine of conservation of forces, by which it is shown that light, heat, electricity, are all simply modes of motion, and convertible into each other. Chemistry has become almost a new science, aided by the revelations of the spectroscope, by which, by merely examining the spectrum, or colored image of a luminous body refracted through a prism, we can determine its chemical structure. This discovery, due to Frauenhofer, a distinguished optician of Munich, enables the chemist to determine the constituents not only of bodies at hand, but of the sun, stars and planets. The discoveries in magnetism and electricity, by Sir William Thomson, Wheatstone, Morse, Bell, and others, and the application of these discoveries to practical ends in the telegraphic wires and cables are among the most marvellous triumphs of science, and are contributing to unite all the civilized nations of the earth into one great family. Scarcely is their application in the cases of the telephone, the phonotype, and numerous other reproductive appliances less wonderful or less useful to man. Geology, the youngest of all the sciences, has also made immense strides, Murchison, Lyell, Geikie, being among its most distinguished exponents. Nor in this

ST. PAUL'S CATHEDRAL, LONDON.

hasty review would it be proper to pass over Owen's contributions to comparative anatomy and physiology. No notice of English scientific progress, however brief, ought to omit the names of Huxley and Tyndall, the two men who, by their writings—at once profound, clear, and eloquent—have done more to popularize science than almost any other men. Among Huxley's works may be cited "Man's Place in Nature," "Lectures on Comparative Anatomy," "Lessons in Physiology," "Lay Sermons." Tyndall's "Faraday as a Discoverer," "Notes on Electricity," "Notes on Light," "Address delivered before the British Association," are no less worthy of recognition. One fact regarding the last-named eminent man we take pleasure in recording. In the course of a tour through the United States, he netted, after paying expenses, $13,000. Not one cent of this did he carry home with him. Before leaving for Europe he placed the amount in the hands of a committee authorized "to expend the interest in aid of American students who devote themselves to original research."

The English school of painting or rather of the fine arts is the youngest in Europe. In early times foreign artists were employed in the court. Henry VIII. secured the services of the German, Hans Holbein; Charles I. patronized Rubens and brought over Van Dyck. Sir Godfrey Kneller, a German, and court portrait-painter to Charles II., was the last of the foreigners. In 1734-1735 from thirty to forty artists combined to establish an academy in London for the study of the human figure, Hogarth being at the head of the movement. This, after thirty-four years, developed into the Royal Academy. At first the English artists were much indebted to the French school. Hogarth was the first to introduce originality, vigor and true humor into native works, in which he has been followed by Wilkie, Leslie, etc. The English school has acquired a very high position in portrait-painting, witness the beautiful likenesses of Sir Joshua Reynolds, Gainsborough, Raeburn, etc. In landscape, also, England holds a lofty place, as shown by the works of R. Wilson, Gainsborough, and especially Turner, who for wide range of subject and rendering of atmospheric effect stands alone. Constable, Calcott, Collins, Nasmyth, J. Thomson and Muller, also have reached high eminence in this branch. Landseer in animal-painting has scarcely been equalled, and he has many worthy disciples. An important department in painting is water-colors, which in England has attained far higher excellence than in any other country.

We have thus endeavored briefly to give our readers a view of that country—England—which, small in itself, has filled a place so large in the world's history. That Englishmen are proud of their country and apt to be boastful of it, all the world knows. We opened our narrative with a quotation from England's greatest literary son, Shakespeare; we close it with a yet more detailed and vaunting eulogium, put by him into the mouth of one of his grandest historical characters. It, at least, shows us how Englishmen estimate their island home:

> "This royal throne of kings, this sceptred isle,
> This earth of majesty, this seat of Mars
> This other Eden, demi-paradise,
> This fortress built by nature for herself
> Against infection and the hand of war,
> This happy breed of men, this little world,
> This precious stone set in the silver sea,
> Which serves it in the office of a wall . . .
> Against the envy of less happier lands,
> This blessed plot, this earth, this realm—this England."

IRELAND.

"Erin, O Erin, thy winter is past,
And the hope that lived through it shall blossom at last."

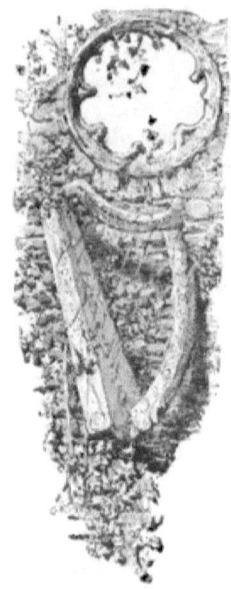

OF all the countries Ireland is *par excellence* the land of contrasts. Nowhere else will you find such genuine drollery and light-hearted mirth; nowhere greater depths of pathos and heart-rending woe; nowhere else are brighter intellects and keener wits; nowhere minds more beclouded by ignorance and darkened by superstition; in no country on earth are there more generous hearts or warmer friends; nowhere a fiercer spirit of revenge and more deadly enemies; in devotion to its religion and in purity of morals, Ireland stands at the head of all lands, yet nowhere do the passions rage wilder and more uncontrolled.

It is the same with the aspects of outward nature. The perennial verdancy and richness of her meadows and pasture lands have won for Ireland the title of "The Emerald Isle;" her crystal streams, her lovely vales, her lakes unequalled for their charms, attract admirers of the picturesque and beautiful from every land; her soil in respect of natural fertility is not surpassed anywhere, and offers to the industrious, skilful cultivator the richest reward for his toil; yet nowhere will the traveller meet with more gloomy stretches of unreclaimed bogs and morasses, more uninviting expanses of unproductive stone-covered uplands; nowhere do the actual cultivators of the soil, as a class, live in such abject poverty and wretchedness; from no country in Europe does so large a proportion of its children emigrate in search of a living.

"'O! sad is my fate,' said the heart-broken stranger;
'The wild deer and wolf to a covert can flee!
But I have no refuge from famine and danger;
A home and a country remain not to me.

"'O Erin, my country! though sad and forsaken,
In dreams I revisit thy sea-beaten shore;
But, alas! in a far, foreign land, I awaken
And sigh for the friends that can meet me no more.'"

The reader naturally inquires the reason for such a seemingly paradoxical condition of matters. We answer freely that it is due to seven centuries of unprecedented oppression and misrule. The Irish have been treated as having scarcely a right to live on their own soil, far less to exercise freedom of judgment or liberty of conscience. The keen sense of injustice operating on minds naturally sensitive has often turned the milder blood of humanity into gall; the peasant seeing himself despoiled of the fruit of his toil to enrich the alien land-owner, has no encouragement to attempt improvement, and has learned to content himself with a mode of living scarcely superior to that of the beasts around him. The one redeeming feature in the whole case is, that England now has begun to awaken to a consciousness of the fact that her treatment of Ireland has hitherto been scandalous and unprofitable to herself; and, whether from a sense of justice or of her own advantage (or both combined), is now disposed to act in a more generous spirit.

The social and political differences distinguishing Ireland from Britain are to be referred largely to its position and physical structure. While it is separated from America by the whole width of the Atlantic ocean, it is cut off from Europe by the greater island to the east of it. This isolated position has till a recent period shut out Ireland from contact with the civilizing influences of Europe, and preserved the bulk of its inhabitants much in their primitive condition. The remarkable unity of its physical structure has had even greater social results, being reflected in the unvaried character of its industry. The centre of the island appears as a basin composed of flat or gently swelling land, broken only by lakes and traversed by one large river (the Shannon). Round this central plain runs a circle of hills and mountains forming a fringe round the island. The principal ranges are the Mourne mountains in Down, the Wicklow mountains, and Macgillicuddy Reeks in Kerry, of which the loftiest peak (Carran-Tual) rises to a height of 3,114 feet. Another leading feature of Ireland is its lakes or loughs. Lough Neagh, in Antrim, is the greatest lake in the British Isles, covering 150 square miles. Associated with this lough there is a legend we must not omit. Every one knows there are no snakes nor toads in Ireland, and that the country is indebted for this immunity to the blessed St. Patrick, who from the top of the Hill of Howth banished them from all the land.

The "king of the serpents" alone, the oldest and wildest of his tribe, objected to being thus disposed of, and withdrew to the borders of Lough Neagh, where he took up his winter-quarters. The saint came on him one bitterly cold day. He let him sleep on till he had provided a strong box, comfortably lined with blankets, and furnished with the strongest lock and key Ireland could supply, and an awfully heavy lid. When all was ready, Patrick awoke the serpent and courteously invited him to enter the fine dwelling he had prepared for him. The royal reptile hesitated, till the saint urged him to lie down in it, just to see whether it would fit. To this the astute beast consented on condition that a bit of his tail was left out. The moment Patrick got him so far in, he slipt instantly round, and putting his shoulder under the lid raised it so that it came down with a crash. The serpent pulled in its tail just in time to save it. The saint at once locked the chest, and with the help of willing hands placed it in a boat, rowed it out to the deepest part of the lough and dropped it overboard. When the aged king found himself entrapped, his pleadings were piteous to hear. "When will you let me out?" he asked. "To-morrow," replied the saint; and to this day the lonely sailor on the lough can hear the deceived reptile wailingly inquire, "Is it to-morrow yet?" We know there are variations of the legend, but we tell the tale as it was told to us.

Other expanses of fresh water are the lakes of the rivers Shannon and Erne, the lakes of Connemara, and the three exquisitely beautiful lakes of Killarney, lying at the base of the Macgillicuddy Reeks. A less attractive feature in the landscape are its bogs or morasses occupying about a seventh part of the island. Of these the largest is the Bog of Allen, stretching in a broad plain across the centre of the island and occupying a large part of the counties of Kildare, Carlow, and King's County. These bogs in some measure compensate Ireland for its comparative want of coal, supplying it with fuel in the shape of turf or peat.

The river system of Ireland is peculiar, all its streams, save the Shannon, rising in the heights that fringe the coast and after a short course falling into the sea on the same side of the island on which they rise. The Shannon, on the other hand, rises in the north, and after passing through the central plain in a series of lakes, along which lies the most fertile soil of the country, falls into the Atlantic by a magnificent estuary, after a course of 224 miles. It is the largest stream in the British Isles and the only really navigable river in Ireland. The rivers on the north and east of Ireland are unimportant, only the Liffey commanding our notice, because at its mouth stands Dublin, the capital of the country. In the south we note the Slaney and Barrow, forming Wexford and Waterford harbors; the Blackwater, forming at its mouth Youghal harbor; the Lee, constituting the magnificent port of Cork; and the Brandon, Kinsale harbor. Several canals intersect the island and render one or two of the rivers navigable to inland towns.

The moisture of Ireland resulting from its situation in the Atlantic produces a constant rainfall that makes pasturage more profitable than tillage, which, except in Ulster, is generally in a very backward state. The vast central plain, excepting the portions covered by bogs, is clothed with almost continual verdure and constitutes one of the finest tracts of grazing-land to be found anywhere in the world. Of the vast herds of cattle fed on it a large proportion goes to England for beef, and the same market takes the bulk of its mutton, pork, dairy produce, etc. The potato is the staple agricultural crop and main article of diet, especially on the small farms in Connaught and Munster; but on the larger and better cultivated farms wheat is also largely raised and yields good returns, a large portion of the crop being exported to England.

The comparative absence of coal and the poverty of its rocks in metals operate to check the development of manufacturing industry, and to restrict the people to agriculture. Linen is the staple textile product, Belfast and the surrounding districts of Ulster being the chief seats. About 300,000 persons, chiefly females, are engaged in this industry. Poplin is also manufactured to a considerable extent in Dublin. Whiskey is largely produced, especially in Leinster and Munster. In its fisheries Ireland might possess an almost exhaustless source of wealth, but unfortunately these are by no means adequately developed. Its mercantile marine is inconsiderable, being mainly engaged in carrying produce and cattle to England.

By far the greatest number of American travellers who visit Ireland approach it by way of Queenstown and Cork. Cork harbor is one of the most beautiful and spacious in the kingdom, being a basin of ten square miles shut in by finely wooded hills, while several islands give variety and luxuriance to the scene. Queenstown, where passengers from America land, is finely situated on Great Island, fourteen miles east of Cork, with which it is joined by a railway. But by far the finest approach to Cork is by steam-boat up the river Lee, the short sail being one of the richest treats the island can supply.

THE JAUNTING CAR.

The hills fringing the rivers are clad from summit to base with every variety of foliage; graceful villas and ornamental cottages are scattered in profusion over the heights, while every here and there some ancient ruin recalls some tradition of the past.

Unhappily, the first peculiarity to strike the stranger on landing is the multiplicity of beggars. Their wit and humor are as proverbial as their rags and wretchedness. "You've lost all your teeth," said a tourist to a female beggar. "Time for me to lose them when I had nothing to eat," was the ready rejoinder. "Go to ———," was the coarse repulse received by a persevering woman from an irate traveller: "Ah, thin, it's a long journey yer honor's sending us on; maybe yer honor'll give us something to fill our mouths on the way."

The characteristic vehicle of Ireland is the jaunting car. The peculiarity of this car is that the occupants sit with their sides to the horses, overlooking the wheels. When there are more passengers than one, they sit back to back,

BESSBROOK LINEN MILLS AND VILLAGE, COUNTY ARMAGH, IRELAND.

with a "well" for the luggage between them. The drivers are no less pertinacious and no whit less comical than the beggars, and the play of wit between the numerous competitors who shout and struggle to secure your patronage is annoying or amusing, according to the humor of the stranger. So soon as you have made your selection, or had it made for you by some carman securing your baggage and depositing it in his "well," you scarcely ever fail to find that you have got an admirable guide, good-humored, obliging, and intelligent as regards the objects worthy of notice. Cork used to be the second city of Ireland, but is now surpassed in population by Belfast, and still more in manufactures and commerce. It is pleasant by reason of the antique picturesqueness of its streets, its situation on the Lee, and the fine overhanging heights. As in most Irish towns, there are many mean streets, inhabited by the poorer classes. It was here that Father Matthew, a Catholic priest, opened his temperance campaign in 1838, which conferred such blessings on Ireland, the fruits of which are still visible. The objects that meet the eye in every direction around Cork go to justify its appellation of "the beautiful city." Undoubtedly the most famous of these are

"The groves of Blarney that are so charming,"

with the still more renowned stone. The "Blarney Stone" is one of the stones of the ruined Castle of Blarney, which stands embosomed amid the "charming groves," some four miles north-west from Cork. He who kisses this stone is ever after master of a mellifluous and persuasive tongue, although not necessarily a sincere one. Especially is he endued with the faculty of putting the "Cornhidher" upon the girls, or the gift of "soft sawder." The true stone can only be reached by the visitor by being let down some twenty feet from the northern angle of the lofty castle. It bears an inscription:

"Cormac McCarthy, fortis, me fieri fecit, A. D. 1446;"

that is, "Cormack McCarthy, the strong, caused me (the castle) to be erected, 1446." A touching story is told in connection with the castle. The descendants of the McCarthys, like those of nearly all the ancient families of Ireland, are now among the poorest of the poor, often working as day-laborers around the castles their forefathers erected. The proprietor of a portion of the great McCarthy estates observed one evening an aged man stretched at the foot of an old tree, "sobbing as though his heart would break." On expressing sympathy with him, the old man exclaimed: "I am a McCarthy, once the possessor of this castle and these broad lands; this tree I planted, and have returned to water it with my tears. To-morrow I sail for Spain, where I have been an exile since the revolution. To-night I bid a last farewell to the place of my birth and the home of my ancestors." The village of Blarney was once clean, neat and thriving, with linen and cotton factories. These works have been swept away, and the hamlet, like the castle, is now a collection of ruins. We note this as a specimen of the case of many an Irish village.

The lakes of Killarney, lying at the base of the gigantic Macgillicuddy Reeks, are world-famed for their loveliness. They are three in number, and the

FATHER MATTHEW.

beauty of the scenery consists in the gracefulness of the mountain outlines, the rich and varied coloring of the wooded shores, deepening through gray rock and light green arbutus to brown mountain heath and dark firs. The largest is the Lower Lake, about five miles long by three broad, and studded by no less than thirty luxuriant islets. The legend which accounts for the existence of the lakes narrates how a fair young peasant girl was wont to meet her lover every night by the side of an enchanted fountain, whose waters could be kept in check only by the pronunciation of a magic spell. The lovers, forgetful of all else save the spell that love cast over them, were lulled to sleep in each other's arms by the side of the fountain without pronouncing the restraining words. At daybreak the girl awoke, screaming: "The well! the well!" Too late! the waters rushed forth and overtook them as they ran. They were drowned, along with the inhabitants of the district, for in a single

ROSS CASTLE, KILLARNEY.

night fair and fertile fields, houses, castles and palaces were covered with water, which lies there yet to testify to the truth of the legend. Several other Irish lakes, notably Lough Neagh, originated in a similar way. In ancient times O'Donoghue of Ross was lord of the great lake and its islands. He was brave and generous, and the defender of the oppressed. Annually he revisits the pleasant places amid which he lived.

> "So sweet is still the breath
> Of the fields and the flowers in our youth we wandered o'er."

Every May morning he may be seen mounted on a white horse, richly caparisoned, while youths and maidens strew flowers in his way.

> "When last April's sun grows dim,
> The Naiads prepare his steed for him,
> Who dwells, bright lake, in thee."

Many another fair and romantic scene, many a legend-haunted ruin of castle, monastery and abbey, dots the County Kerry, but we must pass them over.

The most noted of Kerry's sons was Daniel O'Connell, liberator of Ireland, born in 1775 at Darrynane Abbey, of which, with a moderate estate, he was proprietor. He studied at St. Omer, France, and afterwards was a law-student at Lincoln's Inn. He rose to be the first barrister in Ireland, but it was as leader of the party who demanded equal rights for the Catholics that O'Connell won his fame. Notwithstanding that Catholics were legally excluded from the British Parliament, O'Connell procured himself to be elected member for Clare in 1828, and although he failed to obtain admission at first, this decisive step led to the passage of the Catholic Emancipation Act in 1829. He shortly thereafter began to agitate for Repeal of the Union, and although he did not live to see his dreams of Irish legislative independence realized, yet he bequeathed the question and the struggle to his countrymen, and now it is only a question of time when Ireland shall have her claim conceded.

MONUMENT TO DANIEL O'CONNELL.

> "Freedom's battle once begun,
> Bequeathed by bleeding sire to son,
> Though baffled oft, is ever won."

O'Connell died at Rome in 1847, honored by all. He was a man of transcendent ability, and especially a man of peace.

The mention of O'Connell's name naturally suggests that of Parnell, his successor in maintaining the cause of Ireland. Charles Stewart Parnell was born in 1846, at Avondale, County Wicklow, Ireland, of which property he is owner. His mother is daughter of Admiral Stewart of the United States navy. His paternal grandfather was the last chancellor of the exchequer in the Irish Parliament. Educated at Cambridge College, England, Mr. Parnell was in 1875 elected member of Parliament for Meath, and sat for that county till 1880, when he was chosen by three constituencies, including the city of Cork, for which he decided to sit. He is, although a Protestant, head of the Irish Home Rule party; and it is worthy of note that several Irish popular leaders, as Smith O'Brien, John Mitchell, etc., have belonged to this faith. In 1881 Mr. Parnell, although a land-owner, was made first president of the Land League, the objects of which are, first, a reduction of rents, and, next, the substitution of peasant proprietors for landlords. In 1881 Mr. Parnell was imprisoned as a suspect, but speedily released. His able conduct of the Irish cause seems to promise it early success. "There are," says an able writer, "three hundred years of irrefutable arguments that the English cannot govern Ireland by any modes hitherto resorted to." During the last few years, since Mr. Parnell has taken the lead, the Irish party have shown an insight, a patience and ability quite equal to any section of British administration.

It would be easy to extend the bead-roll of Irish patriots almost indefinitely. The names of Grattan, Curran, Shiel, Smith O'Brien, Mitchell, Butt, etc., etc., rise uncalled for to the memory. We satisfy ourselves, however, with speaking in briefest detail, of only two other great Irishmen, both distinguished ornaments of literature as well as patriots, namely, Edmund Burke and Thomas Moore. Edmund Burke, distinguished above all men of his times for eloquence and political foresight, was born in 1730, in Dublin, where his father was an attorney. Educated at Dublin University, he early gained fame as a writer, his most renowned work being his *Essay on the Sublime and Beautiful*. He became member of successive Parliaments, a member of the Privy Council, and held high office under several governments. He was an able advocate of the claims of the Roman Catholics, while towards America he always advocated a policy of conciliation and justice. Few men have received higher panegyrics than Burke, and few so well deserved them. He was noble-minded, pure in morals, and richly endowed intellectually. He

CHARLES STEWART PARNELL

died in 1798, in his sixty-eighth year. Thomas Moore, one of the finest lyrical poets the world has seen, was also born in Dublin, in 1779, his father being a small tradesman. He studied at Dublin University, where he translated the "Odes of Anacreon." Other well-known poetical works are: "Irish Melodies," "Lalla Rookh," "Loves of the Angels," "Two-penny Post-bag." He published also an excellent life of his friend Byron. He died in 1852. He was a lover of his country, but too much of a courtier to advocate its claims effectively.

The chief part of the County of Limerick consists of a broad plain, bordering the Shannon, called from its fertility the Golden Vale. This, with the plains of Boyle, in Roscommon, is the richest land in Britain. Limerick is an ancient city, on both sides of the Shannon, of 40,000 inhabitants. Before its walls were defeated, first the Anglo-Norman chivalry, then the Ironsides of Cromwell, and last, the victorious army of William III. The treaty made after this victory was broken by William; hence Limerick is known as the "city of the violated treaty." The "treaty stone" still marks the spot where the document was signed. Galway is the largest city in Connaught, having a population of about fifteen thousand. Some of the older houses have a Spanish appearance, from the close connection between Galway and Spain in bygone times. To one house an interesting legend appertains. The mayor, James Lynch, in 1493, condemned his own son to death for murder. The lad was a favorite with the people, and to prevent him from being rescued, his father caused him to be hanged from his own window; some say he hanged him with his own hand, and never after was seen to smile or even look up. In this we probably see the origin of the term "Lynch Law." One suburb of Galway is the Claddagh, inhabited by fishermen, who exclude all strangers from their society, and marry only among themselves. These fishermen still speak the Irish language, and the women wear the Irish costume. Sailing north-east from Derry we come to the Giant's Causeway, one of the most remarkable natural objects anywhere to be seen. It is impossible, indeed, for painter to portray or the imagination to conceive a scene more wonderful than this, consisting of innumerable octagonal pillars of basalt, towering to the height of several hundred feet along the sea margin; with many groined caves, natural bridges, chasms, etc., interspersed. The shore between the base of the pillared cliffs and the water is paved, as it were, by the bases of multitudinous other pillars, dipping gradually to the sea, and giving the impression of a regular causeway

BIRTHPLACE OF TOM MOORE.

formed by giants. Legendary tradition tells us that the causeway was constructed by the Irish giant, Finn McCoul, to enable the Scottish giant Banandonner to come over and receive the benefit of a beating without wetting his feet.

Turning southward, a visit to the thriving manufacturing and commercial town of Belfast will well repay the traveller, and still farther south he finds Dublin, the capital of Ireland, on a bay beautiful as that of Naples, at the mouth of the Liffey. The leading features of Dublin are its castle, its university, its four courts, its custom-house, its ancient Parliament-house in Stephen's Green, shortly to be reoccupied, its noble Phœnix Park, and the Lord-Lieutenant's Lodge. Some of its streets, as Sackville street, Westmoreland street, etc., are

THE GIANT'S CAUSEWAY.

very fine, and it possesses several excellent statues and monuments, notably that to the hero Nelson. The population is about 300,000.

No traveller can leave Ireland without seeing the Vale of Avoca in the County Wicklow, celebrated by the poet Moore. It is formed by the junction of two streams, Avon and Avoca, which uniting here into one, run for nine miles through an exquisitely picturesque vale only a quarter of a mile wide, with wooded banks 300 to 500 feet high.

> "There's not in the wide world a valley so sweet
> As that vale in whose bosom the bright waters meet;
> Oh! the last ray of feeling and life must depart,
> Ere the bloom of that valley shall fade from my heart.

> "Sweet vale of Avoca! how calm could I rest
> In thy bosom of shade with the friends I love best,
> Where the storms that we feel in the cold world should cease,
> And our hearts, like thy waters, be mingled in peace."

The primitive inhabitants of Ireland were Kelts, akin to the Kelts of Britain. Little is known of the island till the time of Laegaire McNeill, chief monarch of Ireland (430), when St. Patrick converted the natives to Christianity. In early times there were five provinces in Ireland—Ulster, Leinster, Meath, Connaught, Munster—and the head monarch or ardrigh ruled over the central district of Meath, residing at Tara. By the sixth century extensive monasteries had been founded, from which rayed forth culture to the surrounding countries, and missionaries issued to carry Christianity to pagan nations. Among the most celebrated of these missionaries was Columba, who converted Scotland. The progress of Irish civilization was checked by the incursions of the Danes towards the close of the eighth century, who harrassed the land for 300 years, till overthrown by Brian Boru, monarch of Ireland, at Clontarf, near Dublin, in 1014. From the eighth to the twelfth century Ireland produced many scholars of eminence, and several books, as the "Book of Kells," survive to prove their acquirements. Under the history of England we have told how Ireland fell under English rule. Gradually the old chiefs were expelled, and their estates confiscated on the charge of treason or rebellion and given to Englishmen. Many times did the Irish revolt and attempt to expel their English rulers. After the suppression of an insurrection under Fitzgerald, son of the viceroy of Henry VIII., in 1534, some of the native princes were induced to acknowledge Henry, and accept peerages. The attempts of the English government to introduce the Reformed faith stirred up the revolt of the Earl of Desmond, whose vast estates in Munster were, after his death in 1583, parcelled out to English settlers.

In the beginning of the seventeenth century the great Ulster chiefs, O'Neill and O'Donnell, made a successful stand till they were recognized as the earls of Tyrone and Tyrconnell. Fearing danger, these nobles in 1608 retired to the Continent, and James I. carried out a project of parcelling out the north of Ireland to Scotch and English settlers. This was the famous "Plantation of Ulster." In 1641 the Irish rose and massacred some 40,000 Protestants. The country continued troubled till 1649, when Cromwell overran it. At the revolution the Irish Catholics took the part of James II., while the Scotch and English colonists stood for William and Mary. The war raged for four years (1688–1692) the most memorable battle being that on the banks of the Boyne (July 12th, 1690,) in which William completely defeated James. The supporters of William are represented by the Orangemen, so called because he was Prince of Orange. From this time for nearly a century history records little but the passing of penal statutes against Catholics, and the disaffection caused by these gave birth to the rebellion of 1798. On the suppression of this in 1800, the legislative union of Ireland and England was consummated, and since then the history of the two countries has been the same.

Ireland has contributed nobly to English literature, witness the names of Oliver Goldsmith, Laurence Sterne, Miss Edgeworth, Sheridan Knowles,

Carleton, Lover, Lever, Maginn, etc. Burke and Moore have been previously mentioned. The country cannot be said to have a distinct school of art, but it has given to the British school Sir Martin Shea, president of the Royal Academy; Maclise, one of the greatest British masters of the human figure; Barry, architect of the British Parliament-house; Hogan, the sculptor, and

Balfe, the composer. In science, she boasts the names of the Earl of Rosse, the astronomer; Kane, the chemist; Hull, the geologist, and many others.

Moore, the great Irish national poet, whilst meditating upon the wrongs and sufferings of his native land, compared it to Sion, in that it too had been

CUSTOM HOUSE, DUBLIN.

compelled to drink of "the cup of trembling." Nevertheless the impression was strong in his mind that there was a bright future before it. And under the influence of this conviction he sang:

"The nations have fallen, and thou still art young,
    Thy sun is but rising, when others are set,
   And though slavery's cloud o'er thy morning hath hung,
      The full moon of freedom shall beam round thee yet.
   Erin, oh Erin, though long in the shade,
   Thy star will shine out when the proudest shall fade."

EDINBURGH.

SCOTLAND.

> "O Caledonia! Stern and wild!
> Meet nurse for a poetic child!
> Land of brown heath and shaggy wood;
> Land of the mountain and the flood."

SUCH are the enthusiastically patriotic lines with which Sir Walter Scott salutes "his own, his native land," and surely, if ever any land merited the love and devotion of its children, it is this little rugged land of Scotland. Separated from its powerful neighbor, England, by only an imaginary line, with not one-tenth part of its population, and not one-twentieth of its resources and wealth, it yet maintained its independence through centuries of arduous struggle; and, though devastated and impoverished, preferred freedom with penury to submission and humiliation with ease and abundance. Well has her earliest real poet, Barbor, the contemporary of Chaucer, who so nobly sung "The Bruce," voiced the national sentiment:

SCOTLAND.

> "Ah! freedom is a noble thing!
> Freedom makes man to have liking;
> Freedom all solace to man gives;
> He lives at peace that freely lives."

"The fundamental difference" said Gladstone, in his speech on Home Rule for Ireland, delivered at Glasgow, June 21st, 1886, "between the union of England and Scotland, and England and Ireland, was, that Scotland was always able to hold her own with England. Scotland met England on a footing of equality; while the case was altogether different with unfortunate Ireland."

No country in Europe has made such advances in material prosperity, during the last century, as Scotland, and few have kept pace with her in literary advancement. In 1780 Scotland was one of the poorest and least known of nations; in 1887 it is scarcely surpassed by any in wealth and industrial activity, or in material, intellectual and moral civilization. This re-

HOME OF ROBERT BURNS.

markable progress is to be traced to various causes. Undoubtedly, at the basis lies the character of its people, who for energy, intelligence, foresight, perseverance and thrift are famed the world over. Not less clearly the admirable system of religious and educational training instituted at the Reformation by John Knox, her "Great Reformer" (which provided that there should be a church and school for every thousand people), had much to do in laying the foundation, and developing many of the best traits of this national character. Over and above these, Scotland possesses in abundance those treasures of mineral wealth (especially of coal and iron) in which Ireland is so deficient; while her peculiar topographical conformation affords to her inland districts facilities for water communication quite unequalled.

It is worth our while, therefore, to survey, for a brief space, the salient features of this rugged little land, than which none more picturesque is anywhere to be found, as well as a few of the leading events in its history. The mainland of Scotland is the northern and smaller division of the island of Great Britain, lying between 54° 38' and 58° 40' 30" N. The longest line that can be drawn on it is between its most southerly point (the Mull of Galloway) and its most northerly (Dunnet Head), 287 miles. Its breadth is extremely irregular, varying from 182 miles at its broadest part, to 24 at the narrowest; but the whole coast is so interpenetrated by arms of the sea, in the forms of firths or estuaries, and lochs, that there is but one spot on the mainland more than 40 miles from the shore. No country has so many islands lying off its coasts. These islands may be classed into three groups, viz.: the Hebrides or Western Isles, dotting all the western coast, and the Orkney and Shetland groups, stretching northward to latitude 60° 50'. The entire area of the country is 31,300 square miles, of which 26,000 are in the mainland, and the balance in the islands. The population is over 4,000,000, of which 333,000 are Highlanders, the remaining 3,750,000 being Lowlanders. One-third of the population lies within a radius of 20 miles round Glasgow.

As compared with England, the general aspect of Scotland is rough and mountainous, a very small proportion of the country spreading out into level plains. Assuming its whole acreage (exclusive of the lakes) to be 19,000,000, it is estimated that not more than 6,000,000 are arable; but it may be safely said that from no other six millions of acres in the world of only equal fertility is so much produce taken for human consumption. Although there are no great plains, there are numerous valleys and tracts of comparatively level land, known as "dales" or "straths," lying between the mountain ranges, and many stretches of rich alluvial land, known as "carses," "haughs" and "holms," lying along its coasts or on the margins of its estuaries and streams.

Scotland consists of two great divisions inhabited by two distinct races of people, differing from each other in origin, customs, speech and dress. If the reader will look at a map of Scotland, he will observe a range of mountains, with numerous spurs and outliers, bearing the general name of Grampians, starting from Dumbarton, on the Clyde, and running in a north-easterly direction towards Aberdeen. All west of this line is known as Highlands; all east and south as Lowlands. The range dies away before reaching the Murray Firth, so that, in reality, all the east-coast country up to the extreme north may, with certain exceptions, be properly regarded as Lowland. The Highland district is generally characterized by romantic scenery, wild, precipitous mountains, dreary moorlands, lochs or lakes, and rushing streams, deep glens and wild, hanging woods; the Lowlands, though presenting several considerable mountain ranges, is much less rugged in its general character. The Highlands are inhabited by a Keltic race akin to the native Irish, and speaking a dialect of Irish known as Gaelic, and having for their national garb the tartan kilt or philabeg, plaid, etc. The Lowlanders are a Teutonic race speaking a pure form of early English, and wearing practically the same dress with the people of England. In the extreme north is the county of Caithness, a level district inhabited by a Norse population of the same race with the natives of the Orkney and Shetland islands, in some of the most northerly of which the Norwegian language continued to be spoken down to near the commencement of the present century.

If the reader would learn the condition of the Highlanders down to the end of the last century, we must refer him to the pages of Sir Walter Scott, who may be said to have discovered this region to the civilized world. Each separate glen was inhabited by its own clan, all bearing the name of their chieftain —Cameron, Macdonald, Macleod, Campbell, Grant, etc.—to whom they were bound by real or supposed ties of family relationship, and for whom they fought and died without question; devotion to their chief being almost their sole idea of religion. War may be said to have been almost their normal condition, feuds between clans being incessant and handed down from father to son for generations. Their more peculiar weapons were the claymore or broadsword, dirk and targe. Says Scott:

> "Ill fared it then with Roderick Dhu,
> That on the ground his targe he threw,
> Whose brazen studs and tough bull-hide
> Had death so often dashed aside."

The bag-pipe was, and is, their national instrument of music, and to its martial strains the Highland regiments still march to "death or glory."

> "And wild and high the 'Cameron's gathering' rose,
> The war-note of Lochiel, which Albyn's hills
> Have heard, and heard, too, have her Saxon foes:
> How in the noon of night that pibroch thrills
> Savage and shrill! but with the breath which fills
> Their mountain pipe, so fill the mountaineers
> With the fierce native daring which instils
> The stirring memory of a thousand years,
> And Evan's, Donald's fame, rings in each clansman's ears!"

The people lived largely on the produce of the chase and fishing. Settled industry they despised as unmanly, the women doing all the drudgery, even on their miserable patches of cultivation. Their grand resources were "forays" into the Lowlands, whence they were wont to return with whole herds of "lifted" cattle. These systematic raids gave rise to the practice of blackmailing, it being the custom of the rich Lowland proprietors living near the Highland line to pay some powerful chief a percentage on the value of his stock, to insure it against being stolen, or if stolen by others, followed by his clan and returned. Robert McGregor—better known as Rob Roy—chieftain of the outlawed clan McGregor, is the type of the Highland robber-chief and blackmailer. No name is more popular in the Highlands.

Roads there were none, nor wheeled carriages. After the rebellion of 1715 General Wade constructed excellent roads in all directions for military purposes. This was the beginning of civilization. The gratitude of the poor people for the unmeant blessing is tersely expressed in the distich:

> " Had you seen these roads, *before they were made,*
> You would hold up your hands and bless General Wade."

In 1746 the chiefs were deprived of the power of life and death over their vassals. Then schools and churches began to be planted, and in 1784 the Highland Agricultural Society was established, with the greatest benefit to the district. Since then progress has been rapid. Much money has been brought into the Highlands by sheep-farming and the letting of deer forests (in which, by the way, there is seldom a tree) to southern noblemen and gentlemen, and now this region promises shortly to be as flourishing as the Lowlands or England.

Space will not permit us to dilate on the former state of the Lowlands. Gibson, describing Glasgow (now the second city in the empire) in 1707, says: " The number of people did not exceed 14,000, and they were in general poor; manufactures were almost unknown, and commerce was carried on to a very trifling extent." Now a greater number of the largest and finest class of steam-ships are built on the Clyde, at and below Glasgow, than on any other river in the world. It is there that nearly all " the greyhounds of the ocean " are designed, fabricated and engined. Agriculture was equally backward. There were no inclosures, no green crops, no clover, potatoes or turnips. The land was cultivated " runrig," that is, ridge and ridge about by neighbors in common. The farmers dwelt in houses little better than hovels. Now, Scotland stands at the head of the agricultural world. The larger tenant farmers, especially in the richer districts, as East and Midlothian, Berwickshire, Easter Ross, Aberdeen, etc., live in a state of comfort and even dignity that must be seen to be realized. Many of them pay annual rents of £1,000, and some far more, and their solid, stone-built mansions are an ornament to the country. The average rental of the available land is from £1 to £3 per acre a year. Even more carefully and more scientifically than in England, every rood is cleared, and made to yield its utmost. It is held that a farmer ought to have a capital of £10 for every acre of his farm. In the more improved districts this is deemed insufficient. The crops raised are oats, wheat (in the more kindly districts), barley, potatoes, beans, etc. In no country are turnips cultivated with such success. Oats yield from fifty to seventy bushels an acre, the standard weight of the bushel being forty-two pounds, but this is generally exceeded. Barley is largely grown to be distilled into whiskey, which manufacture is more extensively pursued here than elsewhere. The principal seats of this industry are the Isle of Islay and Campbelltown in Argyleshire, and Glenlivet in Banff. The finest cattle that reach the London market are the "prime Scots" from Aberdeenshire and Banffshire, bringing when two and a half years old from $150 to $180 a head. Ten years ago prices were even higher, and the feeders were among the wealthiest farmers in the world, but the introduction of American beef has reduced prices, and correspondingly diminished or abolished the farmers' profits. Agricultural servants are generally hired by the half-year, the men receiving at the rate of from £10 to £15 for six months, with board. Laborers are commonly housed in well-built stone houses. They earn from $3.50 to $4.50 a week. The land of Scotland is in fewer hands than that of any other country, several of its nobles, as the Dukes of Buccleuch, Sutherland, Richmond, Hamilton, Argyle, Athole, the Earls of Breadalbane, Fife, Seafield, etc., owning estates each covering hundreds of thousands of acres. As an offset their tenants are much better off than those of the smaller proprietors and lairds. The princely castles of these and other peers, and the stately mansions of hundreds of other great proprietors, with their beautiful gardens and surroundings, confer grace and dignity on the landscape.

The fisheries of Scotland are of high importance and pursued with skill and enterprise. The herring and salmon fisheries, in particular, are the most important of their kind in the world. From one river, the Spey, the Duke of Richmond, the chief proprietor of the salmon fishing, is said to derive an income of £12,000 a year. Nothing connected with the Scottish fisheries so greatly arrests the attention of spectators as the "Newhaven Fishwives." Large brawny women, clean and tidy, clad in a picturesque costume, which is not to be found, in all points, worn by any other class of women in any country, walk, three or four times a week, early in the morning, to Edinburgh from Newhaven—a distance of three miles—carrying large baskets of fish, which have been freshly caught by their husbands. Their singular cry of "caller herrin" (fresh herring), mingling with the sound of church bells on a week-day, suggested to the Scottish violinist, Neil Gow, a song of that name.

The national religion of Scotland is Presbyterianism, about four-fifths of the people adhering to this form. But the original Presbyterian Church has now been split into four branches, viz.: the Established, the Free, the United, and the Reformed. In the thirty-three counties of Scotland there are about 1,300 parishes, and in each of these there is an established church. The average income of the parish minister is £300 a year, with a manse and glebe. But now not more than half of the Presbyterian people are found in the state church. The Free Church has nearly 1,000 churches; the United Presbyterian, 620; the Reformed, 44. The aristocracy largely profess Episcopacy, which has 180 churches. In a few districts there are found native Catholics, but the Catholic Church is mainly attended by immigrant Irish. There are besides, especially in the towns, congregations of Methodists, Congregationalists, Baptists, etc.

Scotland has four universities—Edinburgh, Glasgow, Aberdeen, St. Andrews—with an average attendance of over 5,000 students. Its common-school system is among the most perfect in the world, attendance being compulsory and rigidly enforced. The teachers' incomes range from £140 to £250 a year in country districts, with dwelling-house and garden.

No country of equal size has furnished a greater number of illustrious names to literature, science and art, than Scotland. Her misfortune is that her most eminent sons are apt to emigrate to England and to become recognized as Englishmen. In the sixteenth and seventeenth centuries William Dunbar, Gavin Douglas, Sir David Lindsay and Drummond, of Hawthornden, were distinguished poets; and Bishop Burnet a historian of high repute. In the eighteenth she produced the sweet song-writers, Miss Elliott, Mrs. Cockburn and Baroness Nairn, whose fine songs, "The Flowers of the Forest," "Land o' the Leal" and "Laird o' Cockpen," are known to all; as well as Thomson, bard of the seasons; Reid and Dugald Stewart, philosophers; Adam Smith, political economist; Robertson, historian, and David Hume, Britain's best metaphysician and historian. High over all these towers her national bard, Robert Burns. In the present century space permits us to name only Hogg, the Ettrick shepherd, a true peasant son of genius; Allan Cunningham; William Black and George Macdonald, novelists; and, again surpassing all their coevals, Sir Walter Scott and Thomas Carlyle. Macaulay and Gladstone, though Scotch by blood, were born and trained in England. Byron and Brougham were half Scotch and partly reared in Scotland. In science, Scotland has the names of Napier, inventor of logarithms; James Watt, discoverer of the power of steam; the Hunters (William and John), comparative anatomists; Sir James Simpson (anæsthetics); Murchison, Lyell, Hugh Miller, Ramsay, Geikie, greatest of geologists; and Sir William Thomson, probably the foremost of living men in several departments of natural science. In art, the annual exhibitions in Edinburgh testify to her high place. We name only Sir David Wilkie, Raeburn, Thorburn (miniaturist, etc.), the Faeds, Nicol, Sir Noel Paton.

ROBERT BURNS.

JAMES WATT DISCOVERING THE POWER OF STEAM.

We have distinguished three names as illustrious in literature above others, Burns, Scott, Carlyle. We devote a few special words to each.

Robert Burns, bard of Scotland, was born in a poor "clay-biggin" by the banks of Doon, Ayrshire, January 25th, 1759. His father was a poor working gardener, and afterwards became a yet poorer man as a farmer. Burns, like all Scotch children, received such a common-school education, that he tells us that at the age of ten or eleven he was "a critic in substantives, verbs, and particles." He soon became a critic in a more dangerous lore, and love for his youthful companion in the harvest-field inspired his first song, written in his sixteenth year. In 1781 he entered, with his brother Gilbert, on the farm of Mossgiel, where he continued the struggle with poverty and misfortune that accompanied him all his too short life. In 1786 his first volume of poetry was

TWA BRIGS O' AYR.

published at Kilmarnock; subsequent editions were published in Edinburgh. Among his pieces, marked by wondrous graphic power, dramatic spirit and humor, we may instance his "Tam O'Shanter," "Jolly Beggars," "Twa Dogs," "Death and Dr. Hornbook," "Twa Brigs o' Ayr." Tenderness, truth and sensibility characterize his "Cotter's Saturday Night," and his addresses to the "Mountain Daisy" and the "Mouse." His love songs are instinct with passion and exquisite in their beauty, while no such patriotic lyric as "Bruce's Address" was ever penned. Burns, after failing as a farmer, became an excise-officer, residing in Dumfries, where he fell into somewhat dissipated habits and died, at the early age of thirty-six, July 21st, 1796.

Sir Walter Scott, the "Ariosto of the North," was born at Edinburgh, August 15th, 1771, his father being a lawyer of good standing, allied to the good old border family of Scott, of Harden. He was educated at Edinburgh

University, and, on leaving college, was called to the bar. Subsequently he was appointed sheriff of Selkirkshire, with a salary of £300 a year, and, at a later period, clerk of the Court of Session, with £1,300 a year. Ballad minstrelsy had great charms for him, and he used to hunt up old ballads in Liddesdale and the borders generally, which he afterwards published. His first orig-

inal work was a translation of Burger's "Lenore," and "The Wild Huntsman;" but he was comparatively unknown till, in 1805, appeared his "Lay of the Last Minstrel," which instantly stamped him as one of the greatest of living poets. This was followed by "The Lady of the Lake," "Marmion," "Lord of the Isles," etc. But it was when his first novel, "Waverly" appeared in 1814, that he was recognized as the true "Wizard of the North." This was followed by a long and magnificent series of prose fictions, comprising "Guy Mannering," "Antiquary," "Old Mortality," "Rob Roy," "Ivanhoe," etc. It was Scott's ambition to found a family seat, and with this view, he made many purchases of land on the banks of his favorite Tweed, where he erected his magnificent mansion or castle of Abbotsford. To crown his honors a baronetcy was conferred on him. He was associated with the business of James Ballantine & Co., publishers, Edinburgh, and in 1826 this house failed for close on $600,000. In four years Scott paid off $280,000, but he succumbed under the

THOMAS CARLYLE

strain, and died, universally beloved and lamented, at Abbotsford, September, 1832. He was buried in Dryburgh Abbey.

Thomas Carlyle, essayist, biographer and historian, the most powerful, original, and brilliant writer that Britain has seen since the days of Shakespeare, was born in 1795, at Ecclefechan, Dumfries-shire, his father being a stone-mason and later a small farmer. He was educated at the School of Annan, and latterly at the University of Edinburgh, where he studied seven years with a view to the church. At college his habits were lonely and contemplative, and the stories told of his immense reading are almost fabulous. About the middle of his curriculum he felt disinclined to enter the ministry, and after a short period spent in teaching at Dysart, Fifeshire, he adopted literature as his profession. His first efforts appeared in Brewster's "Encyclopædia." In 1824 appeared his translation of "Willhelm Meister's Apprenticeship." In 1827 he married, and retired to his wife's lonely little estate of Craigen-puttock, amid the hills of Dumfries-shire. Here, from 1830 to 1833, he was employed upon probably his ablest work, "Sartor Resartus," which appeared in *Fraser's Magazine*. During the negotiations for its publication he removed to Chelsea, London, where he was recognized by the title of the "sage of Chelsea." Here he produced his "French Revolution," "Latter Day Pamphlets," "Life of John Stirling," "Oliver Cromwell's Letters and Speeches," "Life of Frederick the Great," etc., etc. The honors conferred on Carlyle are almost too numerous to enumerate, the culminating one being his election as lord rector of Edinburgh University. In 1875, he declined an offer of the Grand Cross of the Bath. He died in 1880, and was interred, by his own request, beside his mother, in the humble churchyard of his native Ecclefechan.

The irregular surface of Scotland has given rise to much picturesque and beautiful scenery. Her rivers, hurrying to the sea from their lofty sources, are especially pure and limpid, and their praises have been sung by many a Scottish bard, as well as by the nature-loving Wordsworth. None excels the "pastoral Tweed," on whose banks stand many a lordly hall and ruin of keel-house, castle, and monastery. Noticeable among these is Abbotsford, the seat of Sir Walter Scott, and Dryburgh Abbey, where he lies. Foremost of all the gems of fair Tweedside, however, is Melrose Abbey, the finest monastic ruin in Europe. It is to it that Scott addresses his famed apostrophe, beginning:

> "If thou wouldst view fair Melrose aright
> Go visit it by the pale moonlight;
> For the gay beams of lightsome day
> Gild but to flout the ruins grey."

On this river stand the towns of Innerliethen and Galashiels, noted for the manufacture of the famous Scotch Tweeds, and at its mouth is Berwick, a town which at the union was left neither in Scotland nor England. For several miles before falling into the sea, the Tweed forms the boundary between the two countries. Passing the lonely Yarrow flowing amid its green hills and famed St. Mary's Loch, we reach the Forth, which rising near Ben Lomond, flows east past the town of Stirling, with its castle-crowned rock, and then in various "links" through the rich "Carse of Stirling," till it widens into the Firth of Forth. The view from the castle of Stirling is one of the finest in the world, being rivalled only by that from the hill of Kinnoul, on the Tay, from which can be surveyed the renowned "Carse of Gowrie," with its fine farms and smiling villages, the city of Perth, and, it is said, the castles of seven noblemen. Edinburgh, the capital of Scotland, is situated about two miles to the south of the Firth of Forth. From the beauty of its buildings, monuments and gardens, and above all for the picturesque grandeur of its situation, Edinburgh is by many held to be the finest city in the world. Its port is Leith. The population of both towns is 250,000. North of the Forth is the Tay, the largest river in Scotland, on whose banks stands Perth, already mentioned. Farther down, on the Firth of Tay, stands the busy town of Dundee, with immense manufactories of jute, coarse linen, sail cloth, and a very large shipping trade. Its population is upwards of 120,000, being the third town in Scotland. To the north of Dundee lie the ports of Arbroath and Montrose, both with large linen manufactories. Still farther north we reach the "Highland Dee," Byron's river, over whose source broods the "dark Lochnagar." This is a grandly romantic stream, famous for the excellent sport it affords to the rod-fisher. On its banks stand the royal castle of Balmoral, as well as several other noble residences. Aberdeen, a town of some 90,000 inhabitants, a flourishing sea-port, lies at its mouth.

Pursuing our journey north and westward we pass Peterhead and Fraserburgh, on the Moray Firth, great seats of the herring and whale fisheries, and Elgin, with a ruined cathedral which ranks next to Melrose. We then reach the Spey, whose strath gives name to the dance-music of Scotland known as "Strathspeys." We are now fairly into the Highlands, and, a few miles west from Speymouth, we reach Inverness, the capital of the Highlands, a prosperous town of 15,000 inhabitants, with a fine old castle, vitrified fort, etc. In Inverness-shire are the islands of Iona and Staffa. In the former, Columba, an Irish Saint, who Christianized Scotland, built his church and cell in the sixth century. The ruins of several churches are still to be seen, and in the holy ground the kings of Scotland used to be interred. Staffa is noted for a cave with basaltic columns of the same character as those of the Giant's Causeway.

Scotland is essentially a country of mountains, the highest peaks being in the Highlands. Of these we note only Ben Nevis, a solitary mountain in the Grampian group, reaching a height of 4,400 feet. Ben Macdhui, and three others in the Cairngorm group, exceed 4,000 feet. The main range in the Lowlands separates Dumfries from Peebles and Lanarkshires. Broadlow and the Lowthers in this range approach 3,000 feet.

It is impossible with the space at our disposal even to name the many natural objects of interest in Scotland. We cannot, however, omit its many fine passes, of which the Trosachs, famed by Scott, is an example; nor its inland lochs or lakes, as Lochlomond, Lochkatrine, etc.; nor its waterfalls, as the Falls of Clyde, of Foyers, Gray Mare's Tail, etc.

Scottish history becomes of interest only after the death of Alexander III., one of the ablest and best of Scotland's kings, in 1286. An old rhyme tells how, under him, the land had blessed peace, and plenty of "meal and malt." His heiress was his granddaughter, Margaret, the maiden of Norway, who died in 1290, on her way to assume the crown. Forthwith there began a struggle for the succession, the two chief claimants being Edward Baliol and Robert Bruce. The question was referred to Edward I., of England, who decided in favor of Baliol, on his promising to recognize Edward as his over-lord. The bondage and humiliation of his position became intolerable to Baliol and his people, and they rose in opposition. Edward defeated Baliol's army at Dunbar, and Baliol having surrendered himself to Edward was, after being kept prisoner for three years, allowed to retire to France. Edward now treated Scotland as a conquered country. Earl Warenne was appointed governor, and all the offices were given to Englishmen. The Scots groaned under the degradation, and in 1297 William Wallace, whose name will be revered as long as patriotism, undaunted courage, and love of freedom is held in respect among men, appeared as the champion of his native land. He was but the son of a country gentleman of small estate; yet, when he stood forth to rescue his country, he was joined by several of the nobility, and, notwithstanding the jealousies of many nobles, he held the foe at bay for eight years, pushing at one time his victorious arms into England. At last, in 1304, he was betrayed into the hands of Edward, who ungenerously put him to a cruel death. But the struggle did not terminate with the patriot's death. Robert Bruce, son of the competitor, now stood forth to enforce his claim to the Scottish throne. He collected an army; and the crown of Scotland was placed on his head by the Countess of Buchan, at Scone, Bruce sitting on the same "stone of fate" on which Queen Victoria sat

when she was crowned queen of Great Britain. Long and bitter was the struggle between Edward, the "Hammer of the Scots," and the gallant and skilful Bruce. At last, in 1307, Edward, determined to crush the Scots, sent for all his forces to meet him at Carlisle. But a sterner summons awaited himself, and he died near that city on July 7th, 1307. Bruce now drove the English out of the country step by step, till, in 1314, Edward II. raised an immense host and marched north to crush Bruce and the Scots forever. The armies met on the 24th of June, at Bannockburn, and the result was the complete and final discomfiture of the English, who never again ventured to attempt the conquest of Scotland. Constant wars there were between the lands, but this was greatly because the Scotch thus lent aid to France in defending itself against England, so that it passed into a proverb:

"He that would France win must with Scotland first begin."

Scotland has been the scene of much partisan warfare, both secular and religious. Her great wars of this class have been in conjunction with affiliat-

ROYAL REGALIA OF SCOTLAND.

ing parties in her southern neighbor, England. Under the head of "England" we have already alluded to the most prominent of those wars, but none have furnished the literature of the world outside of Scotland with so great interest as the trial and execution of the unfortunate Mary, Queen of Scots. Totally defeated at the battle of Langside, she fled to England in 1568, and threw herself upon the protection of Elizabeth, by whom she was kept a prisoner for nineteen years, and then tried by a commission on the charge of engaging in a conspiracy against that unscrupulous queen's life. Her death was heroic, and her sad fate has drawn towards her the sympathy of the world.

The next great event in Scottish history is the Reformation. The grand

MARY STUART RECEIVING HER DEATH-SENTENCE.

(159)

distinction between this great change in Scotland and England was, that in Scotland the Reformation originated among the people themselves; in England it was dictated by a lustful king. The key to the movement in Scotland is to be found in the popular rhyme:

> "The priests o' Melrose made good kale on Fridays when they fasted,
> They neither wanted beef nor ale as lang's their neibor's lasted."

Then followed some lines we do not print. John Knox, the reformer of Scotland, was but the type and outcome of the national mind. It has been said that no great national change of religion has been made by people on account of conviction of the error of the doctrines taught, but only by reason of the dissolute lives of the teachers. This was the case in Scotland. Had the priests and monks been temperate and chaste, Scotland might to this day have been Catholic. John Knox, by whose influence popery was extirpated in 1560, merely therefore embodied the will of the mass of the people, the way having been prepared for him by earlier reformers, as Patrick Hamilton and Wishart. One circumstance to be deplored in connection with the Scottish reformation is the destruction of the fine old abbeys, cathedrals and other religious structures. It is said this was done in accordance with Knox's counsel: "Ding down the nests and the corbies will flee awa'." Glasgow cathedral alone was rescued through the energy of the "trades." Knox's grand characteristic was fearlessness. He braved an adverse court with Mary, the Catholic queen, at its head, as well as a stern nobility. When he was laid to rest in the churchyard of St. Giles, Edinburgh, the Earl of Morton, looking on the face of the dead, said, "there lies one who never feared the face of man." In Scotland he did a grand work by insisting on the establishment of its then unrivalled system of parish schools.

The persecution of the Presbyterians by Laud, under Charles II., only served to attach the people more firmly to their own faith, and embitter them against episcopacy. At the accession of William and Mary to the throne of Great Britain in 1688, all endeavors at spiritual compulsion ceased, and the people dwelt at peace. In 1707 the union of England and Scotland was accomplished, after which the history of England and Scotland became identified. On the whole, this survey, brief as it is, justifies Gladstone's proud statement that "Scotland was always able to hold her own with England;" and that she was thus able "to meet England on terms of equality" has been a blessing to both countries.

AMERICA.

"Westward the star of empire takes its way."

SO wrote Bishop Berkeley over a hundred and fifty years ago. And gazing with prophetic eye down the vista of the future, as if the glorious destiny of the as yet unborn republic to him was as clear as the noonday, and as if witnessing its emblem in that flag which is an image of the everlasting heaven with its bright stars against the blue background of the sky, and the red bands which accompany the sun in the west, he added the inspired words:

"Time's noblest offspring is his last."

Four hundred years have not yet passed away since Christopher Columbus, a sailor of Genoa, in Italy, made his first voyage to the American continent. Two hundred and eighty years ago there was not a settler within the boundaries of the United States or its territories, and now it contains a population of 50,000,000, and with every day the number is increasing. It also contains one-sixth of the whole wealth of the world. "Every night," says a professor in Princeton College, "it is stronger by a regiment of fighting men and richer by $2,000,000, than the night before." Nowhere in history can a parallel of such progress be found.

In the United States we have almost every variety of climate, indeed it might almost be called a world of itself. Fruits of all climates grown upon its own soil can be brought to the door of almost every inhabitant. The United States consumes every year 300,000,000 bushels of wheat, and still it has 150,000,000 bushels to sell to other nations. And beneath its surface all the metals and minerals needed by man are stored away for his use. Coal, iron, gold, silver, copper, lead and oil, are to be found in abundance.

The central portion of North America, from the Atlantic ocean to the Pacific, is included in the territory of the United States. Thirteen States, one by one, were founded along the Atlantic coast, and twenty-five others have been founded since. Its area equals twenty-five times that of Great Britain, or fifteen times those of such countries as France, Germany or Spain. Indeed Texas alone or California alone is larger than either.

In 1882 there were more miles of railroad in the United States than in all Europe, and nearly as many as in all the world outside of the United States. The number is increasing at the rate of about 10,000 miles each year. There were three times as many miles of telegraph in the United States in 1882 as in any other country. This quantity is increasing at the rate of about 20,000 miles each year.

In the United States there are nearly a quarter of a million public schools, and over six million pupils in daily attendance. In addition to schools of medicine, law, and theology, there are nearly four hundred colleges. There are more than 11,000 newspapers and periodicals. There are about 90,000 congregations belonging to the various Christian denominations, all supported by the freewill offerings of those who belong to them, and all are more generally prosperous than if they depended on government aid such as is the case in other countries.

When we look forward into the future, so far as we are able to judge from the present conditions of progress, we can hardly avoid being startled at the result. It was noticed long ago that the population of the United States doubled every twenty-five years. This condition has steadily continued. Now this will make the population of the United States twenty years from now 100,000,000. About the year 1930, it ought to be 200,000,000; and it has been supposed that before the end of the next century the population may be 800,000,000 ; the number which good judges think the territory of the United States will support.

But that which is even more startling than the increase in numbers is the increase in power. Every year 1,000,000 sewing machines are produced, and they can do more work than 12,000,000 women could do by hand. Thus the working power of the country as to sewing, grows far faster than even its women increase. It is the same with steam machinery in regard to men. It is true that the people of Great Britain and other civilized countries have the same advantages of machinery, but they have not the same resources for its continuous growth and development. Great Britain's coal supply will be used up in a century. We know already of 200,000 square miles of coal territory in the United States, forty times as much as in Great Britain, and twenty times as much as in all Europe together.

It is thus evident that fifty years hence there will be no power on earth to be compared to the United States of America. There are no enormous armies required for self-protection, as in Russia, France, and Germany, and which exhaust a nation's resources. We judge of what the future will be from the conditions at present at work, and from the changes which have taken place from the past to the present. It is the story of these changes, and the incidents connected therewith which we intend to make the subject of our special attention. Nevertheless, as it is our purpose to review the history of the whole American continent, a preliminary glance at its more northern region and at the nations of South and Central America will be requisite for the completeness of our undertaking.

SCENE IN CENTRAL AMERICA.

About the year 1000 the Northmen or people of Norway and Denmark, after having settled in Iceland and Greenland, pushed their way to the coast of North America. Some of them settled in Rhode Island. These discoverers sent back to their native country descriptions of the places discovered. Nevertheless, there is no reason to suppose that Columbus had any knowledge of these discoveries which had been forgotten long before his time. Even Greenland itself, in the fifteenth century, was known to the Northmen only by the name of the *lost Greenland*.

Most persons supposed, at that time, that the earth was a flat surface, and few had any correct notions of its form. Among those who believed it to be round, was Christopher Columbus, a native of Genoa, in Italy, and who was born in the year 1447, whose parents were poor, and who were able to give him but little education.

Columbus was sent to sea at an early age, yet he, improving all his opportunities for observation and study, became one of the most intelligent mariners of the age. Believing the earth to be round, and that the shortest route from Europe to the eastern coasts of Asia would be found by sailing in a westerly direction, he anxiously sought the means for making the experiment.

He visited Portugal—laid his plans before the king of that country—and requested that he might be supplied with a ship and seamen to navigate it; but he was laughed at. He applied to his native country, Genoa, where he met with a like ill success. He then went to Spain, where he arrived in great poverty, having previously exhausted the little fortune which his industry had acquired.

The first notice we have of his being in Spain, is as a stranger, on foot, stopping at the gate of a convent near the seaport of Palos, and asking for some bread and water for himself, and his little son Diego, who accompanied him. While they were partaking of this humble refreshment, the priest of the convent, Juan Perez, happened to pass by, and perceiving that Columbus was a foreigner, he entered into conversation with him.

He soon learned from him the object of his travels; detained him several days as a guest; became a believer in his scheme of a western route to Asia; and, after promising to maintain and educate his son Diego at the convent, he and some friends furnished Columbus with the means of continuing his journey to Cordova, to visit Ferdinand and Isabella, the king and queen of Spain.

When Columbus arrived at Cordova, he found the king and queen so busily engaged in preparations for war against the Moorish kingdom of Grenada, that they could find no time to listen to him, and he was therefore obliged to wait until a better opportunity offered, and in the meantime he supported himself by making and selling maps and charts.

Finally, however, although most persons at Cordova regarded him as a kind of madman, or wild adventurer, yet some distinguished men became convinced of the justness of his theory, and, through their influence, he was enabled to see the king, and explain to him his plans.

Ferdinand was highly pleased with the idea of so important a discovery as Columbus hoped to make; but, being doubtful about the success of such a voyage as was proposed, he ordered the most learned men of the kingdom to assemble at Salamanca, to hear Columbus explain his theory, and then give their opinion of its merits.

Several years, however, passed away, during which time he was kept in suspense by the repeated promises of the king and queen, that, when the war should be ended, and they could find a little more leisure, they would give his project a more attentive consideration.

PORTRAIT OF PIZARRO.
From the authentic portrait preserved in the Museum at Lima.

At length Columbus, losing all patience after so many delays, gave up all hope of assistance from the throne, and was on the point of leaving Spain for the purpose of laying his plans before the king of France, when Queen

Isabella resolved to engage in the enterprise, and pledged her jewels to raise the necessary funds. Columbus, who was already on his way to France, was called back to court, where all the necessary arrangements were soon made.

It was agreed that he should be high admiral of all the seas, and governor of all the lands that he should discover; and that he should have a tenth part of all the profits arising from the merchandise and productions of the countries under his government. Three small vessels were fitted out in the little seaport of Palos, the largest of which, called the Santa Maria, Columbus himself commanded. The names of the other vessels were the Pinta and the Nina.

On board this fleet were ninety seamen, and a number of private adventurers—in all, 120 persons. On the 3d of August, 1492, Columbus sailed from Palos, a small town on the seaboard of Andalusia, northwest of Cadiz. He first directed his course to the Canary Islands, where he remained several weeks, refitting one of his vessels, and taking in wood and water and provisions for the voyage.

On the 6th of September he departed from the Canaries, and sailed directly westward into the unknown ocean, where no ship had ever before ventured. When the seamen lost sight of land their hearts failed them, for they seemed to have taken leave of the world; and after they had sailed onward twenty days in the same direction, they began to be filled with dismay at the length of the voyage, and were anxious to return.

So alarmed did they finally become that they threatened to throw Columbus overboard, and return without him. Still Columbus adhered to his purpose, and used every expedient to dispel the fears of the seamen, and encourage them to proceed. The favoring breeze, blowing steadily from the east, wafted the vessels rapidly forward over a tranquil sea, and Columbus found it necessary to keep his crews ignorant of the great distance they had gone.

About the first of October several patches of herbs and weeds drifting from the west were seen, and many birds came singing around the vessels in the morning, and flew away at night. These signs of land were very cheering to the hearts of the poor mariners, and every one was eager to be the first to behold and announce the wished-for shore. But still day after day passed, and although signs of land became more and more frequent, yet the seamen became so impatient and clamorous, that it was with the greatest difficulty that Columbus could prevent an open mutiny.

Beautifully does the German poet Schiller allude to his situation at this time:

"Steer on, bold sailor—wit may mock thy soul that sees the land,
And hopeless at the helm may droop the weak and weary hand;
Yet ever—ever to the West, for there the coast must lie,
And dim it dawns and glimmering dawns before thy reason's eye;
Yea, trust the guiding God—and go along the floating grave.

Though hid till now—yet now behold the New World o'er the wave,
With Genius, Nature ever stands in solemn union still;
And ever what the one foretells, the other shall fulfil."

On the 11th of October, however, the signs of land had become so certain, that all murmuring ceased. On that day a green fish, such as keeps near the land, swam by the ships; and a branch of thorn, with berries on it, floated by; they picked up, also, a reed, a small board, and a staff artificially carved. All were now on the lookout for land, and during the following night not an eye was closed in sleep.

About ten o'clock Columbus himself saw a light which seemed to be on shore; and on the morning of the 12th the sailors saw land, and then arose

"The cry
That told the Indian isles were nigh
To the world-seeking Genoese,
When the land-wind from woods of palm,
And orange-groves and fields of balm
Blew o'er the Haytien seas."—*Halleck.*

During the ceremony of taking possession, the natives looked on with wonder and awe. When at the dawn of day they beheld the ships at a distance, moving about without any apparent effort, they thought they were mighty sea-monsters, which had issued from the deep during the night. The shifting and furling of the sails, which resembled huge wings, filled them with astonishment. But when they saw the boats approach the shore, and a number of strange beings, clad in glittering steel, or raiment of different colors, landing on the beach, they fled in affright to the woods.

When, however, they saw that no attempt was made to pursue or molest them, they gradually recovered from their terror and approached the Spaniards, frequently prostrating themselves with their faces to the earth, and making signs of adoration. They finally ventured to touch the Spaniards, and to examine their hands, faces and clothing. They expressed great admiration at the white complexion of the strangers, whom they believed to be children of the sun.

Nor were the Spaniards much less surprised at the sight of these strange, but simple and artless people, whose color, of a dark copper or dusky brown, was so different from that of Europeans. They wore no clothing; their hair was coarse, straight and black; they had no beards; and their bodies, hands and faces, were painted with a variety of colors. Columbus, supposing that the land which he had discovered was a part of eastern or southern Asia, which was known by the name of India, called the inhabitants *Indians.*

The world which Columbus discovered, and which should have received the name of *Columbia*, has been called *America*, from the name of a distinguished Italian navigator, Americus Vespucius, who visited the country several times before the death of Columbus, and wrote a glowing description of it. It is supposed that the first voyage of Americus was made in the year 1497, when he discovered the continent itself on the coast of Brazil, before it was seen by Columbus, and that this is the reason why it has been called America, after his name.

Spanish adventurers never rested from their eager search after the treas-

SOUTH AMERICAN INDIANS.

ures of the new continent. An aged warrior called Ponce de Leon, fitted out an expedition at his own cost. He had heard of the marvellous fountain whose waters would restore to him the years of his wasted youth. He searched in vain. The fountain would not reveal itself to the foolish old man, and he had to bear without relief the burden of his profitless years. But he found a country hitherto unseen by Europeans, which was clothed with mag nificent forests, and seemed to bloom with perpetual flowers. He called it Florida. He attempted to found a colony in the paradise he had discovered. But the natives attacked him, slew many of his men, and drove the rest to their ships, carrying with them their chief, wounded to death by the arrow of an Indian.

Ten or twelve years after Columbus had discovered the mainland there was a Spanish settlement at the town of Darien, on the isthmus. Prominent among the adventurers who prosecuted, from this centre of operations, the Spaniard's eager and ruthless search for gold was Vasco Nuñez de Balboa— a man cruel and unscrupulous as the others, but giving evidence of wider views and larger powers of mind than almost any of his fellows. Vasco Nuñez visited one day a friendly chief, from whom he received in gift a large amount of gold. The Spaniards had certain rules which guided them in the distribution of the spoils, but in the application of these rules disputes continually fell out. It so happened on this occasion that a noisy altercation arose. A young Indian prince, regarding with unconcealed contempt the clamor of the greedy strangers, told them that, since they prized gold so highly, he would show them a country where they might have it in abundance. Southward, beyond the mountains, was a great sea; on the coasts of that sea there was a land of vast wealth, where the people ate and drank from vessels of gold. This was the first intimation which Europeans received of the Pacific ocean, and the land of Peru on the western shore of the continent. Vasco Nuñez resolved to be the discoverer of that unknown sea. Among his followers was Francisco Pizarro, who became, a few years later, the discoverer and destroyer of Peru.

Vasco Nuñez gathered about 200 well-armed men and a number of dogs, who were potent allies in his Indian wars. He climbed with much toil the mountain-ridge which traverses the isthmus. After twenty-five days of difficult journeying his Indians told him that he was almost in view of the ocean. He chose that he should look for the first time on that great sight alone. He made his men remain behind, while he, unattended, looked down upon the Sea of the South, and drank the delight of this memorable success. Upon his knees he gave thanks to God, and joined with his followers in devoutly singing the *Te Deum*. He made his way down to the coast. Wading into the tranquil waters, he called his men to witness that he took possession for the kings of Castile of the sea and all that it contained—a large claim, assuredly, for the Pacific covers more than one-half the surface of the globe.

POPOCATEPETL.

MEXICO.

IN 1518 the Spanish governor of Cuba sent an officer, Ferdinand Cortez, with ten ships and 600 men to conquer the empire of Mexico. Having founded the colony of Vera Cruz as a basis of operations, Cortez then broke all his ships to pieces. This he did to insure success, for he thus shut himself and his soldiers up in the invaded land.

Montezuma was the emperor of the Mexicans. Gradually advancing through his territories, the Spanish force at last reached the capital. Everywhere they were regarded as deities—children of the sun. Scrolls of cotton cloth were carried far and wide through the terror-stricken land, on which were pictured pale-faced bearded warriors, trampling horses, ships with spreading wings, and cannons breathing out lightning, and dashing to the earth tall trees far away. The emperor admitted Cortez to his capital, but at the same time sent a secret expedition to attack Vera Cruz. The hopes of the Mexicans revived when they saw the head of a Spaniard carried through the land; for then they knew that their foes were mortal. At this crisis Cortez resolved on a bold stroke. Seizing Montezuma, he carried him to the Spanish quarters, and forced him to acknowledge himself a vassal of Spain.

Having held Mexico for six months, Cortez left it to defeat Narvaez, whom the Cuban government, jealous of his success, had sent against him with nearly a thousand men.

During his absence all was uproar in the capital. Two thousand Mexican nobles had been massacred for the sake of their golden ornaments; and the Spanish quarters were surrounded by a furious crowd. The return of Cortez, with a force increased by the troops of the defeated Narvaez, was oil cast on flame. Montezuma, striving to mediate, was killed by a stone flung by one of his angry subjects. The Spaniards were, for a time, driven from the city; but in the valley of Otumba (1520), the Mexicans were routed, and their golden standard was taken. Soon afterwards the new emperor was made prisoner, stretched on burning coals, and gibbeted. The siege of Mexico, lasting seventy-five days, was the final blow.

The fall of Peru followed soon after the conquest of Mexico, and from Peru the tide of Spanish conquest flowed southward to Chili. The river Plata was explored, Buenos Ayres was founded, and communication was opened from the Atlantic to the Pacific. Forty years after the landing of Columbus the margins of the continent bordering on the sea had been subdued and possessed, and some progress had been made in gaining knowledge of the interior. There had been added to the dominions of Spain vast regions, whose coast-line on the west stretched from Mexico southward for the distance of 6,000 miles—regions equal in length to the whole of Africa, and largely exceeding in breadth the whole of the Russian Empire.

For 300 years Spain governed the rich possessions which she had so easily won. At the close of that period the population was about sixteen millions—a number very much smaller than the conquerors found on island and continent. The increase of three centuries had not repaired the waste of thirty years. Of the 16,000,000, two were Spaniards; the remainder were Indians, negroes, or persons of mixed descent.

At length the time came in which Mexico, in concert with the other colonies of Spanish America, threw off the intolerable yoke of the mother country.

When the Mexicans gained their independence they raised to the throne a popular young officer, whom they styled the Emperor Augustine First.

They were then a people utterly priest-ridden and fanatical; and the clergy whom they superstitiously revered were a corrupt and debased class. The reformers had avowed the opinion that the church was the origin of most of the evils which afflicted the country. The emperor, while he offered equal civil rights to all the inhabitants of Mexico, sought to gain the clergy to his cause by guaranteeing the existence of the Catholic Church. But a monarchy proved to be impossible, and in less than a year a republican uprising, headed by Santa Anna, forced the emperor to resign. A federal republic was then organized, with a constitution based on that of the great republic whose territories adjoined those of Mexico.

HIDALGO Y. COSTELLO.
Father of Mexican Independence.

For the next thirty years Santa Anna is the prominent figure in Mexican politics. He was a tall, thin man, with sun-browned face, black curling hair, and dark, vehement eye. He possessed no statesmanship, and his generalship never justified the confidence with which it was regarded by his countrymen. But he was full of reckless bravery and dash, and if his leading was faulty, his personal bearing in all his numerous battles was irreproachable. His popularity ebbed and flowed with the exigencies of the time. He repelled an invasion by Spain and an invasion by France, and these triumphs raised him to the highest pinnacle of public favor. Then his power decayed, and he was forced to flee from the country. When new dangers threatened the unstable nation he was recalled from his banishment and placed in supreme command. At one period one of his legs, which had been shattered in battle, was interred with solemn funeral service and glowing patriot oratory. A little later the ill-fated limb was disinterred, and kicked about the streets of Mexico with every contumelious accompaniment. His public life was closed by a hasty flight to Havana—his second movement of that description.

In 1846 war was declared between Mexico and the United States. At Palo Alto, Resaca de la Palma, and at Buena Vista the Mexicans were totally defeated by General Taylor. General Scott, of the United States army, besieged Vera Cruz and captured it. He then proceeded against the capital. At length the Mexican army, under Santa Anna, were routed by Generals Shields and Pierce, and the city government sent to ask a truce. On the 7th of September the army was again in motion ; the great fortress of Chapultepec, commanding the city, was taken by storm; Santa Anna and his officers fled ; and on the 4th the flag of the United States floated over the ancient home of the Montezumas. With the surrender of her capital the power of Mexico was broken. By the treaty of Guadalupe Hidalgo, Upper California, with Nevada, Utah, Arizona, and New Mexico, was ceded to the United States. The latter agreed to pay $15,000,000, and assume debts due American citizens from the Mexican government. The other captured places were restored.

On account of abuses in the government, there came a demand for reform, and the Mexicans took a large step towards the vindication of their liberties. The leader in this revolution was Benito Juarez, a Toltec Indian, one of that despised race which the Aztecs subdued centuries before the Spanish invasion. This man had imbibed the liberal and progressive ideas which now prevailed in all civilized countries ; and his personal ability and skill in the management of affairs gained for him the opportunity of conferring upon Mexico the fullest measure of political blessing which she had ever received. The Liberals were now a majority in Congress, and the gigantic work of reformation began. But Juarez and his government were afterwards driven for a time from the capital. The aims of his enemies concurred with an ambition which at that time animated the restless mind of Emperor Napoleon III. The Mexican clergy, supported by the court of Rome, gave encouragement to his idle dream. An expedition was prepared, in which England and Spain took reluctant and hesitating part, and from which they quickly withdrew.

A French army entered the capital of Mexico. Juarez and his government withdrew to maintain a patriot war, in which the mass of the people zealously upheld them. An Austrian prince sat upon the throne of Mexico without support, excepting that which the clerical party of Mexico and the bayonets of France supplied. A few years earlier or later these things dared not have been done ; but when the French troops entered Mexican territory the United States waged, not yet with clear prospect of success, a struggle on the results of which depended their own existence as a nation. They had no thought to give to the concerns of other American states, and they wisely suffered the empire of Mexico to run its sad and foolish course. But now the southern revolt was quelled, and the government at Washington, having at its call a million of veteran soldiers, intimated to Napoleon that the farther stay of his troops on the American continent had become impossible. The emperor waited no second summons. When the French were gone the patriot armies swept over the country, and this deplorable attempt to set up imperialism came to an ignominious close. The Emperor Maximilian fell into the hands of his enemies, and was put to death according to the terms of a decree which his own government had framed.

BENITO JUAREZ, EX-PRESIDENT OF MEXICO.

Juarez was again elected president, and returned with his Congress to the city of Mexico. During his whole term of office he had to maintain the Liberal cause in arms against the tenacious priesthood and its followers. When he died, a Liberal president, named Porfirio Diaz, was chosen to succeed him.

Benito Juarez was an unmixed Toltec. Porfirio Diaz, the strongest Mexican of his times, and in many respects the General Grant of his country, is of mixed blood. Everywhere the Aztec face, unmistakable in its pathetic features, goes with the best and worst types of Mexican character.

It may be at first a matter of surprise that the average Mexican seems to know so little of his own country, and to have so little local pride in its history and interesting antiquities. It is not strange to him; he has always been there, and has never thought much about it. It is not yet a show country. When this feature changes, it will, as usual, change too much.

Another strange thing is, that with an advancement in art that surprises every visitor, the country has no literature. The galleries of the capital are filled with specimens of the old and new schools, many of which would be masterpieces in any country. Yet there is not a publishing house in the republic, and the three or four bookstores of the city are filled with French works, either scientific or novels.

Chihuahua, to the traveller from the United States, may be regarded as the first Mexican city. It contains some 18,000 inhabitants, and is a permanent departure from the adobe style of architecture, which has always been regarded by us as the inevitable and unavoidable building material of the Mexican.

A hundred miles south of Chihuahua is Santa Rosalia, famous among Mexicans for its sanitary hot-springs. It is reported by the few foreigners who have yet visited it to be, as to the quality of its waters, probably the finest health resort in America.

The City of Mexico, with a population variously estimated at from 225,000 to 300,000, is situated upon ground that was once the bed of a lake. The lake was what is now the Valley of Mexico.

CYPRESS TREES AT CHAPULTEPEC.

The streets are some sixty feet wide, with wide sidewalks, and the city lies closely built in regular squares. The buildings are mostly of two, though sometimes of three or four stories. The square in front of the cathedral, called the Zócalo, is the place of universal resort, though there are two or three others, handsome and clean, but not so well kept nor so expensively ornamented.

It is the city of churches, as Mexico is unquestionably the land of churches. Their towers, always handsome, assist very much in making up the general view.

Fenced by impassible barriers for some three hundred years, this old, rich, quaint and isolated empire has suddenly become the coming country of the capitalist and the tourist; a land in which, by the invitation of its people, we have already begun an endless series of beneficent and bloodless conquests.

PERU.

THE conqueror of Peru was Francisco Pizarro, a man who could neither read nor write, and whose early days were spent in herding swine. Running away from home in early life, he became a soldier, and saw much service in the New World. Between 1524 and 1528, while exploring the coast of Peru, he formed the design of conquering that golden land, being tempted by the abundance of the precious metals, which glittered everywhere, forming not merely the ornaments of the people, but the commonest utensils of everyday life.

He sailed from Panama with 186 men, in February, 1531. A civil war then raging in Peru between two brothers, who were rivals for the throne, made his task an easier one than it might otherwise have been. The strife seems to have been to some extent decided when the Spaniards landed, for Atahualpa was then Inca of Peru—so they called their kings.

Pizarro found the Inca holding a splendid court near the city of Caxamarca; and the eyes of the Spanish pirates gleamed when they saw the glitter of gold and jewels in the royal camp. The visit of the Spanish leader was returned by the Inca, who came in a golden chair, encompassed by 10,000 guards. A friar, crucifix in hand, strove to convert this worshipper of the sun, telling him at the same time that the pope had given Peru to the King of Spain. The argument was all lost on the Inca, who could not see how the pope was able to give away what was not his, and who, besides, scorned the idea of giving up the worship of so magnificent a god as the sun. The furious priest turned with a cry for vengeance to the Spaniards. They were ready, for it was all a tragedy well rehearsed beforehand. The match was laid to the levelled cannon, and a storm of shot from great guns and small burst upon the poor huddled crowd of Peruvians, amid whose slaughter and dismay Pizarro carried off the Inca. As the price of freedom, Atahualpa offered to fill his cell with gold. The offer was accepted, and the treasure divided among the Spaniards; but the unhappy Inca was strangled after all. The capture of Cuzco completed the wonderfully easy conquest of Peru.

THE INCA HUASCAR.

(176)

Pizarro founded Lima in 1535; and, six years later, was slain by conspirators, who burst into his palace during the mid-day siesta.

Of all the cities of South America, Lima has an aspect most peculiar and original, the buildings being little more than huge cages of canes plastered over with mud. The city is said to be "the paradise of women, the purgatory of husbands, and the hell of donkeys."

In the war for independence by the South American provinces Peru was the last stronghold of Spanish authority. Spain put forth her utmost effort to maintain her hold upon the mineral treasures which were almost essential to her existence. The desire for independence was less enthusiastic here than in the other provinces; the insurrectionary movement was more fitful and more easily suppressed. When independence had triumphed everywhere besides, the Peruvian republic was struggling hopelessly for existence. The Spaniards had possessed themselves of the capital; a reactionary impulse had spread itself among the soldiers, and numerous desertions had weakened and discouraged the patriot ranks. The cause of liberty seemed almost lost in Peru; the old despotism which had been cast out of the other provinces seemed to regain its power over the land of the Incas, and threatened to establish itself there as a standing menace to the liberty and peace of the continent.

At length on the plain of Ayacucho, 12,000 Royalists encountered the Republican army under Bolivar, numbering scarcely more than one-half the opposing forces. The outnumbered independents fought bravely, but the fortune of war seemed to declare against them, and they were being driven from the field with a defeat which must soon have become a rout. At that perilous moment an English general commanding the Republican cavalry struck with his force on the flank of the victorious but disordered Spaniards. The charge could not be resisted. The Spaniards fled from the field, leaving their artillery and many prisoners, among whom was the viceroy. A final and decisive victory had been gained. The war ceased; Peru and Chili were given over by treaty to the friends of liberty, and the authority which Spain had so vilely abused had no longer a foothold on the soil of the great South American continent.

Peru is believed to extract silver from her mines to the annual value of a million sterling—an amount somewhat smaller than these mines yielded down to the war of independence. Peru exports chiefly articles which can be obtained without labor or thought. The guano, heaped in millions of tons on the islands which stud her coasts, was sold to European speculators and carried away by European ships. But these vast stores seem to approach exhaustion. Fortunately for this spendthrift government, discovery was made some years ago of large deposits of nitrate of soda, from the sale of which an important revenue is gained.

For Peru, lying chiefly between lofty mountain ranges remote from the sea, railway communication is of prime importance. In the time of one of her best presidents there was devised a scheme of singular boldness; and by the help of borrowed money, on which no interest is paid, it has been partially executed. A railway line, setting out from Lima, on the Pacific, crosses the barren plain which adjoins the coast, climbs the western range of the Andes to a height of nearly sixteen thousand feet, and traverses the table-land which lies between the great lines of mountain. When completed, it will reach some of the tributaries of the Amazon at points where these become navigable, thus connecting the Pacific with the Atlantic where the continent is the broadest. There are, in all, about fourteen hundred miles of railway open for traffic in Peru, three-fourths of which are government works.

VENEZUELA.

THE provinces which bordered on the Gulf of Mexico had a larger intercourse with Europe than their sister states, and were the first to become imbued with the liberal ideas which were now gaining prevalence among the European people. Seven of these northern provinces formed themselves into a union, which they styled the Confederation of Venezuela. They did not yet assert independence of Spain; but they abolished the tax which had been levied from the Indians; they declared commerce to be free; they gathered up the Spanish governor and his councillors, and, having put them on board ship, sent them decisively out of the country. Only one step remained, and it was speedily taken. Next year Venezuela declared her independence, and prepared as she best might to assert it in arms against the forces of Spain.

One of the fathers of South American independence was Francis Miranda. He was a native of Caraccas, and now a man in middle life. It was this man who laid the foundations of independence, but he himself was not permitted to see the triumph of the great cause. The patriot arms had made some progress, and high hopes were entertained; but the province was smitten by an earthquake, which overthrew several towns and destroyed 20,000 lives. The priests interpreted this calamity as the judgment of heaven upon rebellion, and the credulous people accepted their teaching. The cause of independence thus supernaturally discredited, was for the time abandoned. Miranda himself fell into the hands of his enemies, and perished in a Spanish dungeon, and his lieutenant, Don Simon Bolivar, was the destined vindicator of the liberties of the South American continent.

CHILI.

F all the Spanish provinces of America, Chili furnishes the best example of a well-ordered, settled, and prosperous state. Its area is only one-fifth and its population one-fourth that of Mexico, but its foreign commerce is nearly one-half larger. For this commerce its situation is peculiarly favorable. Chili, a long and narrow country, lies on the Pacific, with which it communicates by upward of fifty seaports. It is, therefore, only in small measure dependent for its progress upon railways and navigable rivers.

For sixteen years after throwing off the Spanish yoke, Chili was governed despotically, without a constitution. During those years constant disorders prevailed. At length the general wish of the nation was gratified. A constitution was promulgated, under which the franchise was bestowed on every married man of twenty-one years, and on every unmarried man of twenty-five, who was able to read and write. With this constitution the people have been satisfied. The government has been throughout in the hands of a moderate conservative party, which has directed public affairs with firmness and wisdom, and has manifested zeal in the correction of abuses. Opposing parties have not in Chili, as in the neighboring states, wasted the country by their fierce contentions for ascendency. In the exercise of a wise but rare moderation, the views of either party have been modified by those of the other. A method of government has thus been reached which men of all shades of opinion have been able to accept, and under which the prosperous development of the country has advanced with surprising rapidity.

THE ARGENTINE CONFEDERATION.

UENOS AYRES, a city founded during the early years of the conquest, was the seat of one of the viceroyalties by which the Spaniards conducted the government of the continent. It stands on the right bank of the river Plate, not far from the ocean. The Plate and its tributary rivers flow through vast treeless plains, where myriads of horses and cattle roam at will among grass which attains a height equal to their own. When the dominion of Spain ceased, Buenos Ayres naturally assumed a preponderating influence in the new government. The provinces which had composed the old viceroyalty formed themselves into a confederation, with a constitution modelled on that of the United States. Buenos Ayres was the only port of shipment for the inland provinces. Her commercial importance, as well as her metropolitan dignity, soon aroused jealousies which could not be allayed. Within a few years the confederation was repudiated by nearly all its members, and for some time each of the provinces governed itself independently of the others.

The twenty-three years of despotism had done nothing to solve the political problems which still demanded solution at the hands of the Argentine people. The tedious and painful work had now to be resumed. The province of Buenos Ayres declared itself out of the confederation, and entered upon a separate career. The single state was wisely governed, and made rapid progress in all the elements of prosperity. Especially it copied the New England common-school system. The thirteen states from which it had severed itself strove to repress or to rival its increasing greatness; but their utmost efforts could scarcely avert decay. They declared war, in the barbarous hope of crushing their too prosperous neighbor. Buenos Ayres was strong enough to inflict defeat upon her assailants. She now, on her own terms, re-entered the confederation, of which her chief city became once more the capital.

CENTRAL AMERICA.

SINCE the time of the Spanish Conquest, in the sixteenth century Central America has been the theatre of tribal wars, fierce religious animosities, dictatorial usurpations, and volcanic eruptions and earthquakes, carrying widespread destruction and death.

Guatemala—then Central America—originally composed all the narrow part of the continent, extending over 800 miles in length, and covering an area of 130,000 square miles. As a geographical division, what is now known as Central America would include the entire stretch of territory from the Isthmus of Tehuantepec to the Isthmus of Darien, which forms the nexus between the two great continents of North and South America. But the political inter-relationship has so influenced the use of the name, that it now distinguishes that area confined in the five independent republics of North America, Costa Rica, Nicaragua, Honduras, San Salvador and Guatemala. The Isthmus of Panama belongs to the division of South America, as a part of New Granada, while the Peninsula of Yucatan and the Isthmus of Tehuantepec are incorporated with North America, as parts of Mexico. The five provinces do not greatly vary in their physical characteristics. The surface of of the country is hilly, and in most parts mountainous, and the climate warm and very moist.

BAY OF RIO.

BRAZIL.

KING John, of Portugal, to whom Columbus first made offer of his project of discovery, was grievously chagrined when the success of the great navigator revealed the magnificence of the rejected opportunity. Till then Portugal had occupied the foremost place as an explorer of unknown regions. She had already achieved the discovery of all the western coasts of Africa, and was now about to open a new route to the East by the Cape of Good Hope. Suddenly her fame was eclipsed. While she occupied herself with small and barren discoveries, Spain had found, almost without the trouble of seeking, a new world of vast extent and boundless wealth.

Portugal had obtained from the Pope a grant of all lands which she should discover in the Atlantic, with the additional advantage of full pardon for the sins of all persons who should die while engaged in the work of exploration. The sovereigns of Spain were equally provident in regard to the new territory which they were now in course of acquiring. The accommodating Pope, willing to please both powers, divided the world between them. He stretched an imaginary line from pole to pole, one hundred leagues to the westward of the

Cape de Verd islands: all discoveries on the eastern side of this boundary were given to Portugal, while those on the west became the property of Spain. Portugal, dissatisfied with the vast gift, proposed that another line should be drawn, stretching from east to west, and that she should be at liberty to possess all lands which she might find between that line and the South Pole. Spain objected to this huge deduction from her expected possessions. Ultimately Spain consented that the papal frontier should be removed westward to a distance of 270 leagues from the Cape de Verd islands, and thus the dispute was happily terminated.

Six years after this singular transaction, by which two small European states parted between them all unexplored portions of the earth, a Portuguese navigator—Pedro Alvarez Cabral—set sail from the Tagus in the prosecution of discovery in the East. He stood far out into the Atlantic, to avoid the calms which habitually baffled navigation on the coast of Guinea. His reckoning was loosely kept, and the ocean currents bore his ships westward into regions which it was not his intention to seek. After forty-five days of voyaging he saw before him an unknown and unexpected land. In searching for the Cape of Good Hope he had reached the shores of the great South American Continent, and he hastened to claim for the King of Portugal the territory he had found, but regarding the extent of which he had formed as yet no conjecture. Three Spanish captains had already landed on this part of the continent and asserted the right of Spain to its ownership. For many years Spain maintained languidly the right which priority of discovery had given. But Portugal, to whom an interest in the wealth of the New World was an object of vehement desire, took effective possession of the land. She sent out soldiers; she built forts; she subdued the savage natives; she founded colonies; she established provincial governments. Although Spain did not formally withdraw her pretentions, she gradually desisted from attempts to enforce them; and the enormous territory of Brazil became a recognized appendage of a petty European state whose area was scarcely larger than the one-hundredth part of that which she had so easily acquired.

For 300 years Brazil remained in colonial subordination to Portugal. Her boundaries were in utter confusion, and no man along all that vast frontier could tell the limits of Portuguese dominion. Her Indians were fierce, and bore with impatience the inroads which the strangers made upon their possessions. The French seized the Bay of Rio de Janeiro. The Dutch conquered large territories in the north. But in course of years these difficulties were overcome. The foreigners were expelled. The natives were tamed, partly by arms, partly by the teaching of zealous Jesuit missionaries. Some progress was made in opening the vast interior of the country and in fixing its boundaries. On the coast population increased and numerous settlements sprung up. The cultivation of coffee, which has since become the leading

GALLERY OF DOM PEDRO I. (By R. Pulsch.)

Brazilian industry, was introduced. Some simple manufactures were established, and the country began to export her surplus products to Europe. There was much misgovernment; for the despotic tendencies of the captains-general who ruled the country were scarcely mitigated by the authority of the distant court of Lisbon. The enmity of Spain never ceased, and from time to time burst forth in wasteful and bloody frontier wars. Sometimes the people of cities rose in insurrection against the monopolies by which wicked governors wronged them. Occasionally there fell out quarrels between different provinces, and no method of allaying these could be found excepting war. Once the city of Rio de Janeiro was sacked by the French. Brazil had her full share of the miseries which the foolishness and the evil temper of men have in all ages incurred. These hindered, but did not altogether frustrate, the development of her enormous resources.

During the eighteenth century the Brazilian people began to estimate more justly than they had done before the elements of national greatness which surrounded them, and to perceive how unreasonable it was that a country almost as large as Europe should remain in contented dependence on one of the most inconsiderable of European states. The English colonies in North America threw off the yoke of the mother country. The air was full of those ideas of liberty which a year or two later bore fruit in the French Revolution. A desire for independence spread among the Brazilians, and expressed itself by an ill-conceived rising in the province of Minas Geraes. But the movement was easily suppressed, and the Portuguese government maintained for a little longer its sway over this noblest of colonial possessions.

During the earlier years of the French Revolution, Portugal was permitted to watch in undisturbed tranquillity the wild turmoils by which the other European nations were afflicted. At length it seemed to the Emperor Napoleon that the possession of the Portuguese kingdom, and especially of the Portuguese fleet, was a fitting step in his audacious progress to universal dominion. A French army entered Portugal; a single sentence in the *Moniteur* informed the world that "the House of Braganza had ceased to reign." The French troops suffered so severely on their march, that ere they reached Lisbon they were incapable of offensive operations. But so timid was the government, so thoroughly was the nation subdued by fear of Napoleon, that it was determined to offer no resistance. The capital of Portugal, with a population of 300,000, and an army of 14,000, opened its gates to 1,500 ragged and famishing Frenchmen, who wished to overturn the throne and degrade the country into a French province.

Before this humiliating submission was accomplished, the royal family had gathered together its most precious effects, and with a long train of followers set sail for Brazil. The insane queen was accompanied to the place of embarkation by the prince regent and the princes and princesses of the family, all in tears; the multitudes who thronged to look upon the departure lifted up their voices and wept. Men of heroic mould would have made themselves ready to hold the capital of the state or perish in its ruins; but the faint-hearted people of Lisbon were satisfied to bemoan themselves. When they had gazed their last at the receding ships they hastened to receive their conquerors and supply their needs.

The presence of the government hastened the industrial progress of Brazil. The prince regent (who in a few years became king) began his rule by opening the Brazilian ports to the commerce of all friendly nations. Seven years later it was formally decreed that the colonial existence of Brazil should cease. She was now raised to the dignity of a kingdom, united with Portugal under the same crown. Her commerce and agriculture increased; she began to regard as her inferior the country of which she lately had been a dependency.

The changed relations of the two states were displeasing to the people of Portugal. The council by which the affairs of the kingdom were conducted became unpopular. The demand for constitutional government extended from Spain into Portugal. The Portuguese desired to see their king again in Lisbon, and called loudly for his return. The king consented to the wish of his people reluctantly; for besides other and graver reasons why he should not quit Brazil, his majesty greatly feared the discomforts of a sea-voyage. His son, the heir to his throne, became regent in Brazil.

The Brazilians resented the departure of the king. The Portuguese meditated a yet deeper humiliation for the state whose recent acquisition of dignity was still an offence to them. There came an order from the Cortes that the prince regent also should return to Europe. The Brazilians were now eager that the tie which bound them to the mother country should be dissolved. The prince regent was urged to disregard the summons to return. After some hesitation he gave effect to the general wish, and intimated his purpose of remaining in Brazil. A few months later he was proclaimed emperor, and the union of the two kingdoms ceased. Constitutional government was set up. But the administration of the emperor was not sufficiently liberal to satisfy the wishes of his people. After nine years of deepening unpopularity he resigned the crown in favor of his son, Dom Pedro, whose reign extended over the long period of forty-nine years.

Brazil covers almost one-half the South American Continent, and has therefore an area nearly equal to that of the eight states of Spanish origin by which she is bounded. She is as large as the British dominions in North America; she is larger than the United States, excluding the untrodden wastes of Alaska. One, and that not the largest, of her twenty provinces is ten times the size of England. Finally, her area is equal to five-sixths that of

Europe. She has a sea-coast line of 4,000 miles. She has a marvellous system of river communication; the Amazon and its tributaries alone are navigable for 25,000 miles within Brazilian territory. Her mineral wealth is so ample that the governor of one of her provinces was wont, in religious processions, to ride a horse whose shoes were of gold; and the diamonds of the royal family are estimated at a value of £3,000,000 sterling. Her soil and climate conspire to bestow upon her agriculture an opulence which is unsurpassed and probably unequalled. An acre of cotton yields in Brazil four times as much as an acre in the United States. Wheat gives a return of thirty to seventy-fold; maize, two hundred to four-hundred-fold; rice, a thousand-fold. Brazil supplies nearly one-half the coffee which the human family consumes. An endless variety of plants thrive in her genial soil. Sugar and tobacco, as well as cotton, coffee, and tea, are staple productions. Nothing which the tropics yield is wanting, and in many portions of the empire the vegetation of the temperate zones is abundantly productive. The energy of vegetable life is everywhere excessive. The mangrove seeds send forth shoots before they fall from the parent tree; the drooping branches of trees strike roots when they touch the ground, and enter upon independent existence; wood which has been split for fences hastens to put forth leaves; grasses and other plants intertwine and form bridges on which the traveller walks in safety.

But the scanty population of Brazil is wholly insufficient to subdue the enormous territory on which they have settled and make its vast capabilities conduce to the welfare of man. The highest estimate gives to Brazil a population of from eleven to twelve million. She has thus scarcely four inhabitants to every square mile of her surface, while England has upward of 400. Vast forests still darken her soil, and the wild luxuriance of tropical undergrowth renders them well-nigh impervious to man. There are boundless expanses of wilderness imperfectly explored, still roamed over by untamed and often hostile Indians. Persistent but not eminently successful efforts have been made to induce European and now to induce Chinese immigration. The population continues, however, to increase at such a rate that it is larger by nearly two million than it was ten years ago. But these accessions are trivial when viewed in relation to the work which has still to be accomplished. It is said that no more than the one hundred and fiftieth part of the agricultural resources of Brazil has yet been developed or even revealed.

Among the people of the cities of Brazil we find several classes. The enterprising business class, planters, etc., is made up of native Brazilians, Portuguese, and Europeans generally. The lower class forms a mixed multitude of Portuguese, aborigines and negroes. The children of this class go about nearly naked until ten or twelve years old. All of the lower orders have a passion for jewelry—gold, if practicable; if not, gilt being acceptable—the main point being that it shall be big and brilliant. Negro girls, selling fruit,

NIAGARA OF BRAZIL.

dress in white, and carry large trays on their heads, while their necks and ears are loaded down with massive chains, charms, and rings.

Nowhere can an honest, hard-working man get on so well with such a minimum of money or ability as in the interior and smaller towns of Brazil. The services of a useful hand, whatever be his specialty, will be paid for at once, and at the highest possible value, and will always remain in demand, and it is simply his own fault if employment does not lead on to fortune, and to what we may call rank.

Altogether, if we consider the present condition of Brazil as regards its government, the nature of its population, and the character of its industries and natural products, it will be seen that there is here offered to the world a field for the exercise of human intelligence and energy quite unsurpassed, a climate and soil possessing peculiarly advantageous qualities, and a wealth of natural production almost unsurpassed.

The Emperor of Brazil, Dom Pedro II., was born in Rio Janeiro, December 2d, 1825. He was crowned July 18th, 1841, and since his accession to the throne Brazil has been steadily increasing in power and usefulness. The emperor possesses remarkable literary and scientific acquirements, is a just and liberal sovereign, and enjoys the warm affection of his people. He is also a member of the French Academy of Sciences.

On November 14th, 1889, and the succeeding days a revolution broke out in the Empire of Brazil, which in many respects was a remarkable event. The outside world had no suspicion that a strong republican feeling existed in Brazil, or that any dissatisfaction was felt at the course of the aged Emperor, who had reigned in peace and prosperity for well nigh fifty years. The leader of the revolution was General Da Fonseca, who is now President of the Brazilian Republic. The revolution was notable for the swiftness with which it succeeded, and for the absence of riot and violence during its brief progress. It appeared that the Emperor had no partisans, even in his own capital, to strike a blow for him; nor does the Emperor himself seem to have for a moment thought of resisting the revolutionary tide. He simply awaited the good pleasure of the successful chiefs of the republican party; and their good pleasure was that he should sail for Portugal. Set sail he did, without a word of remonstrance or even of regret.

Thus quickly and quietly passed away the only monarchy remaining on either American continent; thus was the circle of American republics made at last complete by the memorable accession to them of the United States of Brazil. It is important to note that for a certain period at least monarchy as a political institution has been absolutely repudiated from the Canada line to Cape Horn, and that the republican principle has been accepted and adopted throughout the area of the self-governing American nations.

The revolution in Brazil was not, however, the result of an uprising against tyranny, for Dom Pedro was a liberal-minded monarch. The following poem composed by him many years ago for a lady's album exhibits his keen sense of duty:

> If I am pious, clement, just,
>   I am only what I ought to be;
> The sceptre is a mighty trust,
>   A great responsibility;

DOM PEDRO II.

> And he who rules with faithful hand,
>   With depth of thought and breadth of range,
> The sacred laws should understand,
>   But must not at his pleasure change.
>
> The chair of justice is the throne;
>   Who takes it, bows to higher laws;

1882

The public good, and not his own,
   Demands his care in every cause.
Neglect of duty—always wrong—
   Detestable in young or old—
By him whose place is high and strong
   Is magnified a thousand-fold.

When in the East the glorious sun
   Spreads o'er the earth the light of day,
All know the course that he will run,
   Nor wonder at his light or way;
But if, perchance, the light that blazed
   Is dimmed by shadows lying near,
The startled world looks on amazed,
   And each one watches it with fear.

I, likewise, if I always give
   To vice and virtue their rewards,
But do my duty thus to live:
   No one his thanks to me accords.
But should I fail to act my part,
   Or wrongly do, or leave undone,
Surprised, the people then would start
   With fear, as at the shadowed sun.

1884

CANADA.

HARBOR AND CITY OF QUEBEC.

THE dazzling success which had crowned the efforts of Columbus awakened in Europe an eager desire to make fresh discoveries. Henry VII. of England had consented to equip Columbus for his voyage; but the consent was withheld too long, and given only when it was too late. England and France had missed the splendid prize which Columbus had won for Spain. They hastened now to secure what they could. A merchant of Bristol, John Cabot, obtained permission from the king of England to make discoveries in the northern parts of America. Cabot was to bear all expenses, and the king was to receive one-fifth of the gains of the adventure. Taking with him his son Sebastian, John Cabot sailed straight westward across the Atlantic. He reached the American continent, of which he was the undoubted discoverer. The result to him was disappointing. He landed on the coast of Labrador. Being in the same latitude as England, he reasoned that he should find the same genial climate. To his astonishment he came upon a region of intolerable cold, dreary with ice and snow. John Cabot had not heard of the Gulf Stream and its marvellous influences. He did not know that the western shores of northern Europe are rescued from perpetual winter, and warmed up to the enjoyable temperature which they possess, by an enormous river of hot water flowing between banks of cold water eastward from the Gulf of Mexico. The Cabots made many voyages afterwards, and explored the American coast from extreme north to extreme south.

The French turned their attention to the northern parts of the New World. The rich fisheries of Newfoundland attracted them. Jacques Cartier, a famous sea-captain, sailed, on a bright and warm July day, into the gulf which lies between Newfoundland and the mainland. He saw a great river flowing into the gulf, with a width of estuary not less than 100 miles. It was the day of St. Lawrence, and he opened a new prospect of immortality for that saint by giving his name to river and to gulf. He erected a large cross, thirty feet high, on which were imprinted the insignia of France; and thus he took formal possession of the country in the king's name. He sailed for many days up the river between the silent and pathless forests, past great chasms down which there rolled the waters of tributary streams, under the gloomy shadow of huge precipices, past fertile meadow-lands and sheltered islands where the wild vine flourished. The Indians in their canoes swarmed around the ships, giving the strangers welcome, receiving hospitable entertainment of bread and wine. At length they came where a vast rocky promontory, 300 feet in height, stretched far into the river. Here the chief had his home; here, on a site worthy to bear the capital of a great state, arose Quebec; here, in later days, England and France fought for supremacy, and it was decided by the sword that the Anglo-Saxon race was to guide the destinies of the American continent.

Numerous tribes of savages inhabited the Canadian wilderness. They ordinarily lived in villages built of logs, and strongly palisaded to resist the attack of enemies. They were robust and enduring, as the climate required; daring in war, friendly and docile in peace. The torture of an enemy was their highest form of enjoyment; when the victim bore his sufferings bravely the youth of the village ate his heart in order that they might become possessed of his virtues. They had orators, politicians, chiefs skilled to lead in their rude wars. Most of their weapons were of flint. They felled the great pines of their forests with stone axes, supplemented by the use of fire. Their canoes were made of the bark of birch or elm. They wore breastplates of twigs. It was their habit to occupy large houses, in some of which as many as twenty families lived together without any separation. Licentiousness was universal and excessive. Their religion was a series of grovelling superstitions. There was not in any Indian language a word to express the idea of God; their heaven was one vast banqueting-hall where men feasted perpetually.

The origin of the American savage awakened at one time much controversy among the learned. Had there been a plurality of creative acts? Had Europeans at some remote period been driven by the contrary winds across the great sea? If not, where did the red man arise, and by what means did he reach the continent where white men found him? When these questions were debated, it was not known how closely Asia and America approach each other at the extreme north. A narrow strait divides the two continents, and the Asiatic savage of the far north-east crosses it easily. The red men are Asiatics, who, by a short voyage without terrors to them, reached the north-western coast of America, and gradually pushed their way over the continent. The great secret which Columbus revealed to Europe had been for ages known to the Asiatic tribes of the extreme north.

In course of years it became evident that England and France must settle by conflict their claims upon the American continent. So many conflicting grants were made by the monarchs of the respective nations that no lawyer could reconcile them. The region called Nova Scotia was claimed by both British and French, the latter calling it by the name of Acadia.

The opening lines of Longfellow's beautiful poem, "Evangeline," are descriptive of the region of Acadia:

> "This is the forest primeval. The murmuring pines and the hemlocks,
> Bearded with moss, and in garments green, indistinct in the twilight,
> Stand like druids of eld, with voices sad and prophetic,
> Stand like harpers hoar, with beards that rest on their bosoms.
> Loud from its rocky caverns, the deep-voiced neighboring ocean
> Speaks, and in accents disconsolate answers the wail of the forest.
> . . . .
> In the Acadian land, on the shores of the Basin of Minas,
> Distant, secluded, still, the little village of Grand-Pré
> Lay in the fruitful valley. Vast meadows stretched to the eastward,
> Giving the village its name, and pasture to flocks without number.
> Dikes, that the hands of the farmers had raised with labor incessant,
> Shut out the turbulent tides; but at stated seasons the floodgates
> Opened, and welcomed the sea to wander at will over the meadows.

West and south there were fields of flax, and orchards and cornfields
Spreading afar and unfenced o'er the plain ; and away to the northward
Blomidon rose, and the forests old, and aloft on the mountains
Sea-fogs pitched their tents, and mists from the mighty Atlantic
Looked on the happy valley, but ne'er from their station descended."

At the beginning of the war success was mainly with the French. The English were without competent leadership. An experienced and skilled officer—the Marquis de Montcalm—commanded the French, and gained important advantage over his adversaries. He took Fort William Henry, and his allies massacred the garrison. He took and destroyed two English forts on Lake Ontario. He made for himself at Ticonderoga a position which barred the English from access to the western lakes. The war had lasted for nearly three years ; and Canada not merely kept her own, but, with greatly inferior resources, was able to hold her powerful enemy on the defensive.

DEATH OF MONTCALM.

But now the impatient English shook off the imbecile government under which this shame had been incurred, and the strong hand of William Pitt assumed direction of the war. He found among his older officers no man to whom he could intrust the momentous task. Casting aside the routine which has brought ruin upon so many fair enterprises, he promoted to the chief command a young soldier of feeble health, gentle, sensitive, modest, in whom his unerring perception discovered the qualities he required. That young soldier was James Wolfe, who had already in subordinate command evinced courage and high military genius. To him Pitt intrusted the forces whose arms were now to fix the destiny of a continent.

While Wolfe lay on a sick-bed, a council of war was called, and Colonel Townshend proposed the skilfully audacious plan which was adopted by all. Above Quebec, a narrow path had been discovered winding up the precipitous cliff, 300 feet high ; this was to be secretly ascended, and the Heights of Abraham gained, which overlook the city. Part of the British fleet, containing that portion of the army which had occupied the northern shore, sailed past Quebec to Cap-Rouge. The rest of the troops marched up the south shore till they arrived opposite the men-of-war. Here embarking in flat-bottom boats, they dropped down the river the same night to Wolfe's cove, and almost unopposed, division after division scaled the Heights. When morning dawned, Wolfe's whole disposable force, in number 4,828, with one small gun, was ranged in battle-array upon the Plains of Abraham.

The Heights of Abraham stretch westward for three miles from the defences of the upper town, and form a portion of a lofty table-land which extends to a distance from the city of nine miles. They are from two to three hundred feet above the level of the river. Their river-side is well-nigh perpendicular and wholly inaccessible, save where a narrow footpath leads to the summit. It was by this path—on which two men could not walk abreast—that Wolfe intended to approach the enemy. The French had a few men guarding the upper end of the path; but the guard was a weak one, for they apprehended no attack here. Scarcely ever before had an army advanced to battle by a track so difficult.

The troops were all received on board the ships, which sailed for a few miles up stream. During the night the men re-embarked in a flotilla of boats and dropped down with the receding tide. They were instructed to be silent. No sound of oar was heard, or of voice, excepting that of Wolfe, who in a low tone repeated to his officers the touching, and in his own case prophetic, verses of Gray's "Elegy in a Country Churchyard." Quickly the landing-place was reached, and the men stepped silently on shore. One by one they climbed the narrow woodland path. As they neared the summit, the guard, in panic, fired their muskets down the cliff and fled. The ships had now dropped down the river, and the boats plied incessantly between them and the landing-place. All night long the landing proceeded. The first rays of the morning sun shone upon an army of nearly five thousand veteran British soldiers solidly arrayed upon the Heights of Abraham, eager for battle and confident of victory. Wolfe marched them forward till his front was within a mile of the city, and there he waited the attack of the French.

Montcalm had been wholly deceived as to the purposes of the British, and was unprepared for their unwelcome appearance on the Heights. He had always shunned battle; for the larger portion of his troops were Canadian militia, on whom little reliance could be placed. He held them, therefore, within his intrenchments, and trusted that the approaching winter would drive away his assailants and save Canada. Even now he might have sheltered himself behind his defences, and delayed the impending catastrophe. But his store of provisions and of ammunition approached exhaustion, and as the English ships rode unopposed in the river, he had no ray of hope from without. Montcalm elected that the great controversy should be decided by battle.

13

He marched out to the attack with 7,500 men, of whom less than one-half were regular soldiers, besides a swarm of Indians, almost worthless for fighting such as this. The French advanced firing, and inflicted considerable loss upon their enemy. The British stood immovable, unless when they silently closed the ghastly openings which the bullets of the French created. At length the hostile lines fronted each other at a distance of forty yards, and Wolfe gave the command to fire. From the levelled muskets of the British lines there burst a well-aimed and deadly volley. That fatal discharge gained the battle, gained the city of Quebec, gained dominion of a continent. The Canadian militia broke and fled. Montcalm's heroic presence held for a moment the soldiers to their duty; but the British, flushed with victory, swept forward on the broken and fainting enemy. Montcalm fell, pierced by a mortal wound; the French army in hopeless rout sought shelter within the ramparts of Quebec.

Both generals fell. Wolfe was thrice struck by bullets, and died upon the field, with his latest breath giving God thanks for this crowning success. Montcalm died on the following day, pleased that his eyes were not to witness the surrender of Quebec. The battle lasted only for a few minutes; and having in view the vast issues which depended on it, the loss was inconsiderable. Only fifty-five British were killed and 600 wounded; the loss of the French was twofold that of their enemies.

From this time Canada remained in the hands of the English. When the American colonists revolted they desired the Canadians to act with them, and assist them in their efforts against the British government. This the Canadians declined to do, and the Americans invaded their territory, but were, however, repulsed. During the course of the peaceful years which followed, Canada increased steadily.

In 1812, Canada was again involved in war, and subjected to the miseries of invasion.

Many Americans clung to the belief that the Canadians were dissatisfied with their government, and would be found ready to avail themselves of an opportunity to adopt republican institutions. But no trace of any such disposition manifested itself. The colonists were tenaciously loyal, and were no more moved by the blandishments than they were by the arms of their republican invaders.

Soon after the declaration of war an American army of 2,500 men set out to conquer western Canada. The commander of this force was General Hull, who announced to the Canadians that he had come to bring them "peace, liberty, and security," and was able to overbear with ease any resistance which it was in their power to offer. But victory did not attach herself to the standards of General Hull. The English commander, General Brock, was able to hold the Americans in check, and to furnish General Hull with reasons for withdrawing his troops from Canada and taking up position at Detroit. Thither he was quickly followed by the daring Englishman, leading a force of 700 soldiers and militia and 600 Indians. He was proceeding to attack General Hull, but that irresolute warrior averted the danger by an ignominious capitulation.

A little later a second invasion was attempted, the aim of which was to possess Queenstown. It was equally unsuccessful, and reached a similar termination—the surrender of the invading force. Still further, an attempt to seize Montreal resulted in failure. Thus closed the first campaign of this lamentable war. Everywhere the American invaders had been foiled by greatly inferior forces of militia, supported by a handful of regular troops. The war had been always distasteful to a large portion of the American people. On the day when the tidings of its declaration were received in Boston, flags were hung out half-mast high in token of general mourning. The New England States refused to contribute troops to fight in a cause which they condemned. The shameful defeats which had been sustained in Canada encouraged the friends of peace, and the policy of invasion was loudly denounced as unwise and unjust.

The close of the war was equally disastrous to the invaders. Since then peace has reigned in Canada; and it is with pleasure we note the friendly feeling that is constantly growing between the great Republic and the great Dominion.

There still remain in the various provinces of the Dominion about 90,000 Indians to represent the races who possessed the continent when the white man found it. Canada has dealt in perfect fairness with her Indians; and the Indians have requited with constant loyalty the government which has treated them with justice. A rebellion was indeed raised by the French half-breed population, upon the Dominion of Canada desiring to add to its possessions the vast domain of the Hudson Bay Company.

Their leader in the rebellion by which they hoped to throw off the authority of Canada and Great Britain, and establish themselves as an independent nation, was Louis Riel, an ambitious but reckless young French Canadian. Riel became president of the new republic, and gathered an armed force of 600 men to uphold the national dignity. He turned back at the frontier the newly appointed governor; he seized Fort Garry, in which were ample stores of arms and provisions; he imprisoned all who offered active opposition to his rule. The distant Canadian government looked on at first as amused with this diminutive rebellion. They did not think of employing force to restore order; they sought the desired end by persuasion.

A party of loyal inhabitants made a hasty and ill-prepared rising against the authority of the provisional government. They were easily beaten back by the superior forces under Riel's command, and some of them were taken prisoners. Among these was a Canadian named Scott, who had distinguished himself by his obstinate hostility to the rule of the usurpers. Riel determined to overawe his enemies and compel the adherence of his friends by an act of most conspicuous and unpardonable severity. Poor Scott was subjected to the trial of a mock tribunal, whose judgment sent him to death. An hour later he was led forth beyond the gate of the fort. Kneeling, with bandaged eyes, among the snow, he was shot by a firing-party of intoxicated half-breeds almost before he had time to realize the cruel fate which had befallen him.

This shameful murder invested the Red River rebellion with a gravity of aspect which it had not hitherto worn. There then arose in Canada a vehement demand that the criminals should be punished and the royal authority restored. The despatch of a military force sufficiently strong to overbear the resistance of the insurgent Frenchmen was at once resolved upon.

THE THOUSAND ISLANDS.

Happily there was at that time in Canada an officer endowed with rare power in the department of military organization. To this officer, now well known as Sir Garnet Wolseley, was intrusted the task of preparing and commanding the expedition. No laurels were gained by the forces which Colonel Wolseley led out into the wilderness; for the enemy did not abide their coming, and their modest achievements were unnoticed amid the absorbing interest with which men watched the tremendous occurrences of the war then raging between Germany and France. Nevertheless, the Red River expedition claims an eminent place in the record of military transactions. It is probably the solitary example of an army advancing by a lengthened and almost impracticable route, accomplishing its task, and returning home without the loss of a single life either in battle or by disease. And the wise forethought which provided so effectively for all the exigencies of that unknown journey is more admirable than the generalship which has sufficed to gain bloody victories in many recent wars.

Under the constitution of Canada executive power is vested in the queen and administered by her representative, the governor general. This officer is aided and advised by a Privy Council, composed of the heads of the various great departments of state. The Senate is composed of seventy-eight members appointed by the Crown, and holding office for life. The House of Commons consists of 206 members. These are chosen by the votes of citizens possessing a property qualification, the amount of which varies in the different provinces. Canada gives the franchise to those persons in towns who pay a yearly rent of six pounds, and to those not in towns who pay four pounds; New Brunswick demands the possession of real estate valued at twenty pounds, or an annual income of eighty pounds; and Nova Scotia is almost identical in her requirements. The duration of Parliament is limited to five years, and its members receive payment. The Parliament of the Dominion regulates the interests which are common to all the provinces; each province has a lieutenant-governor and a legislature for the guidance of its own local affairs. Entire freedom of trade exists between the provinces which compose the Canadian nation.

Canada is, in respect of extent, the noblest colonial possession over which any nation has ever exercised dominion. It covers an area of 3,330,000 square miles. Europe is larger by only half a million square miles; the United States is smaller to nearly the same extent. The distances with which men have to deal in Canada are enormous. From Ottawa to Winnipeg is 1,400 miles—a journey equal to that which separates Paris from Constantinople. The adventurous traveller, who would push his way from Winnipeg to the extreme north-west, has a farther distance of 2,000 miles to traverse. The representatives of Vancouver island must travel 2,500 miles in order to reach the seat of government. The journey from London to the Ural mountains is not greater in distance, and is not by any means so difficult. From Halifax, the capital of Nova Scotia, to New Westminster, the capital of British Columbia, there is a distance of 4,000 miles.

The occupation of about one-half of the Canadian people is agriculture. In the old provinces there are nearly 500,000 persons who occupy agricultural lands. Of these, nine-tenths own the soil which they till; only one-tenth pay rent for their lands, and they do so for the most part only until they have gained enough to become purchasers. The agricultural laborer—a class so numerous and so little to be envied in England—is almost unknown in Canada. No more than 2,000 persons occupy this position, which is to them merely a step in the progress toward speedy ownership. Land is easily acquired; for the government, recognizing that the grand need of Canada is population, offers land to every man who will occupy and cultivate, or sells at prices which are little more than nominal. The old provinces are filling up steadily if not with rapidity. During the ten years from 1851 to 1861 the land under cultivation had become greater by about one-half. During the following decade the increase was in the same proportion. Schools of agriculture and model farms have been established by government, and the rude methods by which cultivation was formerly carried on have experienced vast ameliorations. Agriculture has become less wasteful and more productive. Much attention is given to the products of the dairy. Much care has been successfully bestowed upon the improvement of horses and cattle. The manufacture and use of agricultural implements has largely increased. The short Canadian summer lays upon the farmer the pressing necessity of swift

SCENE ON THE EASTERN COAST OF CANADA.

harvesting, and renders the help of machinery specially valuable. In the St. Lawrence valley the growing of fruit is assiduously prosecuted; and the apples, pears, plums, peaches, and grapes of that region enjoy high reputation. Success almost invariably rewards the industrious Canadian farmer. The rich fields, the well-fed cattle, the comfortable farm-houses, all tell of prosperity and contentment.

The fisheries of the Dominion form one of its valuable industries. The eastern coasts are resorted to by myriads of fishes, most prominent among which is the cod-fish, whose preference for low temperatures restrains its farther progress southward. Sixty thousand men and 25,000 boats find profitable occupation in reaping this abundant harvest. A minister of fisheries watches over this great industry. Seven national institutions devote themselves to the culture of fish, especially of the salmon, and prosecute experiments in regard to the introduction of new varieties.

Besides the outlays incurred in carrying on the ordinary business of government, large sums, raised by loan, are annually expended on public works. Navigation on the great rivers of Canada is interrupted by numerous rapids and falls. Unless these obstructions be overcome, the magnificent water-way with which Canada is endowed will be of imperfect usefulness. At many points on the rivers and lakes canals have been constructed. The formidable impediment which the great Fall of Niagara offers to navigation is surmounted by the Welland canal, twenty-seven miles in length, and on which, with its branches, two and a half million sterling have been expended. Much care is bestowed, too, upon the deepening of rivers, and the removal of rocks and other obstructions to navigation. The vast distances of Canada render railways indispensable to her development. The Canadian government and people have duly appreciated this necessity. They have already constructed 7,000 miles of railway, and are proceeding rapidly with farther extension.

Between the Rocky mountains and the Pacific there lies a vast tract of fertile land, possessing an area equal to six times that of England and Wales. This is British Columbia—the latest-born member of the confederation, which it entered only in 1871. The waters of the Pacific exert upon its climate the same softening influence which is carried by the Gulf Stream to corresponding latitudes in Europe, and the average temperature of Columbia does not differ materially from that of England. Gold is found in the sands of the rivers which flow down from the Rocky mountains; coal in abundance lies near the surface; large tracts are covered with pine-forests whose trees attain unusual size; many islands stud the placid waters which wash the western shores of the province; many navigable inlets sweep far into the interior—deep into forests, for the transport of whose timber they provide ample convenience. In the streams and on the coasts there is an extraordinary abundance of fish; on the banks of the Fraser river the English miner and the Indian fisherman may be seen side by side pursuing their avocations with success. The wealth of Columbia secures for her a prosperous future; but as yet her development has only begun. Her population is about 12,000, besides 30,000 Indians. Her great pine-forests have yet scarcely heard the sound of the axe; her rich valleys lie untilled; her coal and iron wait the coming of the strong arms which are to draw forth their treasures; even her tempting gold-fields are cultivated but slightly. Columbia must become the home of a numerous and thriving population, but in the meantime her progress is delayed by her remoteness and her inaccessibility.

THE CAPITOL AT WASHINGTON.

THE UNITED STATES.

"Lord of the Universe! shield us and guide us,
　Trusting Thee always, through shadow and sun:
　Thou hast united us, who shall divide us?
　　Keep us, O keep us, the Many in One!
　　　Up with our banner bright,
　　　Sprinkled with starry light,
　Spread its fair emblems from mountain to shore;
　　　While through the sounding sky,
　　　Loud rings the nation's cry,—
Union and Liberty!—one evermore!"—*O. W. Holmes.*

EIGHTY years had passed since the discoveries by the Cabots before Englishmen made any serious effort to establish homes in North America. Under a patent from Queen Elizabeth in 1585, Sir Walter Raleigh sent 108 colonists to occupy Virginia, which had been so named by Elizabeth in honor of her own state as a maiden queen. This attempted settlement ended in total failure, a result brought about by the hardships of the wilderness and massacre by Indians.

Another attempt at colonization was made, and in course of time a permanent settlement was formed.

The most enterprising and useful man among the settlers was Captain John Smith. He was a man of great strength—bold, active, judicious, and enterprising; and by his exertions alone the colony was often saved from famine, and prevented from being destroyed by the Indians.

When the welfare of the colony was in some measure secured, Smith set forth with a few companions to explore the interior of the country. He and his followers were captured by the Indians, and the followers were summarily butchered. Smith's composure did not fail him in the worst extremity. He produced his pocket-compass, and interested the savages by explaining its properties. He wrote a letter in their sight—to their infinite wonder. They spared him, and made a show of him in all the settlements round about. He was to them an unfathomable mystery. He was plainly superhuman. Whether his power would bring to them good or evil, they were not able to determine. After much hesitation they chose the course which prudence seemed to counsel. They resolved to extinguish powers so formidable, regarding whose use they could obtain no guarantee. Smith was bound and stretched upon the earth, his head resting upon a great stone. The mighty club was uplifted to dash out his brains. But Smith was a man who won golden opinions of all. The Indian chief had a daughter, Pocahontas, a child of ten or twelve years. She could not bear to see the pleasing Englishman destroyed. As Smith lay waiting the fatal stroke, she caught him in her arms and interposed herself between him and the club. Her intercession prevailed, and Smith was set free.

From lands originally belonging to Virginia a new colony had been formed, with a more liberal constitution both as to civil and religious rights. George Calvert, the first Lord Baltimore, obtained from Charles I., in 1629, a grant of lands north of the Potomac, where all persons, but especially Catholics, might enjoy freedom of worship. The country was called Maryland in honor of the queen, Henrietta Maria.

Great religious differences now existed in England. Many hundreds of Puritans, finding that there was no toleration for their views in England, separated themselves from the church, and as many as were able sought an asylum in Holland.

Eleven quiet and not unprosperous years were spent in Holland. The pilgrims worked with patient industry at their various handicrafts. They quickly gained the reputation of doing honestly and effectively whatever they professed to do, and thus they found abundant employment. Mr. Brewster established a printing-press, and printed books about liberty, which, as he had the satisfaction of knowing, greatly enraged the foolish King James. The little colony received additions from time to time as oppression in England became more intolerable.

The instinct of separation was strong within the pilgrim heart. They could not bear the thought that their little colony was to mingle with the Dutchmen and lose its independent existence. But already their sons and daughters were forming alliances which threatened this result. The fathers considered long and anxiously how the danger was to be averted. They determined again to go on pilgrimage. They would seek a home beyond the Atlantic, where they could dwell apart and found a state in which they should be free to think.

The Mayflower, in which the pilgrims made their voyage, was a ship of 160

PLYMOUTH ROCK.

tons. The weather proved stormy and cold; the voyage unexpectedly long. It was early in September when they sailed; it was not till the 11th of November that the Mayflower dropped her anchor in the waters of Cape Cod bay.

It was a bleak-looking and discouraging coast which lay before them. Nothing met the eye but low sand-hills, covered with ill-grown wood down to the margin of the sea. The pilgrims had now to choose a place for their settlement. About this they hesitated so long that the captain threatened to put them all on shore and leave them. Little expeditions were sent to explore. At first no suitable locality could be found. The men had great hardships to endure. The cold was so excessive that the spray froze upon their clothes, and they resembled men cased in armor. At length a spot was fixed upon. The soil appeared to be good, and abounded in "delicate springs" of water. On the 23d of December, the pilgrims landed, stepping ashore upon a huge bowlder of granite which is still reverently preserved by their descendants. Here they resolved to found their settlement, which they agreed to call New Plymouth.

Twenty-three years after the landing of the pilgrims the population of New

AN INDIAN ATTACK.

England had grown to 24,000. Forty-nine little wooden towns, with their wooden churches, wooden forts, and wooden ramparts, were dotted here and there over the land. There were four separate colonies, which hitherto had maintained separate governments. They were Plymouth, Massachusetts, Connecticut, and New Haven. There appeared at first a disposition in the pilgrim mind to scatter widely, and remain apart in small self-governing communities. For some years every little band which pushed deeper into the wilderness settled itself into an independent state, having no political relations with its neighbors. But this isolation could not continue. The wilderness had other inhabitants, whose presence was a standing menace. Within "striking distance" there were Indians enough to trample out the solitary little English communities. On their frontiers were Frenchmen and Dutchmen—natural enemies, as all men in that time were, to each other. For mutual defence and encouragement, the four colonies joined themselves into the United Colonies of New England. This was the first confederation in a land where confederations of unprecedented magnitude were hereafter to be established.

During the first forty years of its existence the great city which we call New York was a Dutch settlement, known among men as New Amsterdam. That region had been discovered for the Dutch East India Company by Henry Hudson, who was still in search, as Columbus had been, of a shorter route to the East. The Dutch have never displayed any aptitude for colonizing; but they were unsurpassed in mercantile discernment, and they set up trading-stations with much judgment. Three or four years after the pilgrims landed at Plymouth the Dutch West India Company determined to enter into trading relations with the Indians along the line of the Hudson river. They sent out a few families, who planted themselves at the southern extremity of Manhattan island. The whole country in their possession they called New Netherlands.

The Dutch retained possession of New Netherlands until the year 1664, a period of about fifty years, when an English fleet arrived and demanded the surrender of the country. The Dutch governor at that time was Peter Stuyvesant. He did all in his power to induce his people to take up arms and resist the English, and it was not until two days after the magistrates of New Amsterdam had agreed to the surrender that he reluctantly yielded it. During the next year a Dutch fleet arrived and reconquered the country; but in the succeeding year it was restored to the English, who held it until the American Revolution.

The name of William Penn will ever be associated with all that is interesting in the early history of Pennsylvania. This man was the only son of Admiral Penn, who long served his country with ability and honorable reputation as an officer in the English navy. At an early age the son was sent to the University of Oxford, but becoming imbued with the principles of a religious sect called Quakers, or Friends, he was fined for boldly avowing their sentiments, and afterwards expelled from the university, at the age of sixteen.

As the English government was indebted to his father, he applied for and obtained a grant of territory in America, in payment of the debt. In honor of Penn's father, the territory thus granted was named Pennsylvania. In the year 1681, Penn sent out several ships with emigrants, mostly Quakers, and he gave instructions to his agent that he should govern the little colony in harmony with law and religion—that he should gain the good will of the natives—and that if a city should be commenced as the capital of the province, it should not be like the crowded towns of the old world, but should be laid out with a garden around each house, so as to form "a green country-town."

Penn dealt justly and kindly with the Indians, and they requited him with a reverential love such as they evinced to no other Englishman. The neighboring colonies waged bloody wars with the Indians who lived around them—now inflicting defeats which were almost exterminating—now sustaining hideous massacres. Penn's Indians were his children and most loyal subjects.

PENN'S TREATY WITH THE INDIANS.

No drop of Quaker blood was ever shed by Indian hand in the Pennsylvania territory. Soon after Penn's arrival he invited the chief men of the Indian tribes to a conference. The meeting took place beneath a huge elm tree. The pathless forest has long given way to the houses and streets of Philadelphia, but a marble monument points out to strangers the scene of this memorable interview. Penn, with a few companions, unarmed, and dressed according to the simple fashion of their sect, met the crowd of formidable savages. They met, he assured them, as brothers "on the broad pathway of good faith and good will." No advantage was to be taken on either side. All was to be "openness and love;" and Penn meant what he said. Strong in the power of truth and kindness, he bent the fierce savages of the Delaware to his will. They vowed "to live in love with William Penn and his children as long as the moon and the sun shall endure." They kept their vow. Long years after, they were known to recount to strangers, with deep emotion, the words which Penn had spoken to them under the old elm tree of Shakamaxon.

The fame of Penn's settlement went abroad in all lands. Men wearied with the vulgar tyranny of kings heard gladly that the reign of freedom and tranquillity was established on the banks of the Delaware. An asylum was opened "for the good and oppressed of every nation." Of these there was no lack. Pennsylvania had nothing to attract such "dissolute persons" as had laid the foundations of Virginia. But grave and God-fearing men from all the Protestant countries sought a home where they might live as conscience taught them. The new colony grew apace. Its natural advantages were tempting. Penn reported it as "a good land, with plentiful springs, the air clear and fresh, and an innumerable quantity of wild-fowl and fish—what Abraham, Isaac, and Jacob would be well contented with." During the first year twenty-two vessels arrived, bringing 2,000 persons. In three years Philadelphia was a town of 600 houses. It was half a century from its foundation before New York attained equal dimensions.

When Penn, after a few years, revisited England, he was able truly to relate that "things went on sweetly with friends in Pennsylvania; that they increased finely in outward things and in wisdom."

The thirteen States which composed the original Union were Virginia, Massachusetts, Connecticut, Rhode Island, New Hampshire, Delaware, Maryland, Pennsylvania, New York, New Jersey, North Carolina, South Carolina, and Georgia.

Of these the latest born was Georgia. Only fifty years had passed since Penn established the Quaker State on the banks of the Delaware. But changes greater than centuries have sometimes wrought had taken place. The Revolution had vindicated the liberties of the British people. The tyrant house of Stuart had been cast out, and with its fall the era of despotic government had closed. The real governing power was no longer the king, but the Parliament.

Among the members of Parliament during the rule of Sir Robert Walpole was one almost unknown to us now, but deserving of honor beyond most men of his time. His name was James Oglethorpe. He was a soldier, and had fought against the Turks and in the great Marlborough wars against Louis XIV. In advanced life he became the friend of Samuel Johnson. Dr.

Johnson urged him to write some account of his adventures. "I know no one," he said, "whose life would be more interesting; if I were furnished with materials I should be very glad to write it." Edmund Burke considered him "a more extraordinary person than any he had ever read of." John Wesley "blessed God that ever he was born." Oglethorpe attained the great age of ninety-six, and died in the year 1785. The year before his death he attended the sale of Dr. Johnson's books, and was there met by Samuel Rogers, the poet. "Even then," says Rogers, "he was the finest figure of a man you ever saw; but very, very old—the flesh of his face like parchment."

This kind-hearted man, observing that there were great numbers of poor people in England, who could with difficulty obtain a living there and were often imprisoned for debts which they could not pay, conceived the project of improving their condition by transporting them to America, and giving them the lands on which they should settle.

Without difficulty Oglethorpe found associates to unite with him in his benevolent enterprise, and in the year 1732 the King of England gave them a grant of the country between the rivers Altamaha and Savannah, which they were to hold, not for their own benefit, but, as was expressed in the charter, "in trust for the poor."

In November of the same year Oglethorpe sailed with 120 emigrants, mainly selected from the prisons—penniless, but of good repute. He surveyed the coast of Georgia, and chose a site for the capital of his new State. He pitched his tent where Savannah now stands, and at once proceeded to mark out the lines of streets and squares.

Next year the colony was joined by about a hundred German Protestants, who were then under persecution for their beliefs. The colonists received this addition to their numbers with joy. A place of residence had been chosen for them which the devout and thankful strangers named Ebenezer. They were charmed with their new abode. The rivers and the hills, they said, reminded them of home. They applied themselves with steady industry to the cultivation of indigo and silk; and they prospered.

The fame of Oglethorpe's enterprise spread over Europe. All struggling men, against whom the battle of life went hard, looked to Georgia as a land of promise. They were the men who most urgently required to emigrate; but they were not always the men best fitted to conquer the difficulties of the immigrant's life. The progress of the colony was slow. The poor persons of whom it was originally composed were honest but ineffective, and could not in Georgia more than in England find out the way to become self-supporting. Encouragements were given which drew from Germany, from Switzerland, and from the Highlands of Scotland, men of firmer texture of mind—better fitted to subdue the wilderness and bring forth its treasures.

THE AMERICAN REVOLUTION.

Up to the year 1764 the Americans cherished a deep reverence and affection for the mother country. They were proud of her great place among the nations. They gloried in the splendor of her military achievements; they copied her manners and her fashions. She was in all things their model. They always spoke of England as "home." To be an Old England man was to be a person of rank and importance among them. They yielded a loving obedience to her laws. They were governed, as Benjamin Franklin stated it, at the expense of a little pen and ink. When money was asked from their assemblies, it was given without grudge. "They were led by a thread"— such was their love for the land which gave them birth.

Ten or twelve years came and went. A marvellous change has passed upon the temper of the American people. They have bound themselves by great oaths to use no article of English manufacture—to engage in no transaction which can put a shilling into any English pocket. They have formed "the inconvenient habit of carting"—that is, of tarring and feathering and dragging through the streets such persons as avow friendship for the English government. They burn the acts of the English Parliament by the hands of the common hangman. They slay the king's soldiers. They refuse every amicable proposal. They cast from them forever the king's authority. They hand down a dislike to the English name, of which some traces lingered among them for generations.

By what unhallowed magic has this change been wrought so swiftly? By what process, in so few years, have 3,000,000 people been taught to abhor the country they so loved?

The ignorance and folly of the English government wrought this evil.

For many years England had governed her American colonies harshly, and in a spirit of undisguised selfishness. America was ruled, not for her own good, but for the good of English commerce. She was not allowed to export her products except to England. No foreign ship might enter her ports. Woollen goods were not allowed to be sent from one colony to another. At one time the manufacture of hats was forbidden. In a liberal mood Parliament removed that prohibition, but decreed that no maker of hats should employ any negro workman, or any larger number of apprentices than two. Iron-works were forbidden. Up to the latest hour of English rule the Bible was not allowed to be printed in America.

In 1765, the famous "Stamp Act" was made a law. All legal documents were to bear a government stamp, costing from three-pence to thirty dollars, according to the importance of the transaction. Every newspaper and pamphlet must be stamped, and every advertisement must pay a tax. The Americans remonstrated.

Benjamin Franklin told the House of Commons that America would never submit to the Stamp Act, and that no power on earth could enforce it. The Americans made it impossible for government to mistake their sentiments. Riots, which swelled from day to day into dimensions more "enormous and alarming," burst forth in the New England States. Everywhere the stamp distributors were compelled to resign their offices. One unfortunate man was led forth to Boston Common, and made to sign his resignation in presence of a vast crowd. Another, in desperate health, was visited in his sick-room and obliged to pledge that if he lived he would resign. A universal resolution was come to that no English goods would be imported till the Stamp Act was repealed. The colonists would "eat nothing, drink nothing, wear nothing that comes from England" while this great injustice endured. The act was to come into force on the 1st of November. That day the bells rung out funereal peals, and the colonists wore the aspect of men on whom some heavy calamity had fallen. But the act never came into force. Not one of Lord Grenville's stamps was ever bought or sold in America. Some of the stamped paper was burnt by the mob; the rest was hidden away to save it from the same fate. Without stamps, marriages were null; mercantile transactions ceased to be binding; suits at law were impossible. Nevertheless, the business of human life went on. Men married; they bought, they sold; they went to law—illegally, because without stamps. But no harm came of it.

England heard with amazement that America refused to obey the law. There were some who demanded that the Stamp Act should be enforced by the sword. But it greatly moved the English merchants that America should cease to import their goods. William Pitt—not yet Earl of Chatham—denounced the act, and said he was glad America had resisted. Pitt and the merchants triumphed, and the act was repealed.

The repeal of the Stamp Act delayed only for a little the fast-coming crisis. A new ministry was formed, with the Earl of Chatham at its head. But soon the great earl lay sick and helpless, and the burden of government rested on incapable shoulders. Charles Townshend, a clever, captivating, but most indiscreet man, became the virtual prime minister. The feeling in the public mind had now become more unfavorable to America. Townshend proposed to levy a variety of taxes from the Americans. The most famous of his taxes was one of three-pence per pound on tea. All his proposals became law. Several ships were freighted with tea, and sent out to America.

Cheaper tea was never seen in America; but it bore upon it the abhorred tax which asserted British control over the property of Americans. Will the Americans, long bereaved of the accustomed beverage, yield to the temptation, and barter their honor for cheap tea? The East India Company never doubted it; but the company knew nothing of the temper of the American people. The ships arrived at New York and Philadelphia. These cities stood firm. The ships were promptly sent home—their hatches unopened—and duly bore their rejected cargoes back to the Thames.

When the ships destined for Boston showed their tall masts in the bay, the citizens ran together to hold council. It was Sabbath, and the men of Boston were strict. But here was an exigency, in presence of which all ordinary rules are suspended. The crisis has come at length. If that tea is landed it will be sold, it will be used, and American liberty will become a by-word upon the earth.

Samuel Adams was the true king in Boston at that time. He was a man in middle life, of cultivated mind and stainless reputation—a powerful speaker and writer—a man in whose sagacity and moderation all men trusted. He resembled the old Puritans in his stern love of liberty, his reverence for the Sabbath, his sincere, if somewhat formal, observance of all religious ordinances. He was among the first to see that there was no resting-place in this struggle short of independence. "We are free," he said, "and want no king." The men of Boston felt the power of his resolute spirit, and manfully followed where Samuel Adams led.

It was hoped that the agents of the East India Company would have consented to send the ships home; but the agents refused. Several days of excitement and ineffectual negotiation ensued. People flocked in from the neighboring towns. The time was spent mainly in public meetings; the city resounded with impassioned discourse. But meanwhile the ships lay peacefully at their moorings, and the tide of patriot talk seemed to flow in vain. Other measures were visibly necessary. One day a meeting was held, and the excited people continued in hot debate till the shades of evening fell. No progress was made. At length Samuel Adams stood up in the dimly lighted church, and announced, "This meeting can do nothing more to save the country." With a stern shout the meeting broke up. Fifty men disguised as Indians hurried down to the wharf, each man with a hatchet in his hand. The crowd followed. The ships were boarded; the chests of tea were brought on deck, broken open and flung into the bay. The approving citizens looked on in silence. It was felt by all that the step was grave and eventful in the highest degree. So still was the crowd that no sound was heard but the stroke of the hatchet and the splash of the shattered chests as they fell into the sea. All questions about the disposal of those cargoes of tea, at all events, are now solved.

This is what America has done; it is for England to make the next move. Lord North was now at the head of the British government. It was his lordship's belief that the troubles in America sprung from a small number of ambitious persons, and could easily, by proper firmness, be suppressed. "The Americans will be lions while we are lambs," said General Gage. The king believed this, and Lord North believed it. In this deep ignorance he proceeded to deal with the great emergency. He closed Boston as a port for the landing and shipping of goods. He imposed a fine to indemnify the East India Company for their lost teas. He withdrew the charter of Massachusetts. He authorized the governor to send political offenders to England for trial. Great voices were raised against these severities. Lord Chatham, old in constitution now, if not in years, and near the close of his career, pleaded for measures of conciliation. Edmund Burke justified the resistance of the Americans. Their opposition was fruitless. All Lord North's measures of repression became law; and General Gage, with an additional force of soldiers, was sent to Boston to carry them into effect.

In September, 1774, the first Continental Congress met at Philadelphia. Fifty-three of the best and ablest men in the country were there; men deeply versed in English law, and who knew well that king and Parliament were violating the constitution which they were sworn to maintain. Awed by a feeling of the tremendous results which depended upon their conduct, a long and deep silence fell on all the members of the assembly. It was broken by Patrick Henry, of Virginia—the greatest orator of his day, and perhaps the greatest that America has yet produced —who recited the wrongs of the colonies with magnificent eloquence, and yet with strict adherence to the truth. Patrick Henry was born in the year 1736, and died in 1799.

He was a man of limited education and in early years displayed few indications of his future greatness. He was exceedingly fond of fishing and hunting, and of social pleasures, all of which were allowed to interfere with his duties. He married at eighteen, failed twice in business, once in an attempt at farming, and finally, when twenty-four years of age, entered the profession of law after six weeks' study of the subject.

Henry was a man of high moral courage, and the instinctive champion of the wronged and the oppressed. The opening scenes of the Revolution fired his patriotic soul; evidently the time and purpose for which he had been born had arrived. His speech before the Virginia House of Burgesses electrified the country, and gained him the reputation, at the age of twenty-nine, of being "the greatest orator and political thinker of a land abounding with public speakers and statesmen." From this time forth he was prominent in the political conventions and congresses of the colonies, and, in 1776, he was elected the first republican governor of the State of Virginia. He held this office until 1779, when, being no longer eligible, he returned to the legislature. At the close of the war he was again chosen governor, and served until 1786, when he resigned. In 1794, he retired from the law, and removed to his estate. After this he declined several honorable positions in public life, but was finally persuaded by Washington and others to become a candidate for the Virginia

LEXINGTON.

senate, in 1799, in order to oppose certain measures there. He was easily elected, but death interposed before he could take his seat.

The colonists endeavored by every peaceable means in their power to have their wrongs redressed; but as Britain showed no signs of relenting in her treatment of them, they then settled down to the conviction that they must either fight for their liberty, or forego it. They at once prepared themselves for the contest.

General Gage had learned that considerable stores of ammunition were collected at the village of Concord, eighteen miles from Boston. He would seize them in the king's name. Late one April night 800 soldiers set out on this errand. In the early morning they reached Lexington where a body of militia awaited them. The patriot volunteers were ordered to disperse, there being only about seventy of them altogether. Firing ensued, by whom first is not known; but eighteen of the seventy lay dead or wounded on the village green, whilst the rest fled. The British pushed on to Concord, and destroyed all the military stores they could find. Their march homeward was mainly on a road cut through dense woods. The people of the surrounding country had been gathering in the meanwhile, and now hung upon their flanks and rear. From the woods throughout the whole line of that return march came shot thick and heavy. It was sunset ere the soldiers, half dead with fatigue, got home to Boston. This fatal expedition had cost them nearly three hundred men. The blood shed at Lexington had been swiftly and deeply avenged.

The battle of Bunker Hill followed soon after. Two thousand British soldiers charged up the hill against the American intrenchments, which they carried, after having been twice repulsed, but with a loss of nearly eleven hundred men, whilst the American loss was less than five hundred.

The time was now ripe for the consideration by Congress of the great question of independence. It was a grave and most eventful step, but it could no longer be shunned. On the 7th of June, 1776, a resolution was introduced declaring "That the United Colonies are and ought to be free and independent;" and on the 4th of July the Declaration of Independence was adopted, with the unanimous concurrence of all the States.

Our illustrious poet Bryant vividly depicts the spirit which animated the patriots at this time, in his poem entitled, "Seventy-Six."

> "What heroes from the woodland sprung,
>   When through the fresh-awakened land,
> The thrilling cry of freedom rung
> And to the work of warfare strung
>   The yeoman's iron hand!
>
> "Hills flung the cry to hills around,
>   And ocean-mart replied to mart,
> And streams, whose springs were yet unfound,
> Pealed far away the startling sound
>   Into the forest's heart.
>
> "Then marched the brave from rocky steep,
>   From mountain-river swift and cold;
> The borders of the stormy deep,
> The vales where gathered waters sleep,
>   Sent up the strong and bold;
>
> "As if the very earth again
>   Grew quick with God's creating breath,
> And, from the sods of grove and glen,
> Rose ranks of lion-hearted men
>   To battle to the death.

"The wife whose babe first smiled that day,
    The fair fond bride of yester-eve,
And aged sire and matron gray,
    Saw the loved warriors haste away,
    And deemed it sin to grieve.

"Already had the strife begun;
    Already blood on Concord's plain,
Along the springing grass had run,
    And blood had flowed at Lexington,
    Like brooks of April rain.

"That death-stain on the vernal sward
    Hallowed to freedom all the shore;
In fragments fell the yoke abhorred—
    The footsteps of a foreign lord
    Profaned the soil no more."

For some time after the Declaration of Independence, the English were generally victorious in the conflicts of the revolution. But in the winter following, the tide of victory turned in favor of Washington and his compatriots. On the day after Christmas he gained the battle of Trenton; and on the 3d of January, 1777, he defeated the British at Princeton.

In the month of June, a British army set out from Canada to conquer the northern parts of the revolted territory. General Burgoyne was in command. In July he reached Ticonderoga, which he captured without difficulty. Being in want of provisions, Burgoyne sent Colonel Baum, with 500 men, to seize a quantity of stores which the Americans had collected at Bennington. They were met by Colonel John Stark, at the head of the New Hampshire militia, and totally defeated. The British loss was about 800; that of the Americans fifty-four. Stark's speech to his men before the battle is said to have been: "There they are, boys; we must beat them to-day, or this night Molly Stark's a widow." The record of this remarkable victory inspired the muse of Bryant, who thereupon produced a poem which cannot be too widely known.

"THE BATTLE OF BENNINGTON.

"On this fair valley's grassy breast
    The calm, sweet rays of summer rest,
And dove-like peace divinely broods
    On its smooth lawns and solemn woods.

"A century since, in flame and smoke,
    The storm of battle o'er it broke;
And ere the invader turned and fled,
    These pleasant fields were strown with dead.

"Stark, quick to act and bold to dare,
And Warner's mountain band, were there;
And Allen, who had flung the pen
Aside to lead the Berkshire men.

"With fiery onset—blow on blow—
They rushed upon the embattled foe,
And swept his squadrons from the vale,
Like leaves before the autumn gale.

"Oh! never may the purple stain
Of combat blot these fields again,
Nor this fair valley ever cease
To wear the placid smile of peace.

"But we, beside this battle-field,
Will plight the vow that ere we yield
The right for which our fathers bled,
Our blood shall steep the ground we tread.

"And men shall hold the memory dear
Of those who fought for freedom here,
And guard the heritage they won
While these green hillsides feel the sun."

This defeat was the forerunner of still greater disasters to Burgoyne. In his march southward he found himself at Saratoga destitute of provisions, and surrounded by the enemy. Night and day a circle of fire encompassed them. There was but one thing to do, and it was done. The British army surrendered. Nearly six thousand men, in sorrow and in shame, laid down their arms.

The summer of 1788 was signalized by a terrible massacre of old men, women and children in the valley of Wyoming, on the Susquehanna, by a combined force of British and Seneca Indians. All the strong men were absent in the army, while their wives tilled the fields. The forts in which they had found refuge on the enemy's approach, were taken and burnt. Three hundred old men and boys fought valiantly until they were surrounded and slain. The British leaders could not, if they would, restrain their savage allies; every dwelling was burnt, and the beautiful valley became a solitude.

The surrender of Burgoyne brought an important ally to the American side; France offered to come to her aid. A treaty was signed by which France and America engaged to make common cause against England. Soon afterwards Spain joined France and America in the league, and declared war against England.

The fleets of France and Spain appeared in the English Channel, and England had to face the perils of an invasion. But the black cloud passed harmlessly away. The invading admirals quarrelled. One of them wished to land at once; the other wished first to dispose of the English fleet. They could not agree upon a course, and therefore they sailed away home, each to his own country, having effected nothing.

During the later years of the war the English kept possession of the Southern States. When the last campaign opened, Lord Cornwallis, with a strong force, represented British authority in the South, and did all that he found possible for the suppression of the patriots. He marched into Virginia and took post at Yorktown.

ON THE WAR-PATH.

One event of some interest, although of little importance in its results, should not be passed over here. We allude to the treason of Arnold.

This man, a general in the American army, having obtained the command of the fortress of West Point, on the Hudson, privately engaged to deliver it up to the British General Clinton, for the sum of £10,000 sterling, and a commission as brigadier-general in the British army.

By the fortunate arrest of a Major Andre, whom Clinton had sent to confer with Arnold, the project was defeated. Andre was hung as a spy, while Arnold fled to the British camp, where he received the stipulated reward of his treason. But even the British themselves scorned the traitor, and the world now execrates his name and memory.

About midsummer (1781), the joyous news reached Washington that a powerful French fleet, with an army on board, was about to sail for America. With this reinforcement, Washington had it in his power to deliver a blow which would break the strength of the enemy and hasten the close of the war. The French fleet sailed for the Chesapeake, and Washington decided in consequence that his attack should be made on Lord Cornwallis. With all possible secrecy and speed the American troops were moved southward to Virginia. They were joined by the French, and they stood before Yorktown a force 12,000 strong.

The siege of Yorktown was pushed on with extraordinary vehemence. The English made a stout defence, and strove by desperate sallies to drive the assailants from their works. But in a few days the defences of Yorktown lay in utter ruin, beaten to the ground by the powerful artillery of the Americans. The English guns were silenced; the English shipping was fired by red-hot shot from the French batteries. Ammunition began to grow scarce. The place could not be held much longer. Lord Cornwallis must either force his way out and escape to the North, or surrender. One night he began to embark his men in order to cross the York river and set out on his desperate march to New York; but a violent storm arose and scattered his boats. The men who had embarked got back with difficulty, under fire from the American batteries. All hope was now at an end. In about a fortnight from the opening of the siege, the British army, 8,000 strong, laid down its arms.

The final treaty of peace between the British and Americans was made in 1783. Great Britain acknowledged the United States to be free and independent, with Canada as a boundary on the north, the Mississippi river on the west, and Florida, extending west to the Mississippi, on the south.

Having now arrived at our beginning as a nation, we may well pause to take a glance at the most prominent characters to whom our country is so greatly indebted for its independent existence. There are, indeed, many names worthy of all remembrance, which the space at our command will hardly allow us even to mention. Still the reader is aware that our purpose is not to enter into the minute details of historical fact, for there are innumerable works which are devoted to that object alone. Our purpose is to give a running summary of the political, social, artistic, literary, and scientific progress of our country—to show how it came to be an independent nation, and what it has achieved since then. And as

"The proper study of mankind is man,"

brief sketches of our most prominent men in any branch of human industry will be given, as well as of those upon whom the nation has bestowed the gift of its highest office. The mind of the reader will thus not be confined to one narrow view of what is involved in the history of the country.

George Washington naturally comes first in our record of great names. He was born February 22d, 1732, and died December 14th, 1799. George's father died when he was eleven years old, so that his training devolved upon his mother, who was a woman of very noble character; and, as events proved, fully equal to the task.

Washington was a good mathematician, and at the age of sixteen had thoroughly fitted himself as a practical surveyor. One of Washington's early friends was Lord Fairfax, an eccentric Englishman, who owned an immense estate in Virginia. He employed Washington to survey this land; and while engaged in this work, cut off from civilization and compelled to undergo numerous hardships, he learned many lessons that afterward proved useful to him.

GEORGE WASHINGTON.

When Governor Dinwiddie arrived in Virginia he appointed Washington, with the rank of major, over one of the four military districts into which he divided the colony. It was at this time, and when only twenty-one years of age, that Washington was despatched on his mission to Venango. The soundness of his judgment was shown on that expedition, and disregard of his advice was followed by disaster to Braddock's expedition.

When called upon to take command of the army of the United States, he replied with his usual modesty: "Though I am truly sensible of the high honor done me in this appointment, yet I feel great distress from a consciousness that my abilities and military experience may not be equal to the extensive and important trust." His generosity and devoted patriotism are also shown in another passage of this same reply: "As to pay, sir, I beg leave to assure Congress that as no pecuniary consideration could have tempted me to accept the arduous employment at the expense of my domestic ease and happiness, I do not wish to make any profit from it. I will keep an exact account of my expenses. Those, I doubt not, they will discharge, and that is all I desire." At this time Washington was forty-three years old. He had married Mrs. Martha Custis, a wealthy young widow, in 1759, and being heir himself to large estates, he had devoted himself to agriculture.

In appearance Washington was of commanding presence. He was six feet and two inches tall, broad-shouldered and muscular. His face was unusually calm and dignified in expression, and his manner was formal. In private, however, he was gracious, and even genial, especially with the young.

While taking his usual ride over the plantation, during the morning of the 12th of December, 1790, he was caught in a cold storm of rain and sleet. Returning home, after two or three hours' exposure to this weather, he sat down to dine without changing his clothes. The second day following he was attacked with "acute laryngitis," a disease of the throat not then understood,

MT. VERNON.

and died within twenty-four hours. Europe vied with America in mourning his loss and eulogizing his name. General Henry Lee, of Virginia, at the request of Congress, pronounced his funeral oration, using the memorable words, "First in war, first in peace, and first in the hearts of his countrymen."

Bryant thus writes of the 22d of February:

> "Pale is the February sky,
>   And brief the mid-day's sunny hours;
> The wind-swept forest seems to sigh
>   For the sweet time of leaves and flowers.

"Yet has no month a prouder day,
  Not even when the summer broods
O'er meadows in their fresh array,
  Or autumn tints the glowing woods.

"For this chill season now again
  Brings in its annual round the morn
When, greatest of the sons of men,
  Our glorious Washington was born."

LITERATURE AND GENERAL PROGRESS IN THE COLONIAL PERIOD.

It may be believed that the first settlers in America found enough to do in subduing the wilderness and devising the laws under which their children were to live, without writing books. But so anxious were they to be remembered and understood in England, and to be reinforced by new parties of emigrants; so full of wonder and delight in the new world that was thrown open to them, and so desirous that their children should not lack the advantages that they would have enjoyed at home, that a mass of literature does in fact date from the very earliest years of the colonies.

The first book written in America was Captain John Smith's "True Relation of Virginia," which he sent home in 1608. A few months later he despatched the London Company a report of the Jamestown colony, with a map of the Chesapeake bay and its tributary rivers, and a very lively description of the surrounding country.

Besides many other descriptive works, Virginia made one contribution to elegant letters; for George Sandys, treasurer of the colony, A. D. 1621-1625, beguiled the loneliness of his absence from polished society and the horror attending the Indian massacre by translating Ovid into English verse. Not only in description and poetry, however, did the colonial authors prove their ability, but in philosophy and science as well.

Among the writers of the later colonial period the greatest, perhaps, was Jonathan Edwards (born 1703, died 1758), whose "Essay on the Freedom of the Will" revealed to the world the most acute and original mind which America has produced. It was written at the little village of Stockbridge, Massachusetts, when he was a missionary to the Indians. But the mind which most perfectly represented and most strongly influenced the character of American institutions was that of Benjamin Franklin (born 1706, died 1790), the printer-boy of Boston, the self-taught sage of Philadelphia, the representative of the colonies at London, the ambassador of the United States at Paris, whose plain, good sense, genial humor, and honest self-respect made him the favorite of all ranks and classes. His writings fill ten octavo volumes. A great statesman spoke of him as being the greatest diplomatist of the eighteenth century.

Among his great services to his country was his organization of its postal service as early as 1754. "Every penny stamp is a monument to Franklin." His simple experiment with the kite, proving lightning and thunder to be caused by electric currents, and his subsequent invention of the lightning-rod, gave him a high place among scientific men.

From the beginning the colonies contained many noted students of natural science. The soils, minerals, plants and animals of the new continent were all objects of keen research. Linnæus, the noted Swedish naturalist, declared John Bartram, the Quaker gardener of Philadelphia, to be the "greatest natural botanist in the world." Virginia and the more southerly colonies had several botanists of European fame. But the scientific reputation of America was established when Franklin, in 1744, drew about him other gentlemen of kindred tastes and formed the American Philosophical Society. It was an important bond of union among the best men in all the colonies.

THE THIRTEEN STATES BECOME A NATION.

Washington saw from the beginning that his country was without a government. Congress was a mere name. There were still thirteen sovereign States—in league for the moment, but liable to be placed at variance by the differences which time would surely bring. Washington was satisfied that without a central government they could never be powerful or respected. Such a government, indeed, was necessary in order even to their existence. European powers would, in its absence, introduce dissension among them. Men's minds would revert to that form of government with which they were familiar. Some ambitious statesman or soldier would make himself king, and the great experiment, based upon the equality of rights, would prove an ignominious failure.

Hamilton proposed that a convention of delegates from the several States should be held, in order to decide upon a form of government. The convention met at Philadelphia, in May, 1787. Fifty-five men composed this memorable council. Among them were the wisest men of whom America, or perhaps any other country, could boast. Washington himself presided. Benjamin Franklin brought to this—his latest and his greatest task—the ripe experience of eighty-two years. New York sent Hamilton—regarding whom Prince Talleyrand said, long afterward, that he had known nearly all the leading men of his time, but he had never known one, on the whole, equal to Hamilton. With these came many others whose names are held in enduring honor. Since the meeting of that first Congress, which pointed the way to independence, America had seen no such assembly.

Alexander Hamilton (born 1757, died 1804), born in the West Indies, was one of the most remarkable characters of the Revolution. His mother died when he was a child, and his father being in destitute circumstances Hamilton was taken charge of by his mother's relatives. They placed him in a commercial house when twelve years of age, and, although the life was very distasteful to him, he applied himself faithfully to the discharge of his duties. A newspaper article, written when he was but fifteen years old, was so remarkable that his friends determined to give him the benefit of a good education, and he was accordingly sent to New York, where he graduated at King's College. He became much interested in politics, and a speech made by him at a public meeting, 1774, attracted general attention to him. Soon after this he wrote a number of political pamphlets that at once gave him a high position in the community. When nineteen years old he obtained a commission as captain of artillery, and in this capacity he first attracted the attention of Washington, to whom he finally became *aide-de-camp*. So implicit was Washington's confidence in this stripling of twenty that he intrusted to him the sole management of his most delicate correspondence with the British commanders and others. After the war he studied law, in which profession he at once rose to eminence, but politics continued to absorb much of his time. He was a member of the constitutional convention, and wrote the majority of a series of papers called "The Federalist," which appeared in a New York paper, in defence of the Constitution, and no doubt had much weight in causing its adoption by the several States. Party feeling now ran very high, and Hamilton's great ability and untiring energy won him many strong friends among the Federalists, and many bitter enemies in the opposite party. As Washington's first secretary of the treasury, Hamilton's career was brilliant and successful, and he readily refuted all the charges brought against him for mismanagement and dishonesty by the Democrats. A split occurring in the Federalist party, Hamilton, by his opposition, gave deep offence to Aaron Burr, who finally challenged him to a duel and shot him.

Hamilton is described as being under the medium height and slight in figure. His complexion was fair and delicate, and his manners were most engaging.

The first step to be taken under the new Constitution was to elect a President. There was but one man who was thought of for this untried office. George Washington was unanimously chosen. Congress was summoned to meet in New York on the 4th of March; but the members had to travel far on foot, or on horseback. Roads were bad, bridges were few; streams, in that spring-time were swollen. It was some weeks after the appointed time before business could be commenced.

That Congress had difficult work to do, and it was done patiently, with much plain sense and honesty. As yet there was no revenue, while everywhere there was debt. The general government had debt, and each of the States had debt. There was the foreign debt—due to France, Holland and

Spain. There was the army debt—for arrears of pay and pensions. There was the debt of the five great departments—for supplies obtained during the war. There was a vast issue of paper-money to be redeemed. There were huge arrears of interest. And, on the other hand, there was no provision whatever for these enormous obligations.

Washington, with a sigh, asked a friend, "What is to be done about this heavy debt?" "There is but one man in America can tell you," said his friend, "and that is Alexander Hamilton." Washington made Hamilton secretary of the treasury. The success of his financial measures was immediate and complete. "He smote the rock of the national resources," said Daniel Webster, "and abundant streams of revenue gushed forth. He touched the dead corpse of the public credit and it sprung upon its feet." All

THE WHITE HOUSE, HOME OF THE PRESIDENTS.

the war debts of the States were assumed by the general government. Efficient provision was made for the regular payment of interest, and for a sinking fund to liquidate the principal. Duties were imposed on shipping, on goods imported from abroad, and on spirits manufactured at home. The vigor of the government inspired public confidence, and commerce began to revive. In a few years the American flag was seen on every sea. The simple manufactures of the country resumed their long interrupted activity. A national bank was established. Courts were set up, and judges were appointed. The salaries of the President and the great functionaries were settled. A home was chosen for the general government on the banks of the Potomac—where the capital of the Union was to supplant the little wooden village—remote from the agitations which arise in the great centres of population. Innumerable details connected with the establishment of a new government were discussed and fixed. Novel as the circumstances were, little of the work then done has required to be undone. Succeeding generations of Americans have approved the wisdom of their early legislators, and continue unaltered the arrangements which were framed at the outset of the national existence.

Washington entered on the duties of his office on the 30th of April, 1789. The people at this time had formed themselves into two political parties. Those who felt that the new Federal government was absolutely necessary, took the name of Federalists, and supported the new constitution. Those who liked the old State government better, took the name of Anti-Federalists, and opposed the new constitution. Most of the leading men were Federalists at this time, and the Anti-Federalists had but two great leaders, Samuel Adams and Patrick Henry. Subsequently, in 1792, the Anti-Federalists took the name of Republican party (similar to the present Democratic party). Jefferson and Randolph became the Republican leaders, and Hamilton and Knox the Federalist leaders. Washington, although he tried to be impartial, was really a Federalist.

At the second Presidential election, in 1792, all the electors again voted for Washington, and John Adams, who was a Federalist, was re-elected Vice-President. In this year Kentucky became a State. In 1796, Tennessee was admitted into the Union as a State, being the third State that was formed during Washington's administration. He declined to be a candidate for a third term of office.

JOHN ADAMS.

Washington was President during the first eight years of the constitution. He survived his withdrawal from public life only three years, dying, after a few hours' illness, in the sixty-eighth year of his age. To this day there is an affectionate watchfulness for opportunities to express the honor in which his name is held. To this day the steamers which ply upon the Potomac strike mournful notes upon the bell as they sweep past Mount Vernon, where Washington had spent the happiest days of his life, and where he died.

John Adams, of Massachusetts, became President of the United States in 1797, and Thomas Jefferson, of Virginia, having received only three votes less from the electoral college, became Vice-President. These two great men were leaders of opposite parties, and during their four years of office the country was disturbed by a violent conflict of opinions. The inconvenience of such a division of sentiment in the administration led, a few years later, to a change in the mode of election—a distinct ballot being held for the Vice-President, who has ever since been of the same political party with his chief.

John Adams was born at Braintree, Massachusetts, in October, 1735. He was a graduate of Harvard College in the class of 1755, and was admitted to the bar three years later. In 1764 he was married. He was an active and influential member of both the first and second Continental Congresses, and by his energy and eloquence did more, perhaps, than any other man to crystallize the American sentiment in favor of independence.

Many of the acts of President Adams were violently denounced by his partisan opponents, and the press was very bitter in its criticism; but the sober judgment of later years has approved most of his public measures. He and Jefferson became widely alienated for a time; but before their death, which by a singular coincidence occurred on the same day—the fiftieth anniversary of the Declaration of Independence—a happy reconciliation had taken place.

Difficulties with France filled almost all Adams' administration. The French government turned the American minister out of the country, and encouraged their naval officers to capture and sell American vessels and cargoes. Special ministers were sent by President Adams to remonstrate, but the French rulers demanded a large sum of money as a bribe for peace. The American ministers replied that they would spend "millions for defence, not one cent for tribute;" and the American people backed them and prepared for war.

THOMAS JEFFERSON.

Congress increased the navy, and ordered it to capture French vessels. A number of French privateers were captured, when Napoleon, who had overturned the former French government, offered fair terms of peace to the United States, and they were accepted.

In the year 1800, the seat of government was removed from Philadelphia to the new city of Washington, then a struggling, half-built village, with a few public buildings.

In the year 1800, parties were so evenly balanced that no President could be chosen by the electors. By a provision of the constitution the choice, therefore, devolved upon the House of Representatives. After a close ballot Thomas Jefferson was declared to be President-elect, and Aaron Burr, of New York, Vice-President.

Jefferson was one of the ablest men that our country has produced. It was Jefferson who wrote the celebrated Declaration of Independence. To him we are indebted for the present convenient denominations of Federal money, such as cents, dimes, dollars, etc., in place of the old English system of pounds, shillings and pence.

During his administration American commerce increased enormously, for nearly all Europe was now at war, and it was not safe to send goods in European vessels, which were liable to capture by their enemies. Money came in rapidly to the government of the United States. Ohio was admitted in the year 1802.

Previous to the year 1803, the territory of the United States extended west only to the Mississippi river—all the region beyond, then called Louisiana, being owned by Spain. This latter power, however, ceded the country to France in the year 1800, and in the year 1803 the United States purchased it from France, for $15,000,000. Thus the territory of the United States was extended west to the Pacific ocean. Thomas Jefferson was born at Shadwell, Virginia, 1743, and died at Monticello, 1826.

Aaron Burr was arrested and tried for treason in 1807. He was, however, acquitted, since he had not actually borne arms against the United States, although he had intended to set up a government of his own in the Mississippi valley. The year 1807 is memorable for the earliest success of steam navigation. Several ingenious men had been experimenting on the application of Watt's invention to modes of travel; but to Robert Fulton, a native of Pennsylvania, is due the credit of having persevered until all obstacles were overcome. He was liberally aided by Chancellor Livingston of New York. His first boat, the Clermont, ascended the Hudson from New York to Albany in 1807. Five years later he built at Pittsburgh the first Mississippi steamer, which, descending the Ohio and Mississippi rivers, reached New Orleans in December, 1812.

Robert Fulton (born 1765, died 1815) was in his earlier years more of an artist than a mechanic, and he went to London to perfect himself in portrait painting under the famous Benjamin West. While there he met Earl Stanhope, James Watt, and others engaged in finding practical uses for the recently invented steam-engine, and his mind was directed to the solution of the same problem. His first application of steam-power for propelling boats was on the Seine, in 1803, but the experiment was not very successful. After the success of the Clermont, Fulton's reputation was world-wide. He built many river steam-boats, and constructed the first United States steam war-vessel, named "Fulton the First." Among his inventions were an improvement in canal-locks, a submarine torpedo, and machines for marble-sawing, flax-spinning and rope-making.

Jefferson, having followed the example of Washington in declining a third term of office, was succeeded by James Madison, of Virginia, who was inaugurated March 4th, 1809. George Clinton, of New York, was re-elected as Vice-President. The same principles continued to control the government, and the same harmony was visible in the cabinet.

JAMES MADISON.

During many years England had been forcibly taking seamen from our vessels, and compelling them to serve in her navy, under the pretence that they were natives of England, and were therefore still British subjects. After many years of suffering and remonstrance, the United States finally declared war against Great Britain, in the month of June, 1812. The war ended with the defeat of the British at New Orleans, 1815.

James Madison (born 1751, died 1836) was born at King George, Virginia, of English descent. He had unusual educational advantages from his earliest years and, after graduating at Princeton, when twenty years of age, he pursued an extensive course of study, embracing law, theology, philosophy, and general literature. At this period of his life he permanently impaired his bodily vigor by over-study, and by allowing himself only three or four hours' sleep each day. He interested himself at once in politics, and in 1776 was elected a member of the Virginia convention. On the return of Jefferson from France, Madison was offered that mission, but declined it. He also refused the position of secretary of state when Jefferson vacated it, feeling that he would create a discord in Washington's cabinet. At the time of the Constituent Convention he was an ardent Federalist, but later changed his views, and was before long recognized as the leader of the Democratic party.

James Monroe, of Virginia, the fifth President of the United States, had a happy and popular administration. He was inaugurated in 1817. The country speedily recovered from the disasters occasioned by the war; the fame of its rich, unoccupied lands drew a tide of immigrants from Europe, whose labor helped to develop the natural wealth of the country, and, by making roads, bridges and canals to supply outlets for its productions. A ten years' revolution had now resulted in the separation of most of the Spanish colonies from their mother-country. In recognizing Mexico and five South American republics as independent states, President Monroe announced the principle of his foreign policy: "The American continents, by the free and independent position which they have assumed and maintained, are not to be considered as subject to future colonization by any foreign power." "Friendship with all, entangling alliances with none," has been the spirit of international relations founded upon the "Monroe Doctrine."

In 1824, the Marquis Lafayette, now an old man, came to see once more, before he died, the country he had helped to save, and took part with wonder in the national rejoicing. The poor colonists, for whose liberties he had fought, had already become a powerful and wealthy nation. Everywhere there had been expansion. Everywhere there were comfort and abundance. Everywhere there were boundless faith in the future and a vehement, unresting energy, which would surely compel the fulfilment of any expectations, however vast.

During his administration, upon the application of Missouri for leave to form a State constitution, the important question arose in Congress whether any more slave-States should be admitted. After long discussion it was supposed to be settled by the Missouri Compromise, which admitted that State with its slaves, but prohibited the extension of slavery into any Territory of the United States north of 36° 30' north latitude.

Henry Clay, of Kentucky, was the chief advocate of the compromise, and he used all his eloquence in calming the angry passions which the discussion had excited, and in promoting peace and brotherly confidence.

The first ocean steamer crossed the Atlantic, from Savannah to Liverpool, in 1819. The same year a treaty was made by which Spain ceded Florida, of which she had

JAMES MONROE.

again obtained possession, to the United States, the latter undertaking to pay $5,000,000, due from the former power to American citizens. Florida became a Territory under the control of Congress, and the President appointed General Jackson to be its governor.

James Monroe (born 1758, died 1831) was a Virginian by birth, and was educated at William and Mary College. During the Revolution he fought as a subordinate officer at Trenton, Brandywine, Germantown and Monmouth, and after the war took a prominent part in politics, both in the Virginia assembly and in Congress. He died in New York City, July 4th, 1831, and was buried there; but in 1858 his remains were removed in state to Richmond, Virginia, and there re-interred in the Hollywood cemetery.

Henry Clay (born 1777, died 1852) was born near Richmond, Virginia. His father, a Baptist preacher, died when Henry was five years old. His mother married a second time, and removed to Kentucky, leaving Henry at work as clerk in a retail store in Richmond. He soon abandoned this position, however, and became a copyist in a law office. Licensed as a lawyer in 1797, he removed to Lexington, Kentucky, and soon established a flourishing practice through his remarkable power of influencing juries. Clay retired from public life in 1842, but in 1848 he was again sent to the Senate, where he struggled hard to avert the great battle on the slavery question. Unfortunately his health gave way, and in 1851 he was compelled to retire to private life, and in the following year, on the 29th of July, he died. Congress adjourned on the news of his death, and the following day eulogies were delivered in both Senate and House. New York and the chief cities of Kentucky honored the day of his funeral.

John Quincy Adams was inaugurated in the year 1825, and John C. Calhoun, of South Carolina, became Vice-President. In internal affairs this administration was marked by an uncommon prosperity. The important event was the introduction of the first railroads.

JOHN QUINCY ADAMS.

John Quincy Adams was born at Braintree, Massachusetts, July, 1767. As a boy he was very precocious, and attracted attention wherever he went for his vigor of mind and body. In the presidential election of 1824 the three candidates besides John Quincy Adams were Andrew Jackson, Henry Clay, and William H. Crawford—all four belonging to the same political party. Jackson received ninety-nine electoral votes, Adams eighty-four, Crawford forty-one, and Clay thirty-seven. Henry Clay threw his influence in favor of Adams, which secured his election. The friends of the other two defeated candidates formed a coalition against the new President, which made his office very uncomfortable, and insured his defeat for a second term. He entered Congress in 1831, and ably represented his district for seventeen years, until stricken with death on the floor of the House of Representatives, February 21st, 1848.

John Caldwell Calhoun (born 1782, died 1850). This great statesman, champion of southern rights and opinions, was born in Abbeville district, South Carolina. His ancestors on both sides were Irish Presbyterians. In youth he was very studious, and made the best use of such opportunities for education as the frontier settlement afforded. He graduated at Yale College in 1804, and studied law at Litchfield, Connecticut. In 1808, he was elected to the legislature of South Carolina; and, three years later, he was chosen to the national House of Representatives. During the six years that he remained in the House, he took an active and prominent part in the stirring events of the time. In 1817 he was appointed secretary of war, and held the office seven years. From 1825 to 1832 he was Vice-President of the United States. He then resigned this office, and took his seat as senator from South Carolina. In 1844 President Tyler called him to his cabinet as secretary of state; and in 1845 he returned to the Senate, where he remained till his death.

JOHN C. CALHOUN.

One hundred and fifty years before the United States achieved their independence, Roger Williams taught that every man is answerable for his belief to God alone, and that governments have no right to interfere in matters of religion. This principle, although rejected at that time, has been a fundamental one with the United States government. This will account for its non-interference with the religion of the Mormons, which, about this time, came into general notice, and to which there has been individual objection in regard to its permission within the Territories of the United States.

In 1823, Joseph Smith, at Palmyra, New York, proclaimed that he had had a vision, wherein an angel stood before him, who declared that he had been chosen a prophet to reveal to the world a new religion of Christ, and who pointed out to him the place where were hidden some golden plates, on which were inscribed the new faith and the history of the Indian races of this country. From this he produced what is called the Book of Mormon. After various attempts at settlement in Ohio and New York, he and his followers moved West, where Smith was killed by a mob. Brigham Young was chosen president in place of the dead prophet and, in 1847, he set out with his fol-

A MORMON HOME.

lowers for the valley of the Great Salt lake, where he founded Great Salt Lake City, and where the community have since lived in peace and independence. The present number of Mormons in this country is about forty or fifty thousand, made up in great part of proselytes from Europe. The most notable feature of Mormonism, as it now exists, is polygamy—each saint taking as many wives as his circumstances and position appear to justify, besides forming *spiritual* unions with others whom he does not marry, but who will accompany him to paradise.

President Adams absolutely refused to employ the influence of the government to secure his re-election; he was opposed by many of his own officers, and General Andrew Jackson received the greatest number of votes at the autumn election of 1828. During the administration of General Jackson violent debates arose in Congress on questions concerning the public lands and the raising of a revenue for the government. The opposing in-

ANDREW JACKSON.

terests of the North and the South now became more fiercely clamorous. Daniel Webster, of Massachusetts, and Robert Hayne, of South Carolina, argued with great eloquence, the one for "Liberty and Union, now and forever," the other for "State Rights" of nullification or secession.

Andrew Jackson was born at the Waxhaw settlement, North Carolina, March 15th, 1767. He was admitted to the bar in 1786, and had a large and lucrative law practice. He may be said to have begun his military career in the Creek war of 1813.

His foreign policy was highly creditable. The nullification movement, the bank war, the Indian troubles, and the hot debates on the currency, tariff and slavery questions—all together made Jackson's term of office an exciting one. He was glad to retire to the quiet scenes of his "Hermitage," where he died of dropsy, June, 1845.

Daniel Webster (born in Salisbury, New Hampshire, 1782, died at Marshfield, Massachusetts, 1852) had as a boy no educational advantages beyond the home instruction of his father and mother, and a few terms in the district schools of the neighborhood. He passed nine months of diligent study at Phillips' Exeter Academy, and finished his preparation for college in the family of a minister at Boscawen. He was graduated from Dartmouth with high honors in 1801.

In 1805 Daniel Webster was admitted to the bar in Boston, and located in Portsmouth, New Hampshire, in 1807; in 1808 he was married to Miss Grace Fletcher; in 1812 he was elected to Congress by the Federalists, and was a prominent member of the House for two terms. Then he removed to Boston, and, during the busy practice of his profession for the next seven years, attained the reputation of the greatest lawyer of his time. In 1823 Webster was again sent to the national House of Representatives, and was twice re-elected; but, in 1827, he was transferred to the Senate, of which body he was, perhaps, the most conspicuous figure during the next twelve years. Webster married a second time in 1829. As secretary of state under Harrison and Tyler, and again under Fillmore, he managed the foreign affairs of the nation with consummate skill. He was returned to the United States Senate in 1845, where he continued until he entered Fillmore's

DANIEL WEBSTER.

cabinet, in 1850. In May, 1852, he was thrown from a carriage and severely injured. This accident, no doubt, hastened his death.

Robert Young Hayne (born 1791, died 1840) entered the United States Senate in 1823 and served two terms. He was educated for the law, fought in the war of 1812, was speaker of the House in the South Carolina legislature and attorney-general for the State, before coming to Washington. Before his senatorial term was ended, he was chosen governor of South Carolina, and boldly defied President Jackson to enforce his proclamation in regard to the nullification acts.

Hayne possessed brilliant talents, and was especially strong in debate.

At the autumn election of 1836, Martin Van Buren, of New York, was chosen to be President. The electors failed to unite upon a Vice-President, and the Senate chose for its presiding officer Richard M. Johnson, of Kentucky.

Martin Van Buren was the first President born after the struggle for independence. His success was due to his abilities as lawyer, politician and statesman. He was born at Kinderhook, New York, December 5th, 1782; died there July 24th, 1862. He enjoyed only a moderate education, and in 1796 began the study of law, which he continued until 1803, when he was admitted to the bar. He had meanwhile taken an active part in politics, and in 1808 was appointed surrogate of Columbia county. In 1812 he was elected to the State Senate. He continued a member of that body until 1820, having been, during that period, a supporter of the war and the canal project. A portion of this time he also held the office of attorney-general. He was a member of the constitutional convention of the State of New York in 1821, and in February of the same year he was elected to the United States Senate, and re-elected in 1827, serving until 1829. The following year the gubernatorial chair of the State of New York became vacant by the death of Governor Clinton, and Mr. Van Buren was selected as the candidate for that office by the Democratic party of the State. He was elected, but his career as governor was brief, for he soon afterwards accepted, from President Jackson, the office of secretary of state. He received a large majority of the electoral votes for Vice-President in 1832, which office he continued to fill during President Jackson's term.

MARTIN VAN BUREN.

Martin Van Buren died at his native place in 1862.

In 1837 occurred a great business revulsion, which brought ruin to thousands. Speculation had been rampant; importations ruinously large; business had been too much expanded, and an unsound credit system prevailed. The banks were obliged to suspend specie payments; a commercial panic and failures to an enormous amount were the consequence. Congress in vain tried to relieve the country; the recovery was very slow and tedious.

The financial difficulties under which the country had labored being charged by many to the administration, Van Buren was not re-elected. The Whigs had nominated General William H. Harrison, whose military services the country remembered with gratitude. Second on their ticket was John Tyler, of Virginia, who had been governor of that State and had also represented it in the United States Senate. The presidential campaign was an exciting one. Log-cabin and hard cider barrels figured largely in it, as emblematical of Harrison's plain farmer-life in Ohio, and the song of "Tippecanoe and Tyler too" rang through the land. The Whig nominees were elected by a large majority.

GENERAL WILLIAM H. HARRISON.

President Harrison lived only one month after his inauguration. "Killed by office-seekers" would probably be the true verdict; for, anxious to do justice to all men, he gave to the throng of applicants time which he needed for repose. He died April 4th, 1841. John Tyler, of Virginia, became President, retaining the same cabinet which Harrison had appointed and the Senate had confirmed.

John Tyler, the successor of President Harrison, was born in Virginia in 1790. He had barely attained manhood when he was elected to the State legislature. Five years afterwards he was elected to Congress, and in 1826 to the gubernatorial chair of his native State. Before the expiration of the term of his office he was chosen to fill a vacancy in the Senate of the United States, where he officiated as president *pro tem.* of that body. He served in this capacity till, a difference of opinion having arisen between General Jackson and himself, he resigned his seat in 1836. In 1840 he was selected by the Whig party as their candidate for Vice-President. He was elected to that office by a large majority, and entered upon the discharge of his duties in March, 1841, when the death of the President, General Harrison, shortly after, raised him to the chief-magistracy of the Republic. His term of office expired in 1845, after which he lived in retirement in Virginia until early

JOHN TYLER.

in 1861, when he re-appeared at Washington as a delegate to the Peace Congress, of which body he was president. A few weeks later he became a member of the Virginia convention which passed the ordinance of secession, and subsequently of the Confederate Congress. He died in Richmond, January 17th, 1862.

James K. Polk was inaugurated President in 1845, with George M. Dallas as Vice-President. The electro-magnetic telegraph, invented by Professor Samuel F. B. Morse, was now first put to practical use. Congress appropriated $30,000 to test the invention, and a line was built from Washington to Baltimore. The first public despatch ever sent over the wires was the announcement of Polk's nomination, May 29th, 1844.

In March, 1845, Texas was received into the Union. Mexico was displeased with the annexation of Texas and, without the formality of any declaration of war, a Mexican army of 6,000 men attacked an American army of 4,000 in the south-western part of that State, but received a severe defeat.

President Polk hastened to announce to Congress that the Mexicans had "invaded our territory, and shed the blood of our fellow-citizens." Congress voted men

JAMES K. POLK.

and money for the prosecution of the war, and volunteers offered themselves in multitudes. Their brave little army was in peril—far from help, and surrounded by enemies. The people were eager to support the heroes of whose victory they were so proud.

The war was pushed with vigor, at first under the command of General

Taylor, and finally under General Scott, who, as a very young man, had fought against the British at Niagara, and, as a very old man, was commander-in-chief of the American army when the great war between North and South began. Many officers were there whose names became famous in after years. General Lee and General Grant gained here their first experience of war. They were not then known to each other. They met for the first time, twenty years after, in a Virginian cottage, to arrange terms of surrender for the defeated army of the Southern Confederacy.

The Americans resolved to fight their way to the enemy's capital, and there compel such a peace as would be agreeable to themselves. The task

THE ALAMO.

was not without difficulty. The Mexican army was greatly more numerous. They had a splendid cavalry force and an efficient artillery. Their commander, Santa Anna, unscrupulous even for a Mexican, was yet a soldier of some ability. The Americans were mainly volunteers, who had never seen war till now. The fighting was severe. At Buena Vista the American army was attacked by a force which outnumbered it in the proportion of five to one. The battle lasted for ten hours, and the invaders were saved from ruin by their superior artillery. The mountain passes were strongly fortified, and General Scott had to convey his army across chasms and ravines which the Mexicans, deeming them impassable, had neglected to defend. Strong in the consciousness of their superiority to the people they invaded—the same consciousness which supported Cortez and his Spaniards three centuries before—the Americans pressed on. At length they came in sight of Mexico, at the same spot where Cortez had viewed it. Once more they routed a Mexican army of greatly superior force; and then General Scott marched his little army of 6,000 men quietly into the capital. The war was closed, and a treaty of peace was, with little delay, negotiated.

Winfield Scott (born 1786, died 1866) was born at Petersburg, Virginia. After graduating at William and Mary College he adopted the profession of law, but almost immediately abandoned it, entering the army as a captain in 1808. His brilliant career in the war of 1812, the Creek war and the war with Mexico, has made him one of the most renowned of American generals, while the tact and judgment displayed in managing the delicate questions of the tariff trouble in South Carolina, and the Canadian agitation of 1837, marked him as a skilful diplomate. He was retired in 1861 on full pay and rank, and passed his remaining days at West Point. He has left behind him several military works, a few letters, and a book of memoirs of his life.

Zachary Taylor was one who, previous to his election to the Presidency, never held a civil office. He was born in Virginia in 1786. His father, who had fought at the side of Washington during all the war of independence, at its conclusion settled in Kentucky, and conducted his family to their forest-home, where his son, amid the perils of savage life, had ample opportunity of developing those military qualities of which he afterwards gave so signal a proof. At the outbreak of the war with England, in 1812, he hastened to join the army, and was appointed to guard the banks of the Wabash. In that year, while in command of the garrison of Fort Henderson, consisting only of fifty-two men, he was suddenly attacked at midnight by a hostile party, who succeeded in setting fire to the fort. But Taylor, with his handful of men, extinguished the flames and forced the enemy to retreat. For this exploit he was raised to the rank of major. In the war against the Indians, both in Florida and Arkansas, he passed successively through all the grades of his profession, till he reached the rank of general. Nominated, in 1846, to the command of a corps of observation on the frontiers of Mexico, an attack of the Mexicans gave him an opportunity of crossing the Rio Grande, and of gaining his first battle, at Palo Alto. The vic-

ZACHARY TAYLOR.

tories of Resaca de la Palma, Monterey and Buena Vista, proved him at once a valiant soldier and an able general, and marked him out to the suffrages of his countrymen for the Presidency. Chosen in November, 1848, he entered on his high office in March, 1849; but he had only filled the chair for sixteen months when he was attacked by the cholera and died, July, 1850. His last words were, "I have tried to do my duty; I am not afraid to die." Millard Fillmore, of New York, the Vice-President, now came to the head of the government. Daniel Webster was appointed secretary of state. Part of the duties of that office were devolved upon the new "Department of the Interior," which has charge of the public lands, of dealings with the Indians, and of issuing patents.

Millard Fillmore was born in Cayuga county, New York, in 1800, which at that time was very sparsely settled, and the young boy had the simplest of rudimentary education. He was apprenticed to a trade when fourteen, but, being ambitious, he studied hard during spare hours, and finally obtaining a release from his master he entered a law office as a clerk. After two years of drudgery there he went to Buffalo, and although at first almost penniless and an entire stranger, he succeeded in making a living and in winning friends who secured his admission to the bar. His abilities soon made him known, and his rise was rapid.

MILLARD FILLMORE.

His political life commenced in 1828, when he was elected to the State legislature. In 1832 he was first elected to Congress, and served one term. He was re-elected in 1836, and held his seat until 1842, when he declined a renomination. In doctrine he was a staunch Whig, and took an active part in the debates in Congress. He was appointed chairman of the committee of ways and means, a most important post, and took the leading part in drawing up the tariff of 1842. After retiring from Congress Mr. Fillmore was a candidate for Vice-President, but failed to secure the nomination. He was also defeated as the Whig nominee for governor of New York in 1844; but in 1847 he was elected comptroller of the State, and displayed great ability in that office.

As President, Fillmore won the sincere admiration of his cabinet. His messages to Congress contained many suggestions of great value to the country, but none of them were carried out, owing to purely political reasons. Fillmore signed the various acts comprised in Mr. Clay's compromise measures, being convinced of their constitutionality; but the Fugitive Slave Law, which was included, was so offensive to the Abolition party that, when Mr. Fillmore was again nominated for President in 1856 by the "American" party, he was unable to secure the electoral vote of a single Northern State. He then retired to private life in Buffalo, New York, where he died in 1874, of paralysis.

Franklin Pierce was elevated to the Presidency in 1853. The great political events of Pierce's administration arose from a bill introduced into Congress by Senator Stephen A. Douglas, of Illinois, "to organize the Territories of Kansas and Nebraska." Disregarding the Missouri Compromise, this bill left to the majority of people in each Territory the choice whether to enter the Union as a slave or a free State. It became a law after five months of violent debate. Then began a rush for the first possession of the land.

Franklin Pierce, of New Hampshire, was born 1804, and died 1869. He graduated at Bowdoin College in the class of 1824, and was admitted to the bar three years later. He was very successful as a lawyer. His political life began in the legislature of his State, from which, in 1833, he was transferred to the lower house of Congress. In 1837 he was chosen United States senator. Twice Mr. Pierce refused cabinet appointments by President Polk, and once declined the nomination of his party for governor of New Hampshire. He favored the annexation of Texas, and was among the first to volunteer for the Mexican war.

FRANKLIN PIERCE.

For bravery in action he rapidly rose from the ranks to a brigadier-generalship, and was commissioned by General Scott to arrange an armistice after the battle of Churubusco. When made President, in 1852, he received 254 electoral votes to forty-two cast for Winfield Scott. Pierce's entire administration was one of intense political excitement. Party feeling ran high in all parts of the country. The President was an advocate of the doctrine of "State Rights," and opposed every anti-slavery movement. After the expiration of his term of office Mr. Pierce made an extended European tour, and then settled down in his quiet New Hampshire home.

Stephen Arnold Douglas was born in Brandon, Vermont, 1813, and died at Chicago, 1861. He emigrated to the West in 1833, and a year later commenced the practice of law in Jacksonville, Illinois. He showed such ability in his profession that at the youthful age of twenty-two years he was chosen attorney-general of the State. In 1840 he was appointed secretary of state, and the same year a judge on the supreme bench of Illinois. Douglas first became a candidate for Congress in 1837, but was defeated. Again nominated by the Democrats in 1843, he was more successful. He was re-elected to the House of Representatives the two following terms, and in 1847 was promoted to the Senate. He was an acknowledged leader in this high body for the remainder of his life. During his long congressional career Mr. Douglas took part ably in the discussion of every important political question before the nation. He was a master of constitutional law, a powerful debater, and exerted a strong personal influence over his audiences. He was a man of large frame, though not tall, and was popularly styled "the little giant." His Kansas-Nebraska bill, which embodied the doctrine of "squatter sovereignty" (as termed by the papers of the day), was the cause of exciting controversy throughout the land, and led to the formation of the Republican party. At the Baltimore convention, in 1852, Mr. Douglas received ninety-two votes as candidate for the Presidency; and at Cincinnati, in 1856, 121 votes. In 1860 he was the nominee of the northern wing of the Democratic party, and received a very large popular vote. He greatly deplored the civil war, and strongly denounced the doctrine of secession.

James Buchanan, the Democratic candidate, became the fifteenth President of the United States; John C. Breckenridge being Vice-President.

This President was born in Franklin county, Pennsylvania, 1791, and died near Lancaster, Pennsylvania, in 1868. He was admitted to the bar in 1812, and practised at Lancaster. Beginning as a Federalist, he was a member of Congress in 1821-31; minister to Russia in 1832-4; United States senator, 1834-45; secretary of state under President Polk, 1845-9, opposing the anti-slavery movement; United

JAMES BUCHANAN.

States minister to England, 1853-6. In 1856 he was Democratic candidate for President, and was elected. In Congress he favored a tariff merely for revenue. As President he soon announced his intention to make it his special study to suppress the slavery agitation, and to restore the harmony between the States that had been disturbed by sectional violence. His well-intentioned efforts in this direction were not successful. It was clear long before the close of his administration that a severer struggle than the country had yet gone through was fast becoming inevitable. After Mr. Buchanan had retired from the Presidency on the 4th of March, 1861, he withdrew to the privacy of Wheatland, his country home, near Lancaster, Pennsylvania. Here he spent the remainder of his days, taking no prominent part in public affairs. Always a keen observer of public events as well as a most patriotic man, he watched the progress of the war of the Rebellion with the greatest solicitude. In 1866 he published a volume entitled "Mr. Buchanan's Administration," in which he explained the policy he had pursued while in the presidential office. He died at Wheatland, on the 1st of June, in the year 1868.

The Democratic party, in convention at Charleston, became divided on the question of slavery in the Territories. The seceding minority formed a new convention at Richmond, and nominated John C. Breckenridge, of Kentucky, to be the next President. The majority adjourned to Baltimore and nominated Stephen A. Douglas, of Illinois. A third party named John Bell, of Tennessee, and Edward Everett, of Massachusetts, for President and Vice-President. The Republicans meanwhile nominated Abraham Lincoln, of Illinois, and Hannibal Hamlin, of Maine.

By dividing its forces the Democratic party lost the power which it had held for twelve out of fifteen presidential terms since the accession of Jefferson. Mr. Lincoln was, therefore, elected by a plurality of votes. The threat of withdrawing from the Union was put into force, and an ordinance of secession passed by South Carolina. Within a few weeks Georgia and all the Gulf States had followed the example.

A convention of delegates from six of the seven seceding States met at Montgomery, Alabama, in February, 1861, and organized a new government under the title of "The Confederate States of America." The main features of its constitution were modelled upon those of the United States, but the sovereign rights of each State were recognized; the favor of foreign nations was sought

ABRAHAM LINCOLN.

by pledges of free trade; and slavery was guaranteed protection not only in existing States, but in Territories yet to be acquired.

Jefferson Davis, of Mississippi, and Alexander H. Stephens were elected President and Vice-President of the new confederacy.

It is not our purpose to dwell upon the details of the late war, which is yet fresh in the memory of many, and of which there are many histories.

The blockade of the Southern ports effected for many months an almost complete isolation of the Confederates from the world outside. Now and then a ship, laden with arms and clothing and medicine, ran past the blockading squadron and discharged her precious wares in a Southern port. Now

VICKSBURG.

and then a ship laden with cotton stole out and got safely to sea. But this perilous and scanty commerce afforded no appreciable relief to the want which had already begun to brood over this doomed people. The government could find soldiers enough, but it could not find for them arms and clothing. The railroads could not be kept in working condition in the absence of foreign iron. Worst of all, a scarcity of food began to threaten. Jefferson Davis begged his people to lay aside all thought of gain, and devote themselves to the raising of supplies for the army. Even now the army was frequently on half-supply of bread. The South could look back with just pride upon a long train of brilliant victories, gained with scanty means by her own valor and genius. But, even in this hour of triumph, it was evident that her position was desperate.

The North had not yet completely established her supremacy upon the Mississippi. Two rebel strongholds—Vicksburg and Port Hudson—had successfully resisted Federal attack, and maintained communication between the revolted provinces on either side the great river. The reduction of these was indispensable. General Grant was charged with the important enterprise, and proceeded in February to begin his work.

For six weeks Grant pressed the siege with a fiery energy which allowed no rest to the besieged. General Johnston was not far off, mustering an army for the relief of Vicksburg, and there was not an hour to lose. Grant kept a strict blockade upon the scantily-provisioned city. From his gun-boats and from his own lines he maintained an almost ceaseless bombardment. The inhabitants crept into caves in the hill to find shelter from the intolerable fire. They slaughtered their mules for food. They patiently endured the inevitable hardships of their position; and their daily newspaper, printed on scraps of such paper as men cover their walls with, continued to the end to make light of their sufferings, and to breathe defiance against General Grant. But all was vain. On the 4th of July—the anniversary of independence—Vicksburg was surrendered with her garrison of 23,000 men.

During the later years of the war the North exerted her giant strength to the utmost, in order to crush the stubborn defence of the revolted States. She had 1,000,000 men under arms. She had 600 ships-of-war. Her people supplied freely, although on terms whose severity patriotism did not appear to modify, the means of an enormous expenditure. Her own factories worked night and day to provide military stores; and their efforts were freely supplemented by the dockyards and foundries of Europe. Peaceful America was for the time the greatest military power of the world. Her soldiers had gained the skill of veterans. Among her generals men had been found worthy to direct the vast forces of the republic.

The poor Confederates were habitually ill-supplied with food. Every available man was already in the ranks; if men could have been found, there were no arms to give them. The strength of the Confederacy waned so steadily that Grant became anxious lest General Lee should take to flight and renew the war on other fields. He prepared an attack with overwhelming numbers upon the enfeebled Southern lines. He stormed a fort in the centre of Lee's position, cutting his army in two, and making an immediate retreat inevitable. The rebel government fled from Richmond, and General Lee, a few days afterward, laid down his arms. The North had triumphed. After four years of war the Rebellion was quelled, and the authority of the Federal government was undisputed from Atlantic to Pacific, from the great lakes to the Gulf of Mexico.

Mr. Lincoln was elected President and entered upon his second term of office a few weeks before the close of the war. He was with the army when its final triumphs were gained, and he visited Richmond on the day of surrender, walking through the streets with his little boy by his side. No heart in all the rejoicing land was more thankful and more glad than his. He occupied himself with measures for healing the nation's wounds. No thought of vengeance for the past was entertained. Security for the future was necessary, but it was to be sought for with all leniency and gentleness. Possessing, as no man but Washington had ever done, the confidence of the American people, Lincoln was pre-eminently fitted to soothe the humiliated South and reunite the severed sisterhood of States. But the nation was to lose him when its need was at the greatest.

A few days after the fall of Richmond, Mr. Lincoln visited one of the Washington theatres. He went with some reluctance, moved by the consideration that the people expected him to go, and would be disappointed by his absence. As the play went on, a fanatical adherent of the fallen Confederacy, an actor called Booth, made his way stealthily into the President's box. He crept close up to Mr. Lincoln, and holding a pistol within a few inches lodged a bullet deep in the brain. The President sat motionless, save that his head sank down upon his breast. He never regained consciousness, but lingered till morning, and then passed away.

Before dismissing our reference to the war we may mention a fight which occurred upon the sea.

On the 8th of March, 1862, a strange-looking craft appeared in Hampton Roads. It was the old United States steamer Merrimac, now in Confederate service, cut down to the water's edge and fitted with a sharp steel prow and a sloping iron-plated roof. Steering directly for the sloop-of-war Cumberland, it so disabled her by one blow of her steel beak that she sank, with her flag flying and with all her men on board.

The United States frigate Congress was next attacked. She was run ashore, but the Merrimac poured into her such a storm of shot and shell that she was forced to surrender. The new sea-monster then retired to Norfolk, intending to complete its work of destruction the next day. Early in the morning it steamed out again, and approached the steam-frigate Minnesota; but before it had fired a gun a new champion appeared upon the scene.

It was the iron-clad Monitor of Captain Ericsson, which had arrived from New York during the night, just in time for its first trial of strength. Its deck near the surface of the water was protected by a heavy iron sheathing; it was surmounted by an iron tower, which, slowly revolving, turned its two enormous guns in every direction. The duel between these odd antagonists was not unlike David fighting Goliath, for the Monitor was less than one-fifth the burden of the Merrimac. But the shot and shells of the latter rolled harmlessly off the iron sheathing of her little opponent, while her huge beak passed above the deck and could not reach the tower. The Monitor glided nimbly away from every charge, and found out every weak spot in the Merrimac's armor where a heavy ball from her guns could make a leak, thus preventing her from engaging any other vessel. The Merrimac withdrew to Norfolk for repairs. She was blown up by the Confederates two months later, on the surrender of Norfolk to the United States. The national government immediately contracted with Captain Ericsson for a fleet of " Monitors," which effectually defended the coast, and made the United States for a time the greatest naval power in the world.

JOHN ERICSSON.

John Ericsson was born in 1803 in the province of Vermeland, Sweden ; and at an early age displayed great mechanical ability. After serving some years as an engineer in the Swedish army he went to England, where he introduced several important inventions which attracted great attention and gained the inventor several medals and prizes. His invention of the propeller not being well received, however, he came to the United States in 1839, and two years later built a war-steamer, the Princeton, for the government, which was the first steamship ever built with the propeller machinery. This vessel was also furnished with numerous other ingenious inventions of Ericsson's, which have since come into common use. The revolving turret, however, is the most important of Ericsson's inventions, and has caused a complete change in the naval architecture of the world.

ANDREW JOHNSON.

Andrew Johnson, the seventeenth President of the United States, was born at Raleigh, North Carolina, in 1808. At the age of ten was apprenticed to a tailor in Raleigh. Without a single day's schooling he taught himself to read. In 1826 he removed with his mother to Tennessee, where he married and settled in Greenville. His wife taught him to write and cipher. He was elected alderman, mayor, member of the legislature, and finally a member of Congress in

1843-53; was governor of Tennessee from 1853 to 1857, and United States senator from 1857 to 1863. The resolute opponent of secession, he was tireless in his efforts to uphold the national cause during the early stages of the Rebellion, and, on the reoccupation of Nashville in 1862, he was appointed by President Lincoln military governor of Tennessee; was nominated Vice-President by the Baltimore convention of 1864, and, on the assassination of President Lincoln, succeeded him in the presidential chair. At first he displayed a spirit of much severity to the rebels, but was afterwards more liberal in his policy, and so hostile to the reconstruction policy of Congress that he was impeached by that body, tried and acquitted May 26th, 1868—thirty-five voting him guilty, nineteen voting not guilty. During his Presidency the submarine telegraphic cable was successfully laid, and congratulatory messages were exchanged July 28th, 1866.

By the elections in the autumn of 1868 General Ulysses S. Grant became the eighteenth President, and Schuyler Colfax, of Indiana, Vice-President of the United States.

Ulysses S. Grant was born in 1822 at Point Pleasant, Clermont county, Ohio, and passed his boyhood in the neighboring village of Georgetown. At the age of seventeen he entered West Point, where he graduated four years later without having distinguished himself, being twenty-first in a class of thirty-nine. As a second lieutenant he was stationed on the frontier until the breaking out of the Mexican war. He was in every important battle of the latter except that of Buena Vista, and received the warmest praise from his superior officers for gallant conduct. He was rewarded by brevets on two occasions. He resigned his commission as captain in 1854, and attempted farming near St. Louis. Not meeting with much success, however, he accepted a position in his father's tannery at Galena, Illinois. Here he lived in comparative obscurity, and at the breaking out of the civil war was entirely unknown to the public. When President Lincoln issued his call for volunteers Grant organized and drilled a company at Galena, and at the same time offered his services by letter to the adjutant-general, but was ignored. Marching his company to Springfield, Illinois, he was appointed by the governor to muster the State volunteers, and five weeks later was made colonel of a regiment. He first reported to General Pope, in Missouri, and shortly after, having been appointed brigadier-general of volunteers, he was placed in command of the district of south-east Missouri. His first act of importance was the seizure of Paducah, which had great influence in keeping Kentucky in the Union; and the capture of Fort Donelson, which followed soon after, gave him a national reputation and won him his commission of major-general of volunteers. His career was now a series of brilliant successes, and his generalship at Chattanooga is considered by military authorities as the masterpiece of the war. He has been severely criticised for recklessly sacrificing the lives of his soldiers, but without just cause; for although the battles during his advance on Richmond were unusually severe and costly to the Union side, yet Grant felt that he was pursuing the shortest and best course to put an end to the horrors of civil war, and the result proved the correctness of his judgment.

Grant was included in the plot of the conspirators who murdered Lincoln, and probably escaped death through declining the latter's invitation to join the party at the theatre.

The years 1871 and 1872 were marked by several dreadful fires. For two days Chicago was burning—solid masses of stone, iron, and brick making scarcely more resistance to the fierce heat than the lightest wooden buildings. Nearly 100,000 persons were deprived of homes; and the property destroyed was worth $200,000,000. About the same time the great lumber-lands of Wisconsin and Michigan were visited by immense conflagrations. The flames spread from forests to villages; people plunged into lakes or rivers to escape them, but uncounted hundreds perished.

Boston was visited in November, 1872, by a similar disaster, though with less loss of life and property. More than sixty acres, covered with magnificent structures of granite and brick, were laid in ashes. The disaster was greater from an epidemic which had disabled all the horses in Boston, so that the heavy fire-engines had to be drawn by men.

INDIAN CHIEF.

Though the government had pursued a conciliatory course to the Indians, a hostile disposition was manifested early in 1876 by the Sioux in Dakota, Montana and Wyoming. They refused to settle upon a reservation, and attacked friendly Indians under the protection of the United States. It was necessary to reduce them by force. In June, General Custer, with part of his regiment, came upon the hostile Sioux, 2,500 strong, near the Little Big-Horn river, and without waiting for support dashed upon them. His whole force was overwhelmed and destroyed, Custer himself being slain while fighting gal-

GENERAL GRANT.

lantly. A brave, who was in the battle, afterwards related how "the White Chief," when his comrades had all fallen and his fire-arms were emptied, undauntedly defended himself with his sword until a bullet laid him in the dust. The Federal army, reinforced, subsequently pursued and broke up the Sioux, and compelled most of them to surrender.

The election of 1876 was unusually exciting. The candidate on the Republican side was Rutherford B. Hayes, of Ohio, and the candidate on the Democratic side Samuel J. Tilden, of New York. The contest was close, and the issue for some time doubtful. Charges of fraud were made by the one side, and intimidation by the other. From several States two opposing certificates were handed in. When Congress met, there was a long debate. It was agreed at last that a commission consisting of five judges of the Supreme Court, five senators, and five representatives, should hear the evidence and decide. Their conclusion was reached two days before the end of General Grant's term. It was to the effect that the Republicans had cast one hundred and eighty-five electoral votes for Rutherford B. Hayes, of Ohio; the Democrats had cast one hundred and eighty-four for Samuel J. Tilden, of New York. So the vexed question was settled, and President Hayes was inaugurated (the 4th being Sunday) on the 5th of March, 1877.

Rutherford Birchard Hayes was born at Delaware, Ohio, in 1822. He graduated at Kenyon College, in that State, and after taking his degree at the Harvard Law School, commenced the practice of law at Fremont, Ohio. In 1849 he moved to Cincinnati, and soon established a flourishing practice. He was made major of the Twenty-third Ohio Volunteers in 1861, and served throughout the war. He was badly wounded at South Mountain, and shortly after was promoted to a colonelcy. His gallant service in many of the hardest battles of the army of the Potomac was rewarded by successive advances in rank, and at the close of the war Hayes was a brevet major-general. After the battle of Cedar Creek, in which he took part, Hayes was notified of his election to Congress from the second district of Ohio. He resigned from the army in June, 1865, and the following December took his seat in Congress. He was re-elected in 1866, but resigned his seat to accept the governorship of Ohio: the latter office was held for two successive terms, when he

RUTHERFORD B. HAYES.

again became a candidate for Congress and was defeated. In 1875 he received an unprecedented honor in his native State, being elected governor for the third time. His popularity in Ohio, and the stand taken by him on the issues at stake in his last contest for the governorship, brought him prominently before the country, and resulted in his nomination for the Presidency in 1876.

Samuel J. Tilden, the Democratic candidate for the Presidency, and who was believed by many to have been actually elected, performed great service to his country in the way of political reform. Purity of government seems to have been dearer to him than mere party success. This is now conceded by those whose political views were different from his own.

SAMUEL J. TILDEN.

His great work in destroying the Tweed and the Canal rings in New York would entitle him to a permanent place among the greatest of political reformers, even if his prominence as a public-spirited citizen for fifty years, his devotion to important public questions and his discussions of great principles of law, finance and State during that long period did not constitute an example of unselfish and patriotic statesmanship which has been rarely equalled in our annals. In the highest relations of public life Mr. Tilden has always combined more nearly, perhaps, than any of his contemporaries, the two great kinds of quality—theoretic and practical—which form the true statesman, a profound understanding of the philosophic grounds of political opinion, and the sagacious tact and energy of the man of business. He died August 4th, 1886.

The four years' term of Mr. Hayes was chiefly remarkable as a period of peace and prosperity. Bounteous harvests supplied an enormous export of grain to European markets. Immigrants arrived at our ports in greater numbers than ever before, and an unusual proportion of these were industrious people, who were likely to be an advantage rather than a burden to the country. The census taken in June, 1880, showed the population of the United States to be more than fifty millions.

The election in the following November resulted in the choice of James A. Garfield, of Ohio, to be the twentieth President of the United States, and of Chester A. Arthur, of New York, to be Vice-President. The Democratic candidate for the Presidency was General Winfield S. Hancock.

Not far from Cleveland, Ohio, on November 19th, 1831, a very humble home was brightened by the birth of a son, now known to the world as James Abram Garfield. Living on the frontier, his early life was one full of the struggles that accompany poverty. On the farm helping his mother; at the carpenter's bench; on the canal, he studied hard, reading all the while. At eighteen years old he was fitted to teach country-school, and became a popular teacher. From 1851 to 1854 he studied at Hiram Institute, Ohio, teaching in the winter, working as a carpenter, in the haying or harvest fields, in summer and autumn, keeping up with his studies. He entered Williams College, Massachusetts, in 1854, and graduated in 1856, having accomplished his "definite purpose," but he was $500 in debt. He was soon elected president of Hiram Institute. His success as an instructor was marked. While attending to his multifarious duties as teacher, giving lectures on a great variety of subjects, preaching on Sundays, he began, in 1857, the study of law. By the year 1859 his strength of mind and character, and his ability as an orator were so well known, that he was elected to the State senate, and immediately took high rank as a speaker and debater.

JAMES A. GARFIELD.

While factional animosities were rankling in their greatest degree of bitterness, the President was stricken down by the assassin Guiteau. He lay, alternating between life and death, from the 2d of July until the 19th of September, when he died at Long Branch, to which place he had been recently removed from Washington. Upon the morning of September 20th, Vice-President Chester A. Arthur took the oath of office as chief executive of the United States, the country having been without a President for the space of three hours and a half.

CHESTER A. ARTHUR.

Chester A. Arthur, the son of a New England minister, was born at Fairfield, Vermont, in 1830. Early in life his father moved to Troy, New York, and in 1844 sent young Arthur to Union College, Schenectady, New York,

GENERAL HANCOCK.

then under the presidency of Rev. Eliphalet Nott, one of ablest men in his profession at that time. He graduated in 1848 and, studying law, was admitted to the bar in 1850. During the three or four years following he confined himself strictly to his profession, winning some reputation as an advocate.

On the formation of the Republican party in 1856, young Arthur supported Fremont, and afterwards Lincoln, in 1860. He was appointed collector of the port of New York by Grant in 1871, and when his term expired was reappointed, and the Senate, by a unanimous vote, confirmed the appointment without reference to a committee—a high and unusual compliment. He died November 18th, 1886.

Winfield Scott Hancock, the Democratic candidate for the Presidency, was born in Montgomery county, Pennsylvania, February 14th, 1824, and died February 9th, 1886. His mother's father was a Revolutionary soldier and was captured at sea and confined in the Dartmoor prison, England. His great-grandfather on his mother's side was also a soldier under Washington and rendered good service, dying at the close of the Revolution from exposure and hardships endured in the field. Hancock's father served in the war of 1812, and afterwards became a lawyer of distinction in Montgomery county, Pennsylvania. At the age of sixteen Hancock was sent to West Point, and had for classmates, U. S. Grant, George B. McClellan, J. F. Reynolds, J. L. Reno, Burnside, Franklin and W. F. Smith. He graduated in 1844. June 30th, and in 1845-6 served with his regiment in the Indian Territory as a second lieutenant of the Sixth Infantry. In 1847 we find him in Mexico and conspicuous for his gallantry at the Natural Bridge, San Antonio, Contreras, Churubusco, Molino del Rey and the capture of the City of Mexico. He was brevetted for gallantry at the battles of Contreras and Churubusco.

When he heard of the Rebellion he took high ground in favor of the Union, and did much in 1861 to check the secession spirit then seizing upon the State of California.

General Hancock's services on the Peninsula and at Antietam were as brilliant and striking as those of any of the lieutenants of the commanding general, and for his gallantry at Chancellorsville he was made permanent commander of the Second Corps.

It was at Gettysburg Hancock again loomed up before the country as a hero. He was commanding the rear-guard of the army in its advance on Gettysburg, and had reached Tarrytown, the place where his grandfather, one hundred years before, had started to escort one thousand Hessian prisoners of Burgoyne's army to Valley Forge, when General Meade sent him an order to hasten to the front and assume command of all the troops there. It is well known that Gettysburg might have been a Confederate victory, had it not have been for Hancock turning the tide in favor of the Union forces.

We have come now to the late Democratic administration. In what was forty years ago the hamlet and is still the obscure town of Caldwell, Essex county, New Jersey, there stands yet a little two-story-and-a-half white house with wooden shutters, and there, in the year 1837, was born Stephen Grover Cleveland. His career has been carelessly characterized as brief and uneventful, because his name has not been in every man's mouth and mind for a quarter of a century; because it has been unmarked by sensational episodes and is lacking in the romantic incidents which make biography fascinating; but if less brilliant and extravagant and eventful than that of the lives of some of the men who have been President of the Republic or who have aspired to that exalted station, the career of Stephen Grover Cleveland is typical of our time and our country, and in its comparatively few pages the youth of our land will find a story of trial, struggle and triumph, inspiring the highest ideals, illustrating the noblest virtues and teaching the truest lessons of the citizenship into which they are born.

STEPHEN GROVER CLEVELAND.

We have now reached the period of the present administration. On the 19th day of June, 1888, the Republican National Convention, which met at Chicago, nominated Benjamin Harrison for the presidency, to which office he was elected November 6th. The Hon. Levi Parsons Morton was elected Vice-President. Benjamin Harrison comes of good stock on both sides of the family. His mother was a woman of character and ability, and his father came of a family distinguished for courage, patriotism and statesmanship. The great-grandfather was conspicuous during the revolutionary period. He voted for and signed the Declaration of Independence.

President Harrison was born at North Bend, Ohio, August 20th, 1833. On October 20th, 1853, he was married to Miss Carrie W. Scott, of Oxford, Ohio. When the war broke out he recruited the Seventieth Regiment of Indiana Volunteers. He was a faithful, brave, efficient commander, and did valuable service in the many battles in which he was engaged.

On February 15th, 1889, the House of Representatives agreed with the Senate on the admission of the four new States of Montana, North Dakota, South Dakota and Washington. The bill was finally passed by both Houses February 20th, and in the following November these States were all admitted into the Union.

The greatest disaster of which we have any record in the history of Pennsylvania was the sweeping away of the greater part of Johnstown and adjoining villages by the collapsing of the South Fork Dam, which had been originally constructed to supply the old State canal with water. Heavy rains had filled the dam to overflowing, when suddenly the sides gave way, and an immense body of water rushed down through the thickly populated and narrow valley of the Conemaugh. The loss of life and property was enormous.

It is a remarkable fact that the three ablest captains, Grant, Sherman and

BENJAMIN HARRISON.

Sheridan, who fought for the Union, were born in the State of Ohio. Grant died July 23, 1885, and Philip Henry Sheridan died suddenly of heart disease on Sunday, August 5th, 1888, in his fifty-eighth year.

Sheridan was a restless spirit. His appetite for war was not gone when the civil strife ended. It is known that Mexico and Canada alike fired his active imagination, and that he would have gone into any movement where he could have been a leader.

An anecdote of his boyhood may not be uninteresting as showing how the man is often foreshadowed in the boy. Patrick McNauly, Sheridan's school-teacher, tried to punish "Phil" because some boy had thrown a bucket of water over him. But "Phil," who saw that suspicion had fallen upon him, ran home, the teacher chasing him until "Phil's" dog, Rover, treed the teacher and kept him there. He begged "Phil" to call off the dog, for it was bitter cold. But the boy would not. Mr. Sheridan at last came out of the house.

"Did you throw any water upon your teacher?" inquired the father.

"No, sir," was the prompt reply.

As Mr. Sheridan had implicit confidence in the boy's veracity under all circumstances, he refused to call off the dog until the teacher had promised not to lick "Phil."

This may be regarded as the first surrender to Sheridan.

In the present age, and more especially in our own country, events which in an earlier period of the world's history would have occupied many years now take place in a day. This was notably the case in the opening up of the Oklahoma lands in accordance with a proclamation by President Harrison. On the morning of the 22d of April, 1889, Guthrie, the capital of Oklahoma, had but twenty inhabitants; and on the night of that same day 8,000 souls slept there under tents; whilst carpenters were at work all around them. Next day—April 23d—the sun shone upon hotels, law-offices, doctors' offices, shops, banks, job-printing offices, and even gambling-houses, all engaged there in active business.

PHYSICAL FEATURES OF NORTH AMERICA.

If we take a glance at the physical aspect of North America we will find that two great mountain systems form the rocky framework of the continent. The eastern or Appalachian system, extending in a direction nearly parallel with the Atlantic coast, is divided by several river-valleys into the White mountains of New Hampshire, the Green mountains of Vermont, the Adirondacks of New York, the Alleghenies of Pennsylvania and Virginia, the Blue Ridge and Cumberland mountains of the Southern States. The gentle slope and frequent divisions of these mountains permit the navigation of many rivers far from the sea; and the two thousand miles of coast which now form the eastern and part of the southern limit of the United States, are broken by bays, inlets, and fine harbors, large enough to shelter the shipping of all the world.

The Cordilleras of the western part of the continent form a grand mountain-system 1,100 miles across its greatest width, consisting of elevated tablelands cut by narrow cañons and bounded by still higher ridges and peaks. The coast range descends abruptly to the Pacific, and its westward-flowing rivers are short and rapid. It is broken in the north by the gorges, or dalles, of the Columbia river, and farther south by San Francisco bay, which extends so far into the interior as to receive the Sacramento and San Joaquin rivers from the eastern slope.

On the various elevations west of the Sierra Nevada, nearly all the grains

GIANT TREES OF CALIFORNIA.

and fruits of the world can be made to grow; but the date-palm, most bounteous of the gifts of nature, has been found best adapted to the river-valleys of Arizona. The greatest growth of the soil is the gigantic sequoia of California, whose trunk, twenty feet or more in diameter near the base, rises often to a height of 300 feet. There are ten groves of these big trees. Some of the trees, by actual measurements, have been found to be 450 feet in height, whose huge trunks measure 116 feet in circumference.

North-westward from the Mississippi valley is a chain of five great lakes, containing collectively nearly half the fresh water in the world. Before reaching the last of the lakes, the mass of water plunges over a precipice 160 feet in height,

NIAGARA FALLS.

making the great cataract which is known as the Falls of Niagara.

Niagara falls are situated on the river of the same name, a strait connecting the floods of Lakes Erie and Ontario, and dividing a portion of the State of New York on the west from the Province of Ontario. The cataracts thus lie within the territory both of Great Britain and the United States.

Niagara, in the Iroquois language, signifies "Thunder of Waters." The waters for which the Niagara is the outlet cover an area of 150,000 square miles—floods so grand and inexhaustible that the loss of the hundred millions of tons which they pour every hour, through succeeding centuries, over these stupendous precipices is totally imperceptible.

The Horseshoe Fall, always marvellous from whatever position it is viewed, forms the connecting link between the scenes of the American and Canadian sides of the river. This mighty cataract is 144 rods across, and it is said by Professor Lyell, that 1,500,000,000 cubic feet of water pass over its ledges every hour.

Gull Island, just above the Horseshoe Fall, is an unapproachable spot upon which it is not likely

YOSEMITE VALLEY.

that man has ever yet stood, and it is hardly possible that he can ever do so.

Three miles below the falls on the American side is the Whirlpool, resembling in its appearance the celebrated Maelstrom on the coast of Norway.

The Yosemite falls in California are amongst the most wonderful in the world. Yosemite, in the Indian tongue, means "Large Grizzly Bear." There is first a vertical leap of 1,500 feet; then a series of cascades down a descent equal to 626 feet perpendicular, and then a final plunge of 400 feet to the rocks at the base of the precipice. The rumble and roar of the falls are heard at all times, but in the quiet of the evening they are so great that it seems as if the very earth were shaking. No falls in the known world can be compared with these in height and romantic grandeur. The renowned Staubbach of Switzerland is greatly inferior, both in height and volume. There are other remarkable falls in the Yosemite valley. One, bearing the romantic name of Bridal Veil Fall, leaps over a cliff 900 feet high into the valley below. The water, long ere it reaches its rocky bed, is converted into mist, and descends in a white sheet of spray. The Virgin's Tears creek, on the other side of the valley, directly opposite the Bridal Veil, makes a fine fall over 1,000 feet high, inclosed in a deep recess of the rock. This is a beautiful fall while it lasts, but the stream which produces it dries up early in the season.

In the United States there are many places which will afford as grand panoramic views of mountain and valley as can be found in Switzerland itself. This is notably so amongst the coal regions of Pennsylvania. Mauch Chunk, for instance, is noted for being situated in the midst of some of the wildest and most picturesque scenery in America, the village lying in a narrow gorge between and among high mountains, its foot resting on the Lehigh river and its body lying along the hillsides. The village is but one street wide, and the valley is so narrow that the dwelling houses usually have their gardens and outhouses perched above the roof. Prospect Rock is a projecting bluff from which a pleasant view may be had; but the view from Flagstaff Peak, just above, is much finer, and the ascent is easily made. Glen Onoko is a wild and beautiful ravine on the side of Broad mountain, about two miles from the village. It is 900 yards long and from forty to eighty feet wide, and presents a continuous succession of cascades, rapids and pools, which afford a fine spectacle in seasons of high water.

SWITZERLAND OF AMERICA.

The celebrated "Switch-Back" railroad, which at one time was used to bring coal from Panther-Creek valley, is now used only as a pleasure road. It is run by gravity. The cars are drawn to the top of Mount Pisgah by a powerful engine on the summit, whence they descend six miles, by gravity, to the foot of Mount Jefferson, where they are again taken up by means of an inclined plane, which ascends 462 feet in a length of 2,070 feet, and then run on to Summit Hill. From that point the cars return, all the way, by the "back-track" or gravity road, to Mauch Chunk, landing the passengers but a short distance from the spot where they commenced the ascent of Mount Pisgah.

Chautauqua lake, long the pride of western New York, and now the admiration of the whole country, claims here a word from us. It lies 700 feet above Lake Erie, which is but seven miles distant. It is about twenty miles

POINT CHAUTAUQUA.

in length, and o. an average depth of twenty feet, ranging from shallows of but a few inches to eighty feet. Its banks are of gentle slope, stretching upward on every side into a beautiful landscape of forest and field.

At Chautauqua, what is known as the Sunday-School Assembly was projected by members of the Methodist Episcopal Church, and organized under the auspices of the normal department of the Sunday-School Union of that church.

With its National Sunday-School Assembly, Church Congress, Scientific Congress and temperance conventions; with wise men in control, and calling together the best talent of the nation to its yearly feasts of science and religion; with its Park of Palestine, Jewish Tabernacle, model of Jerusalem oriental house and Great Pyramid; with its book bazaar and museum; with Ostrander and orientals in full dress, together with Van Lennap, the Turk; with an auditorium of 5,000 capacity, a pavilion of 2,000 capacity, a children's temple in amphitheatre form to seat also 2,000; with its vocal concerts, instrumental concerts, stereopticon exhibitions, fire-works, music on the lake and croquet; with its cool, clear springs, health-giving breezes and gentle showers; with boating, bathing and fishing, and its unlimited go-to-meeting privileges—every day three first-class lectures or sermons; five services for Bible-study, etc., etc.—Chautauqua is already a household word in thousands of American homes.

Our work would be incomplete did we omit all reference to Mount Wash-

TIP-TOP HOUSE, MOUNT WASHINGTON.

ington, the loftiest of the White mountains in New Hampshire. The summit, 6,293 feet high, is an acre of comparatively level ground, on which stand the Mount Washington Summit Hotel, the old Tip-Top House, the engine-house of the railway and the United States signal-service observatory. At this station, which is occupied in winter, observers have recorded a temperature of 59° below zero, while the wind blew with a velocity of 190 miles an hour. The range of the thermometer, even in midsummer, is from 30° to 45°.

The view from Mount Washington is incomparably grand; but its use as being a signal-service station gives it a special interest. The importance of the signal service calls for some slight description of it.

The Signal Service is a military organization which takes note of the development and progress of storms and other atmospheric phenomena, and which reports the same to the public, when not engaged in the duties of warfare.

The observers of the signal corps are trained not only in the art and practice of military field-signalling, but in the ordinary army drill and rules and habits of discipline; they constitute a part of the regular military establishment of the nation, always ready for active service. Occupied in time of peace with scientific work of acknowledged value, the cost of their maintenance is but a small additional burden upon the country, fully requited by their meteorological services to it. Experience has shown that arduous meteorological labors such as they perform have not been secured from any civil corps. As the signal-service observers must report several times a day to the Washington office, each regular report serves in effect as a telegraphic roll-call of all the stations spread over the country from the Atlantic to the Pacific, and from the lakes to the Gulf of Mexico, insuring promptitude, vigilance and steadiness in the entire signal corps.

The net-work of the signal-service stations now extends over the continent from the Atlantic to the Pacific coast, and the intervening territory from the Gulf (including the West Indies) to the Canadian frontier, and is in receipt, by comity of exchange, of daily telegraphic intelligence of the weather from the Canadian Dominion and its outlying posts. These reports from 147 stations of observation are not infrequently concentrated at the central office in the space of *forty minutes*. The stations at which cautionary signals are displayed are equipped with flags, lanterns, etc., for exhibiting the cautionary day or night signals, and also for communicating with vessels of any nationality.

In addition to the regular force of military observers, there was transferred to the signal service on February 2d, 1874, at the instance of Professor Joseph Henry, secretary of the Smithsonian Institution, the entire body of Smithsonian weather observers in all parts of the United States.

In organizing the service of simultaneous weather observations, the first problem that presented itself was to devise a system of observations which would, when mapped accurately, represent the aerial phenomena at the same instant of time, and in their actual relations to each other, and thus enable the investigator to discover the laws of storms and their rates of movement over the earth's surface. Certainly no solid foundation for the science of the weather could have been laid in 1870 upon any of the then existing systems. The European weather stations at that date, and long after, were engaged in making non-simultaneous reports; no two of them, unless they happened to be on the same meridian, read off their instruments at the same time.

The perfectly simple scheme of simultaneous observations aimed at the rescue of weather research from the chaos in which for ages it had lain. Its cardinal principle of observation is to gain frequent views of the atmospheric condition and movements over the country as they actually are, and as they would be seen, could they, so to speak, be photographed.

The cautionary storm-signals which accompany the "Synopsis and Indications," issued to the press three times each day, constitute a very important part of the signal-service work, and it was the possibility of preparing such storm-warnings for the benefit of navigation that originally gave the chief stimulus to the establishment of a weather bureau.

The cautionary signals are of two kinds: 1. Those premonishing dangerous winds to blow from any direction. 2. Those premonishing off-shore winds, likely to drive vessels out to sea. Both kinds are needed by mariners as the storm-centres approach or depart from a maritime station. The first, distinctively termed the "Cautionary Signal," consists of a red flag with a black square in the centre, for warning in the daytime, and a red light by night. The second, or "Cautionary Off-Shore Signal," consists of a white flag with black square in the centre, shown above a red flag with square black centre by day, or a white light shown above a red light by night, indicating that, while the storm has not yet passed the station and dangerous winds may yet be felt there, they will probably be from a northerly or westerly direction; this second signal, when displayed in the lake region in anticipation of high north to west winds, is designated the "Cautionary North-west Signal." The display of either signal, however, is always intended to be cautionary, and calls for great vigilance on the part of vessels within sight of it.

LITERATURE.

The true glory of a nation becomes manifest in its literature, and an account of our country would be incomplete did we omit reference to those of our nation who have shown the pen to be still mightier than the sword. We have already alluded to the first books published in America, and will now mention the names of some of our most celebrated authors whose works have appeared since the opening of the nineteenth century.

Joseph Rodman Drake was born in 1795, and died in 1820. He was a poet of brilliant promise. He was the author of the patriotic poem, entitled "The American Flag." His genius, however, shone pre-eminent in the imagery of the exquisite fairy tale, "The Culprit Fay." This poem was written in three days, on a wager laid between Cooper the novelist, Halleck the poet, and himself.

Fitzgreene Halleck, the friend of Drake, was also born in 1795. He died in 1867: but he wrote little or nothing after 1830, although before that year he had become famous. His immortal lyric, "Marco Bozzaris," alone gained him literary celebrity. Upon the death of his brother-poet, Drake, he wrote a beautiful tribute to his memory, from which we extract the following lines:

> "Green be the turf above thee,
> Friend of my better days!
> None knew thee but to love thee,
> None named thee but to praise."

William Cullen Bryant, the Wordsworth of America, a native of Cummington, Massachusetts, was born in 1794. He resided for over half a century in New York city, where he held the position of editor of the *Evening Post*. A lover of nature, the reverence he felt for her is seen in strongly marked lines throughout his writings. "Thanatopsis" was written and delivered by the author, in his nineteenth year, at a college commencement. His finest poems are "To a Waterfowl," "Death of the Flowers," "Forest Hymn," "Song of the Stars," "The Planting of the Apple-Tree," "Waiting by the Gate," "Our Country's Call" and "The Flood of Years," the last being written at the age of eighty-two. In 1871 he completed a translation of the "Iliad and Odyssey" of Homer, upon which he had been engaged for six years. He died in 1878.

WILLIAM C. BRYANT.

Henry Wadsworth Longfellow, our loved and revered poet-laureate, the first American author to be honored with a memorial in Westminster Abbey, was born in Portland, Maine, in the year 1807, "in an old square wooden house upon the edge of the sea." Graduating from Bowdoin College in 1825, he was, four years afterwards, elected professor of modern languages and literature in his *alma mater*, which position he relinquished to accept a similar one in Harvard in 1835. His duties as a "teacher" were varied by occasional travels to Europe, and his writings are thus enriched with legendary, historic and biographical notes. From 1836 he resided in the "Craigie House," which was purchased for him by his father-in-law in 1843, the year in which he married Miss Appleton. Mary Flora Potter, his first wife, who died suddenly at Rotterdam, four years after their marriage, was a daughter of Judge Potter, of Portland, very lovely in person and rarely gifted in mind.

It may be a consolation to poets who receive little for their verses to know that the "Psalm of Life" first appeared in the *Knickerbocker*, and was never paid for.

Longfellow has a fruitful imagination, under the control of the most perfect taste, and a remarkable power of illustrating moods of mind and states of feeling by material forms. He has a great command of beautiful diction, and equal skill in the structure of his verse. His poetry is marked by tenderness of feeling, purity of sentiment, elevation of thought and healthiness of tone. He understands and can express all the affections of the human heart. The happy delight in his poems; and they fall with soothing and sympathizing touch upon those who have suffered. His readers are more than admirers; they become friends. And over all that he has written there hangs a beautiful ideal light—the atmosphere of poetry—which illuminates his page as the sunshine does the natural landscape.

HENRY W. LONGFELLOW.

Of his leading works are "Hyperion," a romance; "The Spanish Student, Kavanagh," a tale; "The Golden Legend," "Tales of a Wayside Inn," "Outre Mer," "The Building of the Ship," "The Day is Done," "Morituri Salutamus," "Hiawatha," "Miles Standish," "Flower de Luce," "New England Tragedies," "Wreck of the Hesperus," "Paul Revere's Ride," "Children's Hour," "Village Blacksmith," "The Divine Tragedy," "Translation of Dante's Divina Commedia," and "Michael Angelo," a drama.

Longfellow died in 1882.

Oliver Wendell Holmes, M. D., was born in Cambridge, Massachusetts, August 29th, 1809, was graduated at Harvard College in 1829, and commenced the practice of medicine in Boston in 1836. He has been for many years one of the professors in the medical department of Harvard College, and he is understood to be highly skilful, both in the theory and practice of his profession. He began to write poetry at quite an early age. His longest productions are occasional poems which have been recited before literary societies, and received with very great favor. His style is brilliant, sparkling and terse; and many of his heroic stanzas remind us of the point and condensation of Pope. In his shorter poems he is sometimes grave, and sometimes gay. When in the former mood, he charms us by his truth and manliness of feeling, and his sweetness of sentiment; when in the latter, he delights us with the glance and play of the wildest wit and the richest humor. Everything that he writes is carefully finished, and rests on a basis of sound sense and shrewd observation. Dr. Holmes also enjoys high reputation and wide popularity as a prose writer. He is the author of "The Autocrat of the Breakfast Table," "The Professor at the Breakfast Table" and "Elsie Venner," works of fiction which originally appeared in the *Atlantic Monthly Magazine*, and of various occasional discourses.

The following extracts are very characteristic of Holmes:

> "Day hath put on his jacket, and around
> His burning bosom buttoned it with stars."—*Evening—by a Tailor.*

> "Give us men! A time like this demands
> Great hearts, strong arms, true faith and willing hands,
> Men, whom the lust of office does not kill;
> Men, whom the spoils of office can not buy;
> Men who possess opinions and a will;
> Men who have honor, men who will not lie;
> For while the rabble, with their thumb-worn creeds,
> Their large professions and their little deeds,
> Wrangle in selfish strife—lo! Freedom weeps,
> Wrong rules the land, and waiting justice sleeps."—*Give Us Men.*

John Greenleaf Whittier was born in Haverhill, Massachusetts, in 1808. He has written much in prose and verse; and his writings are characterized by earnestness of tone, high moral purpose and energy of expression. His spirit is that of a sincere and fearless reformer; and his fervent appeals are the true utterances of a brave and loving heart. The themes of his poetry have been drawn, in a great measure, from the history, traditions, manners and scenery of New England; and he has found the elements of poetical interest among them without doing any violence to truth. He describes natural scenery correctly and beautifully; and a vein of genuine tenderness runs through his writings. We subjoin a poem of Whittier's, because it is only in our country that the verses are applicable.

"THE POOR VOTER ON ELECTION DAY."

> "The proudest now is but my peer,
>   The highest not more high;
> To-day, of all the weary year,
>   A king of men am I.

> To-day, alike are great and small
>   The nameless and the known;
> My palace is the people's hall,
>   The ballot-box my throne!

"Who serves to-day upon the list
   Beside the served shall stand;
Alike the brown and wrinkled fist,
   The gloved and dainty hand!
The rich is level with the poor,
   The weak is strong to-day;
And sleekest broadcloth counts no more
   Than homespun frock of gray.

"To-day let pomp and vain pretence
   My stubborn right abide;
I set a plain man's common-sense
   Against the pedant's pride.

To-day shall simple manhood try
   The strength of gold and land;
The wide world has not wealth to buy
   The power in my right hand!

"While there's a grief to seek redress,
   Or balance to adjust,
Where weighs our living manhood less
   Than Mammon's vilest dust—
While there's a right to need my vote,
   A wrong to sweep away,
Up! clouted knee and ragged coat!
   A man's a man to-day!"

Edgar Allan Poe (1809–1849), "the poet of morbid anatomy," was born in Boston, and died in Baltimore, where, after life's fitful fever, he sleeps well. The victim of melancholia, a morbid disposition, and an insatiate thirst for intoxicants, in rebellion against a world that misunderstood the man and has attempted to falsify the reputation of one with whom "poetry was not a purpose, but a passion," his life displayed some irregularities, though it is on record by one who, from business association, had every opportunity of estimating his character, that he was "a winning and well-mannered gentleman." His first literary production, "Al Aaraaf and Minor Poems," was unsuccessful. This was followed by "The Narrative of Arthur Gordon Payne," and the weird and powerful romances that bear the impress of a master-mind, of "The Mystery of Mary Roget," "The Murders of the Rue Morgue," "The Gold Bug," "The Fall of the House of Usher," and the poems "The Raven," "The Bells," "Ulalume," "The Haunted Palace" and "Annabel Lee."

Suffering induced by Poe's dissipated habits brought his wife to an early grave, and he wrote of his loss in some very musical lines:

   "The moon never beams without bringing me dreams
      Of the beautiful Annabel Lee;
   And the stars never rise, but I feel the bright eyes
      Of the beautiful Annabel Lee.
   And so, all the night-tide I lie down by the side
   Of my darling, my darling, my life and my bride,
      In her sepulchre there by the sea—
      In her tomb by the sounding sea."

John Howard Payne, the sixth of nine children, was born in New York, June 9th, 1792. He came of a family of conspicuous literary ability and of gentle breeding. Robert Treat Payne, a signer of the Declaration, and Robert Treat Payne, Jr., were of the same family. Miss Dolly Payne, also, who became the wife of President Madison, was his kinswoman.

Payne was the author of some noble and lasting literary work in his day—one of the grandest of heroic tragedies now played, "Brutus, or the Fall of Tarquin," being from his pen. He was both in America and England recognized as an actor of advancing reputation, and as an author of merit. In one of his plays he introduced the song of "Home, sweet Home." The song at once became popular. In less than a year 100,000 copies were sold by a publisher who did not even put Payne's name on the title-page. As this song is, and always will be, a favorite wherever the English language is spoken, we give the words as they appear in Payne's original manuscript.

> "'Mid pleasures and palaces though we may roam,
> Be it ever so humble, there's no place like home!
> A charm from the sky seems to hallow us there,
> Which, seek through the world, is ne'er met with elsewhere!
> Home, home, sweet, sweet home!
> There's no place like home!
> There's no place like home!
>
> "An exile from home, splendor dazzles in vain;
> O give me my lowly thatched cottage again!
> The birds, singing gayly, that came at my call,
> Give me them—and the peace dearer than all!
> Home, home, sweet, sweet home!
> There's no place like home!
> There's no place like home!"

There are two of the original verses which are now commonly omitted, but as they appear to express the poet's own personal feelings in regard to himself as being a wanderer from his native land, we think it well to give them here.

> "To us, in despite of the absence of years,
> How sweet the remembrance of home still appears!
> From allurements abroad, which flatter the eye,
> The unsatisfied heart turns, and says, with a sigh,
> 'Home, home—sweet, sweet home,
> There's no place like home—there's no place like home!'
>
> "Your exile is blessed with all fate can bestow,
> But mine has been checkered with many a woe;
> Yet, though different our fortunes, our thoughts are the same
> And both, as we think of Columbia, exclaim,
> 'Home, home—sweet, sweet home,
> There's no place like home—there's no place like home!'"

Payne was appointed American consul at Tunis in 1842, and sailed thither the year following.

From Tunis, Payne was recalled in 1845. He was reappointed in 1851. In April he sailed from New York, and he died in Tunis, June, 1852, in his sixtieth year. The United States government caused a marble slab to be placed at his grave, which bears the following inscription:

<blockquote>
In memory of
COLONEL JOHN HOWARD PAYNE,
Twice Consul of the United States of America to the Kingdom
of Tunis,
This stone is placed here by a grateful country.
</blockquote>

The slab has also engraven on it these lines, written by Mr. R. S. Chilton:

<blockquote>
" Sure, when thy gentle spirit fled
   To realms beyond the azure dome,
With arms outstretched God's angels said,
   ' Welcome to heaven, " Home, Sweet Home." ' "
</blockquote>

BIRTHPLACE OF JOHN HOWARD PAYNE.

In 1883, the remains of Payne were brought to Washington, and on June 9th, the ninety-first anniversary of the poet's birth, were buried with appropriate ceremonies in Oak Hill Cemetery, Georgetown, District of Columbia.

The following verses were written by Will Carleton, on the removal of the remains of John Howard Payne to this country:

<blockquote>
" The banishment was overlong,
   But it will soon be past;
The man who wrote Home's sweetest song
   Is coming home at last!
For years his poor abode was seen
   In foreign lands alone,
And waves have thundered loud between
   This singer and his own.
</blockquote>

> But he will soon be journeying
> To friends across the sea ;
> And grander than of any king
> His welcome here shall be."—*Coming Home at Last.*

Carleton was born in 1845, and in 1869 graduated at Hillsdale College, and then entered the journalistic profession, to which he still belongs. He is the author of "Betsey and I are out," "Over the Hills to the Poor-House," and other well-known ballads.

Space will not permit our dwelling upon many other worthy names in poetry. Bayard Taylor was alike eminent as a poet, novelist, and traveller. Read won fame both with brush and pen. Boker is a lyric and dramatic writer of great excellence, and has represented the United States at Constantinople and St. Petersburg. Bret Harte has given us some able dialect poetry, and Walt Whitman has shown remarkable originality. Nor ought we to omit Alice Carey, who was born in 1820 and died in 1871, and who was the greatest female genius that our country has produced, was born at Mount Healthy, near Cincinnati, and died at her home in New York City. Contributing verses to the Cincinnati press at the age of eighteen, which were well received, she first attracted attention by a series of sketches of rural life. Removing with her sister Phœbe (1824–1871) to New York, the two issued a volume of poems. She wrote "Married, not Mated," and "Hollywood," novels; "Pictures of Country Life," "The Bridal Veil," "Thanksgiving," "Krumley," "The Bishop's Son," and "Snow Berries."

Phœbe Carey wrote many beautiful poems, such as "Nearer Home," and, among other amusing parodies, one on the "Psalm of Life."

If we turn to prose we will find names equal in ability to those mentioned in poetry.

Washington Irving, the most popular of American authors, and one of the most popular writers in the English language during his time, was born in New York, April 8th, 1783, and died November 28th, 1859. His numerous works are too well known to need enumeration; and his countrymen are so familiar with the graces of his style and the charm of his delightful genius, that any extended criticism would be superfluous. His writings are remarkable for their combination of rich and original humor with great refinement of feeling and delicacy of sentiment. His humor is unstained by coarseness, and his sentiment is neither mawkish nor morbid. His style is carefully finished, and in his most elaborate productions the uniform music of his cadences approaches monotony. He is an accurate observer, and his descriptions are correct, animated and beautiful. In his biographical and historical works his style is flowing, easy and transparent. His personal character was affectionate and amiable, and these traits penetrate his writings and constitute no small portion of their charm. Few writers have ever awakened in their readers a stronger personal interest than Irving; and the sternest critic could not deal harshly with an author who showed himself to be so gentle and kindly a man.

James Fennimore Cooper, the author of "The Spy," "The Pilot," "Leather-stocking Tales," etc., was born at Burlington, New Jersey, on the 15th of December, 1789. The distinguished novelist was also author of the "History of the Navy of the United States." He died in 1851.

William Ellery Channing was born at Newport, Rhode Island, April 7th, 1780, was graduated at Harvard College in 1798, and died October 2d, 1842.

Dr. Channing's style is admirably suited for the exposition of moral and spiritual truth. It is rich, flowing and perspicuous; even its diffuseness, which is its obvious literary defect, is no disadvantage in this aspect. There is a persuasive charm over all his writings, flowing from his earnestness of purpose, his deep love of humanity, his glowing hopes and his fervent religious faith.

William Hickling Prescott was born in Salem, Massachusetts, May 4th, 1796, and died in Boston, January 28th, 1859. His grandfather was Colonel William Prescott, who commanded in the redoubt at Bunker Hill. He is the author of four historical works—"The History of the Reign of Ferdinand and Isabella," "The History of the Conquest of Mexico," "The History of the Conquest of Peru" and "The History of the Reign of Philip the Second;" which last was left unfinished at the time of his death. These are all productions of great merit, and have received the highest commendations at home and abroad. Among their most conspicuous excellences may be mentioned their thoroughness of investigation and research. Mr. Prescott examined, with untiring industry, all possible sources of information, whether in print or in manuscript, which could throw light upon the subjects of which he treated. This was the more honorable to him, as, in consequence of an accident in college, he was deprived, to a considerable degree, of the use of his eyes, and was constantly obliged to make use of the sight of others in prosecuting his studies.

Ralph Waldo Emerson, the sage of Concord, was born in Boston, in 1803, graduated at Harvard in 1821, taught for a short time, ministered thought to a congregation for three years in his native city, and then retired to the classic town, where he lived till the end, only varying the studious retirement of his life by lecturing in this country and abroad. His writings are observant and speculative: display a quaintness of language and a philosophic taste and power that has made a vivid impression upon the literature of the nineteenth century. He died in 1882.

Henry Ward Beecher was born in Litchfield, Connecticut, June 24th, 1813, graduated at Amherst College in 1834, studied theology under his father, the Rev. Lyman Beecher, and from 1847 until his death (March 8th, 1887) was pastor of the Plymouth Church, Brooklyn, New York. As a lecturer he enjoyed an unrivalled popularity, earned by the happy combination of humor, pathos, earnestness and genial sympathy with humanity, which his discourses present. He was a man of great energy of temperament, fervently opposed to every form of oppression and injustice, and with a poet's love of nature. His style was rich, glowing and abundant.

Harriet Beecher Stowe was born at Litchfield, Connecticut, in 1812; but resided for several years, with her husband, Professor Stowe, at Mandarin, on the St. John's river, Florida. Her fame was established by the publication of "Uncle Tom's Cabin" (in 1852), the most widely read book ever written in America.

In George Bancroft and John Lothrop Motley we have historians whose reputation worthily reaches wherever the English language is read.

THE FINE ARTS.

In the generation which immediately succeeded the American Revolution, there was very little devotion to art. The adjustment of commercial and political relations at home and abroad, naturally required all the energies of the people. In the beginning of this century, however, the art principle began to develop itself side by side with literature. Still at no time was there a total lack of tendency towards pictorial representation.

If we take into account all the drawbacks incident to a new country which the study of art necessarily meets with, we will find that its progress in the United States has been wonderfully rapid. There are branches of art unknown in ancient times, which have attained remarkable development within the present century. And in engraving, and the illustration of books and periodicals, the palm of superiority has been freely conceded to American artists by the critics in the art centres of the old world. Indeed, it is those branches of pictorial art which conduce to the education, the comfort and even luxury of universal mankind, which it has been the mission of the great Republic to bring to perfection, as it has been in corresponding branches of science and mechanical invention. Its work in art as in science has been for the good of the many, and not, as in the old world, mainly for the benefit of the few, as may be seen in the strides it has made in chromolithography, which has made the works of the world's most eminent artists familiar to the commonest and poorest.

But even in the arts of painting and sculpture America has been productive of great names. It will be sufficient to mention the names of West, Allston, Church, Leslie, Weir, Bierstadt, Cole, Rothermel, Hamilton and Moran in painting; Greenough, Powers and Harriet Hosmer in sculpture, as evidence that the highest order of genius in art can exist side by side with the most unwearied industry in commerce and manufactures.

In the kindred art of music, the United States has also been a benefactor to the world. The compositions of Bliss and Sankey in sacred music; and of Stephen Foster in his plaintive negro melodies, are the delight of many homes in the old world, as well as homes in the New.

But it is inventive talent by which Americans are most distinguished. The inventive genius which the subduing of a great, wild continent first called into action has been only heightened by prosperity. The soil of South Africa, Australia and Japan is turned by American plows, and their harvests are gathered by American mowers and reapers; fires in European cities are extinguished by American steam fire-engines; American palace-cars roll over European railways; and American steam-boats ply on the Rhine, the Danube, and the Bosphorus. Great London newspapers are printed on the type-revolving press invented by Richard Hoe, of New York.

Viewing then the rapid progress, vast extent, and present prosperity of our country, well might our poet-laureate Longfellow sing:

> "Thou, too, sail on, O Ship of State!
> Sail on, O Union, strong and great!
> Humanity, with all its fears,
> With all the hopes of future years,
> Is hanging breathless on thy fate!
> We know what Master laid thy keel,
> What Workmen wrought thy ribs of steel,
> Who made each mast, and sail, and rope,
> What anvils rang, what hammers beat
> In what a forge, and what a heat,
> Were shaped the anchors of thy hope.
>
> . . . . . .
>
> "Sail on, nor fear to breast the sea!
> Our hearts, our hopes are all with thee,
> Our hearts, our hopes, our prayers, our tears,
> Our faith triumphant o'er our fears,
> Are all with thee—are all with thee."

GRAND CANAL, VENICE.

ITALY.

HE limits of the Italian peninsula have been most distinctly traced by nature. The Alps, which bound it on the north, from the promontories of Liguria to the mountainous peninsula of Istria, present themselves like a huge wall, the only breaches in which are formed by passes situated high up in the zones of pines, pastures, or eternal snows. Its delightful climate, beauteous skies and fertile fields distinguish it in a marked manner from countries lying beyond the Alps.

For nearly two thousand years Italy remained the centre of the civilized world. Two of the greatest events in history, the uniting of the Mediterranean world under the laws of Rome, and at a later age the regeneration of the human mind, to which the term "renaissance" has been given, originated in Italy.

There is no other country in the world which can boast of an equal number of cities remarkable on account of their buildings, statues, paintings and decorations of every kind. There are provinces where every village, every group of houses even, delights the eye either by a fresco painting or a work of the sculptor's chisel, a bold staircase or picturesque balcony.

Italy owes the rank it has held for more than two thousand years not merely to its monuments and works of art, which attract students from the extremities of the earth, but also to its historical associations. Every fortress, every country house, marks the site of some ancient citadel, or of the villa of a Roman patrician; churches have replaced the ancient temples, and though the religious rites have changed, the altars of gods and saints arise anew on the spots consecrated of old.

The Italian is the most richly endowed of all the European nations. When we look to the splendid achievements of this race in all its subdivisions—to the artists, authors, soldiers, natural philosophers, and civil engineers, which the peninsula has produced—we other peoples are compelled to bow our heads before them in every department of intellectual exertion.

ROME.

Rome, the most celebrated of European cities, famous in both ancient and modern history, formerly for being the most powerful nation of antiquity, and afterward the ecclesiastical capital of Christendom and the residence of the pope, and since 1871 the capital of United Italy and the residence of the king, is situated on both banks of the Tiber, about sixteen miles from its mouth.

The earliest history of Rome is legendary, or to some extent fabulous, with a basis of historical truth. It is said that Rhea Silvia, a female descendant of Æneas, one of the Trojan heroes, was compelled by her uncle to become a vestal virgin, whereby she was obliged to remain unmarried. But by the god Mars she became the mother of twin sons, Romulus and Remus. Thereupon her uncle caused her to be killed, and her infants to be thrown into the river Tiber. The river at the time happened to have overflowed its banks, so that after a short time, when the waters subsided, the basket containing the babes remained standing on dry land. There they were suckled by a she-wolf and fed by a woodpecker, until they were found by a shepherd, who took them to his wife.

When the boys had grown up to manhood they resolved to build a town near the spot where they had been saved. When the new town was finished, a dispute arose as to which of the two brothers should give it its name; from words it came to blows, and Romulus slew his brother. In order to increase the number of inhabitants, Romulus opened an asylum, inviting all to come and settle in the new place. Vagabonds of every description came, and all were welcome. But as there were no women among them, the population would soon have died out, and in order to prevent this Romulus applied to the neighboring communities of Latins and Sabines to obtain wives for his subjects. This request was scornfully rejected, and Romulus then resolved to obtain by a cunning device what had been refused to his fair demand. He invited the neighboring tribes to a festival to be celebrated in honor of the god Neptune; and while the strangers were witnessing the games, the Romans suddenly seized their daughters and carried them by force to their homes. To avenge this outrage, the Latins and Sabines took up arms against Rome. The former were easily defeated, but during the heat of the fight with the Sabines, the Sabine women threw themselves between the combatants, imploring them to desist from destroying one another, and declared themselves willing to remain with their new husbands.

After the death of Romulus, a whole year passed away without a successor being elected, and in the meantime the government was conducted by the senate. At length the Ramnes or Romans chose from among the Sabines Numa Pompilius, of Cures, a man renowned for his piety and wisdom. The legend represents him as the founder of all the great religious institutions, just as Romulus is described as the author of the political organization of the state. Numa's reign was a period of uninterrupted peace, during which the people were engaged in the peaceful pursuit of agriculture and in the worship of the gods. In all he did the king was supported by the counsels of the nymph Egeria, with whom he had interviews in a sacred grove near Aricia.

After the death of Numa Pompilius the Romans chose Tullus Hostilius for their king. His reign, extending from B. C. 672 to 640, is described as the very opposite of that of Numa, for he is said to have neglected the worship of the gods and to have been engaged in perpetual wars with his neighbors. The first of these wars was waged against Alba Longa, in consequence of certain acts of violence for which reparation was refused by that city. The contest between the two little states remained for a long time undecided, until at length the commanders arranged that the dispute should be determined by a combat of three Roman brothers, called the Horatii, with three Alban brothers called the Curiatii, who happened to be serving in their respective armies; and it was agreed that the conquering party should rule over the vanquished. When the three champions of each party met, two of the Horatii were killed, while all the three Curiatii were indeed wounded, but still able to fight. The surviving Horatius then took to flight, and the three Curiatii pursued him at such intervals as their wounds permitted. This was what Horatius had foreseen, and turning round, he slew them one after another. It was thus decided that Rome should rule over Alba. When the Romans returned home in triumph, Horatius met his sister, who burst into tears and lamentations, when she saw among the spoils won by her brother a garment she had woven with her own hands for one of the Curiatii, to whom she had been betrothed. Horatius, enraged at her conduct on such an occasion, ran her through with his sword. For this outrage he was tried and sentenced to death; but he availed himself of his right to appeal to the people, who, moved by the recollection of what he had done for his country, and by the entreaties of his father, who by his death would have been left childless, acquitted him.

The kingly government of Rome came to an end with the expulsion of Lucius Tarquin, in 510 B. C.

During the latter part of his reign, Tarquin was involved in a war with Ardea, a fortified town of the Rutulians, who had probably refused to acknowledge the supremacy of Rome. The town accordingly was besieged, but with little success; and one day, while the king's sons and their cousin, Collatinus, were feasting in their tents and discussing the virtues of their wives, it was arranged that the three should go home unexpectedly by night, to see how the princesses were spending their time. The wives of the two brothers were found at Rome, revelling at a luxurious banquet; but when they came to Collatia, they found Lucretia, the wife of Collatinus, engaged in domestic occupations with her maid-servants. She accordingly was acknowledged to be the best of the three; but in her humble occupation she appeared so lovely and beautiful, that a few days later Sextus Tarquin, one of the princes, returned to Collatia, where, as a kinsman, he was hospitably received. But in the dead of night he entered her chamber, and threatened to expose her name to everlasting shame, if she refused to gratify his lust. By intimidation he gained his end. But on the following morning Lucretia sent for her father and husband, who came accompanied by Publius Valerius and Lucius Junius Brutus. To these four men Lucretia revealed the crime committed upon her, and having called upon them to avenge the wrong, plunged a dagger into her own breast. Brutus, throwing off the mask of idiocy, which had been assumed by him in order to escape the danger of being put to death, a fate which had befallen others, drew the dagger from the wound, and vowed destruction to the royal house of the Tarquins. The three others took the same oath. Brutus then gained over the people and the army of Rome, and drove out the Tarquins.

In the first year of the republic a conspiracy was formed among a number of young patricians for the purpose of restoring the exiled monarch; they were joined even by the sons of Brutus. When it was found out, the guilty were put to death, and Brutus, with a sternness peculiarly characteristic of a Roman, ordered his own sons to be executed.

The fall of Tarquin has been the subject of many poems and dramatic works. Shakespeare made "The Rape of Lucrece" the subject of his longest poem. And our own poet, John Howard Payne, the author of "Home, Sweet Home," has, in his tragedy entitled "Brutus, or the Fall of Tarquin," surpassed all other authors who have treated dramatically of the same subject.

Tarquin afterwards went and obtained the assistance of Porsenna, King of Etruria, who marched against Rome and pitched his camp on the right bank of the Tiber. On one occasion, it is said, the Romans crossed the Tiber with the intention of driving the enemy from his strong-hold, but were repulsed and returned to the city; and the enemy would have pursued them

across the river, had not Horatius Cocles, a bold and powerful Roman, who was guarding the wooden bridge with two comrades, kept the whole hostile army at bay, while his countrymen were busily engaged in breaking down the bridge. He is even said to have dismissed his two comrades and alone to have resisted the whole army until the bridge was demolished. He then threw himself into the river, and safely swam across, amid showers of darts from the Etruscans.

Macaulay, in his "Lays of Ancient Rome," has, in vigorous verse, vividly depicted this fight:

> "Then out spake brave Horatius, the captain of the gate:
> 'To every man upon this earth death cometh, soon or late.
> Hew down the bridge, Sir Consul, with all the speed ye may;
> I, with two more to help me, will hold the foe in play.
>
> "'In yon straight path a thousand may well be stopped by three.
> Now, who will stand on either hand, and keep the bridge with me?'
> Then out spake Spurius Lartius, a Ramnian proud was he:
> 'Lo! I will stand at thy right hand, and keep the bridge with thee.'
>
> "And out spake strong Herminius, of Titan blood was he:
> 'I will abide on thy left side, and keep the bridge with thee.'
> 'Horatius,' quoth the Consul, 'as thou sayest, so let it be.'
> And straight against that great array forth went the dauntless three."

In the year B. C. 509, Rome concluded a commercial treaty with the wealthy city of Carthage, a Phœnician colony on the north coast of Africa. The same treaty had been twice before renewed, and the relation between the two republics had always been of an amicable kind, but the Carthaginians seem to have become apprehensive of the growing power of Rome. Disputes arose between the two powers, and at length Rome declared war against Carthage, and finally compelled it to sue for peace, which was only granted on most humiliating conditions. This was called the First Punic War.

The Second Punic War arose by Hannibal, a young man of nineteen, laying siege to Saguntum, a city of Spain in alliance with Rome. The Romans remonstrated, but in vain, and war was the consequence. Saguntum was destroyed, and the inhabitants put to the sword. The contest was now between Rome and Hannibal. Hannibal, with a force of 90,000 foot, 12,000 horse and thirty-seven elephants, began his memorable march across the Alps. When he descended on the south side, his forces were reduced to 20,000 foot and 6,000 horse. He then met two Roman armies, and defeated them both. In the following spring he met, at Lake Thrasimenus, the Roman consul Flaminius, who was defeated and slain. In this battle 15,000 Romans perished. At length the Romans prepared to crush their terrible enemy with one blow. They proceeded to Apulia with a large army of 80,000 foot and 6,000 horse, and pitched their camp near the little town of Cannae. Here Hannibal again totally defeated the Romans, leaving 47,000 of them dead on the field. But the support necessary for Hannibal to carry on his career of victory to a successful issue was denied him, and at Zama he was defeated by Scipio; and the war was decided in favor of Rome. Hannibal returned to Carthage and did all he could to repair the losses which his country had sustained. But the fear and enmity of Rome, and the jealousy of many of his own countrymen, forced Hannibal to quit his own country as an exile. He took refuge with Antiochus, King of Syria, who made war against Rome, but through not following the advice of Hannibal was easily defeated. Hannibal then sought the protection of Prusius, King of Bithynia; but here, too, the Romans pursued him, for they did not feel safe whilst he lived; and Hannibal, seeing that Prusius could protect him no longer, put an end to his life by poison.

Forty years after the death of Hannibal the Romans, seeing that Carthage was recovering to some extent its former prosperity, became bent on destroying it. The Carthaginians were driven to desperation, and, although they suffered from the most terrible famine, they defended every inch of ground, even after the enemy had entered the city. The battle which raged in the streets lasted for six days, after which the fury of the invaders and a fearful conflagration changed the once proud mistress of the Mediterranean into a heap of ruins. Fifty thousand of its inhabitants who escaped from the massacre were sold as slaves; and Scipio, like his great namesake, was honored with the surname of Africanus. The territory of Carthage was changed into a Roman province under the name of Africa, and a curse was pronounced upon the site of the ancient city, so that it should never be rebuilt.

Wars, both foreign and domestic, now followed each other in rapid succession. The Cimbri and Teutons, wild northern tribes, were defeated by the Roman general Marius. Civil war then arose between Marius and Sulla, in which more than 100,000 lives were sacrificed. In this, Sulla was victorious. Pompey, a young partisan of Sulla, gained many victories and, upon the death of Sulla, became the most popular man in Rome.

Ever since the time of Marius and Sulla, the leading object of the men in power was to gain popularity at any cost, and that not with a view to benefit their country, but to gratify their own ambition and avarice. Hence the history of this period down to the establishment of the monarchy, is little more than the personal history of men who endeavored to outdo one another. By far the most eminent and most talented among them was Caius Julius Cæsar, born in B. C. 100, and belonging to one of the most ancient patrician families. He was fast rising in popular favor at the time when Pompey was quietly enjoying the fruits of his victories.

Julius Cæsar was a man of the highest culture, and was indefatigable in everything that he undertook. He was equally great as an orator, an author, a general and a statesman. He has been called "the greatest man in all history;" and Shakespeare styles him

"The foremost man of all this world."

Cæsar was of slender build, fair, of a delicate constitution, and subject to violent headaches and epileptic fits. He did not, however, make these disorders a pretence for indulging himself. On the contrary, he sought in war a remedy for his infirmities, endeavoring to strengthen his constitution by long marches, and by simple diet. Thus he contended with his distemper and fortified himself against its attacks.

He was a good horseman, and brought that exercise to such perfection by practice that he could sit a horse at full speed with his hands behind him. He also accustomed himself to dictate letters as he rode on horseback, and found sufficient employment for two or more secretaries at once.

As an evidence of his naturally ambitious temperament, a remark made by Cæsar whilst coming to a little town near the Alps may be given. His friends, jocularly, took occasion to say, "Can there be any disputes for offices here?" upon which Cæsar answered, "I had rather be the first man here, than the second in Rome."

He seemed totally without fear. On one occasion, when some of his soldiers became panic-stricken, and were fleeing from the enemy, he took one by the neck, and making him face about, said, 'You are taking the wrong road; this is the way towards the enemy."

When Cæsar was at war with Egypt, its princess, Cleopatra, with a friend named Apollodorus, got into a small boat, and in the dusk of the evening made for the palace which Cæsar had captured. As she saw it difficult to enter undiscovered, she rolled herself up in a carpet; Apollodorus tied her up at full length, like a bale of goods, and carried her in at the gates to Cæsar. This strategem of hers, which was a strong proof of her wit and ingenuity, is said to have opened her the way to Cæsar's heart; and he insisted that she should reign with him.

After this, Pharnaces, a king of Pontus, stirred up all the kings and tetrarchs of Asia against the Romans. Cæsar defeated them in a great battle, and ruined their whole army. In the account he gave one of his friends in Rome of the rapidity with which he gained his victory, he made use of only three words, "I came, I saw, I conquered."

Cæsar having conquered all the world then known to Rome, was told by the senate that he must now disband his forces. This Cæsar refused to do, and crossing the Rubicon, a river dividing Gaul from Italy, he marched towards Rome. A Roman army, under Pompey, was sent against him. Pompey was completely defeated, and fled to Egypt, where he was murdered.

Cæsar was now virtually the sole ruler of the Roman empire, and on his

return from Africa he silenced all fears and apprehensions by proclaiming a general amnesty, and by assuring his fellow-citizens that his sole object was to restore peace and order. He celebrated four triumphs, and entertained both soldiers and citizens with every kind of public amusement. During his stay at Rome, in B. C. 46, he introduced his celebrated reform of the calendar, which, through the ignorance or caprice of the pagan pontiffs, had fallen into the greatest disorder. Cæsar not only remedied the existing evil, but made regulations to prevent its recurrence; and the calendar, as reformed by him, remained in use until A. D. 1582, when Pope Gregory XIII. introduced another reformed calendar, which is still in use.

Whilst in Rome a conspiracy was formed against him. He was warned in regard to it, but with characteristic indifference, for he never feared death, he paid no attention to the warning. A soothsayer also forewarned him of a great danger which threatened him on the ides of March, and when the day was come, as he was going to the senate-house, he called to the soothsayer, and said, laughing, "The ides of March are come;" to which he answered softly, "Yes; but they are not gone."

When Cæsar entered the house, the senate rose to do him honor, but the conspirators drew their swords and gathered round him in such a manner that, whatever way he turned, he saw nothing but steel gleaming in his face, and met nothing but wounds. The other senators were seized with consternation and horror, insomuch that they durst neither fly nor assist, nor even utter a word. Cæsar, seeing himself doomed, drew his robe over his face, and yielded to his fate.

The assassination was soon followed by civil war. Mark Antony, a friend of Cæsar, and Octavius, a son of Cæsar's niece, made war against the assassins Brutus and Cassius, and defeated them upon the plains of Philippi. These conspirators afterwards committed suicide by falling upon their own swords.

Antony and Octavius were now the chief rulers in the Roman empire. Antony married Octavia, the sister of Octavius, but afterwards divorced and left her for Cleopatra, Queen of Egypt. Octavius then declared war against Egypt and defeated Antony and Cleopatra, who then put an end to their own existence.

When Octavius, in B. C. 39, returned from the East, the senate and the people vied with each other in their servility and adulation. Two years later he received the title of Augustus, that is, the Venerable, a title which was afterwards assumed by all the Roman emperors.

The most important event which marks the reign of Augustus is the birth of Christ. The reign of Augustus, or more correctly, the period from the death of Sulla to that of Augustus, forms the golden age of Roman literature. The Latin language then reached its highest development, and the greatest poets, orators and historians belong to that period.

In the first century of the Christian era, Jerusalem was besieged by the Romans; and history can show nothing to match the horrors of that siege, or the deadly work produced by war and famine. Mothers snatched the morsels from their children's lips. The robbers broke open every shut door in search of food, and tortured most horribly all who were thought to have a hidden store. Gaunt men, who had crept beyond the walls by night to gather a few wild herbs, were often robbed by these wretches of the poor handful of green leaves for which they had risked their lives. Yet, in spite of this, the starving people went out into the valleys in such numbers that the Romans caught them at the rate of 500 a day, and crucified them before the walls, until there was no room to plant and no wood to make another cross.

The siege lasted 134 days, during which 1,100,000 Jews perished, and 97,000 were taken captive. Some were kept to grace the Roman triumph; some were sent to toil in the mines of Egypt; some fought in provincial theatres with gladiators and wild beasts; those under seventeen were sold as slaves.

Eleven persecutions of the Christians—some fiercer, others fainter—marked the dying struggles of the many-headed monster, Paganism. More than three centuries were filled with the sound and sorrows of the great conflict.

In the tenth year of the brutal Nero's reign the first great persecution of Christians took place. A fire, such as never had burned before, consumed nearly the whole city of Rome; and men said that the emperor's own hand had kindled the flames out of mere wicked sport, and that, while the blazing city was filled with shrieks of pain and terror, he sat calmly looking on and singing verses on the burning of Troy to the music of his lyre.

This story finding ready acceptance among the homeless and beggared people, the tyrant strove, by inflicting tortures on the Christians, to turn the suspicion from himself upon them. On the pretence that they were guilty of the atrocious crime, he crucified many; some, covered with the skins of wild beasts, were worried to death by dogs in the theatres; tender girls and gray-haired men were torn by tigers, or hacked with the swords of gladiators. But the worst sight was seen in the gardens of Nero, where chariot races were held by night, in which the emperor himself, dressed as a common driver, whipped his horses round the goal. There stood poor men and women of the Christian faith, their clothes smeared with pitch, or other combustible, all blazing as torches to throw light on the sport of the imperial demon. In the wider persecutions that followed, for this one was chiefly confined to Rome, there was perhaps, no scene of equal horror.

During these persecutions the Christians took refuge in the catacombs or underground caves. These had been used, at first, simply as places of worship and sepulture. But now an entire change in their construction took place. They became obviously designed for the purposes of safety and concealment. Centuries after this period, during the short and tumultuous career of Cola di Rienzi, the catacombs were the scenes of the plots and counterplots of that troublous time; and were also used as places of refuge and concealment.

Rienzi, the son of an innkeeper and a washerwoman, was, in early youth, deeply read in the great masters of the Latin tongue. Cicero and Livy were his special favorites. His classic enthusiasm gained for him the friendship of Petrarch. He was very poor, reduced to a single coat, when he received the post of apostolic notary, which rescued him from poverty. The feuds of the noble families, Colonna, Orsini and Savelli, filled the streets with daily riot and bloodshed. Rienzi, whose fiery eloquence made him a man of mark in Rome, might often be seen in the centre of an eagerly attentive crowd, interpreting the words of some old brass or marble tablet, and dwelling fondly on the ancient glories of senate and people. Encouraged by the flashes of patriotic fire which from time to time burst from the enslaved people, he formed the bold design of seizing the helm of the state.

Rienzi drove out the nobles from Rome, and was elected tribune. Italy flourished under his government; but his rule was brief. The nobles, secretly gathering strength, rose in arms against him; whilst the citizens seeing his inability to cope with the nobles also revolted. His palace was stormed and burnt, and he himself stabbed to death.

The career of Rienzi has been made the subject of one of Bulwer's finest romances; and the reader will find therein a picture of Italy in mediæval times, more faithful than that usually given in professed history. Rienzi has also been made the subject of a beautiful tragedy by Miss Mitford. Byron thus writes of the great patriot:

> "Then turn we to our latest tribune's name,
> From her ten thousand tyrants turn to thee,
> Redeemer of dark centuries of shame—
> The friend of Petrarch—hope of Italy—
> Rienzi! last of Romans!"

No city in the world can show greater objects of interest than are to be found in Rome. The remains of all the epochs of civilization of which we have any knowledge, can be found there within a day's ride. In its galleries is to be found the most of what we have of antique art.

The greatest of antique structures in Italy is the Colosseum. It was built in honor of Titus, and it is said that 60,000 Jews were engaged on it ten years. In the middle ages it was a feudal fortress for a long time, and finally a quarry from which were built churches and palaces, until by its consecration as holy ground, on account of the number of martyrs supposed to have been immolated there,

INTERIOR OF ST. PETER'S, ROME.

further ravage was stopped. The subsequent repairs, though greatly interfering with its picturesqueness, will doubtless have the effect of preserving the remainder for centuries more. It is said to have given seats to 87,000 spectators, and was inaugurated A. D. 81, the same year in which Titus died, on which occasion 5,000 wild animals and 10,000 captives were slain. The inauguration lasted 100 days.

St. Peter's, the great marvel of Christian Rome, is built on or near the place where stood the Temple of Jupiter Vaticanus, so called because it was the place where the vates, or augurs, made their auguries from the victims sacrificed, and from which is derived the name borne by the papal palace of the Vatican. The first structure on this site was an oratory erected in A. D. 90 to indicate the place where St. Peter was buried. Constantine the Great erected a basilica on the spot. The present structure was commenced by Julius II. about 1503, under the direction of Bramanti; but the present form of the basilica is due more to Michael Angelo than to any other of the many architects employed on it.

The Vatican is the capitol of modern Rome, and its gallery of sculpture the most complete and valuable in existence. It is three stories high, and comprises an infinite number of saloons, galleries, corridors, chapels, a library of 100,000 volumes, a museum which is immense, twenty courts, eight grand stairways and 200 small ones. It is far superior to any palace in the world in history, being the most ancient and decidedly the most celebrated of all the papal palaces, composed of a mass of buildings erected by many different popes, covering a space 1,200 feet in length and 1,000 in breadth. It is the winter residence of the pope.

In the Vatican are to be found the greatest works of Raphael, who is universally acknowledged to be the greatest painter that has ever lived. The "Transfiguration" was the last and greatest painting of the immortal master, painted for the cathedral of Narbonne by order of Cardinal Giulio de' Medici, afterward Clement VII. For many years the picture was preserved in the church of St. Pietro, in Montorio, from which the French had it removed to Paris. In 1815, on its return, it was placed in the Vatican. The idea throughout the piece seems to express the miseries of human life, and lead those who are afflicted to look to heaven for comfort and relief. The upper portion of the composition represents Mount Tabor; on the ground the three apostles are lying, affected by the supernatural light which proceeds from the divinity of Christ, who, accompanied by Moses and Elijah, is floating in the air. On one side are nine apostles; a multitude of people on the other, bringing to them a demoniac boy whose limbs are dreadfully convulsed, which produces on every countenance an expression of terror. Two of the apostles point toward heaven. The figures on the mount of the two prophets and the three disciples are magnificently executed, while the figure of the

Saviour is of surpassing loveliness. Before Raphael had finished the painting, he was himself called away to the land of the blessed, to behold in reality the spiritual beings which inspiration had led him to portray in such a lovely manner. He was but thirty-seven; and while his body lay in state his last work was suspended over the couch, and was carried before him at his funeral while yet the last traces of his master-hand were wet upon the canvas.

RAPHAEL.

"And when all beheld
Him where he lay, how changed from yesterday—
Him in that hour cut off, and at his head
His last great work; when, entering in, they look'd

Now on the dead, then on that masterpiece;
Now on his face, lifeless and colorless,
Then on those forms divine that lived and breathed
And would live on for ages—all were moved,
And sighs burst forth, and loudest lamentations."

FLORENCE.

To Florence has been awarded the title of the fairest city of the earth. Who can doubt it, situated as it is in the rich valley of the Arno, surrounded by beauties of nature and of art, immortalized by Byron and Rogers, and revered as the birthplace of Dante, Petrarch, Boccacio, Galileo, Michael Angelo, Leonardo da Vinci, Benvenuto Cellini, and Andrea del Sarto? What beautiful recollections of the past must naturally be awakened in the appreciative mind while tarrying in a spot which has given birth to such noble contributors to poetry and the arts? Beautiful gardens adorned with statues, vases, fountains, and other decorations, as well as the open squares or piazzas, continually attract the eye of the visitor; and the palaces, which are very numerous, each containing rare paintings and sculptures, form the principal objects of interest in this delightful city, which is the pride of Tuscany. The climate of Florence is delightful, varying but thirty degrees from summer to winter.

The "Divine Comedy" of Dante was the first great Christian poem; and it has been called one of the "landmarks of history." The subject or plot may be thus stated:

Dante, astray in a gloomy wood and beset by wild beasts, is rescued by the shade of the poet Virgil, who has left his proper abode in a painless region of hell for the purpose of guiding Dante through the world of lost souls, at the request of Beatrice, whom Dante had known in his youth, but who is now an inhabitant of heaven. Over hell-gate an awful inscription is placed:

"Through me you pass into the city of woe;
　Through me you pass eternal woes to prove;
Through me among the blasted race you go.
'Twas Justice did my most high Author move,
And I have been the work of Power divine,
　Of supreme Wisdom, and of primal Love.
No creature has an elder date than mine,
　Unless eternal, and I have no end.
O you that enter me, all hope resign."

From agony to agony the pilgrims plunge deeper and deeper into the abyss of hell, meeting sinner after sinner whose ghastly story is told at more or less length, until they reach the visible, abhorrent presence of Lucifer, who from "perfect in beauty" has by rebellion become absolute in hideous horror.

Mid-Lucifer occupies the earth's centre of gravity. Virgil, with Dante clinging to him, clambers down the upper half of Lucifer and climbs up the lower half, whereby the twain find themselves emerging from the depth of hell upon the Mountain of Purgatory.

This purgatory is the domain of pain and hope—finite pain, assured hope. Here the shade of Beatrice assuming in her own person the guidance of her lover, Virgil vanishes.

Under the guardianship of Beatrice, Dante mounts through eight successive heavens to that ninth which includes within itself all blessedness.

Dante was of middle stature, and had a long face and aquiline nose. His complexion was very dark, and his countenance always sad.

The most important church in Florence is the church of Santa Croce. It contains monuments erected to the memory of the most celebrated men of Italy. Byron alludes to it in the fourth canto of "Childe Harold:"

GALILEO.

"In Santa Croce's holy precincts lie
  Ashes which make it holier; dust which is,
Even in itself, an immortality,
  Though there were nothing save the past, and
    this,
The particle of those sublimities
  Which have relapsed to chaos : here repose
Angelo's, Alfieri's bones, and his,
  The starry Galileo, with his woes ;
Here Machiavelli's earth returned to whence it
    rose."

The principal monuments of the church are as follows: Michael Angelo Buonarotti. The three statues of painting, sculpture, and architecture appear as mourners. His bust, by Lorenzi, is considered a most correct likeness. The position of this monument was selected by Michael Angelo himself that he might see from his tomb the dome of the cathedral, the delight and study of his mind; Alfieri's monument, by Canova, erected at the private expense of the Countess of Albany; colossal monument to Dante; monument of Machiavelli; also of Lanzi, writer on Italian art.

VENICE.

The city of Venice, formerly called the "Queen of the Adriatic," is unrivalled as to beauty and situation. It stands on a bay near the Gulf of Venice. In this gulf, or Adriatic sea, the ceremony of espousing the Adriatic took place annually on Ascension day. It was performed by the doge, accompanied by all the nobility and ambassadors in gondolas, dropping into the sea a ring from his bucentaur or state barge. This ceremony was omitted for the first time in many centuries in 1797.

DOGE'S PALACE, VENICE.

In 1172 the appointment of the doge and other magistrates was vested in the grand council of four hundred and eighty members. Change after change took place, until a Council of Ten secured the government to themselves. Under this unchecked oligarchy a reign of terror began. The ten were terrible; but still more terrible were the three inquisitors—two black, one red—appointed in 1454. Deep mystery hung over the three. They were elected by the ten; none else knew their names. Their great work was to kill; and no man—doge, councillor, or inquisitor—was beyond their reach. Secretly they pronounced a doom; and ere long the stiletto or the poison cup had done its work, or the dark waters of the lagoon had closed over a life. The spy was everywhere. No man dared to speak out, for his most intimate companions might be on the watch to betray him. Bronze vases, shaped like a lion's mouth, gaped at the corner of every square to receive the names of suspected persons. Gloom and suspicion haunted gondola and hearth.

No scene in Venice is of greater interest to the traveller than the "Bridge of Sighs," immortalized by Byron in the fourth canto of "Harold Childe:"

> "I stood in Venice, on the Bridge of Sighs;
> A palace and a prison on each hand:
> I saw from out the waves her structures rise,
> As from the stroke of the enchanter's wand:
> A thousand years their cloudy wings expand
> Around me, and a dying glory smiles
> O'er the far times, when many a subject land
> Look'd to the winged lion's marble piles,
> Where Venice sate in state, throned on her hundred isles."

Criminals were conveyed across this bridge to hear their sentence, and from there led to their execution; from this it derives its melancholy but appropriate name.

The Grand Canal, which takes a serpentine course through the city, is intersected by 146 smaller canals, over which there are 306 bridges, which being very steep, and intended only for foot-passengers, are cut into steps on either side. These canals, crossed by bridges, form the water-streets of Venice, the greater part of the intercourse being carried on by means of gondolas. They are long, narrow, light vessels, painted black, according to an ancient law, containing in the centre a cabin nicely fitted up with glass windows, blinds, cushions, etc.; those belonging to private families are much more richly decorated.

PADUA.

A little over twenty miles from Venice lies Padua, the most ancient city of the north of Italy. It abounds in tradition, and its foundation was ascribed to Antenor, after the siege of Troy. It was taken by Alaric, Attila, and the Lombards, but restored by Charlemagne to its former grandeur, and under his successors it became flourishing and independent. The appearance of the city is very singular: large portions of irregular unoccupied ground, situated on the outskirts, adds to its peculiarity. The houses are supported by rows of pointed arches; the city is of a triangular form, surrounded with walls and intersected with canals. It has a low, marshy situation, at the terminus of the Canal of Monselici, between the Brenta and Bacchiglione. Travellers are generally much disappointed in the appearance of this city, it being very damp and exceedingly gloomy; the streets are narrow, unclean, and very monotonous; they are bordered by arcades, and have no leading thoroughfares.

The University of Padua was quite celebrated in the fourteenth and fifteenth centuries; it was not only patronized by an immense number of students from all parts of Europe, but also from Mohammedan countries. Dante and Petrarch were among its pupils; Harvey received his degree of medicine here in 1602; Galileo and Guglielmi were among its professors of philosophy.

VERONA.

Verona is delightfully situated on the river Adige, which flows through it and divides it into two unequal parts, forming a peninsula. The river, being wide and rapid, is crossed by four noble stone bridges.

Verona is particularly celebrated for having been the birthplace of many distinguished men, some of whom are worthy of particular mention: The celebrated Roman poet Catullus, born B. C. 86; he lived and died poor, as many other poets have done, although he possessed a superior genius. At the time of his death he was thirty years old, in the flower of his age, and at the height of his reputation. He had a great admiration for the fair sex; in speaking of Lesbia, and how many kisses would satisfy him, said that he desired as many as there were grains of sand in the deserts of Libya and stars in the heavens. Aurelius Macer, a Latin poet in the age of Augustus acquired considerable fame. Cornelius Nepos, the Latin historian, who flourished in the time of Julius Cæsar; he left the "Lives of the Illustrious Greek and Roman Captains" as a monument to his memory; he died in the reign of Augustus. "Caius Secundus Pliny the elder," one of the most learned of the ancient Roman writers, born A. D. 23.

There was one person who did more to increase, by his own efforts, the fame of the city, than all the rest of its natives. This was the celebrated painter Paul Cagliari, surnamed Veronese from having been born in Verona, which event took place in 1530. He was the son of a sculptor, and at an early age manifested a strong desire to become a painter. He was styled by the Italians "the happy painter." Titian and Tintoretto were selected as his models of perfection.

Verona is distinguished as one of the most industrious towns of Italy. It has nine establishments for weaving silk; sixty silk-twist factories; large leather, earthenware and soap factories; also others for the weaving of linen and woollen fabrics. Its trade consists chiefly in these articles; also in raw silk, grain, oil, sumach and agricultural produce. Two weekly markets are located here; two fairs take place annually, and continue for fifteen days each. The fruits and flowers raised in Verona are remarkably fine. The climate is healthy, but a little keen, on account of its near approach to the Alps.

MILAN.

Milan is the principal city of northern Italy, nearly circular in its formation, and surrounded by a wall which was mostly erected by the Spaniards in 1555. The space between the canal and wall is laid out in gardens and planted with fine trees; the city proper is about eight miles in circumference, and although, like most ancient cities, it is very irregularly laid out, yet it is one of the most interesting in Europe, full of activity and wealth, has some noble thoroughfares, and displays a number of fine buildings kept in thorough repair.

Milan stands at an elevated height of 452 feet above the sea. It was annexed to the Roman dominions by Scipio Nasica, 191 B. C. It ranked the sixth city in the Roman empire in the fourth century. In the twelfth century it was the capital of a republic, and afterward of a duchy in the families of Sforza and Visconti. It was held by Spain, after the battle of Pavia, until it was ceded to Austria in 1714. It was taken by the French in 1796, and also after the battle of Marengo, in 1800. From 1805 until 1814 it was the capital of the kingdom of Italy.

Milan cathedral is the finest Gothic edifice in Italy, and, as a church, ranks next to St. Peter's. No person can fail to be impressed with its sublimity;

and the idea suggests itself to one beholding it that, although nature in her works was so perfectly faultless and impressive, man, in his efforts to compete with her, was brought into very close alliance. If so grand at all times, how greatly must that grandeur be increased when the entire building is illuminated, as it was after the battle of Magenta, and to celebrate at the same time the anniversary of the five days of March, 1848, when the Milanese rose and expelled their Austrian masters? After the entire city was illuminated, gorgeous rays of light, representing the Italian colors, red, green and white, blazed forth simultaneously from this magnificent edifice; spire, roof and body presenting a mysterious grandeur and sublime beauty, with which no one could fail to be everlastingly impressed. The delicate tints of the crimson, as they reflected upon the white marble of the cathedral, were scarcely surpassed by the deeper color which it afterward assumed, and then so mysteriously changed into green, and then to the purest white.

In Milan is to be seen the celebrated painting of "The Last Supper," by Leonardo da Vinci, the greatest painting by one of the greatest painters that has ever lived.

NAPLES.

The country around Naples is rich in beauties of scenery; nothing can well be conceived to be more beautiful. Quite a celebrated author remarks that he congratulated himself upon being delayed on the route, so that he did not arrive at Naples until late at night, for it enabled him to anticipate with brighter hopes the beauty of the scene that opened on his eyes with the light of morning. The situation of Naples is as fine as can be imagined, being partly seated on a spacious bay, upon the shores of which are magnificent villas and gardens.

It is principally in respect to situation that this city surpasses most others. The streets are straight, and paved with square blocks of lava laid in mortar, and said to resemble the old Roman roads. Owing to the mildness of the climate, a great deal of business is carried on in the open streets, and, while walking along, you are accosted by numerous different traders. There is but little real magnificence in architecture; and, though many of the buildings are erected on a very grand scale, they are generally overloaded with ornament. The houses resemble those of Paris, except that they are on a larger scale.

Naples is very ancient. It was founded by the people of Cumæ, a colony from Greece, who gradually spread themselves round the bay of Naples, and was called from this circumstance Neapolis, or "The New City."

In after years it became, as it is now, a seat of pleasure. Its hot baths, the number and excellence of its theatres and other places of amusement, its matchless scenery, the mildness of its climate, and the luxury and effeminacy of its inhabitants, made it a favorite retreat of the wealthy Romans.

The nobility are fond of great show and splendor. The females are proud, even when very poor. They never go out unless to ride, and bestow great pains and time upon their personal charms, to fascinate the other sex. The principal promenade of the ladies is on their own roof, which is generally adorned with shrubs and flowers.

Within a few hours' journey from Naples are the ruins of Pæstum, and also the ruins of Pompeii and Herculaneum, which were destroyed by an eruption of Mount Vesuvius in the year 79.

The grandeur, gloom and majesty of the temples of Pæstum, standing alone as they do amid their mountain wilderness, similar to Baalbec, without a vestige near of any power that could have raised them, surpasses anything of the kind on earth. The principal ruins are the Basilica, the Temple of Neptune, the Amphitheatre, the Temple of Vesta and the Forum.

The early history of Pompeii is involved in obscurity, but the supposition is that it was settled by Osci and Pelasgi prior to the establishment on this coast of the Greek colonies from Eubœa. It fell into the hands of the Samnites about the year 440 B. C., and was taken by the Romans eighty years afterward; during the Social War it revolted with the other Campanian towns, and but little more was known respecting it until it was visited by an earthquake A. D. 63, which occasioned great destruction; it was afterward overwhelmed, in 79, by the eruption of Vesuvius, and continued to be buried under the ashes and other volcanic matter for about 1,669 years. Notwithstanding that the celebrated architect and engineer, Domenico Fontana, who was employed in constructing an aqueduct to convey water to Torre, fell in with the ruins of the city, no particular attention was paid to the discovery until 1748, when the peasants were employed in cutting a ditch, since which time it has continued to be an object of great interest, and since 1755 the progress of excavation has been pretty constantly prosecuted.

Pompeii has the reputation of being "the most wonderful of the antiquities of Italy, and one which it is said never disappoints the traveller who is at all acquainted with the history of ancient Rome."

Herculaneum was destroyed by torrents of volcanic mud, upon which, in subsequent eruptions, ashes and streams of lava fell to a depth varying from seventy to 110 feet: no great loss of life resulted from the destruction of this city. It is said by an eminent historian to have been built on elevated ground between two rivers, thereby rendering the atmosphere perfectly healthy. Some quite distinguished Romans resided in the city and suburbs.

Too much cannot be learned or said of these ruins of antiquity, with the history of which every student must be familiar. The melancholy destruction of such a city, the desolation which spread from dwelling to dwelling, the flight of mother, father, sister and brother from the scene of terror and confusion, must awaken feelings of awe and sympathy in every human heart. Mothers, with infants in their arms, seeking safety and protection, gathering their little ones around them, trying to escape uninjured, and yet how many were plunged into a fearful eternity!

A united Italy had always been the dream of her greatest patriots; but it was not till 1870 that this dream was realized. The main agents in bringing about this result were Count Cavour, one of the greatest of modern statesmen, and the patriots Mazzini and Garibaldi. In 1848, when France had once more cast out her king, the Italians rushed to arms for the purpose of driving

DESTRUCTION OF POMPEII.

out the Austrians from Italy, and of becoming a united nation. Pius IX., who had recently become pope, had given some unexpected evidences of a sympathy with the popular desire. He permitted a body of Roman volunteers to join the patriot ranks, but, being a man of peace, he soon withdrew his permission.

General Garibaldi spent the largest portion of the years 1851, '52, and '53 on Staten Island, and the house in which he lived has been made, in a way, a memorial by the Italian colony of New York, who purchased it, and after suitably marking it with a marble tablet commemorative of the great revolutionist's stay in it, presented it to Antonio Meucci, whose guest he was during most of his stay in the United States.

Signor Meucci knew Garibaldi in South America, and for many years lived in Havana, Cuba. Originally a sculptor, he was but in moderate circumstances when Garibaldi, escaping from Austrian tyranny in Piedmont, took ship at

POPE PIUS IX.

Genoa and arrived in New York. He offered him the shelter of his humble home on Staten Island and the "Liberator" gladly accepted it. The twain, with General Avezzano, formed a partnership in the manufacture of stearine and paraffine candles on a small scale, and the furnace in which they melted and mixed their material before running into the moulds is still standing in the yard of the brewery, where it is slowly crumbling away under the tooth of time, surrounded by huge beer casks.

Dr. Nardyz, who was then an officer of the corvette, and subsequently served on Garibaldi's staff in Italy, thus describes the hero's appearance at that time: "He was about five feet six or seven inches high, and weighed about one hundred and sixty pounds. His eyes were light and his hair and beard red. He was very quick and active on his feet, and very pleasant and agreeable in his manners. At the time he was quite poor, all his property in Italy having been sequestered, and he acted as salesman of the candles he helped to manufacture. They were a novelty at the time, and he was concerned in their invention. He used to carry them to New York in a basket and go about from store to store disposing of them and soliciting orders for more."

Garibaldi was high up in masonry, and while a resident of Staten Island he established the masonic lodge in New York which now bears his name.

GARIBALDI.

The marble tablet affixed to the front of the house bears a legend, of which the following is a translation:

Here lived and labored, from 1851 to 1853,
GUISEPPE GARIBALDI,
THE HERO OF TWO WORLDS.
March 9th, 1884. Erected by Friends.

In return for his services to Italy and Victor Emmanuel (although he had little love for the latter) Garibaldi was given a pension of two hundred thousand francs a year. He retired to the island of Caprera, and on this before rather barren rock he established a home which was truly delightful. He made it a garden spot, but, no doubt, amid its enjoyments his memory often reverted to the time when he was an exile in the humble abode on Staten Island.

Garibaldi for a time governed Naples. The people were asked to declare their wishes in regard to their political future. They voted, by vast majorities, in favor of union with Sardinia. King Victor Emmanuel, in accepting the new trust, summoned the people to concord and self-denial. "All parties," he said, "must bow before the majesty of the Italian nation, which God uplifts."

Humbert IV., King of Italy, the eldest son of King Victor Emmanuel, was born March 14th, 1844. At an early age he obtained an insight into political

KING HUMBERT IV.

and military life under the guidance of his father. He took part in the reorganization of the ancient kingdom of the Two Sicilies, and in 1862 he visited Naples and Palermo, where he shared the popularity of Garibaldi. In 1868 he married his cousin, the Princess Marguerite of Savoy. He succeeded to the throne on the death of his father, in 1878. In the same year, as he was entering Naples, a man named Passanante approached the royal carriage and attempted to assassinate him with a poniard. The king escaped with a slight scratch, but the prime minister, who was with him, was wounded rather badly in the thigh. King Humbert has shown himself to be a good king and brave soldier.

Byron, in his "Childe Harold's Pilgrimage," thus apostrophizes Italy, its remarkable history passing vividly before his mind:

"Italia! O Italia! thou who hast
The fatal gift of beauty, which became
A funeral dower of present woes and past,
On thy sweet brow is sorrow plough'd by shame
And annals graved in characters of flame."

ANGOULEMÉ.

FRANCE.

EUROPE was gradually peopled from Asia. Four great tides of migration may be noted. First came the wave which peopled Greece and Italy; then Celts and Cimbri, who occupied Spain, France and Britain; in the third place the Germans, who filled Central Europe; and lastly, Sarmatian or Sclavonic tribes, who peopled the north-east, and upon whom pressed the Huns from Mount Ural, and Tartars from beyond the Caspian.

Early in the sixth century we find France parcelled out among three nations—Franks in the north and centre, Visigoths in the south-west and Burgundians in the south-east. Underlying these ruling races was a great mass of Celts or Gauls, and some Roman settlers, reduced to a state of vassalage. Clovis, the leader of the Salian Franks, was at first merely a captain of *leudes*, or free warriors, with no title to command except what his personal qualities gave him. He roved from city to city, until the influence of the clergy, and the gift of a gold crown and purple robes from Constantinople, gave him some show of royalty, and then he fixed his court at Paris.

Beginning with Pharamond in 418, the list of Merovingian kings of the

Franks contains thirty-four names. Third of these was Meroveg or Meerwig (sea-warrior), from whom the race derived their name. And the fifth was Clovis, who has been already named as the true founder of the French monarchy.

Charlemagne, or Charles the Great, was born about 742, and when twenty-nine years of age became ruler of the Frankish kingdom.

His reign divides itself into two parts. The one, extending from its opening in 771 to the complete subdual of the Saxons in 804, was spent in constant wars on almost every frontier; the other, from 804 to his death, was devoted to the organization and improvement of the vast empire which his sword had won.

The chief wars of Charlemagne were with the Saxons beyond the Rhine, the Lombards of Italy, the Saracens of Spain, and the Avars, who occupied modern Hungary. He fought also with the Danes, and the Sclavonic tribes on his eastern border.

Charlemagne died of pleurisy in his seventy-second year. A year before, in the cathedral of Aix-la-Chapelle, amid the applause of the assembled nobles, he had caused his only living son Louis to assume the imperial crown.

Louis le Debonnaire, fitter for a monk's cell than a selfish court or brawling camp, succeeded his great father, and did all his gentle nature could for twenty-six years to humanize his subjects. But belted bishops and lawless chiefs were too strong for him. War among his three sons then divided the empire. Lothaire, the eldest, seized the imperial title; but Charles and Louis, uniting, defeated him in 841, on the bloody field of Fontenaille. Two years later a treaty was made at Verdun, by which France and Germany became separate and independent states. Charles held France; Louis ruled Germany; while Lothaire received Italy, with some broken strips along the Rhone and Rhine. As had happened in the family of Clovis, the race of Charlemagne, called Carlovingians, grew very degenerate; and there is nothing in the history of kings branded with nicknames, such as the Stammerer, the Fat, the Foolish, the Lazy, to challenge our notice or respect. Such men misgoverned France, until, in 987, under Hugh Capet, a new dynasty arose. With that date the history of the Franks ends; that of the French begins.

The history of France soon merges, from this period, into that of the Crusades, when all Christendom began to be aroused by the wild eloquence of Peter the Hermit.

This man, said to have been a native of Amiens, was a soldier in his youth. Upon the death of his wife, he retired broken-hearted to a hermit's cell, from which, however, his innate love of change drove him a pilgrim to the Holy Land. Returning thence full of anger at the degradation of the sacred spot, he obtained leave from Pope Urban II. to call all true Christians to arms; and as he passed through Italy and France, a fleshless spectre, clad in mean raiment, with bare head and feet, and staggering under a heavy crucifix, his fierce war-cry woke an echo in millions of hearts.

Within the same year two general councils were called by the pope—one at Placentia, the other at Clermont, in Auvergne. At the latter, both the pope and the hermit spoke in words of fire. With one voice all who heard cried out in the old French, "*Dieu li volt!*"—"It is the will of God!" and few there were who left the old market-place on that day without a red cross on the shoulder, to mark them as soldiers in the sacred cause.

The great captain of the first crusade (war of the cross), was Godfrey of Bouillon, or Boulogne, the Duke of Basse-Lorraine. This leader is the hero of Torquato Tasso's great poem, "Jerusalem Delivered." Godfrey one day, in single combat with a Turk, cut his foe in two; one-half fell into the river, the other sat still on horseback—"by which blow," says Robert the Monk, "one Turk was made two Turks."

At last the capital of Palestine, lovely even in her desolation, rose in their view. The knights, springing from their saddles, wet the turf with tears of mingled joy and grief. Barefooted and weeping the little band advanced. Under a sky of burning copper, with no water in the pools and brooks, they fought for five long weeks before Godfrey and his stormers stood victorious within the walls. The massacre of 70,000 Moslems, and the burning of the Jews in their synagogue, stained the glory of the conquerors.

Forty-eight years passed, and then a second crusade began, which ended disastrously, although Jerusalem still remained in the hands of two orders of military monks—the Hospitallers and Templars. But when the news came that Jerusalem had fallen before Saladin, the great Sultan of Egypt, and that the golden cross, which had glittered for eighty-eight years on the Mosque of Omar, marking its transformation into a Christian church, had been trampled in the streets, Europe for the third time girt herself for war. The three great western princes took the cross—Richard I. of England, Philip Augustus of France and Frederic Barbarossa (Redbeard) of Germany. A tax, called Saladin's tithe, was laid upon Christendom to meet the expenses of the war. As was usual in all the Crusades, complete absolution from sin was promised to every soldier who struck a blow at the infidel.

It was, however, nearly a year after their setting out that the royal warriors appeared before Acre; Philip first, Richard shortly afterwards. New vigor stirred in the besiegers; and Saladin must have trembled for his hold upon the key of Syria when he saw the plain whitened with a new camp of many thousand tents. One glimpse of the great Saracen's character must not be passed by. Even at so great a crisis, this generous foe sent frequent presents of pears and snow to cool the fever, of which Richard and Philip lay sick in their tents. Ere long the broken ramparts of the city yielded to the crusaders, and the sultan fell back towards the south.

Soon after the fall of Acre, Philip returned to France. Other Crusades followed, only to end disastrously. The strangest was the Boy Crusade of 1212.

A shepherd boy, Stephen, of Vendome, gave out that God in a vision had bestowed on him bread, and had sent him with a letter to the King of France. Round him gathered 30,000 children of about twelve years. Boys were there, and girls in boys' clothes, on horseback and afoot. The tears and prayers of their parents could not turn them from their mad design. The strange flame spread through all France; from castle and from hut the little ones fled to follow the car of Stephen. With wax candles in their hands, clad in pilgrim's dress, they moved, singing hymns, over the hot dusty plains of Provence, upheld through all the toils and terrors of the way by the wild hope that the waters of the sea, drying up before them, would open a path to the Holy Land. Robbed by the way, they were yet more pitilessly cheated in Marseilles. Two merchants agreed to take them to Palestine, for the love of God, as the canting scoundrels said. The children set sail in seven ships. Two of these were wrecked, and all on board lost. The other five bore their precious freight to Egypt, where all were sold as slaves. It is some consolation to know that the rascally merchants were soon after hanged in Sicily.

The life of the Middle Ages is deeply colored with the brilliant hues of chivalry. There the knight is the central figure—the model of mediæval art—the hero of mediæval literature—foremost in every court revel and greenwood sport, in the glittering tilt-yard and the dusty battle-field.

The tournament has been well called the link which united the peaceful to the warlike life of the knight. They were first held in France, as the French origin of the name seems to show. England and Germany soon followed the example of their neighbors. The lists, in which the encounters took place, were roped or railed off in an oval form, generally between the city and a wood. The open spaces at each end were filled with stalls and galleries for the ladies and the noble spectators.

Bayard, who fell in France in 1524, was almost the last of the *preux chevaliers* of that knightly land. The Emperor Maximilian I. is still called in Germany "*der letzte Ritter*"—the last knight. In England chivalry, as a system, lasted till the time of Elizabeth.

We find a brilliant reflection of chivalry in the romantic literature which grew up about the time of the Crusades. The Romance pictures the knight in his glory, splendid but clumsy; suave and courteous in the extreme, but very often brutal. The enchanted castle with its beautiful and distressed captives, the monster dragons and other terrors to be overcome by the unconquered arm of the hero, were the allegorical images of evils existing in that terrible time, when might was the only right, highly magnified and colored by the untaught poets, who sang of them. It is a pity to think that the knight-errant is a very doubtful character, whose picture, if ever he existed, must have been drawn from those chevaliers who travelled from tournament to tournament, claiming and receiving hospitality everywhere as citizens of the world. The Romance, owing its birth to chivalry, repaid the benefit by prolonging the life of chivalry for many years. The deeds of Arthur and Charlemagne formed the subjects of some of the earliest romances.

The history of France during the fifteenth and sixteenth centuries brought into prominence the great names of Richelieu, Mazarin and Colbert.

France had already produced one or two great names in literature. Rabelais, the greatest of all humorists, was born at Touraine in 1483. His chief work is a satirical romance, of which a giant, Gargantua, and his son are the heroes. He died in 1553.

Montaigne printed his "Essays" in 1580, and they are by far the best of their kind. Our own great essayist, Emerson, calls Montaigne one of the great "representative men" of the world.

The great brilliance of the court of Louis XIV. was owing to the cluster of wits and literary men whom he gathered round him. Corneille and Racine, the tragedians ; Molière and Régnard, the comedians ; Boileau and La Fontaine, the poets ; La Rochefoucauld and La Bruyère, the wits ; Des Cartes and Pascal, the philosophers ; Bossuet and Arnauld, the divines ; Mabillon and Montfaucon, the scholars ; Bourdaloue and Massillon, the preachers ; all gave lustre to his reign. With such men he lived in close intimacy ; and thus, too, he struck a blow at the old noblesse, for his aristocracy of talent, of which he made so much, was drawn almost altogether from the ranks of the people. The writings of these great stars of French literature bear the stamp of the age. They are highly polished and have a stately grace ; but they were written by men who breathed an atmosphere of splendid artificiality ; and they lack, in consequence, "that touch of nature which makes the whole world kin." They were not written for the whole world, but for the favored few who wore ruffles and brocade. Dryden and Pope, who got their inspiration from Paris, are the best examples in English literature of a similar style.

Louis XV. being only five years old when his great-grandfather died, the government was placed in the hands of Philip, Duke of Orleans, the nephew of the dead king. This prince, whose licentious extravagance was rivalled by that of his worthless minister, the Cardinal Dubois, held the regency for eight years. When, in 1723, Orleans and Dubois sank within a few months of each other into the grave, Louis XV. was a boy of fourteen. Three years later began the administration of Cardinal Fleury, tutor to the king, which, lasting for seventeen years marks the best period of a shameful reign. Then, when Fleury died, France went rapidly down the hill. The court, ruled by the painted favorites of the licentious king, Pompadour and Dubarry, exhausted every shape of costly debauchery. The last *sou* of taxation was wrung from the starving peasants. The soldiers of France were beaten at Dettingen, at Rossbach, and at Minden. Canada, Nova Scotia, and some of the finest of the Antilles were wrested from Louis by the English. The health of the public mind was sapped by the infidelities of Voltaire and the mock sentimentalism of Rousseau.

THE REVOLUTION IN FRANCE.

Louis XVI. succeeded his grandfather on the 10th of May, 1774. Then twenty years of age, he had been already four years married to Marie Antoinette, the beautiful daughter of Maria Theresa. The young couple entered with the fresh joy of their years into the gayeties of the coronation, and all high-born France rang with the noise of feasting. But in every square mile of the land there were men whose wives and children cried to them in vain for bread.

At last, after many muttered warnings, and long-gathering darkness, the tempest broke in awful fury. A fierce mob, whose souls were leavened with infidelity and brutalized by changeless misery and never-satisfied hunger, raged through the Paris streets. The spark which fired the mine was a rumor that the soldiers were marching to dissolve the Assembly. Necker, too, the sole hope of the starving people, had been dismissed. Cockades of green leaves, torn from the trees, became the badge of the rioters. Shots were heard in many quarters. An old man was killed by a bullet from the German guards.

Then the grim old prison of the Bastile was stormed. Within its dark walls hundreds of innocent hearts had broken, pierced through with the iron of hopeless captivity. The terrible *lettres de cachet*—sealed orders from the king to arrest and fling into prison without a trial, and often without any distinct charge—had packed its dungeons with wretched men during the late reign. Little wonder, then, that the first rush of the mob was to the Bastile. Dragging cannon from Les Invalides, they opened a fire upon the walls, burst in, and, seizing the governor, slew him in the Place de Grève.

The flames then burst out all through the land, except in La Vendée. The *chateaux* of the nobles were pillaged and burned to the ground. Tortures were inflicted by the fierce peasants upon their former masters. The royal *fleur de lis* was trampled in the mud, and the Tricolor upraised.

One day in autumn a swarm of women gathered around the Hotel de Ville, crying, "Bread! give bread!" It became the nucleus of a riotous crowd, surging with wild outcries through the street. Then out came Millard with a drum, who said he would lead them to Versailles. Outside the barriers he strove to disperse them, but no—they would go on. Hungry, and wet with heavy rain, when they found that the king and the Assembly would give them only words, they gathered round the palace. Some fool fired on them. Sweeping through an open gate, they spread through all the splendid rooms; and the queen had scarcely time to escape by a secret door, when her bedchamber was filled with a fierce and squalid throng. The timely arrival of Lafayette, and the consent of the king to remove to Paris, alone quelled the tumult.

Dark and still darker grew the sky. Mirabeau, "our little mother Mirabeau," as the fishwomen of the gallery used lovingly to call him, was made president of the Assembly in January, 1791. He exerted all his giant genius to quell the storm, whose rising gusts had been felt at the Bastile and Versailles; and poor Louis clung to the hope that this aristocratic darling of the rabble might yet save him. But Mirabeau died in April; and while the spring blossoms were brightening in all the fields of France, the Bourbon lilies drooped their golden heads. There seemed no hope for Louis but in flight. He fled in despair, but was recognized, stopped at Varennes, and brought back to Paris.

Matters then grew worse than ever at the centre of the Revolution. The Paris mob rose like a sea, swelled by some troops from Marseilles, who, first singing along Paris streets the war-hymn of Rouget de Lisle, caused it henceforth to be known as "The Marseillaise."

King Louis was tried for treason and conspiracy against the nation. He denied the justice of the charge. But denial was useless before judges such as his. Death was the sentence of the court after a discussion of some days. The Reign of Terror began. The Girondists, friends of moderate republicanism, were slain without mercy, or driven over the land, without shelter or food, to die. When Marat met a merited death—he was assassinated in his bath by Charlotte Corday, a young girl from Caen—Robespierre was left sole dictator of France. A frightful carnage followed. Every day saw red baskets of human heads carried from the guillotine, whose dull thud was music to the crowd. Women sat and worked as calmly as in the pit of the theatre, while the fearful tragedy was played out before their eyes. Fathers brought their little ones to see the heads fall. And as fast as the prisons were emptied by this wholesale butchery, fresh victims, denounced often by their nearest neighbors, were thrust into the cells to await their certain doom.

Queen Marie Antoinette followed her husband to the guillotine and the grave in the October of the same year. Bailly, Condorcet, Barnave, and Madame Roland met the same fate. Philip Egalité, whose vote had been given for the death of his royal kinsman, went also to his richly deserved doom.

Still the mob cried for more heads. The guillotine could not be stopped. Some of the Mountain-men, less tigerish than their fellows, were first laid below its edge. Such were Danton and Camille Desmoulins. It is little wonder that Christianity was cast aside in this Reign of Terror. The Goddess of Reason, impersonated by a worthless woman, was openly worshipped, and torches were burnt before her shrine. A thing was then tried, the failure of which is a noteworthy proof how little man's wisdom is when compared with that of the all-wise God. Every tenth day was appointed a day of rest and amusement; but neither man nor beast could bear the strain of ten days' work.

The French Revolution may be said to have come to an end with the opening of the career of Napoleon Bonaparte; indeed we may say that with this man's life a new era dawned upon the world. A British writer says in regard to him, that "Nature had no obstacles that he did not surmount—space no opposition that he did not spurn; and, whether amid Alpine rocks, Arabian sands, or Polar snows, he seemed proof against peril, and endowed with ubiquity!

MARIE ANTOINETTE.

"The whole continent of Europe trembled at beholding the audacity of his designs and the miracles of their execution. Scepticism bowed to the prodigies of his performances—romance assumed the air of history; nor was there aught too incredible for belief when the world saw a subaltern of Corsica waving his flag over her most ancient capitals. All the visions of antiquity became commonplace in his contemplation: kings were his people; nations were his outposts; and he disposed of courts, and crowns, and camps, and churches, and cabinets, as if they were the titular dignitaries of the chess-board.

"Grand, gloomy, and peculiar, he sat upon the throne a sceptred hermit, and wrapt in the solitude of his awful originality. A mind, bold, independent, and decisive; a will despotic in its dictates; an energy that distances expedition, and a conscience pliable to every touch of interest, marked the outline of this extraordinary character, the most extraordinary perhaps, that, in the annals of this world, ever rose, or reigned, or fell.

"Such a medley of contradiction and, at the same time, such an individual consistency, were never united in the same character—a royalist, a republican and an emperor; a Mahometan, Catholic, and a patron of the synagogue; a subaltern and a sovereign; a traitor and a tyrant; a Christian and an infidel—he was through all his vicissitudes the same stern, potent, inflexible original—the same mysterious, incomprehensible self; the man *without a model and without a shadow.*"

At an early age, when others scarcely start in life, Napoleon's years were outnumbered by his victories; and the kings of Europe conquered by his sword, or subjugated by his genius, lowered before the imperial eagle. It would appear that, from his earliest childhood, Napoleon's parents rested all their hopes on him. His father, in the delirium with which he was seized in his last moments, incessantly called Napoleon to come to his aid with his *great sword*.

Napoleon had a very happy knack in speaking, as well as in acting the sublime. At the battle of Lodi, there was a battery of the enemy which was making dreadful havoc amongst the French ranks; and repeated attempts had been made, in vain, to storm it. An officer came to Bonaparte to represent to him the importance of making another effort to silence it; when he

NAPOLEON'S RESIDENCE AT ST. HELENA.

put himself at the head of a party, exclaiming, "Let it be silenced then!" and carried it by storm.

On another occasion he was giving some orders, which were humbly represented to him to be *impossible*; when he burst out "How! *impossible!* That word is not French."

When the marriage of Napoleon with the Archduchess Maria Louisa was about to take place, the French emperor, in answer to some remonstrance on the subject, observed, "I should not enter into this alliance if I did not know that her origin is as noble as my own." This was said for the purpose of showing his indifference for mere rank.

In person Bonaparte was rather under the middle size, being about five feet six inches in height. An anecdote is related of his endeavoring to take down something he desired from a shelf, but which was above his reach. One

of his marshals courteously offered to hand it down to him, using the words:
"Excuse me, Sire; I am higher than you." "You are *taller*," was the rejoinder of Napoleon.

After Napoleon's defeat at Waterloo he went to Rochefort with the view of escaping to America; but this he could not do, because the British cruisers watched all the coast. On the 15th of July he went on board the British ship Bellerophon (Captain Maitland), having previously written to the prince regent to say that "he came, like Themistocles, to claim the hospitality of the British people and the protection of their laws." The ship sailed to Torbay, where Napoleon received word that the British government had resolved to send him to St. Helena.

The Northumberland carried him out to that lonely rock, which he reached on the 15th of October, 1815. And there he lived, first at Briars and then at Longwood for nearly six years, dreaming of the glorious past. In 1818 his health began to fail, and on the 5th of May, 1821, he died of an ulcer in the stomach. His body, laid at first in Slane's Valley, near a clump of weeping willows, was borne to France in the winter of 1840, and placed with brilliant ceremony in the Hotel des Invalides.

TOMB OF NAPOLEON I.

The history of France since 1815 is full of change. When Louis XVIII. died, in 1824, his brother became king, with the title of Charles X. This king, like all his Bourbon kindred, had a mania for despotic rule. He could not—poor blind king—read the lessons written in French blood upon those pages of the national story which had not long been closed.

Louis Philippe succeeded Charles, and his reign lasted from 1830 to 1848, when a revolution in France drove him from his throne and he sought shelter in England. France was now a republic once more, and Louis Napoleon was elected president. He then overturned the government and was crowned emperor. The emperor married Eugénie, Comtesse de Téba, in January, 1853. In the summer of 1859, the Emperor Napoleon in person led the French armies across the Ticino, won on the soil of Lombardy the brilliant fields of Magenta and Solferino, and concluded the mysterious peace of Villafranca.

The result of the Franco-German war, which ended so disastrously for France, put an end to the rule of Napoleon III. He and his army were forced

BLÜCHER'S MARCH TO WATERLOO.

to surrender to the victorious Germans, who then marched upon Paris. At length Paris itself was forced to surrender to the conquerors.

The celebrated Vendôme Column was destroyed by the Communists, the inspiring spirit of that affair being the distinguished French artist and communist, Gustave Courbet. On the 16th of May, 1871, at a quarter after four

PORTE ST. DENIS.

in the afternoon, the Vendôme Column, previously undermined by masons, yielded, but only after many efforts and slowly, to the strain of powerful windlasses. It came down with a great crash, filling the adjacent streets and squares with dust. An immense crowd was in attendance; they saw Napoleon's statue roll headless in the *debris*. The column was subsequently restored by the government.

COLUMN, PLACE VENDÔME, PARIS.

In certain respects Paris is the capital of the world. The strangers who flock to it in thousands proclaim it to be so. No other city offers equal attractions to persons of the most varied tastes. Paris consists of a hundred distinct cities welded into one, and yet, as a whole, it is full of individuality.

Architecturally Paris is one of the finest cities of the world. In its very centre rises the church of Notre Dame, a noble edifice of the twelfth and thirteenth centuries, illustrating one of the most remarkable epochs in the history of architecture. On the same island stands the Sainte-chapelle, a marvel of decoration, erected in the space of two years (1245-1247).

Amongst more modern buildings there are many which challenge admiration. The Louvre; the dome of the Invalides; the Pantheon; the palace of Luxembourg; the Greek temple of the Madeleine, designed by Napoleon to perpetuate his glory; the new Opera House, and the Arc de Triomphe, forming a fitting terminus to the noble avenue of the Champs Elysées, would each separately constitute the fame of a less worthy town. Most of the public buildings of Paris are, however, associated with great historical events. The Hotel de Ville, the Tuilleries, the Palais Royal and the Sorbonne are rich in historical associations.

Scientific and art collections abound. At the Museum of Arts and Industry may be seen a collection illustrating the progress of the mechanical arts. The galleries of the Luxembourg and the Louvre are rich beyond measure in works of art of every age. Several of the theatres, and notably the Theatre Francais, may fitly be enumerated amongst art institutions. The number of scientific societies is exceedingly large.

The Porte St. Denis is an arch of triumph which was erected in 1672, in commemoration of the conquests of Louis XIV. in Germany.

COMTE DE PARIS.

Since the death, a few years ago, of the Comte de Chambord, there is none of the direct line of Louis XIV. possessing any claim to the throne of France. He descended from the eldest son of the Grand Dauphin, who was son of Louis XIV. The second son of the Grand

Dauphin became King of Spain as Philip V., and from him descended the families known respectively as the Spanish Bourbons, the Bourbons of Parma, and the Bourbons of the Two Sicilies; but Philip formally renounced for himself and his descendants all claims upon the throne of France.

Upon the extinction of the elder branch of the French Bourbons—direct descendants of Louis XIV.—the younger branch, descended from the only brother of the great king, has taken its place, and fallen heir to whatever rights or claims it may have possessed. That younger branch is known as the House of Orleans; and its head is Louis Philippe Albert, Comte de Paris.

General Boulanger, the French minister of war, has been called the "Bonaparte without a victory." He is still quite young, very handsome, and a good speaker.

GENERAL BOULANGER

The upper classes in France are brilliantly gifted. In literature and the arts, in science, and in the application of science, they show innumerable names of distinction. For the last two centuries and a half, ever since the reign of Louis XIV., the French biographical dictionary illustrates every department of intellectual labor. Many women have also made themselves famous as authors and artists.

The "Heptameron," stories collected by Margaret of Valois, rivals the "Decameron" of Boccaccio; and Rosa Bonheur, in animal painting, is the equal of Landseer. Angouleme, the birthplace of Margaret of Valois, was also that of the great French authors, Balzac and Montalembert.

France has been termed not inappropriately the vineyard of the earth, its grand red wines for *finesse* and *bouquet* being unrivalled throughout the world, and its wines, led off by Château d'Yquem, rivalling those of any other country, not omitting even the renowned Johannisberg, and the still more renowned Tokay, while as regards its sparkling wines France is universally acknowledged to be without a peer.

ROYAL PALACE, MADRID.

SPAIN.

THERE is more of color, fascination and new sensation in a trip to Spain than to any other European country. The country is strange and beautiful, the habits and manners of its people novel and striking, and it is out of the beaten track.

Spain is divided into three distinct regions: the south and south-east warm and fertile, the productions being those of the temperate and tropical zones; the central consisting of elevated plains, but scantily watered; the northern covered chiefly with mountain ranges, high, broken and rugged; each region being provided by nature with outlets to convey its productions to any quarter of the globe.

No one knows what people first lived in Spain. History begins with the Iberians, of whom it tells us little. The Iberians were followed by the Celts. After much fighting the two nations concluded to dwell peacefully together, and were called the Celtiberians.

During the civil wars of the Roman republic, it often happened that the defeated general fled to Spain. There he collected his followers, hired soldiers, made alliances with the native tribes, and fought again. It was thus during the furious contest of Marius and Sulla for the control of public affairs. Quintus Sertorius, a partisan of Marius, fled to Spain when Sulla became victorious.

Sertorius had a tame fawn which he pretended had been sent to him by the goddess Diana, in order to guide his actions in war. If he learned that the enemy was preparing to attack some city, or was trying to persuade the inhabitants to rebel, he declared that the fawn had warned him to have his forces in readiness for action. If he received intelligence of a victory gained by his officers, he concealed the messenger who brought it. Then he presented the fawn, crowned with flowers, and bade the people rejoice and sacrifice to the gods, for that they would soon hear good news.

The northern tribes who conquered Rome overran Spain also. The Franks, the Suevi, the Alans and the Vandals followed each other, burning and slaying as they marched. Great numbers of these passed into Africa; the remainder were overcome by the Western Goths, or Visigoths, who succeeded them in 411. The Visigoths ruled in Spain until its conquest in the eighth century by the Saracens or Moors.

In 710, Tarik, a lieutenant of the Saracen general Musa, crossing the strait from Tangier with 500 men to reconnoitre the Spanish coast, landed at the rock ever since called Gibraltar (the hill of Tarik). Next year, with 12,000 men, he met and defeated at Xeres, Roderic, last of the Visigothic kings. The beaten monarch, who had come to battle crowned with pearls and lounging in an ivory car, was drowned in the Guadalquivir as he fled from the fatal field. Musa completed the conquest of the peninsula, driving the remnant of the Visigoths into the mountain-land of Asturias.

Among the mountains of Asturias the wreck of the Visigothic nation, shattered on the field of Xeres, survived; and these, breathing the free mountain air and eating the bread of hardship, became steeled into a race of heroes, whose succeeding generations never rested until the infidels, driven continually southward, were at last expelled from the peninsula.

Rising from amid the dust of these early wars was seen the famous hero of the Spanish ballads, Roderigo Diaz de Bivar, called by the Christians Campeador (the Champion), and by the Moors, whom he so often defeated, El Seid, the Cid (lord). He was born at Burgos, in the eleventh century. Driven from Castile by the usurper Alfonso, he began a guerilla warfare against the Moors of Aragon, where he fixed his castle on a crag, which is still called the Rock of the Cid. His great achievement was the conquest, after a long siege, of the Moorish city of Valencia. There he established a little state, over which he ruled until his death in 1099.

The "Cid," it is related, was never defeated: alive, he whipped the Moors, and, dead, his corpse was miraculously strapped to a steed and driven out to attack the invaders, when he routed them with tremendous carnage. Such is the legend; but these legends and proverbs are very solid things in old Spain.

In Granada shone the last blaze of Moorish splendor in Spain. Though shrunken to a circuit of 180 leagues, the kingdom of Granada, under the Alhamarid monarchs, remained strong and glorious for two centuries and a half, defying the chivalry of Spain and enriched by a commerce which carried her silks and sword-blades, her dyed leather, her fabrics of wool, flax and cotton to the bazaars of Constantinople, Egypt, and even India. Mulberry trees and sugar-canes clothed her fertile valleys. The fair Vega, or cultivated plain, sweeping away from the city of Granada for ten leagues, brought forth delicious fruits and heavy grain, nourished by the waters of the Xenil, which were spread through a thousand rills by the industry of the Moorish husbandmen.

To the east rose the white peaks of the Sierra Nevada; and, crowning one of the two hills on which the city stood, was the palace or royal fortress of the Alhambra, still even in its ruins the great sight of Spain.

Outwardly the Alhambra seems to be but a plain, square red tower; but within, in spite of monkish whitewash and the vandalism of Charles V., who pulled down a large part to make room for a winter palace that was never finished, it is a group of halls, courts and colonnades of wonderful grace and beauty. Their slender columns rivalling the taper palm-tree; walls whose stones were cut and pierced into a trellis-work, resembling in its exquisite delicacy lace or fine ivory carving; domes honey-combed with azure and vermilion cells, and bright with stalactites of dropping gold; groves of orange and myrtle, clustering round the marble basins in which cool silver fountains plashed their merry music, formed a scene of fairy splendor, amid which the monarchs of Granada held their brilliant court.

The Moslem power had existed in Spain for nearly eight centuries, when the Christian king, Ferdinand, resolved to win Granada from the Moors, and laid siege to the city. Famine soon began to be felt. Unknown to his people, the besieged monarch and his advisers entered into negotiations with the Spaniards. On a fixed day the Moorish king gave up the keys of the Alhambra; and the great cross of silver, which had been throughout the war the leading ensign of the Christian host, was borne into the Moorish capital amid the pealing notes of the *Te Deum*.

The Moorish name of the city was Karnattah. "The Pomegranate," and the threat of the Spanish king, Ferdinand, that he would pluck the pomegranate leaf and flower to pieces was fulfilled when Boabdil, the last of the Moorish monarchs, was driven out of the beautiful city. Upon the height overlooking Granada, Boabdil, heart-broken, gazed at the exquisite pomegranate that lay beneath him, gazed until compelled to fly, and that spot is called unto the present hour *El ultimo Sospiro del Moro*, or "The last Sigh of the Moor." His eyes were brimming with tears. "Well doth it become thee," said his mother, "to weep like a woman for what thou couldst not defend as a man."

After the expulsion of the Moors, Spain, under Charles V., engaged in a war with France, which was carried on with varying fortune. It then, under his son Philip II., turned its arms against the Netherlands. The Spaniards were beaten, England giving aid to these northern provinces through the terrible struggle.

In 1588, Philip, King of Spain, endeavored to make a complete conquest of England, and for that purpose sent an armament of 130 ships. It was called the "Invincible Armada," because it was believed to be unconquerable. But his hopes proved dreams. The Armada met with nothing but misfortune, both from battle and from storms. Only fifty ships returned to Spain.

THE ARMADA.

The beginning of Spanish literature is found in ballads, which in part express national feelings, opinions and beliefs, and in part celebrate great men and great deeds. The chronicle followed the ballad. It was in part history, in part story; but it described truly the customs and feelings of the age. Romances of chivalry (tales of impossible feats performed by gallant knights) were extremely popular. Many, however, believed that they had a damaging effect upon the mind. At length the greatest genius which Spain ever produced put an end to them by a work which will be read as long as the world lasts. This work is called "Don Quixote," and the author is Miguel de Cervantes. Cervantes, who wrote it while imprisoned, died in 1616. No monument was raised to his memory until 1835, when a bronze statue of him, larger than life, was set up in Madrid. This is thought to have been the first ever erected in Spain in honor of any man of letters or science.

Calderon, one of the greatest, and Lope de Vega, the most prolific dramatist that ever lived, were natives of Spain.

Spain has produced some great painters. Velasquez is the finest court painter, while Murillo is the best painter of religious pictures. Murillo cared little on what material he painted. Once, when employed at a convent, the cook of the establishment served him with great zeal. As he was about to depart, this brother begged for some slight sketch, when it was discovered that there was no more canvas.

"Never mind," said the cook, who feared that he might miss the picture, "take this napkin;" and he held out the one which the artist had used at dinner.

Murillo took it with a laugh, and before evening it was worth more than its weight in gold. He had painted on it a "Virgin and Child," still known as the "Virgin of the Napkin."

Marshal Soult, who was an inveterate looter, was in the habit of seizing all the valuable paintings to be found on the line of his march. Of thirteen Murillos which he managed to collect in Spain, one of them, an "Immaculate Conception," at the Marshal's sale in May, 1852, was bought by the French government for 586,000 francs ($117,200).

There is an amusing story of the circumstances under which Soult secured his prize. In pursuit of Sir John Moore he overtook two Capuchin friars, who turned out, as he suspected them to be, spies. On hearing that there were some fine Murillos in the convent to which they belonged, he ordered them to show him the way to it. Here he saw the Murillo in question, and offered to purchase it. All to no purpose, till the prior found that the only way to save the lives of his two brethren was to come to terms.

"But," said the prior, "we have had 100,000 francs offered for it."

"I will give you 200,000 francs," was the reply, and the bargain was concluded.

"You will give me up my two brethren?" asked the prior.

"Oh," said the marshal, very politely, "if you wish to ransom them, it will give me the greatest pleasure to meet your wishes. The price is 200,000 francs."

The prior got his friars, but lost his picture.

Madrid, the capital of the Spanish monarchy, is situated in the centre of an arid plain. It is the most elevated of all the capitals of Europe, being about 2,200 feet above the level of the sea. The royal picture-gallery is the great lion of the Spanish capital. It is richer in paintings than any other museum in Europe.

The structure for bull-fighting is built of brick, and is capable of holding

14,000 spectators. The interior is well fitted for seeing this spectacle. The fights generally take place on Sunday afternoons.

Seville, the birthplace of Murillo, as a place of permanent residence, is perhaps one of the most desirable in Spain. There is not a day during the whole year on which the sun does not shine. The winter is very pleasant. Byron says that Seville is famous for its oranges and its women, and the women, like the oranges, are of two kinds: bitter and sweet. For a long time it was, however, the centre of letters, science and arts. Its most remarkable and interesting building is the Alcazar, or palace, the residence of the Moorish and Catholic kings of Spain. The name signifies the House of Cæsar. It is a splendid specimen of Moslem architecture. In the royal chapel there is a large assortment of relics, amongst which is a piece of the true cross, the chemise of the Virgin Mary, the crown of thorns, with any quantity of legs, arms and bones of different male and female saints.

Valencia is the smallest province in Spain. The Moors believed that heaven was suspended over this portion of Spain, and imagined that a portion of it had originally dropped here and formed Paradise. Its climate is considered far superior to that of Italy for consumptive invalids.

SPANISH PRIEST.

In one of its churches there is a picture said to have been painted under the following circumstances: the Virgin Mary, having appeared to Martin de Alvaro, a famous Jesuit, and requested him to have her painted just as she appeared, Alvaro described her minutely to the famous artist Joanes, who made several attempts, but invariably failed. At length he joined the church, tried again, and succeeded to a miracle. When the picture was finished, the Virgin descended to examine it, and pronounced it perfect.

St. Vincent is the patron saint of Valencia, "the St. Paul of Spain." He came into the world under peculiar circumstances; in fact, before he came he was continually barking in his mother's womb. His mother, having consulted the bishop on the subject, was assured that she would bring forth a "mastiff which would hunt the wolves of heresy to hell." It is alleged he never changed his one woollen garment, never wore linen, nor washed himself.

The city of Saragossa is chiefly noted for the memorable sieges it has sustained, both in ancient as well as in modern times. It passed from the hands of the Romans into those of the Goths. It was conquered by the Moors, who made it their capital, in 1017. A century later the Moors were expelled by Alphonso of Aragon, after a long siege. Early in the century, Spain, wearied with resistance, succumbed to the genius of Napoleon, and the town of Saragossa alone remained unconquered. Women of all ranks assisted in its defence, forming themselves into battalions of two and three hundred, and shirking no exposure or danger.

The French were so exasperated at the protracted defence offered by this single town, that they bribed the people in charge of a powder magazine to

BRIDGE OF SARAGOSSA.

blow it up during the night. The enemy then pressed forward, and commenced a vigorous cannonade, and the consequent confusion in the city became fearful; the terror-stricken defenders were about to capitulate; the French were already pouring into the town through the breaches made by the explosion and their cannons, when the "Maid of Saragossa" appeared upon the scene, turned the fortunes of the day, and immortalized her name. Dressed in white, a cross hanging from her neck, her dark hair falling upon her shoulders, her eyes sparkling with the excitement of her resolve, she issued from the church of the Donnas del Pillas and, disregarding the insults of the soldiers, passed through the streets to the ramparts. Mounting the breach, she seized a lighted match from the hands of a dying engineer and set fire to his piece; then, kissing the cross, she exclaimed: "Death or victory!" and reloaded the cannon.

The despairing people were seized with fresh hope, enthusiasm filled each saddened heart, a great cry arose. "Long live Agostina!" and the fortunes of the day were changed.

Napoleon, having driven Ferdinand VII. from the Spanish throne, set his brother Joseph up in his place.

In 1868 a revolution took place in Madrid, and Isabella, Queen of Spain, was forced to flee, and take refuge at Paris. Spain remained without either a monarchical or any other form of settled government until 1870, when Bismarck proposed to place on the vacant Madrid throne the dapper little Prince of Hohenzollern, of Kaiser William's royal stock and household. Napoleon III. demurred, and it was on account of this insignificant pretext that the terrible war between Germany and France was fought. Before it had ended, Amadeus, son of Victor Emmanuel of Italy, was offered the throne by General Prim, and agreed to accept it. He was pompously inaugurated as king at Madrid on the 1st of January, 1871. For this work Prim was assassinated while he was passing in his carriage through the street, during the royal ceremony.

Amadeus soon found that he had not got on a bed of roses. He was a foreigner, not a Spanish prince—and that was crime enough in the eyes of those he had come to reign over. The reception that he met with from his new subjects was a freezing one; in their eyes he was not only a foreign intruder, but the son of the blasphemous and excommunicated King of Italy, who was at that moment trampling under his feet the dazzling crown of St. Peter, at Rome. He had fondly hoped that all the Spanish factions and parties would be disposed to unite on him. Nothing of the sort occurred. Carlists, Isabelinos, Republicans, Internationalists, Intransigents—each and all saw in his accession an excellent opportunity to work up the national feeling on their particular side, and their intriguing operations at once commenced.

Amadeus then renounced the crown, and the mock royalty had scarcely left the palace ere a "Republic" was proclaimed, the senate and cortes amalgamated under the title of "National Assembly," in the French style, and a new ministry was seated in the cabinet.

"Spain a republic!—what next?" The news fairly took away the breath of everybody in Europe, so unexpected and stunning was it. Anything rather than that from old Spain! But the telegraphic despatches were emphatic—official. Nevertheless, people at once nodded their heads, giving a sly laugh or wink, and spoke of the new-born as "premature." They knew best. The new republic lasted only the same length of time that Amadeus had reigned; it gave place to King Alfonso on the 1st of January, 1875.

21

Alfonso XII., Francisco d'Assisi Fernando Pio Juan Maria de la Concepción Gregorio, was born November 28th, 1857. He was married, 1878, to Maria de las Mercedes, who died the same year. Alfonso was married again to the Archduchess Christina, of Austria, 1879. He died in 1885.

KING ALFONSO XII.

The Spanish passion for public shows, games and festivals is deeply rooted. In Spain we still meet with that love of pageant which with us barely survives. The bull-fights, so often described, are a remnant of the public circus of imperial Rome; and still attract their thousands of ardent spectators. The great fair of Seville is a centre for all manner of shows; and the natural love of dancing finds vent not only in the theatres, but in every popular reunion throughout Andalusia. Spanish men and women, though reputed grave, dance in all manner of places, and in all styles. How many names of dances betray their Spanish origin, such as the Fandango, the Catucha, the Bolero. Gustave Doré has drawn various groups of Andalusians enjoying this their favorite pastime, all full of grace and spirit, and giving an idea of determined expression of enjoyment to which the phlegmatic nations of the North can afford no parallel. We laugh and sing because we are amused, and with no thought of how we do either. And we dance because we like the motion set to music; but the Spaniard dances to express his emotions of pleasure, and puts mind into the action.

But even more universal than the love of dancing is the love of fighting inherent in the people. They will draw out the knife upon every pretext. Malaga has, perhaps, the worst reputation for street rows and impromptu duels; but other towns are not far behind.

Still, in all these traits of character is the germ of possible restoration in the future—courage, gayety of spirit, a keen eye for beauty in motion, in color, in costume—a capacity for work whenever the backward institutions of the country allow a chance of profit—these things have remained by the Spanish people amidst all their decadence.

PORTUGAL.

PORTUGAL is one of the smallest European states, stretching along the western side of the Spanish peninsula. Its extreme length is 345 miles north and south; the greatest breadth is 140 miles. The climate and resources are similar to those of Spain.

The city of Lisbon, the capital of Portugal, is one of great antiquity; but it has been subject to frequent earthquakes.

In 1755 Lisbon was at the height of its prosperity; but in ten minutes, on November 1st of that year, the greater and most elegant part of the city was one mass of ruins. Fifty thousand souls perished; the number has been put as high as 80,000. The shock was felt nearly all over Europe.

Camoens is the only Portuguese writer that has obtained celebrity in other countries than his own. His works, however, have been translated into most of the modern languages of Europe, and he has been counted worthy of a place among the great epic poets, in the category with Homer, Virgil and Milton.

The subject of his great poem, "The Lusiad," is the pointing out to Europe a hitherto unknown track to India, which was achieved by a Portuguese fleet under command of Vasco de Gama. The eventful and unfortunate life of the poet himself enabled him too truly to depict from his own experience the sorrows of love, the tumults of the battle-field, the dangers of the deep and the luxury of oriental manners, which form the most attractive portions of his poem. There is still to be seen, on the coast of China, a kind of natural gallery formed by the rocks, which is called the Grotto of Camoens. At one time Camoens was shipwrecked; and it was with difficulty he reached the shore, swimming with one hand and bearing his poem above the water with the other, while everything else he possessed was lost for ever.

The people are industrious and commercial; they raise sheep and horned cattle; and have lead and iron mines. They possess two large, flourishing seaports, Lisbon and Oporto; and many colonial dependencies, some in Africa, as Senegambia and Mosambique, and others in Asia and the Oceanic isles.

ON THE COAST OF NORWAY.

SCANDINAVIA.

DENMARK, NORWAY AND SWEDEN.

THE Emperor Charlemagne, looking out one day over the blue Mediterranean, saw the snake-like galleys of the Norsemen stealing along the horizon, and, as he looked on them, he wept for his descendants.

Already, for many a year, as soon as the spring sunshine had unlocked the sea, the Vikings—sea-kings, as they called themselves—stirred by a restless, warlike spirit, had pushed out from the deep, rocky fiords of Scandinavia, steering south and south-west. In the names Norway, and Normandy, we still trace their old home, and the scene of one of their most successful descents. A branch of the great Teutonic family, they had spread over Denmark,

THE VIKINGS.

Norway, and Sweden, from which lands, centuries earlier, had come the famous Goths—Teutons too.

To guard the mouth of the Elbe against the Norsemen, Charlemagne built there a strong castle, which served as a nucleus for the great town of Hamburg. Before his reign their warlike fire had spent itself within the circle of their own lands. We read, in particular, of a desperate battle fought in 740, on the heath of Braavalla, between Harold Goldtooth, the Dane, and Sigurd Ring, the Swedish king. Harold, old and blind, died like a hero on the field; and Sigurd ruled in Scandinavia.

But then, sweeping both shores of the North sea, began their wider rangings, which have left deep and lasting marks upon European history. One of the earliest of these rovers, Regnar Lodbrok, Sigurd's son, seized by Saxon Ella as he was ravaging Lindisfarne, shouted his war-song to the last, while snakes were stinging him to death in a Northumbrian dungeon.

Words cannot paint the ferocity of these northern warriors. Blood was their passion; and they plunged into battle like tigers on the spring. Everything that could feed their craving for war they found in their religion and their songs. The chief god, Odin, was the *beau idéal* of a Norse warrior; and the highest delight they hoped for in Valhalla, their heaven, was to drink endless draughts of mead from the skulls of their enemies. There was, they thought, no surer passport to heaven than a bloody death amid heaps of slain. And their songs, sung by Skalds when the feast was over, and still heard among the simple fur-clad fishermen, who alone remain to represent the wild Vikinger, ring with clashing swords and all the fierce music of battle to the death.

But into the very centre of this dark, raging barbarism sparks of truth fell, which brightened and blazed until the fierce idolatry lay in ashes. Ansgar, the apostle of the north and first archbishop of Hamburg, pressing with a few monks through fen and forest, early in the ninth century, preached the cross at the court of Biörn, on the banks of Maelarn.

England and France, as was natural from their position, suffered most in the descents of the Norsemen. During a part of the time that Harold Haarfager (Fair-haired) reigned in Norway (863 to 931), Alfred, King of Wessex, the mightiest of all the Norsemen's foes, was laying the foundation of British greatness. Little more than a century later, Alfred's crown passed to the Norseman, Canute, and Norsemen wore it for twenty-four years. Then a little gap, and William, no longer a Norseman, but a Norman—mark well the change of name, for it denotes a deeper change of rough sea-kings into steel-clad knights—sat as a conqueror on the English throne, and set the wild Norse blood flowing down through the whole line of British sovereigns.

The empire of Canute, consisting of Denmark and Norway, with territories along the shores of the Baltic, also of England and part of Scotland,

MARGARET AWAITS THE ATTACK OF THE VITALI.

was broken up, and Denmark was distracted by intestine feuds until the reign of Margaret, daughter of King Waldemar, who, upon the death of her son Olaus, mounted the throne, although the female successor was not recognized, and by her beauty so gained the hearts of the people, that she was further elected Queen of Norway. Not content with this, she marched into Sweden, and for seven years carried on a devastating war; and finally, by the treaty of Calmar in 1397, was proclaimed queen of the three Scandinavian countries. She also expelled the Vitali or Victuallers from the Baltic—German pirates who were so named because they had brought provisions to Stockholm whilst it was in a state of siege. By her valor and heroic deeds Margaret deserved and obtained the title of the "Semiramis of the North."

The union of these three nations of Scandinavia existed, however, but nominally and, after being several times ruptured, was finally broken in 1523. In 1448, after the death of Christopher of Bavaria, Christian I., the first of the house of Oldenburg, which still reigns in Denmark, was elected to the throne. Norway and Denmark, however, remained united until 1814, when Norway accepted the sovereign of Sweden as their own.

The yoke of Denmark was shaken off by Sweden in 1523, when Gustavus Vasa, whose father had been slain in a previous insurrection, succeeded in driving out the Danes, and was elected king the same year.

His grandson, the famous Gustavus Adolphus, mounted the throne at the age of eighteen, and by his great ability and military genius soon gained the admiration of all Europe. He was victorious in wars with Denmark, Russia and Poland. He ended his victorious career at the battle of Lutzen in 1632.

The battle of Lutzen was fought between the Austrians, under the celebrated Wallenstein, and the Swedo-German army under Gustavus Adolphus.

Wallenstein would not move, and Gustavus had to attack. A thick mist covered the ground. The armies were close together, but neither could see much of the other.

The king sang, with his soldiers, Luther's hymn, "A mighty fortress is our God!" and then his own battle-song, "Verzage nicht, du Häuflein klein!" He addressed, first to the Swedes, then to the Germans, two of the noblest orations before a battle that history records. In an enthusiasm of heroism he threw off his cuirass, and cried, "God is my armor!" Wallenstein was suffering from gout in the feet. Although his stirrups were thickly padded with silk, he could not ride, and took his place in a litter. He called his officers together and gave them his orders, which were to fight chiefly on the defensive. Gustavus gave out the war-cry, "God with us!" Wallenstein gave to his troops as a battle-cry, "Jesus Maria!" About eleven o'clock the mist cleared a little, and the fiery king himself headed the attack upon the imperialist lines and ditches.

Gustavus, riding alone with his cousin, Duke Franz von Lauenburg, the page, Leubelfing, and a groom, stumbled upon an imperial ambush. His horse, maddened by a bullet, threw its rider and fled. The king received a bullet in the arm and another shot in the back. This second shot was, as the Swedes maintain, fired by Lauenburg, who left the king to his fate, rode away, and afterward joined the imperialist side. German historians speak doubtfully on the point, and the question of Lauenburg's treachery may be considered an open one. The imperialist soldiers did not believe that the king could be alone with so small an escort. They, however, took Gustavus to be an officer of rank until he cried out, "I am the king of Sweden, and seal with my blood the Protestant religion and the liberties of Germany. Alas! my poor queen!" The imperialist soldiers then killed and stripped him, and the tide of battle rolled on past the dead body. The faithful page, who alone remained with Gustavus, tried vainly to mount the king upon his own horse. The poor lad died, five days afterward, in Naumburg, of his wounds.

So fell Gustavus Adolphus. His own side were startled when the king's horse rushed back into their lines. They did not know that he was dead; they supposed him taken prisoner. A kind of fury possessed the troops, and the spirit of Gustavus rendered them invincible. Wallenstein, despite this advantage, could not claim a victory at Lutzen.

Wallenstein was well pleased when the news of the death of Gustavus Adolphus was brought to him. He said in his coarse proverb-like way, "Two cocks could not exist together on one dunghill."

Charles XII., the "Madman of the North," was born in 1682 and ascended the throne in 1697. During his minority Russia, Denmark and Poland combined to despoil him of many of his dominions; but their successes were of short duration. At the head of his troops he advanced from one triumph to another, until, intoxicated with success, he determined upon the conquest of Russia, which ended in a terrible defeat at Pultowa (1709). He was finally assassinated during the siege of Frederikshald in 1718.

According to agreement, Norway was allotted to Sweden in 1814 by the coalition against Napoleon, in payment for her aid in his downfall; and in 1818 Bernadotte, who had been one of the great emperor's generals, but who had joined the coalition against him, ascended the throne with the title of Charles XIV.

Though Denmark looks such a little country on the map, and indeed lost part of her possessions, Sleswig-Holstein, in the war with Prussia, of 1864, she is an active, intelligent state.

The soil of Denmark is very sandy in parts, and flat where the peninsula abuts upon the mainland; but the islands are extremely fertile, and the Danish farms are well cultivated; and there is a fair amount of manufactures. The Dane of to-day is no longer the fiery warrior he once was; but brave, patient, thoughtful. He is thrifty rather than particularly industrious; politically calm and constant in all his affections. Quiet as he seems, the Dane has yet a fund of poetry possible of awakening, since in one generation he has had for countrymen Thorwaldsen, the sculptor, and Hans Christian Andersen, whose beautiful stories have long been so popular in England. Thorwaldsen lived and worked at Rome; but came back to end his days in his native land, and was received with an ardent enthusiasm, of which the history of nations in relation to their great men affords but few parallels.

TYCHO BRAHE.

The celebrated astronomer Tycho Brahe, remarkable for his invention of instruments and his numerous works, was a native of Denmark. He was born December 14th, 1546, and died Octobor 24th, 1601.

The character of the Norwegian is moulded by that of the bold, mountainous country which he inhabits—a country of forests and of fiords. A fiord is a long arm of the sea, stretching so far inland that it comes to resemble an immense winding salt-water lake. The coast of Norway is indented like a huge saw with these fiords, and the coasts are inhabited by farmers and fishermen.

Among the Norwegian mountaineers none exhibit a truer picture of the grand nature which surrounds them, than the race which inhabits the valley of Hallingdal. They are quick, intelligent, robust and agile. The violent jumps and leaps, which distinguish their national dances, are so famous over the whole country, that these dances have got the general name of "Halling," the name also of the music that accompanies them. These dancers are said to touch the rafters of the ceiling with their toes.

The general character of the Swede is not much different from that of the Norwegian, only it is more lowland. Stockholm is a large flourishing town, the seat of the royalty of Sweden and Norway, where the ladies talk good French and the arts are held in high esteem.

The climate of Sweden influences not only the country, but the town life. Sledge-driving is the favorite amusement of the Stockholm ladies during the winter months, and the more severe the cold the greater the enjoyment of the season. The goodness of a winter in Sweden depends on the hardness of the ice and the quantity of the snow. Without these, winter trade and winter pleasures would be sadly impeded. The spring thaw is very unpleasant, the deep snow in the streets of Stockholm has to be broken up with pick-axes, and what we call spring weather hardly exists. As soon as the disagreeable thaw is over, summer is come.

LAKE OF GENEVA

SWITZERLAND.

EARLY in the Christian era Helvetia, which was peopled chiefly by Gallic tribes, formed a part of the Roman empire. Then, overrun by various barbarous races, it was included in the kingdom of Burgundy the Less, and as such fell under the rule of Charlemagne. After his death it was annexed to the Romano-Germanic empire. Conspicuous among the many small sovereignties and states, into which it was broken even while owning a sort of dependence on the empire, were the Forest Cantons of Schweitz, Uri and Underwalden, clustered round the southern shore of Lake Lucerne.

In 1273, Count Rodolph of Hapsburg (Hawk's Castle on the Aar in north Switzerland) was elected King of the Romans, or Emperor of Germany. He is distinguished in history as the founder of the imperial house of Austria. Lord of many lands and towns in Switzerland, he held besides, by the free choice of the foresters themselves, the advocacy or protectorship of the Forest States. He did not allow his elevation to the imperial throne to sever the ties which bound him to the mountain-land. He spent much time among the Swiss; and the many benefits and enlarged privileges they received from him were repaid on their part by unbroken affection and unbounded trust.

But when, in 1298, his son Albert, Duke of Austria—which had been taken by Rodolph from Bohemia—was made emperor, a gloom fell upon Switzerland. It soon became clear that his design was to make himself despotic master of all the land. The Forest Cantons were placed under two bailiffs or governors, Gessler and Beringer, whose insolent tyranny soon became intolerable.

Three of the oppressed foresters, Walter Fürst, Arnold von Melchthal and Werner Stauffacher, met to plan the deliverance of their country. On a November night, in the meadow of Rutli, by Lake Lucerne, these three patriots, in the presence of thirty tried friends, swore beneath the starry sky to die, if need were, in defence of their freedom. And all the thirty joining in the solemn vow, the new year's night was fixed for striking the first blow.

Meanwhile Gessler, the Austrian bailiff, was slain by one of the thirty, William Tell, a native of Burglen, near Altorf, and famous over all the country for his skill with the cross-bow. The romantic story, upon which, however, some doubt has been cast by modern historians, runs thus:

Gessler, to try the temper of the Swiss, set up the ducal hat of Austria on a pole, in the market-place of Altorf, and commanded that all who passed it should bow in homage. Tell, passing one day with his littles on, made no sign of reverence. He was at once dragged before Gessler, who doomed him to die, unless with a bolt from his cross-bow he could hit an apple placed on his son's head. The boy was bound, and the apple balanced. Tell, led a long way off, aiming for some breathless seconds, cleft the little fruit to the core. But, while shouts of joy were ringing from the gathered crowd, Gessler saw that Tell had a second arrow, which he had somehow contrived to hide while choosing one for his trying shot. "Why," cried the bailiff, "hast thou that second arrow?" And the bold answer was, "For thee, if the first had struck my child."

In a violent rage, Gessler then ordered Tell to be chained, and carried across the lake to the prison of Kussnacht. A storm arising when they were half-way over, huge waves threatened to swamp the boat. By order of the governor, Tell, whose knowledge of the lake was remarkable, was unchained and placed at the rudder. Resolved on a bold dash for liberty, he steered for a rocky shelf which jutted into the waters, sprang ashore, and was soon lost among the mountain glens. And some time after, hiding in a woody pass near Kussnacht, he shot the tyrant Gessler dead with his unerring cross-bow.

Thus for a few hours Tell shone out in the story of the world with a lustre that has never since grown dim. Darkness rests on his after-life. We know nothing more than that he fought in the great battle of Morgarten, and that in 1350 he was drowned in a flooded river.

The dawn of 1308 saw the foresters in arms. The Austrian castles were seized. The Alps were all alight with bonfires. Albert, hurriedly gathering an army, was advancing to crush the rising, when he was assassinated at the Reuss by his nephew, Duke John of Suabia. To their lasting honor, be it said that the three revolted cantons refused to shelter the murderer, who lived and died miserably in Italy.

Three great battles—Morgarten, Sempach and Nefels—mark the steps by which the brave Swiss achieved their independence.

Seven years after Albert's death, his son, Duke Leopold of Austria, resolving to pierce the mountains of Schweitz and punish the audacious herdsmen, left Zug with an army of 15,000 men, carrying great coils of rope to hang his prisoners. The pass of Morgarten, which ran for three miles between the steep rocks of Mount Sattel and the little Lake Egeri, was the only way by which heavy cavalry could pass into the doomed canton. With the dawn of a November morning, as the sun shone red through a frosty fog, the Austrians entered the pass—a host of steel-clad knights in front, and the footmen following in close order. Their advance was known and prepared for. Fourteen hundred herdsmen, who had commended their cause and themselves to the God of battles, lined the rocky heights. Fifty exiles from Schweitz, burning to regain an honored place among their countrymen, gathered on a jutting crag that overhung the entrance of the defile, and when the Austrians were well in the trap, hurled down great rocks and beams of wood upon the close-packed ranks. Amid the confusion, which was increased by the fog, the Swiss rushed from the heights, and with their halberts and iron-shod clubs beat down the knights, who fell back upon the footmen, trampling them to death. It was a woful day for Austria, and for chivalry, when the steel cuirass and the knightly lance went down before the pikes and clubs of a few untrained footmen. Duke Leopold scarcely saved himself by a headlong flight over the mountains to Winterthur, where he arrived late in the evening, a haggard, beaten man.

The valor of the Schweitzers was so remarkable in this battle, and throughout the great future struggle, that the name of their canton was extended to the whole country, henceforth named Switzerland.

The three cantons renewed their solemn league of mutual defence. Lucerne joined the Confederation in 1335; Zurich and Zug in 1351; Glarus and Berne soon followed, thus completing a list of the eight ancient cantons of the infant republic. A treaty, ratified at Lucerne, is remarkable as being a distinct acknowledgment on the part of Austria that the Swiss had triumphed and were free. The ceaseless industry and steady economy of the mountaineers proved them worthy of the freedom they had so bravely won.

But their task was not yet done. Bent on crushing the Confederation with one terrible blow, Leopold, Duke of Suabia, one of the Hapsburg line, marched from Baden towards Lucerne. He found his way barred at Sempach by 1,300 men, who held the wooded heights round the lake. The Austrian force consisted of 4,000 horse and 1,400 foot. At the hastily summoned council the arrogant nobles were loud in their cry that the peasant rabble should be crushed at once, without waiting for the rest of the army. And rashly the duke gave orders for the fight. As the broken mountain-ground was unfit for cavalry movements, the knights, dismounting, formed a solid mass of steel, blazing in the hot harvest sun.

A short prayer, and the Swiss were formed for the charge. On they came, the gallant mountain-men, some with boards on their left arms instead of shields. But the iron wall stood fast, with its bristling fence unbroken; sixty of the little band lay bleeding on the earth; the wings of the Austrian line were curving round to hem them in a fatal ring, when Arnold von Winkelried, a knight of Underwalden, dashing with open arms on the Austrian lances, swept together as many as he could reach, and, as they pierced his brave breast, bore their points with him to the ground. Like lightning the Swiss were through the gap; the Austrian line was broken; all was rout and dismay. Two thousand knights perished on the field. Duke Leopold himself died while gallantly defending the torn and bloody banner of Austria.

This brilliant success was followed, two years later, by another at Nefels, in which 6,000 Austrians were scattered by a handful of Swiss. Here, as at Morgarten, rocks flung from the heights caused the first disorder in the Austrian lines.

At the diet of Zurich, held in 1393, a general law-martial, called the Sempach Convention, was framed to bind the eight cantons together in firmer league. It enacted that it was the duty of every true Switzer " to avoid unnecessary feuds, but where a war was unavoidable, to unite cordially and loyally together; not to flee in any battle before the contest should be decided, even if wounded, but to remain masters of the field; not to attempt pillage before the general had sanctioned it; and to spare churches, convents, and defenceless females."

So Switzerland shook off the yoke of Austria; and never since, but once, when for a time Napoleon laid his giant grasp upon her, has the liberty won at Morgarten and Sempach been imperilled.

The land in Switzerland is exceedingly subdivided; the farmers own their own ground, which is chiefly pasture land. When the snow melts, the flocks are sent up to graze on higher levels; in winter they are brought down and housed. A great staple of production and commerce is cheese.

The occupations of the people are exceedingly various; they are herdsmen, hunters, guides, and makers of clocks and watches. In Geneva the watch trade is greatly developed, and gives rise to large exports. The people of Berne are intelligent and progressive, influenced by the excellent university there; and the town ranks the first in Switzerland. Geneva is, however, much resorted to by foreigners as a residence. Every summer, tourists by the thousand pour into the Swiss valleys; then the landlords open the huge hotels, many of which have been shut up in the winter time, and make up hundreds of beds, and kill beasts, and lay in provisions for the *table-d'hôtes*, where all the guests dine in long rows. Then the men of the villages at the foot of the

Alps bestir themselves to go up as guides with adventurous travellers. The majority of these ascents are accomplished in safety, but sometimes fearful falls occur, in which not only the traveller but the guide loses his life; and then there is mourning in the village, and a weeping widow and orphans. The guides generally tie the travellers together with themselves by a long rope, so that if one man slips he is upheld by the others; and so they go winding up and up, often cutting steps in the steep snow with their hatchets, until they reach the top.

The beautiful valley of Chamouni lies 3,000 feet above the level of the sea, and is one of the most popular places of resort in Switzerland. Near Chamouni is Mont Blanc, the far-famed "Monarch of Mountains." The Lake of Geneva or Leman, at the south-west of Switzerland, lies about 1,230 feet above the level of the sea, and has about the same number of feet in depth; its waters are a beautiful blue, and it is considered by many the most beautiful of Swiss lakes.

CALVIN.

Lord Byron passed the summer of 1816 on the banks of the Lake of Geneva; and here he wrote his third canto of "Childe Harold," his "Manfred," and his "Prisoner of Chillon;" and the sublime scenery of this region has been best described in his passionate poetry.

On the lake is the castle of Chillon, immortalized by Byron. His name may be seen here cut in the pillars in connection with those of Eugene Sue, Victor Hugo and George Sand. Here Bonnivard, a Genevese patriot, was imprisoned by order of Charles V. of Savoy for six long years.

Many Swiss have distinguished themselves in intellectual achievements. Jean Jacques Rousseau and Sismondi were both of this nation. Calvin was a preacher at Geneva, and St. Francois de Sales was a Catholic bishop of the diocese. In natural philosophy many Swiss have excelled; in art they have been less known. Tiny as their country is, they have always been a very creditable and much respected part of the great European family. Nor would they exchange their Alps and vales for any country in the world. When absent, their home-sickness is proverbial, and soldiers have sometimes died of it.

THE NETHERLANDS.

"In the market-place of
Bruges stands the belfry,
old and brown;
Thrice consumed and thrice
rebuilded, still it watches
o'er the town.
As the summer morn was
breaking, on that lofty
tower I stood,
And the world threw off the
darkness like the weeds
of widowhood."
—*Longfellow.*

HOLLAND and Belgium were formerly only one country, the Netherlands, and were for a long time under the dominion of Spain. They are, however now divided, and present some difference in the characters of the people, as well as in religious views.

Belgium is a Catholic country, and possesses the most beautiful old churches. The religious orders "are so abundant, both in extent and variety, that, like that of the celestial luminaries, the number is bewildering to the unpractised eye."

Sunday is better kept in Belgium than in France, and really is a day of pious rest. In fact, considering how near it is to France, and that the flat frontier provinces are covered with a network of railways, encouraging constant communication, it is very singular to see how much of the quaint old German spirit lingers in the smaller country, and how serious and quiet she is. Doubtless, had the French occupation under Napoleon continued, the constant pressure of French institutions would in time have somewhat assimilated the habits of the two peoples. The French, however, met with a desperate resistance, which Henri Conscience has well described in his "Peasants' War," and when Napoleon was struck down, Belgium was set free; being, in the first instance, united with Holland, and in 1830 created into a separate kingdom under King Leopold.

Brussels, the capital, is a lively town, and is said by some to be a smaller Paris; but though the new quarters and boulevards might for a moment deceive the traveller, a walk into the grand old market-place would soon undeceive him and show him he was in Belgium. It is a sort of neutral ground—French exiles, who do not like London, settling here. Books for-

A STREET IN GHENT.

bidden in France are turned out of the Brussels presses; and reprints of English and American books are also largely made. Brussels is, moreover, a gay town in regard to theatres, concerts, and balls. Ghent, on the contrary, is rich and manufacturing. Her burghers have been solid people since the days of Philip Van Artevelde, the warrior-brewer. There are crowds of tall, smoking, manufacturing chimneys in Ghent; cottons, woollens, and iron work being produced here. Louvain is the seat of a great university. Bruges is quiet, and full of institutions for the poor, the sick and the insane.

The Hollander or Dutchman is noted for his pertinacity of character. Holland or *Hollow-land* is so-called because large tracts of the land are literally below the sea-level, and the ocean restrained by a gigantic dyke, kept up with the greatest care. Who but Dutchmen would have had the dogged courage and perseverance necessary for such a work, especially as they have been nearly drowned out more than once? But though the land be flat, there are plenty of picturesque things upon it. Spires, church towers, bright farmhouses, their windows glancing in the sun; long rows of willow trees, their bluish foliage ruffling up white in the breeze; grassy embankments of a tender vivid green, partly hiding the meadows behind, and crowded with glittering gaudy-painted gigs and wagons, loaded with rosy-cheeked, laughing country girls, decked out in ribbons of many more colors than the rainbow, all streaming in the wind—these are the objects which strike the eye of the traveller from seaward, and form a gay view of the coast of Holland as he steams along its coast and up its rivers.

The Dutchman's ancestors were a great commercial people. They had colonies in the eastern seas, and fleets upon the waters, and were the Venetians of the North. They are no longer this, and the ancient greatness has departed; but they are still an active, productive people, of very curious manners and habits, and wonderfully unlike the rest of the world. One of their characteristics is exceeding cleanliness. The house-washing of Holland is proverbial. Not only the insides, but the outsides, are sluiced and mopped, and the brick pavements shine with water. In fact, Dutch tiles were made to be washed.

Although we have been of necessity brief in our description of the state of Holland, we will not omit the legend firmly believed in by sailors from generation to generation—that of the "Flying Dutchman," the "Phantom Ship." The sailor believes that a ghostly vessel, governed by a ghostly admiral in full Dutch costume, haunts the high seas, having been condemned for misdeeds done in the flesh, and the wood, to drive eternally before the gale. Again and again have mariners declared that they have been startled by the sudden bearing-down upon them of a huge, square-built barque, which, when they hailed, they saw to be a ship of ghostly transparence, so that the moon could be seen through her sails. This vision they consider an omen of misfortune; and its appearance at midnight, or looming in a dense fog, strikes terror into the seaman's heart. It is wonderful how such tales, once believed, propagate themselves; so that many a harmless ship, passing rapidly and in silence before another, has doubtless been firmly believed to be the dreaded "Flying Dutchman." This legend of the sea appears to have remotely suggested Coleridge's ballad of the "Ancient Mariner."

HEIDELBERG CASTLE, FROM THE NECKAR.

GERMANY.

THE startling events produced by the Austrian and Prussian war of 1866, and still later by the Franco-Prussian war of 1870 and 1871, have realized the fondest dreams of German writers and German politicians, that of a common nationality. The wildest hopes of Prussia have been realized, and not only is Germany to-day united (with the exception of that portion which belongs to the Austrian Empire), but two of France's most populous provinces, viz., Alsace and Lorraine, comprising 5,665 square miles (nearly 1,000 square miles larger than the State of Connecticut), and containing over one million and a half of inhabitants, have been added to its territory.

The states constituting the modern German Empire extend over a large area of Central Europe, between the Baltic sea on the north, and Austria and Switzerland on the south; from the Netherlands and the North sea on the west, to Austria and Russia on the east, embracing nearly a quarter of a million of square miles.

Within this extensive range the people are nearly throughout German, and, with some minor modifications, the language, customs, usages and manners are the same. It is in regard to religious and social institutions that the chief differences are to be noted. Southern Germany is Catholic; Northern Germany has for the most part embraced the doctrines of the Lutheran or Reformed Church.

The German nation has a better right than any other in Christendom to take pride in its reigning House. For nine centuries the Hohenzollerns—as successively counts (*Grafen*) of Zollern, burggraves of Nuremberg, prince-electors of Brandenburg and kings of Prussia—have borne a prominent and ever-increasing part in German history; and in our own days the head of the family has become hereditary head of the newly-created Empire of Germany. Counting from Frederick I., who eight centuries ago became Burggrave of Nuremberg, down to Kaiser William, we find some five-and-twenty names, mostly in direct succession from father to son. Among these are many able men, only a few weak ones, and not a single absolute blockhead or scoundrel. All of them are of pure German blood, for scarcely a Hohenzollern has taken any other than a German wife.

The present ruler of Prussia is Frederick William Victor Albert, born January 27th, 1859. He succeeded his father, Frederick III., under the title of William II. Of his character and promise we have as yet no good grounds for forming a definite opinion, as the various reports concerning him appear to be colored either by partiality or prejudice.

The most prominent struggle in German history during the seventeenth century was what is known as the "Thirty Years' war," of which Gustavus Adolphus, the King of Sweden, on the one side, and Albert, Count Wallenstein, a rich and distinguished Bohemian officer, on the other, were the principal characters. Gustavus Adolphus was killed at the battle of Lutzen, which was fought November 6th, 1632; but his troops gained the victory. In 1634, Wallenstein, being then fifty years of age, was assassinated. France, Spain, Italy and the Netherlands, as well as Sweden and the various German nations, were all drawn into this war, which was really a conflict between Protestantism and Catholicism.

The peace of Westphalia, signed at Munster, closed this eventful war. The leading terms of this celebrated treaty, which is looked upon as having laid the groundwork of modern Europe, were—1. That France should retain Metz, Toul, Verdun and the whole of Alsace except Strasburg and a few other cities; receiving, instead of these, two fortresses—Breisach and Philippsburg, which were regarded as the keys of Upper Germany. 2. That Holland should be a free state, independent alike of Spain and of the empire.

3. That the Swiss Cantons should be free. 4. That Sweden, receiving Stralsund, Wismar and other important posts on the Baltic, should also be paid $5,000,000, as indemnification for the expenses of the war.

The central point of the history of Germany in the eighteenth century, was the Seven Years' war, of which Frederick the Great, of Prussia, was the principal hero. In this war, Austria, France, Russia, Saxony, Sweden and Poland were arrayed against Prussia and England. In this war the life-blood of more than a million had been shed, but the face of Germany, on the whole, remained unchanged.

The beginning of the present century was signalized by the wars with Napoleon I. In the late Franco-German war, to which we will allude further on, Germany again wrested from France what had been ceded to her at the peace of Westphalia.

Frederick the Great of Prussia was one of the cleverest and most arbitrary of mankind; he raised the country from a small German kingdom to be the rival of Austria. He was brought up by a strict, tyrannical father, King William, and was obliged to rise to a signal every morning, and to be clean, neat and completely dressed in ten minutes. When a grown-up man, Frederick set to work to make all Prussians like himself, and the national character has always preserved the stamp. The people look as if they rose to a minute, and turned themselves out perfectly tidy in ten minutes. They are accurate.

The Prussian provinces on the Rhine are somewhat different. In Prussia proper the majority are Lutheran Protestants, and modern in their ways. In the Rhineland they are chiefly Catholics, and the country is full of old legends and quaint traditions.

Our American poet Longfellow has written a charming book, called "Hyperion," about the Rhine and the old cities on its banks; and the French poet Victor Hugo has written another. The Rhine is bordered by steep hills, on which the vine is cultivated and forms the great occupation of the people. On family feast-days it is pretty to see fathers and mothers and children sitting in the inn-gardens drinking coffee together. The young men wear long beards and smoke a great deal.

One of the great industrial centres of Prussia is the mining district of the Hartz, on the confines of Prussia and what was once the Kingdom of Hanover. This mountainous country, of which the Brocken is the chief feature, is rich in silver, lead, and copper; and also in wild legends, ascribing the possession of untold treasures to the demons of the hills.

The greatest of German legends is the old epic poem, the "Nibelungenlied," or the Song of the Nibelungen, one of the greatest poems of the world. Siegfried is represented as having slain a dragon, vanquished the ancient fabulous royal race of the Nibelungen, and taken away their immense treasures of gold and gems. He wooes, and finally wins, the beautiful Chriemhild, but is treacherously killed by the fierce and covetous Hagen, who seeks the treasures of the Nibelungen, and who skilfully draws from Chriemhild the secret of the spot where alone Siegfried is mortal, and fatally plunges a lance between his shoulders in a royal chase.

Berlin, the capital of Prussia, is situated on the river Spree, a small sluggish stream, and is ordinarily the residence of the monarch. It is one of the largest and handsomest cities in Europe, being about twelve miles in circumference. It has a garrison of 20,000 soldiers. The Spree intersects the city, insulating one of its quarters, and is crossed by more than fifty bridges in various parts of the city. The name of this river has given rise to the joke that Berlin is always drunk, because at all times on the Spree.

Berlin has the air of the metropolis of a kingdom of yesterday: no Gothic churches, narrow

STREET IN BERLIN

streets, fantastic gable-ends, no historical stone and lime, no remnants of the picturesque age, to recall the olden time. Voltaire in satin breeches and powdered peruke, Frederick the Great in jack-boots and pigtail, and the French classical age of Louis XIV., are the men and times Berlin calls up to the traveller. Berlin is a city of palaces; that is, of huge, barrack-like edifices, with pillars, statues, etc., etc.

The fixtures which strike the eye in the streets of Berlin are vast fronts of buildings, ornaments, statues, inscriptions, a profusion of gilding, guard-houses, sentry-boxes; the movables are sentries presenting arms every minute, officers with feathers and orders passing unceasingly, hackney droskies rattling about, and numbers of well-dressed people. The streets are spacious and straight, with broad margins on each side for foot-passengers, and a band of plain flag-stones on these margins makes them much more walkable than the streets of most continental towns.

About sixty miles from Berlin, Wittenberg is situated. This town is noted for being the place where Martin Luther commenced his war against the evils and abuses of the Church of Rome. He was professor of philosophy and theology in the University of Wittenberg, the same school where Shakespeare's Hamlet studied. The Schloss Kirche is the principal building. It was against the doors of this church that Luther hung up his ninety-five arguments against the Church of Rome, offering to defend them against all-comers. In the centre of the church are two tablets set into the floor, pointing out the spot where Luther and his friend Melancthon lie buried.

Martin Luther was born November 10th, 1484, in Eisleben, a town in Prussian Saxony. He was the son of a miner. He studied at Eisenach, begging in the meantime to obtain subsistence. A thunderbolt having killed one of his companions at his side, caused him to embrace religion. He entered the convent of the Augustins, and became professor of theology in the University of Wittenberg. Having studied the writings of John Huss, he rapidly acquired a taste for his opinions. The sale of indulgences by the pope furnished him an occasion to open the controversy. He published an argument in which he denied their efficacy. The quarrel soon became excited. Luther, who at first attacked but the abuses of the church, now attacked the authority of the pope, the belief in purgatory, the celibacy of the priests, the possession of temporal wealth, the doctrine of transubstantiation, and the mass. He married a nun named Catherine de Bore, by whom he had six children. He was excommunicated

"MARTIN LUTHER.

by the pope, and Henry VIII., of England, wrote strongly against him. He burnt the bulls of the pope, and responded to Henry VIII. in the strongest terms. The Duchy of Saxony, Denmark and Sweden took the part of Luther in this quarrel. At the Diet of Worms he supported his opinions. The first Diet of Spire, held in 1526, acknowledged the liberty of conscience; that held in 1529, desiring to rescind the acknowledgment of the first, the Lutherans protested against it, from whence is derived the name of Protestants. Luther died at Eisleben, in 1564, in the sixty-third year of his age. He was a man of impetuous eloquence, and exercised an irresistible influence on the multitude.

Eisenach, the capital of Saxe-Weimar, contains 13,000 inhabitants. It is the principal town in the Thuringian forest, and has been rendered famous from the fact of Martin Luther being detained a prisoner in its Castle of Wartburg, which is situated about one mile and a half south of the town.

On the 4th of March, 1521, as Luther was returning to his home from the Diet of Worms, where, in defiance of all threats and the pope's excommunication, he had boldly proclaimed the Protestant religion, as he was entering the borders of the wood his party was attacked by a body of armed knights and dispersed; he alone was made prisoner. He was conducted to the Castle of Wartburg, where he discovered the whole affair was managed by the order of his friend, the Elector of Saxony, who was present at the Diet when he left. Although the Emperor Charles V. had given Luther assurance of safe-conduct, a decree for his arrest was instantly sent after him, and his sentence of death decided on. The elector's band reached him before the warrant of arrest, and he was carried in secret to Wartburg, where he remained for ten months. He cultivated mustaches, and passed at the castle for a young nobleman, thus screened by the friendly Elector of Saxony until the first fury of the storm had passed. The chamber which Luther occupied in the castle contains his portrait and that of his father and mother. This room was the scene of his conflict with Satan. There is a story told and believed, that the evil one appeared before him gnashing his teeth and threatening him with vengeance; whereupon Luther, who had defeated his foes with pen and ink, thought he would try the ink alone on the devil, and, seizing the inkstand, he hurled it with all his power at the head of his satanic majesty, hitting his—imagination and the wall, making a greater impression on the latter than Satan did on the former. The hole in the wall is now shown to the traveller.

In another part of the castle is the picture of St. Elizabeth, of Thuringia, formerly a resident of Wartburg, whose husband was as hard-hearted as she was kind and charitable to the poor. On one occasion, when she had her apron filled with food which she was about to bestow on the hungry, her husband caught her in the act and demanded what she had in her apron; she replied, "Flowers," when, thinking to detect her in a falsehood, he tore open her apron, when, lo and behold! the bread and cheese were transformed into roses and lilies. She stands in the picture as if trembling for fear they will change again.

Dresden, the capital of the Kingdom of Saxony, is delightfully situated on both banks of the Elbe. It has 177,025 inhabitants. Its military museum outstrips all others in the variety and quantity of its offensive and defensive weapons; in its accoutrements of the tournament; the richness and skill evinced in the decoration of the armor and trappings both of man and horse; and the relics it possesses of the greatest warriors of different ages. Among the relics are the robes worn by Augustus II., surnamed "Strong," at his coronation as King of Poland; the horseshoe which he broke with his

MAYENCE.

fingers; his cuirass, weighing 100 pounds, and his iron cap, twenty-five pounds. He is said to have lifted a trumpeter in full armor, and held him aloft in the palm of his hand; to have twisted the iron banister of a stair into a rope; to have made love to a coy beauty by presenting in one hand a bag of gold, and breaking with the other the horseshoe mentioned above. Judging from the great weight of his armor and weapons, he must have been a man of giant strength. There is also a saddle of Napoleon's, his boots worn at the battle of Dresden, and the shoes worn at his coronation.

The city of Mayence is the largest place in the Grand-Duchy of Hesse-Darmstadt. It was annexed to Prussia in 1866. It contains a population of 56,000, including the garrison, which consisted of 7,000 soldiers previous to its Prussian annexation. Its fortifications are of great strength. Mayence is a city of great antiquity; under Charlemagne and his successors it became the first ecclesiastical city of the Roman Empire, and was long the seat of a sovereign archbishopric. In modern times it became celebrated for the memorable siege it endured, when it was successfully defended by the French troops who garrisoned it.

Among the principal edifices of Mayence, which are of great antiquity, is the cathedral, a vast pile of red sandstone buildings, begun in the tenth and finished in the eleventh century; it has suffered considerable damage at different times, having been burned by the Prussians in 1783, and used as a barrack by the French in 1813. The interior is filled with the monuments of the different electors of Mayence, who always presided at the election of the em-

FIRST PRINTING-PRESS.

peror, and were the archbishops and first princes of the German Empire. The site formerly occupied by the dwelling-house of Gutenberg, the inventor of printing, a native of the town, may still be seen. With Gutenberg was associated John Faust, a goldsmith and engraver. Faust died at Paris in 1466.

Luther believed that he threw ink at the devil and forced him to flee; but since the invention of printing the world has been really throwing ink at the devil, *Ignorance*, by means of the first printing-press, and is fast driving him away. The age of the invention of printing produced many great names in Germany, as well as in other countries. Albert Durer, one of the greatest painters and engravers, was born at Nuremberg, May 20th, 1471, and died in 1528. Nicholas Copernicus, the promulgator of the true system of astronomy, was born at Thorn, in Prussia, in 1472, and died in 1543. Following Copernicus came the astronomer John Kepler, who has been called the "Lawgiver of the Heavens." The three laws which lie at the basis of all true astronomical science were discovered after seventeen long years of labor by this great man. His exultation when he found that "the anguish and the sweat of years" had brought him at last to see the truth was unbounded. "Nothing holds me," he wrote; "I will indulge my sacred fury. . . . If you forgive me, I rejoice; if you are angry, I can bear it. The die is cast; the book is written, to be read either now or by posterity, I care not which. It may well wait a century for a reader, since God has waited 6,000 years for an observer."

COPERNICUS.   KEPLER.

The famous town of Weimar is situated on the Ilm, in the midst of beautiful groves and handsome grounds. Its population is 15,000. It possesses great interest as the residence of some of the most distinguished literary men of Germany, drawn thither by the enlightened patronage of the grand duke. Among the great names thus connected with it are those of Schiller, Goethe, Herder and Wieland.

Schiller's remark during his first visit to Weimar, "An affair of the heart is an easy matter here; scarce a woman without her history," proved too true of Goethe, Germany's greatest mind, "whose lute was a woman's broken heart." He was then in the full bloom of a manhood whose like literary history has rarely seen. With a face more beautiful than Byron's or Milton's, nature had endowed him with a physique denied to either. The waving brown hair, the soft dark eyes, the Apollo-like profile, seemed Cupid's arrows, which pierced the hearts of men and women alike. As a specimen of Goethe's poetry we give Carlyle's favorite poem, translated by himself from Goethe, with his comment upon it:

"MASON LODGE.

"The Mason's ways are
  A type of existence,
  And his persistence
  Is as the days are
  Of men in this world.

"The future hides in it
  Gladness and sorrow;
  We press still thorough,
  Naught that abides in it
  Daunting us, onward.

"And solemn before us
  Veiled the dark portal,
  Goal of all mortals;
  Stars silent rest o'er us,
  Graves under us silent.

"While earnest thou gazest
  Comes boding of terror,
  Comes phantasm and error,
  Perplexes the bravest
  With doubt and misgiving.

"But heard are the voices,
  Heard are the sages,
  The world's, and the age's
  Choose well; your choice is
  Brief and yet endless.

"Here eyes do regard you
  In eternity's stillness;
  Here is all fulness,
  Ye brave, to reward you.
  Work and despair not."

"Is not that a piece of psalmody? It seems to me like a piece of marching music to the great brave Teutonic kindred as they march through the waste of time—that section of eternity they were appointed for. Let us all sing it and march on cheerful of heart. 'We bid you to hope.' So say the voices, do they not?"

This poem of Goethe's was on Carlyle's lips to the last days of his life. When very near the end he quoted the last lines of it when speaking of what might lie beyond: "We bid you to hope."

In the new churchyard outside of Weimar may be seen an admirable arrangement to prevent the accident of premature burial in cases of suspended animation. In a dark chamber, lighted with a small lamp, the body lies in a coffin; in its fingers are placed strings, which communicate with an alarm-clock; the least pulsation of the corpse will ring the bell in an adjoining chamber, where a person is placed to watch, when medical attendance is at once supplied. There have been several cases where persons supposed to be dead were thus saved from premature interment.

Cologne is one of the most important cities in the Prussian kingdom. It is built in the form of a crescent close by the river Rhine, and is strongly fortified, the walls forming a circuit of nearly seven miles. The well-known liquid which bears the name of the city (*eau de Cologne*) is an important production of the place, and is exported in very large quantities.

The chief glory of Cologne is its magnificent cathedral, or Minster of St. Peter, which is one of the most magnificent specimens of Gothic architecture in the world.

Behind the high altar is the Chapel of the Magi, or the Three Kings of

Cologne. The custodian will tell you that the silver case contains the bones of the three wise men who came from the East to Bethlehem to present their presents to the infant Christ, and that the case, which is ornamented with precious stones, and the surrounding valuables in the chapel, are worth $6,000,000. These remains were presented to the archbishop of Cologne by the Emperor Barbarossa when he captured the city of Milan, which at that time possessed these valuable relics. The skulls of the Magi, crowned with diamonds, with their names written in rubies, are shown to the curious. Among the numerous relics in the sacristy is a bone of St. Matthew.

COLOGNE CATHEDRAL, SOUTH SIDE

The church of St. Ursula is one of the most remarkable sights in Cologne. The tradition of St. Ursula is this: She was the daughter of the King of Brittany, who sailed up the river Rhine as far as Basle, and then, accompanied by 11,000 virgins, made a pilgrimage to Rome; from Basle she travelled on foot, and was received at the Holy City by the pope with great honors. On her return the whole party was barbarously murdered by the Huns, because they refused to break their vows of chastity. St. Ursula was accompanied by her lover, Conan, and an escort of knights. St. Ursula and Conan suffered death in the camp of the Emperor Maximin. Ursula was placed in the calendar as the patron saint of chastity; and the bones of all the attendant virgins were gathered together, and the present church erected to contain the sacred relics. On every side you turn, skulls, arm- and leg-bones meet your eye, piled on shelves built in the wall. In every direction these hideous relics stare you in the face. Hood says it is the chastest kind of architecture. St. Ursula herself is exhibited in a coffin which is surrounded by the skulls of a few of her favorite attendants. The room in which she is laid contains numerous other relics; among these are the chains with which St. Peter was bound, and one of the clay vessels used by the Saviour at the marriage in Cana.

The church of St. Peter will be visited with interest, as it contains not only the font in which Rubens was baptized—he was born in Cologne—but also one of his masterpieces, the Crucifixion, presented to the church in which he was baptized, a short time before his death. It is used as an altar-piece.

We will now take a glance at that war which made a united Germany possible; and in doing so we must remember that the Emperor William was a full-grown, tall young officer of the Prussian army on the field of Waterloo, and shared in the revels after Waterloo with the Czar Alexander, Wellington and Blucher, in captured Paris. It seems strange that, at the outset of his

PRINCE BISMARCK.

military career, he should have taken part in the overthrow of the first French empire; and that the crowning incident of his later years should be the demolition of the second. And it is one of the most striking evidences of William's shrewdness and foresight in kingcraft that he should discern the one man in all Germany whose brain and will were equal to the task of achieving German unity and a restoration of the ancient empire. The appointment of Bismarck as his chief adviser proved this.

In the nature of things all wars must be studded thick with dramatic incidents—the eagerness for martial distinction; the whirl and turmoil of the battle, the "rapture of the fray," as Kinglake styles it; the spasms of hope of success alternating with those of apprehension of defeat; the long strain of suspense; the cheering of the charge and the groaning of the wounded; the swelling triumph of the victory or the bitter realization of the defeat—all these things present a drama of varied emotional interest, the lurid fascination of which never fails to inthrall the world.

But while this is so, the story of some wars is comparatively prosaic, while others teem with sensations outside that of the actual fighting, and so present an exceptionally wide range of melodramatic incident. Of no war of modern times can this be more truly said than of the Franco-German war of 1870-1. Its story abounds with what in stage parlance are called "situations;" its every episode was sensational. It was a strife, not so much of political friction, but of great nation against great nation. The very hearts of the people were in it: empires and dynasties were the stakes; monarchs and the offspring of monarchs were in the field; it shattered one imperial dynasty and it created another.

The difficulty is not to find its melodramatic incidents, but to make a selection of them out of the wealth of those which are most striking. In the early days of June, 1870, the atmosphere of Europe is that of profound peace. Earl Granville, the British foreign minister, has made the statement that there is not a cloud, or the shadow of a cloud, in the political sky. A few days later King Wilhelm of Prussia is quietly rusticating at the little watering-place of Ems. There besets him there Benedetti, the French ambassador to his court. Benedetti demands, in the name of his master, the Emperor Napoleon, that King Wilhelm will disavow his sanction to the candidature of his kinsman, Prince Leopold of Hohenzollern, for the throne of Spain. Wilhelm replies that his sanction has not been asked, and Prince Leopold simplifies matters, and seemingly resolves the difficulty, by declining to be a candidate. But this does not satisfy Benedetti's master. Benedetti is instructed to obtain from King Wilhelm a categorical promise that, in the future, under no circumstances will he permit a German prince to become a candidate for the throne of Spain. Then the old man's blood is stirred. He declines to give any such promise. Benedetti, pursuant to instruction, persists in the endeavor to exact the promise, or to sting Wilhelm into an angry refusal. He accosts the old king on the promenade. Wilhelm's face flushes with hot wrath; but he forgets not the dignity of his kingship. Looking over Benedetti as if he were a worm on the pavement, he says to his aide-de-camp, Count Lehndorff, "Tell this gentleman I have nothing to say to him!" and then he turns on his heel and stalks away, leaving the Frenchman *planté là*.

And so begins the war that, sought by that Frenchman's master, is to hurl the latter from his throne—a war none the less that the declaration of hostilities comes from France, the preparations for which had been maturing in Germany, under the superintendence of Moltke and Roon, ever since Bismarck, when he left the Tuileries three years before, took away the conviction that war between France and Germany was inevitable, and that the task before him was to get Germany ready for the contest, postpone the crisis till she was ready, and bring it on when that consummation had been attained. Napoleon, Wilhelm and Benedetti were alike the puppets and playthings of the great burly chancellor.

VON MOLTKE.

"On to Berlin!" was the cry of the French soldiers as they marched along the boulevards of Paris amid the frantic applause of the spasmodic boulevardiers. The braggart cry came from an army that never got nearer Berlin than the frontier of France—came from an army which Le Boeuf warranted ready for war to the last button on the last soldier's gaiter, but which in reality lacked every attribute of an army save the gallant courage that, with all his faults, is inherent in the French soldier. In Germany there was infinitely less throat-splitting, but infinitely more of method and alacrity of preparation. Moltke had touched that bell of his in his room in the bureau of the general staff, that bell whose sound is the signal for the telegraph wires to speed to the head-quarters of the respective army corps the signal for the mobilization of the reserves of the German army.

The first great battle took place near the city of Metz, the French army being totally defeated. The great battles of Mars-la-Tour, Gravelotte, Beizeilles, and Sedan rapidly followed, with the same result. Outside of Sedan the French fought with desperation, and the Germans pressed on with overwhelming numbers and characteristic German persistence. In this battle the Germans had 285,000 engaged, while MacMahon's army numbered 115,000— less than half that number. The French, outnumbered two to one, were forced into Sedan, and the Germans commenced shelling the town. The Prussian king ordered the firing to stop, and sent an officer with a flag of truce, offering capitulation. He entered the city and was conducted into the presence of the Emperor Napoleon. The French emperor asked what his orders were, when he replied that he had been sent to summon the army and fortress to surrender.

He was referred to General Wimpffen, who had assumed the command in place of MacMahon, who had been disabled in battle. With much reluctance General Wimpffen consented to an unconditional surrender, and 83,000 Frenchmen laid down their arms. No such shame had ever before fallen upon the arms of France.

And now the way to Paris was cleared of every obstacle, and the Germans without loss of time began their march on the capital. So soon as the disaster of Sedan was known there, the Parisians deposed their emperor and erected a republic. The new government determined upon a strenuous defence. The Germans completely surrounded the city, and effectively cut off communication with the world outside. They did not inflict the horrors of bombardment, and were contented to wait till famine compelled surrender.

Fiction would not have dared to be so strange as the stern truth embodied in that environment of Teuton soldiery that surrounded the queen city of the old world from September, 1870, to February, 1871. While inside Trochu planned, ever unavailingly, outside, in Versailles, Bismarck grimly waited for the "physiological moment," and the palace of the *grand monarque*, with its proud inscription "*A toutes les gloires de la France,*" was in use as an hospital for the wounded German soldiers. But on the 18th of January, 1871, the grandest hall of that palace, the sumptuous Gallery of Mirrors, was cleared of the truckle-beds of the wounded soldiery, that it might be the scene for the proclamation of a new emperor. The great mirrors that once reflected the splendor of the court of Louis reflect to-day the varied uniforms of the German armies. Not Prussian uniforms alone do the mirrors reflect, but Bavarian, Wurtemberger, Saxon, also, for to-day witnesses the consummation of German unity, and the creation, or rather the resurrection, of a German Empire. The raised dais at the upper end of the long hall is thronged with the princes and potentates of Germany, gathered there to proclaim as "the German emperor" the square-shouldered, white-haired monarch who stands in the centre of the forefront of the throng. Behind and on either side of him are the men who have made that empire—Bismarck, the planner; Moltke, the strategist; Roon, the army reformer. By his side, flushed with pride in his father, stands the gallant Crown Prince, scholar, general, patriot. Suddenly there stands forth the Grand Duke of Mecklenburg, with a clash of his sword as its scabbard-point rings on the polished floor. He waves his plumed helmet aloft, and shouts, "Hurrah for the German Emperor!" The deep-noted "Hoch!" is caught up vociferously by the throng; it is repeated over and over again, till the echo of the cheering booms out over the Place d'Armes below. The wounded soldiers in the adjacent galleries hear it as they lie, and they give it back in feebler, but not less earnest, tones. The crown prince is on his knees before the emperor, his father, kissing the hand of father and kaiser. The cannon bellow out the salute, the noise of which

KING WILLIAM PROCLAIMED EMPEROR OF GERMANY.

mingles with the firing of the fighting line out to the front, by Montretout and Ville d'Avray. There is a flush of triumph on Bismarck's dark face, for the unity of Germany has been formally consummated.

The Emperor William I. was a true German in his fondness for the good things of the table. He once had a severe conflict between his appetite and his patriotism, in which, it must be confessed, his appetite won. Before the war with France he had a chief cook who suited him exactly. But the cook

CROWN PRINCE OF GERMANY.

was a Frenchman, and when the war broke out he was dismissed because of his obnoxious nationality. But the German who replaced him only succeeded in giving the monarch a series of fits of violent indigestion. So the former cook, Frenchman as he was, was recalled to his post, where he has remained ever since.

GERMANY.

The day on which King William was hailed Emperor of Germany was the one hundred and eightieth anniversary of the coronation of Frederick the Great as King of Prussia; so that the day was already notable in the history of his family. On the 28th Paris capitulated. With the city of Paris were surrendered 1,900 pieces of artillery and 180,000 prisoners.

EMPEROR WILLIAM II.

By the terms of peace France ceded the greater part of Alsace and Lorraine. The war indemnity amounted to $1,000,000,000.

An attempt was made on May 11th, 1878, to assassinate the Emperor in Berlin. He was returning in his carriage from a drive with his daughter, the Grand Duchess of Baden, when a tinsmith, named Hödel, fired two shots into the carriage from the sidewalk, but both shots missed. Hödel was beheaded for his crime. Another attempt was made on June 2d, when he was driving in the Unter der Linden, by Dr. Nobeling, a Socialist or Nihilist. Though the Emperor received thirty small shot in the face, head and arms, he was not seriously injured.

He died March 9, 1888, and was succeeded by his son, Frederick William Nicholas Charles, "Unser Fritz," who assumed the title of Frederick III. Frederick was a lover of learning and of a noble character. When he and Von Moltke were making a tour of military inspection through the provinces, the alarm of fire was given in one of the cities. He was the first person to reach the fire, and labored hard with his hands till it was extinguished. This act made him tens of thousands of friends, and all Germany boasted a royal son who, though a child of a palace, was a friend of the poor man's home. At the annual picnic for children he always took his family, and bade his sons and daughters mingle with the poorest and humblest of the throng. He believed in greater freedom of the press. When a law restricting the liberty of the press was passed he objected to it, and his father was greatly displeased at his son's opposition to the law. But he said: "Father, you may strip me of all my decorations, you may take away all my commissions, but you cannot compel me to favor what I consider to be so unjust a measure." The obnoxious feature of the law was repealed. He favored freedom of conscience. He encouraged the largest religious freedom.

Frederick married the Princess Victoria of England on the 25th of January, 1858. In 1883, on the occasion of their silver wedding, the citizens of Berlin gave Frederick and Victoria a vessel containing two hundred thousand dollars in gold, which, like the presents received twenty-five years before, they set apart as an endowment for charities.

Frederick died of a disease of the throat on June 15th, 1888. The same heroism which he had displayed on the battle-field was manifested on the bed of sickness. The people of Potsdam spread oak leaves on the road for a mile over which their beloved monarch might pass to the tomb. And they laid him beside Frederick the Great.

On March 18, 1890, Prince Bismarck resigned the Chancellorship of the German Empire, and was succeeded by General Von Caprivi. General Caprivi was born at Berlin on February 24th, 1831. He is a descendant on his father's side of an illustrious Italian family. Entering the regiment in his eighteenth year, he won rapid promotion. He has not only proved himself a great soldier, but also an able administrator.

STREET IN VIENNA.

AUSTRIA.

HE Empire of Austria is bounded on the north by Russia, Prussia, Poland and Saxony; on the west by Bavaria, Switzerland and the Kingdom of Italy; on the south by Italy, the Adriatic sea and Turkey, and on the east by Turkey and Russia. Its greatest length is 860 miles, and its average breadth 400 miles, the total area being nearly twice the size of Great Britain and Ireland, and one-third more than the whole of the Middle and Eastern States of our own country.

The countries brought together under the rule of Austria comprise a greater portion of the European continent than belongs to any other single power excepting Russia. They include provinces inhabited by people of different race and language, and whose only bond is that of political rule. The nucleus of Austrian power is German, and the German provinces of the empire comprehend the portion of its population that is most advanced with regard to civil and social condition. But the German provinces constitute less than a third part of the entire extent of the empire; the Hungarian countries form more than a half of its entire area, and include two-fifths of its population. Galicia, or Austrian Poland, is equal to one-eighth of the whole empire as regards size, and includes more than that proportion of its population. Previous to 1866 the Italian subjects of Austria amounted to one-eighth of the population.

In 1804 Francis assumed the title of hereditary Emperor of Austria, and on the 6th of August, 1806, renounced the title of Emperor of Germany. The latter event had been preceded by the formation of the Confederation of the Rhine, and the entire dissolution of the old Germanic Confederation. His son, Ferdinand I., succeeded him in March, 1835, and he was succeeded by the present emperor, Francis Joseph, born August 18th, 1830, who ascended the throne December 2d, 1848.

As every province in Austria forms a separate land, each has its peculiar language or dialect, and its distinguishing customs and habits. Of the Slavonic languages the Polish possesses the richest literature; but the Bohemian has of late years been highly cultivated, and forms the written language of the Moravians and Slowaks of the north-west counties of Hungary. The dialect of Carniola has been methodized, and is grammatically taught as the written language of Illyria and Croatia. The ephemeral existence of the Illyrian kingdom, established by Napoleon, sufficed to call forth the powers of a lyric poet of considerable merit named Wodnik, who wrote in this dialect.

Vienna, the capital, is a city of ancient origin, and has been the scene of many interesting historical events. It was successively taken by the Goths and Huns, and subsequently by Charlemagne, who placed it under the government of the margraves of the eastern part of his dominions, thence called Oesterreich, and Austria. The margraves, afterward dukes, held Vienna until the middle of the thirteenth century, when it was taken by the Emperor Frederick II., and again by Rodolph I., founder of the Hapsburg dynasty, in 1297. The Hungarians vainly besieged it in 1477, but eight years later it was obliged to surrender to Matthias, who then possessed the united crowns of Hungary and Bohemia and made it the seat of his court. Since the time of Maximilian I., it has been the usual residence of the archdukes of Austria and emperors of Germany. The most memorable event in its history, however, and one that largely influenced the fortunes of Christendom, was its famous siege in 1683 by a Turkish army, 200,000 strong, under the command of Kara Mustapha, when it was only saved from surrender by the timely arrival of John Sobieski, the heroic King of Poland, who defeated the besiegers with great slaughter under the very walls of the city. In 1619 Vienna was unsuccessfully blockaded by the Bohemian Protestants. In 1805 it submitted to the conquering arms of the first Napoleon, and again, after a short resistance, in 1809.

Throughout Germany the name of Vienna has long been synonymous for music. It is the chief national art in Austria, which never had great warriors,

NAPOLEON AND QUEEN LOUISE.

statesmen or orators, but has always had great and good musicians. The musical history of Vienna comprises four grand epochs: that of Haydn and Mozart, that of Beethoven and Schubert, that of Liszt and Thalberg, and the present, which is dubbed the "Renaissance." The citizens are always enthusiastic over music—their weak, or rather strong, point. Misunderstood geniuses are understood by them, and their city is the only one, except Munich and Bayreuth, where Wagner's music has been performed in all its fulness. Composers and musicians receive at their hands that formal consecration which Rome formerly gave to painters and sculptors.

BEETHOVEN.

The environs of Vienna are worthy of notice, and much frequented by pleasure-parties from the metropolis. The principal place is Schönbrunn, the favorite summer residence of the emperor. This palace was begun by Matthias, and finished by Maria Theresa. It possesses a melancholy historical interest on account of Napoleon II., Duke of Reichstadt, having died here, and in the same bed that his imperial father occupied in 1809. This occurred in 1832. His mother was the Archduchess Maria Louisa, who was married to Napoleon I., March 11th, 1810.

BAVARIA.

Bavaria consists of two distinct divisions of territory, which cover an area of 29,628 square miles, and contains a population of 5,000,000. The larger division is bounded on the south and east by the German provinces of Austria; on the west by the Kingdom of Wurtemberg and the Duchy of Baden; and on the north by the smaller German states. The smaller portion is to the westward of the Rhine, and bordering on the French frontier. It has a mean elevation of 1,600 feet above the level of the sea, is 200 miles long, and 150 wide. The greater portion of Bavaria is within the basin of the Danube, which crosses the country from west to east, and is watered by that river and its numerous affluents. The climate is in general temperate and salubrious.

Bavaria is particularly noted for the good quality of its beer, which is far superior to that of any other country; in fact, its flavor is entirely different; *but you must drink it in Bavaria*. The quantity drunk and brewed is incredible. Allowing 25,000,000 gallons to be exported every year, the quantity brewed would leave seventeen gallons per annum to every man, woman and child in the kingdom.

BOHEMIA.

"' Hold your tongues! both Swabian and Saxon!'
A bold Bohemian cries;
'If there's a heaven upon this earth,
In Bohemia it lies.'"—*Longfellow's "The Happiest Land."*

The ancient Kingdom of Bohemia, of which Prague is the capital, has been a dependency of Austria since the Thirty Years' war. The princess Elizabeth, daughter of James I. of England, was for a short time Queen of Bohemia, her husband, the Elector Palatine, having been invited to fill the throne and support the Bohemian Protestants. But Ferdinand II. of Austria drove him out, and this religious war involved the whole of Germany in flames, each principality taking one side or the other, and retaliating on their adversaries by the destruction of churches, schools, libraries, and institutions of all sorts.

The capital city of Bohemia is Prague, which retains many traces of former grandeur. It is situated on a noble river, the Moldau; and the Hradshin, or royal palace, crowns a height overlooking the town. There are many Jews in Prague, and they possess a quaint, picturesque cemetery, which strangers are taken to see. The Bohemians are not of German race; they are Sclavs, a people of oriental derivation, and of finer and less ponderous qualities; they have something of the Tartar in their physiognomy.

In the cathedral of St. Vitus in Prague are kept some very curious relics, among which are some of the bones of Abraham, Isaac and Jacob, a piece of the true cross, two thorns from the dying Saviour's crown, one of the palm-branches over which he rode, the pocket-handkerchief of the Virgin Mary, the bridal robe of Maria Theresa, worked by herself into a mass-robe, with numerous relics used at the coronation of the kings.

Not far from the city stands, at a great height, the Acropolis. These precipices are famous in history. It is said that Queen Libussa, the founder of Prague, who was a notorious wanton, used to pitch her lovers from this giddy height into the river as soon as she got tired of them and wished a new one. A country clown, who was more successful than the rest in retaining her passion, was the ancestor of the long line of Bohemian kings.

Near the palace is situated the Loretto chapel, which is an exact copy of the wandering house of Loretto in Italy (neither of which is anything like the house at Nazareth). This is considered the holiest place in Prague, and pilgrimages are made to it from all parts of Germany. Here you will be shown the leg-bone of Mary Magdalen and the skull of one of the wise virgins!

TYROL.

The Tyrol is the westernmost province of Austria. Its length and breadth are about alike (145 miles), with a population of about 950,000, of which a third are of Italian origin. The main chain of the Alps, including many of its higher summits, traverses it from east to west. In some respects its scenery is as grand as any in the world. The Dolomite mountains, with their fantastical shapes and sharp peaks, extending along, one after the other, in serrated ridges, like alligators' jaws, cleft and fissured thousands of feet deep, form a picture which stands in living contrast with anything known in Europe. The Stelvio Pass, the highest carriage-road in the world (9,200 feet above the level of the sea—nearly 1,000 feet above the level of perpetual snow), is for grandeur of scenery, boldness of design, magnitude of labor, etc., not to be surpassed in Europe. Some of the glaciers, within the limits of the Tyrol, are unsurpassed in grandeur.

GLACIER

The aptitudes of the Tyrolese are many. At six years old the little Tyrolese boys go off into Bavaria, to the great fair of Kempten, and hire themselves out to mind cattle and flocks of geese. In older years they migrate hither and thither in all sorts of capacities—masons, carpenters, miners and picture-dealers. More than 30,000 men thus go out every year. The chamois-hunters of the Tyrol are renowned for their agility, and will go through any fatigue and danger for the valuable chamois' horn. The search after medicinal plants is also actively carried on. The flora of the country is rich and varied, and the inhabitants are very skilful in detecting useful herbs.

The Tyrolese, again, are apt with their hands in mechanical arts. They not only sculpture ornamental articles in wood, but undertake larger works, such as portable wooden shops and houses, of which the pieces are numbered, so as to be put together properly. These are carried as far as the shores of Lake Constance, and there embarked for different localities.

The Tyrolese have a great love of liberty, and when the French, under the first empire, took possession of the country in 1808, an insurrection broke out under the famous Andrew Hofer, an innkeeper and corn-merchant. After considerable success, and the destruction of several detachments of French troops, Hofer was obliged to capitulate and lay down his arms. But the following year (1810) he was arrested on accusation of holding secret intrigues with the Austrians, taken to Mantua, and shot.

In every village is a school which children are obliged to attend; and the University of Innspruck, the capital of Tyrol, is one of the best in the empire.

We conclude with the translation of a few lines from that charming poetess, Cordula Peregrina:

> " Where find another land like thee—Tyrol?
> Where heavenward rears so proud the rock's steep crest?
> Where hushed in dreams do greener valleys rest?
> Where sunlit streams in wilder torrents foam?
> So ask lone wanderers as o'er thee they roam—
> And echo answers to the listening soul:
> God hath blest thee—blessed land, Tyrol!
> God bless thy meadows green,
> God bless thy lakes so blue,
> God bless thy rugged peaks,
> God bless thy hearts so true!"

NOVGOROD.

RUSSIA.

THE early history of that great empire whose boundaries have been gradually extended until it now occupies almost the entire northern portion of the Eastern Hemisphere, embracing in its immense area more than half of Europe and one-third of Asia, is involved in great obscurity. Its earliest annals only furnish occasional glimpses of numerous barbarian hordes roaming over its surface. The Greeks established several colonies in this region, and entered into commercial relations with the various tribes.

In the second century the Goths overran the country, and established themselves from the Don to the Danube. Successive migrations of Alans, Huns, Avarians and Bulgarians followed, and in the fifth century the Slavi, or Slavs, as they are now termed, came from the northern Danube and, spreading themselves along the Dnieper, drove the scattered Finnish tribes dwelling in this territory higher north, toward Finland and the region of the Arctic sea.

The Slavs soon acquired, from commercial intercourse with their southern neighbors, habits of civilized life, and embraced the Christian religion. They founded the cities of Novgorod and Kiev, which early attained considerable importance. Their wealth, however, soon excited the avidity of the fierce nomadic tribes by whom they were surrounded, and with whom they were compelled to maintain a perpetual warfare.

The Slavs, seeing that the warlike races threatened their rising state with destruction, were compelled by the necessity of self-preservation to make terms with them.

Their negotiations resulted, in 862 A. D., in the arrival of a celebrated Varagian chief, named Rurik, with a body of his countrymen, in the vicinity of the lake Ladoga, who laid the foundation of the present Empire of Russia by uniting his people under one government with those who already occupied the soil. Rurik seems to have been a bold and sagacious ruler, and is credited with zeal for the strict administration of justice, and enforcing its exercise on all the boyars or nobles who possessed territories under him. The Christian worship, according to the forms of the Greek Church, was first made known in Russia under Olga, the daughter-in-law of Ruric; and it was formally adopted as the state religion by her grandson, Vladimir I., who was baptized in 980. For 736 years (862-1598) Ruric's descendants, of whom the last was Feodor, filled the Russian throne.

Feodor I. was a feeble and vacillating prince. He died in 1598, and with him ended the dynasty of Rurik, which, during eight centuries, had wielded the Russian sceptre.

A hideous period of internal strife followed, with many rival claimants for the throne. To the horrors of internal warfare was added the shock of invasion by the Poles, who burnt Moscow in 1611 and slaughtered tens of thousands of the inhabitants.

The turmoil was finally ended in 1613 by the elevation to the throne of Michael Feodorovitch Romanoff, the first czar of the present imperial family. He was a son of Feodor, Archbishop of Rostov, whose grandfather had been connected by marriage with the House of Rurik.

In 1689 a new era opened for Russia on the accession of Peter, known in history as the Great. In a brief time he transformed the entire nation; Russia became the most powerful empire of Northern Europe, and henceforth regarded herself, and was generally regarded, as a leading member of the European family of states.

The ruling passion of Peter the Great was a desire to extend his empire and consolidate his power; and consequently his first act was to make war on the Turks, an undertaking which was at the outset imprudently conducted, and consequently unsuccessful. He lost 30,000 men before Azov, and did not obtain permanent possession of the town until the year 1699, and then by an armistice. In the following year he was defeated in his intrenched camp at Narva, containing 80,000 men, by 8,000 Swedes, under Charles XII., then only a boy of seventeen; and on many other occasions the Russians suffered severe checks and reverses.

But at length the indomitable perseverance of Peter prevailed. In 1705 he carried Narva, the scene of his former defeat, by assault; and two years after, by the crowning victory of Poltava, where he showed the qualities of an able general, he sealed the fate of his gallant and eccentric adversary and the brave nation over which he ruled.

PETER THE GREAT.

The emperors of Russia are called Czars. When the Czar Peter was twenty-five years old he left his throne and travelled over Europe in search of knowledge. He did not go to any of the learned universities, nor apply himself to the study of the dead languages. That was not the sort of knowledge which Peter wanted. The first thing he did was to go to Holland, and put himself apprentice to a ship-carpenter. The house is still standing where he used to live while there. He afterward went to England and followed the same trade as in Holland. Besides learning the business of ship-carpentry, he took lessons in other branches of mechanics, and also in surgery. In short, he neglected no kind of knowledge which he thought would be useful to himself or his subjects. In a little more than a year he heard that his sister was endeavoring to make herself empress of Russia. This intelligence compelled him to break off his studies and labors, and hasten back to the city of Moscow. On arriving there he put some of the conspirators to death, and confined his sister in prison. His time was afterward so much occupied in war, and in taking care of the empire, that he never had leisure to finish his education. But he had already learnt a great deal, and the effect of his knowledge was soon seen in the improvement of the condition of Russia.

Peter used to rise at five in the morning, and busy himself all day about the affairs of the empire. But in the evening, when his work was over, he would seat himself beside a big, round bottle of brandy, and drink till his reason was quite gone. This habit, together with the natural violence of his temper, rendered him almost as dangerous to his friends as to his enemies.

He often said that he had corrected the faults of Russia, but that he could not correct his own.

Peter was in the habit of beating those who offended him with his cane. The highest nobleman in Russia often underwent this punishment. Even the Empress Catherine, his wife, sometimes got soundly beaten. It is supposed that the Czar Peter ordered his own son to be put to death, and that he was himself privately executed in prison.

Peter died in 1725, at the age of fifty-three, and was succeeded by his wife, the Empress Catherine. She had been a country girl, and the Czar Peter had married her for the sake of her beauty. In some respects Catherine was a good sort of woman; but, among other faults, she was rather too fond of wine.

She reigned only about two years, and was succeeded by her husband's grandson, named Peter the Second. He died in 1730, and left the throne to Anne, Duchess of Courland, his niece. This empress was a good sovereign, and performed many praiseworthy acts. None of her deeds, however, have been more famous than the building of a palace of ice. This stately and beautiful structure was built on a frozen lake. Instead of wood or hewn stone, it was composed entirely of blocks of ice. The furniture was likewise of ice; and even the beds were of the same material. When it was illuminated within, the whole edifice glittered and sparkled as if it were made of diamonds.

The successor of Anne was the Princess Elizabeth, a daughter of Peter the Great. She mounted the throne in 1740, and reigned twenty-two years. Her successor was Peter the Third, who began to reign in 1762. He, like Peter the Great, had a wife named Catherine. They had not long sat together on the throne when she contrived to depose Peter, and make herself sole ruler of Russia. It is supposed that she afterward caused him to be murdered.

In the early part of her reign she interfered in the affairs of Poland, which produced a civil war and terminated eventually in the conquest and partition of that unfortunate country. In 1769 the Turks declared war against Russia, which was at first favorable to their arms, but they were afterward defeated with great slaughter on the Dneister, and compelled to abandon Choczim. At this period was fought the celebrated action before Tchesme, in which the Turkish fleet was completely destroyed—an achievement mainly owing to the gallant conduct of Admirals Elphinstone and Greig, Englishmen in the Russian service.

In 1791 the intrigues of Russia, Austria and Prussia, for the partition of Poland, commenced, and, carried on for several years, were brought to a conclusion by two sieges of Warsaw. In the first, Kosciusko was made prisoner; and in the second the Poles, unassisted by his genius, gave way in a formal assault, which in 1794 consummated the ruin of Poland as a nation. Catherine's further plans of conquest and aggrandizement were cut short by her death in 1796, after a reign of thirty-five years. She was succeeded by her son Paul, who was then forty-three years old.

The Czar Paul possessed none of his mother's talents, and was of a very stern and unamiable disposition. People suspected him of being insane. His conduct grew so intolerable that some of his principal nobles conspired to kill him.

CATHERINE THE GREAT OF RUSSIA.

Paul was succeeded by Alexander I., his eldest son. This emperor reigned from 1801 till 1825. During his reign Russia was invaded by the Emperor Napoleon Bonaparte, at the head of nearly half a million of men.

The policy of the Russians was to retire before the irresistible force of Napoleon, laying waste the country as they went. At an early period in the campaign it became evident that Napoleon had brought into those thinly-

BURNING OF MOSCOW.

peopled wilds a host of men so great that it was beyond his power to feed them. It was impossible to carry supplies for such multitudes, and the wasted country through which their march led yielded nothing adequate to their enormous wants. Almost from the beginning the soldiers were put on half-rations. Water was scanty and bad; the heat of the weather was intense. Large numbers of the hungry soldiers strayed on marauding expeditions, and were lost. The mortality soon became excessive, and the army left ghastly traces of its presence in the carcasses of horses and the unburied bodies of men scattered thickly along the line of march. Before they reached Moscow, one-half of the men had sunk under the hardships of the journey.

Although the French army had penetrated to Moscow, it was found that they could not remain there. The Russians set the city on fire. Winter was coming on, and the French soldiers had nowhere to shelter themselves. They retreated toward Poland. On their way thither, they fought many battles with the Russians, and the weather was so bitter cold that the bodies of the slain were frozen stiff. The snow was crimsoned with their blood. Before they reached the frontiers of Poland, three-fourths of the army were destroyed. The Emperor Napoleon fled homeward in a sledge, and returned to Paris.

Nicholas succeeded Alexander I. in 1825; he was a man of great abilities and, though of a despotic temper, greatly contributed to the advancement of Russia in civilization. In 1854 he became involved in a war with Turkey, France and England. The latter besieged the Russian town and fortress of Sebastopol in the Crimea, and here about half a million of men became engaged in the mighty contest. This was called the Eastern war.

For many dreary months, while the allied army was being destroyed by official incapacity, the siege went on. The allies never for a moment loosened their hold on the besieged city. Often their fire was intermitted because of the difficulty of conveying from Balaklava the huge masses of iron which it was their business to throw into Sebastopol. Occasionally it was discontinued for a time that preparations might be made for greater efforts. Very soon it could be seen that Sebastopol was a mass of ruins. But that had no tendency to weaken the defence. The Russians fortified a position outside the town by means of earthworks and rifle-pits.

One very strong earthwork, the Malakoff, faced the French position; another, the Redan, was in front of the English. It was determined to carry these works by assault. The French, whose trenches were now within fifteen yards of the enemy, were able, after a brief but violent struggle, to take secure possession of the Malakoff.

The English had a considerable space to traverse under a murderous fire. But they forced their way into the Redan, and looked eagerly for reinforcements which would enable them to hold their conquest. Incapable generalship left them without support, and they were driven out with terrible loss.

Next day the attack was to have been renewed. But the Russian position had become untenable. Their whole army was conveyed across the bay, and the southern side of the city was abandoned. The war was virtually ended. The Emperor Nicholas had died—broken-hearted by the disasters of this calamitous struggle—and his son, the more enlightened Alexander, was now willing to negotiate. He had maintained the contest in this remote corner of his dominions at enormous cost in men and treasure, and he could maintain it no longer. His ships had been sunk to save them from the enemy. Sebastopol—in ruins—was wrenched away from him; his impregnable forts, his splendid docks, were at leisure mined and blown into the air by triumphant foes. His power in the Black sea was for the time utterly overthrown. The allies

THE SIEGE OF SEBASTOPOL.

had two hundred thousand men in the Crimea—a force which he was now powerless to resist. Peace had become a necessity for Russia.

Under the rule of his successor, the despotic system of Nicholas was to an important extent departed from. The newspaper press experienced sudden enlargement. So urgent was the demand for political discussion, that within a year or two from the close of the war seventy new journals were founded in St. Petersburg and Moscow alone.

The enfranchised press began to call loudly for the education of the people, for their participation in political power, for many other needful reforms. Chief among these, not merely in its urgency, but also in its popularity, was the emancipation of the serfs.

Forty-eight million Russian peasants were in bondage—subject to the arbitrary will of an owner—bought and sold with the properties on which they labored. This unhappy system was of no great antiquity, for it was not till the close of the sixteenth century that the Russian peasant became a serf. The evil institution had begun to die out in the west before it was legalized in Russia. Its abolition had long been looked forward to. Catherine II. had contemplated this great reform, and so also had her grandson, Alexander I.; but the wars in which they spent their days forbade progress in any useful direction. Nicholas very early in his reign appointed a secret committee to consider the question; but the Polish insurrection of 1830 marred his design. Another fruitless effort was made in 1836. In 1838 a third committee was appointed, but its work was suspended by "a bad harvest," and never resumed. Finally, it was asserted that the dying emperor bequeathed to his son the task which he himself had not been permitted to accomplish.

ALEXANDER II.

And thus it came to pass that when Alexander ascended the throne the general expectation of his people pointed to the emancipation of the serfs. The emperor shared in the national desire. At his coronation he had prepared the somewhat reluctant nobles for the change which, although it had been long foreshadowed, was to too many of them very unwelcome.

The 17th of March, 1861, will ever be a memorable day in Russian civilization; for 20,000,000 of human beings, who were slaves the day before, then became free men. The law of emancipation bestowed personal freedom on the serfs. For two years those who were household servants must abide in their service; receiving, however, wages for their work. Those who had purchased exemption from the obligation to labor for their lord were to continue for two years the annual payment. At the end of that time all serfs entered on possession of unqualified freedom.

Alexander II. was assassinated in 1881 by the agents of a set of people calling themselves Nihilists, or Destructives. The murder of the czar brought down upon them the execrations of the whole world. Immediately after his death, his son was proclaimed emperor under the title of Alexander III.

The czars have for some time been by blood more than half German. Their mothers have been German, their wives have been German. Alexander II. was more German than Russian. He was trained by his German mother, and under the influence of her German kindred; after marriage he was ruled by his German wife.

When Alexander II. came to the throne, Russia was undergoing the stress of the Crimean war, which was already going against her, and all parties had to unite for a time. It was Russia against all the great powers of Europe, save Prussia, who at least kept Austria in check and had prevented her from actively joining the unnatural coalition between England and France. Alexander II. naturally flung himself into the arms of his kinsmen, the Hohenzollerns, and became more a German and less a Russian than ever.

READING THE EMANCIPATION PROCLAMATION.

Alexander III. came to the throne pledged in a manner to the anti-German party and its foreign policy. He was born March 12th, 1845. He married the Princess Maria Dagmar, daughter of the King of Denmark, in November, 1866. The Nihilists, at whose hands his father came to an untimely end, have made the throne of Alexander fraught with danger, and he is haunted by a constant fear of assassination. Who his friends are he knows not, and his servants he is afraid to trust. The Nihilists work in secret and in the dark. They are, however, thoroughly organized, and have the means of penetrating into the inmost recesses of the imperial palace, and they have shown that they have both the power and the means of disseminating their views by the printing-press. In some of these secret printing-offices desperate conflicts have occurred between government officials and Nihilists, whose work was the printing of sheets distributed by their organization. All this has given the monarch to feel that, let him be ever so much a favorite with his people, he is at every moment in peril of his life. If there be anywhere even a small body of discontented spirits, the more especially if they are banded together by the ties of some political theory, and bent upon assassination as a means to carry

DESTROYING A NIHILIST PRINTING-OFFICE.

it out, they will, most likely, sooner or later, gain their end. Nine attempts may fail, but the tenth will succeed. Nothing works such a change in a weak man as this constant dread of an unseen murderer. It not infrequently shatters the strongest nerves.

The conquests of Russia in Central Asia have within a few years attracted general attention; yet the Russian advance into these regions began centuries ago, when the czars of Moscow, who succeeded Ivan IV., being freed from the Tartar invasion, began to retaliate upon the Mongols, and also endeavored to find markets for their manufactures, which were so inferior in quality as to be unsalable in Europe. Between the Ural river, which is the natural eastern boundary of European Russia, and the Irtish, formerly on the south-west

CROSSING THE STEPPES.

frontier of Siberia, extended boundless, arid plains, called steppes, inhabited only by a few thousand wandering Kirghis. These tribes maintained an almost constant warfare upon the Russian frontier settlements, and compelled the Russians to pursue them far into the interior of their vast territory. In this manner the Russian domain was constantly advancing eastward, but although some of the tribes submitted to the Russian rule, for two centuries no one could say who was really master of the vast tracts of land between the rich Khanates of Central Asia and the banks of the Ural and Irtish. A considerable trade existed between these khanates and the towns of Astrakhan and Orenburg, but it was carried on rather by Bokhara merchants, who crossed the steppes, than by Russian traders: for the latter could not venture abroad without great risk of being robbed and killed in the steppes, or plundered and sold into bondage in the khanates themselves; while the former managed to traverse the wilderness in safety, and to make good bargains with the Muscovites.

The Emperor Nicholas attempted to compel the khanates to a fairer system of trading, but with little success. An expedition sent out in 1839, under Count Petrovsky, perished in the wilderness for want of food and water, their sufferings being aggravated by constant fights with the hostile nomadic tribes and the regular forces of the khans.

Finally, by a succession of Russian victories, the Khan of Khiva was forced to make cessions which brought the entire east coast of the Caspian into the hands of Russia, enabling her to communicate with and supply all her military lines of operation by rail, river and the sea, from St. Petersburg and the Baltic.

Russia estimates the military importance of the Caspian sea so highly, that, while reserving to herself the unrestricted use of its waters, she has forced Persia to accede to a treaty which prevents that power from maintaining any vessels of war upon it, although the south and south-west shores are part of its territory.

We have now traced the gradual rise of Russian power, from the period when the rude Varagian chieftain first established his sovereignty, a thousand years ago. The comparatively small territory which then yielded to his sway is now part of the most majestic empire the world has ever seen. Extending from latitude 38 deg. 20 min. to about 77 deg. 30 min. north, and from longitude 17 deg. 38 min. east to about 170 deg. west, its greatest length from west to east is about 6,000 miles, and its greatest breadth (exclusive of islands) about 2,300 miles. Its total surface is estimated to comprise one-twenty-sixth of the entire surface of the globe, and to represent one-sixth of its firm land. Its total area, in square miles, is 8,360,000, and its population more than 85,000,000 of people!

St. Petersburg, the modern capital of Russia, contains 700,000 inhabitants.

It was founded by Peter the Great in the year 1703 amid the marshes through which the river Neva discharges its waters into the sea. In the number and vast size of its public edifices the Russian capital may compare with any other city in Europe, and even surpasses most of them.

The longest street, and most fashionable, as well as the most animated thoroughfare of the city, is the Newsky Prospect. In St. Petersburg are some of the finest cathedrals in the world, amongst which may be mentioned St. Isaac's cathedral, the foundation-pile alone of which cost over a million of dollars; Smolnoi church, which has twenty-four colossal stoves for heating the building, and representing small chapels; the cathedral of St. Petersburg,

NEWSKY PROSPECT.

built in the shape of a cross, 238 feet in length and 182 feet in width; the cathedral and fortress of St. Peter and St. Paul, which contains the remains of all the deceased emperors and empresses of Russia, from Peter the Great, with the single exception of Peter II., who, dying at Moscow, was also buried there.

Moscow, the ancient metropolis of the Russian Empire, is situated on the banks of the Moskwa river. It was founded in 1147, and is one of the most irregular cities in the world. Its irregularity of design is not so conspicuous as formerly, prior to the conflagration of 1812, when its flames exerted so fatal an influence over the destinies of the first Napoleon. But Moscow is now more splendid than before; half Asiatic and half European.

In the heart of the city stands the celebrated Kremlin, or citadel, which is itself two miles in circuit. It has been completely repaired since the injuries it received in 1812, and is crowded with buildings of almost every imaginable kind.

In the little palace of Moscow, within the Kremlin, on a pedestal of granite, stands the monarch of all bells. Its height is over twenty-one feet, its circumference sixty-seven feet, and its weight is 400,000 pounds.

The cathedral of the Assumption is also within the Kremlin, and here all the emperors are crowned, and a grander sight than this ceremony cannot well be imagined. Amongst the relics and objects of interest which it contains, there is an immense Bible, presented to the cathedral by the mother of Peter the Great. The binding, which is covered with emeralds and other precious

KREMLIN AT MOSCOW.

stones, cost over $1,000,000. Here is also a nail from the true cross, a robe of the Saviour and a portion of that of the Virgin, a picture of the Virgin by St. Paul, and numerous other relics.

Situated behind the cathedral is the "House of the Holy Synod." It is celebrated for being the place where the *Mir*, or holy oil, is kept and made, with which all the children of Russia are baptized. The oil, made every three years, amounting to three or four gallons, is sanctified by some drops of the same oil that Mary Magdalen used in anointing the feet of the Saviour. In christening, the priest uses a small camel's-hair brush, with which, having dipped it in the oil, he makes the sign of the cross on the child's eyes, that it may see only the way to do good; over its mouth, that it may say no evil; over its ears, that it may not listen to evil counsel; over its hands, that it may do no evil; and over its feet, that it may only walk in the path of holiness.

Close to the Kremlin walls on the outside stands the cathedral church of St. Basil the Beatified. It differs in appearance from Russian churches in general, possessing no fewer than twenty domes and towers, which are not only of different shapes and sizes, but are gilded and painted in all possible varieties of color. It was erected by the czar John the Terrible in the sixteenth century, who, it is said, was so well pleased with the work of the Italian

CATHEDRAL OF ST. BASIL.

architect that, after eulogizing his skill, he ordered his eyes to be put out that he might never erect another.

Novgorod, the cradle of the Russian Empire, is situated on the Volkhov river, and contains a population of 20,000. The churches are the only surviving monuments of the greatness of Novgorod. Foremost among them stands the cathedral of St. Sophia, or, as it was formerly styled, "the heart and soul of Great Novgorod," where the princes were crowned.

Odessa, a port on the Black sea, is noted for its bombardment for twelve hours by an Anglo-French squadron on the 22d of April, 1854. There are no less than twenty Jewish synagogues at Odessa, while there are but thirteen Russo-Greek churches. More than half the number of inhabitants is made up of Jews.

Odessa presents a very handsome appearance from the sea. The buildings are modern and imposing. There is a magnificent flight of marble stairs, a hundred feet wide, leading from the sea to the summit of the bluff on which

ODESSA.

the city stands. The streets are broad and well paved, and on each side, flanking the sidewalks, is a double row of shade-trees.

The religion of Russia is Greek Catholic. The Greek Church separated from the Roman Church at the time of the dismemberment of the Roman Empire, when Rome and Constantinople were each striving to be the head. At this period a great controversy about the worship of images began to agitate the mind of Europe. East and West were divided against each other, and against themselves. Leo III., Emperor of the East, believing that the victories of Islam were owing more to Christian weakness than to Moslem strength, resolved to root out the idolatry which had struck its roots so deeply in the church.

All Christendom was severed into two great bands, image-servers and image-breakers. Pope Gregory III. solemnly denounced the sin of image-breaking under pain of excommunication. But, in spite of threat and curse, the work went on, and a gulf, never since bridged over, grew between the Churches of Rome and of Constantinople. The strife lasted for a hundred and twenty years, lulled only for a season, but not settled, by a decision of the second Council of Nicæa in 787, which sought to cast oil on the waves by permitting the veneration, but forbidding the worship of images, until the final triumph of the image party in the Council of Constantinople in 1842. From this controversy we may date the rise of the Greek Church, whose present stronghold is Russia.

ARCHIMANDRITE.

The Greek Church does not acknowledge the supremacy of the pope, nor claim infallibility. It is governed by Patriarchs. Celibacy is not compulsory on its clergy. Like the Church of Rome, it has also monasteries, with governors over them, who are called Archimandrites, and who are the same as abbots in the Roman Church. Cloisters, in which females reside for life, under a vow of chastity and religion, are also numerous in Russia.

The Russian is the strangest mixture of civilization and barbarism, of great talent, polished manners, and domestic affability, combined with qualities and habits which mark him much below the average European level. The reason is partly to be found in history. Peter the Great set himself,

RUSSIAN NUNS BEGGING ALMS.

to work to force his subjects up to the standard of the rest of Europe. He found them semi-savages of Asiatic origin; he left them with many of the externals of London and Paris. He found them with Moscow for their capital, far in the heart of the country; he left them with St. Petersburg, a grand new city on the banks of the Neva, and with immediate connection with the Baltic. He changed army, navy, laws, customs; he actually went and studied as a shipwright in Holland, that he might teach his people how to build ships, for in those days Holland was the great commercial emporium. He went to Paris to learn manners and arts; he eat and drank enough for a giant, but could be a gentleman when he chose; and he did all this by the

RUSSIAN FAMILY.

force of an overwhelming will and the autocratic power of his czarship; but his life and work was in a certain sense artificial. Work as he would, he could not civilize those enormous tracts of Russia proper, of Siberia, and of the East.

The people are exceedingly superstitious in regard to ghosts, house-spirits, and the evil eye. They have been seen to make violent gestures to the wind, to induce it to change and blow the sparks of a burning house away from other property which was being endangered. Some twenty-five years ago a balloon went up from St. Petersburg, under charge of a French aëronaut in the car. It was lost sight of, and the place of its descent could not be ascertained. At last it was discovered that it had come down in a country village at some distance, and that the peasants had murdered the Frenchman, under the conviction that he was a supernatural being, especially as they could not understand a word he said.

Our account of Russia would be quite incomplete without some mention of Siberia, the cold, northern country to which political exiles have been sent in such numbers. It comprises nearly all the northern part of Asia. At present Russia only looks upon Siberia as a country rich in furs, whence tribute-money may be exacted; but snow-covered, thinly-peopled, and poor in provisions and means of communication; and the government officials are detestable. Men who are sent as convicts to Siberia suffer the most wretched fate, and are driven along in chained gangs. The dreaded words, "Siberian

GOLD MINES, SIBERIA.

exile," comprise all degrees of human misery, from dreary banishment to physical sufferings of the most excruciating kind.

When Mr. and Mrs. William Atkinson, in whose books upon Siberia and Tartary are many interesting details, were known to be about to leave Moscow on a prolonged tour in these wild regions, the families and friends of these unhappy exiles, many of them lost for long years to their native land, crowded about the travellers with messages to the objects of their affection; and it is a fact that the Atkinsons constantly went out of their way, that they might deliver these messages in lonely villages, in nameless solitudes, and sometimes even in the very mines. Mr. Atkinson speaks of two Russian noblemen, one of whom worked in a mine, the other cultivated a small farm. In both instances, the wife had voluntarily accompanied her husband,

Even hospitality, that true Sclavonic virtue, has not become acclimatized in this inhospitable region. When a man is going to visit his neighbor, he never goes straight to his house, but walks along the road, and stops as if by chance at the window and begins a conversation; then, if the master or mistress wishes to see him, they invite him in.

When the samovar is ready, they drink tea out of saucers, now and then taking a bite of a piece of sugar. In this way they consume about three cups, and then turn the cups upsidedown, placing on the bottom the remains of the sugar they have been nibbling at.

As soon as tea is over the guest rises to go, and then the following dialogue invariably takes place:

"Why are you in such a hurry?" says the hostess.

"Time to go home," answers the guest.

"Stay a little longer."

"Thank you; you have given us plenty to eat and drink."

"There was but little."

"No; there was quite enough; we had plenty."

This conversation, which always takes place and is almost mechanically repeated, being ended, the guest approaches the host, and taking his hands, says, "I thank you for the vodka, the tea, the cakes, the sugar," etc.

It is indispensable, when thanking the host, to enumerate everything the guest has consumed during his visit. At the end of this catalogue the visitor humbly begs his host to come and see him, which, after a time, he does, and things go on in exactly the same way. Care must be taken that the viands provided are of equal quantity and quality. If at any time a man eats or drinks more than his host did when a guest on a former occasion, quarrels, upbraidings, or sarcastic remarks are the result.

"I gave them tea and sugar," the host will be heard to say, "and they gave me nothing but tea;" or again, "I gave them cake, and had nothing but bread in return."

SIBERIAN DOG-SLEDGE.

CONSTANTINOPLE.

TURKEY.

MIDWAY between Asia and Africa, having the Black sea upon the north and the Mediterranean sea upon the south, lies Turkey. In one sense the centre of the hemisphere which contains it, this country, by its geographical position as well as its political import, is, so to speak, the "hinge" of the eastern continent.

Comprising in Europe 196,770 square miles, with a population of nearly seventeen millions, and in Asia 664,272 square miles, and a population about equal to that in Europe, there are to be added to the area 1,036,350 square miles in Africa, having a population of 11,000,000; making a grand total of about two millions of square miles and forty-four millions of people. This entire country, including all dependencies, is known as the Ottoman Empire.

And the significance borne by its geographical situation has been, almost since its first existence as an empire, sustained by its political import in the affairs of Europe and Asia. For this reason—and equally whether we consider it in its palmy days and under monarchs whose achievements have become matters of high consideration in the history of the world, or at the present time, when, as the "Sick Man," it challenges no less the attention of humanity everywhere—Turkey may not improperly receive the title which we have ventured to give to it, that of the hinge of the eastern continent. Shorn, by the exigencies of war and the devastation of foreign hosts, of much of its ancient dominion, the Ottoman Empire at present comprises, besides Turkey in Asia and Turkey in Europe, the principalities of Moldavia and Wallachia, Servia and Montenegro, in Europe; Egypt, with Nubia, Tripoli and Tunis, in Africa; and a part of Arabia, including the holy cities of Mecca and Medina, in Asia.

The religion of the Turk is Mahomtean. He believes in one God, Allah, and Mahomet, his prophet. The simplicity of the faith and the spirituality of its practice, involving devout prayer to one Supreme Being several times in the course of the day, does produce certain ennobling effects. The Turk faithfully follows out his religious obligations in a way which might put many Christians to shame; and he is sober in regard to wine, as strictly enjoined by his scriptures, the Koran. But the exceedingly coarse nature of the heaven which Mahomet promised to his faithful disciples is such as to undo all the good effects of their abstinence here. Eating and drinking, and all sensual delights, are what the Turk looks forward to when he shall be clothed with his new body, as the reward of the virtues he is commanded to practise on earth; and he is not at all sure, indeed it is more than doubtful, whether his wives and daughters will share the bliss. Thus the domestic affections are unsupported by the spiritual hopes which nourish the beautiful blossoms of love in a Christian home. His paradise is at best a very questionable one in point of goodness, and such as it is, he looks forward to it selfishly.

Some of the leading articles of belief are: 1. There is but one God. 2. There are angels of various ranks; among them a fallen spirit, Eblis, driven from Paradise for refusing to worship Adam; also inferior spirits, liable to death, called Genii and Peris. 3. There are six great prophets—Adam, Noah, Abraham, Moses, Jesus, Mahomet. 4. There is a hell, called Jehennam, and a Paradise of wondrous beauty, full of sensual delights. 5. Men have no free-will; but all things are ruled by an unchanging fate—a doctrine tending at first to kindle reckless fury in battle, but in the hour of peace a source of corroding indolence.

Devout Moslems practise four great religious duties: 1. Washing, of curious nicety, followed by prayers five times a day, with the face towards Mecca. 2. The giving of one-tenth in charity. 3. Fasting from rise to set of sun during the thirty days of the month Rhamadan. Pork and wine are specially forbidden at all times. 4. A pilgrimage to Mecca at least once in a lifetime, which, however, may be performed by proxy.

As the time appointed for the resurrection approaches, the sun will rise in the west; beasts and inanimate things will speak; and, finally, a wind will sweep away the souls of those who have faith, even if equal only to a grain of mustard-seed, so that the world shall be left in ignorance. After this shall come the last day. Then forty years of oblivion, followed by the resurrection.

Next, the day of judgment, when the righteous shall enter paradise, and the wicked hell; both, however, having first to go over the bridge Al Sirat, laid over the midst of hell, finer than a hair, sharper than the edge of a sword and beset with thorns on every side. Upon this uncomfortable thoroughfare the righteous will proceed with ease and swiftness; but the wicked, probably overweighted by their sins, will be precipitated headlong into hell—a place divided by the Koran into seven stories or apartments, respectively assigned to Mahometans, Jews, Christians, Sabians, Magians, idolaters; and the lowest of all to the hypocrites, who, outwardly professing religion, in reality had none.

Of Mahomet himself we will speak hereafter when we come to treat of Arabia. The Arabians who followed Mahomet were called Saracens. The kings or rulers of the Saracen Empire were called Caliphs, and resided at Bagdad, a splendid city which they built on the river Tigris, in Mesopotamia. These caliphs extended their empire over a considerable part of Asia and Africa, and some portions of Europe.

To the north of Mesopotamia there were several tribes of Tartars, among which were some called Turks. These were daring warriors, and such was their fame that the caliphs induced many of them to come to Bagdad and serve as soldiers.

In process of time, the Turks acquired great influence at Bagdad, and finally overturned the Saracen Empire, made themselves masters of nearly all the Saracen possessions, and adopted the Mahometan religion. Thus the Turkish Empire became the successor of the Saracen Empire, and included in its dominions Asia Minor, Syria, Palestine, and other Asiatic countries which the Saracens had conquered from the Greek Empire.

In the year 1356 the Emir (a Turkish name for commander) Solyman crossed the Hellespont and seized a castle on the European shore. This event marks the first firm footing gained by the Turks on European soil; and they never since have lost their hold.

Under Amurath I. (1360-1389) Adrianople, being taken by the Turks, was made for a time the centre of their European possessions. A league was formed by the Sclavonic nations along the Danube to repel the infidel invaders, but in vain. The crescent—such was the device borne on the Turkish banners—still shone victorious in Thrace and Servia.

Bajazet, a drunken sensualist, who, succeeding his father, reigned from 1389 to 1402, exchanged the title Emir for the prouder name of Sultan. At Nicopolis he routed the chivalry of Hungary and France, which had mustered to roll back the dark flood of Moslem war. Classic Greece, too, was ravaged by his victorious hordes. Steadily he seemed to be advancing in the gigantic plan of European conquest sketched out by his ambitious father, when the most terrific warrior Asia has ever borne, rising on his eastern frontier, dashed his power into fragments.

This was Timour the Lame, whose name has been corrupted into Tamerlane, a Mongol descended from Zenghis Khan. From his capital, Samarcand, he spread his conquests on every side—from the Chinese wall to the Nile; from the springs of the Ganges to the heart of Russia. Whenever this demon conqueror took a city, he raised as a trophy of his success a pyramid of bleeding human heads. Bajazet was obliged to forego the intended siege of Constantinople by the attack of the ferocious Mongol upon the eastern frontier of his newly-acquired dominions in Asia Minor. The decisive battle was fought at Angora, where Bajazet, utterly defeated, was made prisoner. Carried about with the Mongol army in a litter with iron lattices, which gave rise to the common story of his imprisonment in an iron cage, the Turkish sultan died, eight months after, of a broken heart. His conqueror, Timour, died in 1405, while on the march to invade China.

Four Turkish sultans reigned between the wretched Bajazet and the conqueror of Constantinople.

Amurath II., last of the four, having died at Adrianople in 1451, his son Mahomet, crossing rapidly to Europe, was crowned second sultan of that name. He was a terrible compound of first literary taste with revolting cruelty and lust. One of his very first acts after he became sultan was to cause his infant brother to be drowned, while the baby's mother was congratulating him on his accession.

The throne of the Eastern Empire was then filled by Constantine Palæologus, no unworthy wearer of the purple. Limb after limb had been lopped from the great trunk. There was still life in the heart, though it throbbed with feeble pulses; but now came the mortal thrust.

After more than a year of busy preparation, 70,000 Turks, commanded by Mahomet II. in person, sat down in the spring of 1453 before Constantinople. Their lines stretched across the landward or western side of the triangle on which the city was built. A double wall, and a great ditch 100 feet deep, lay in their front; and within this rampart the Emperor Constantine marshalled his little band of defenders.

The siege began. On both sides cannon and muskets of a rude kind were used. One great gun deserves special notice. It was cast by a European brass-founder at Adrianople, and threw a stone ball of 600 pounds to the distance of a mile. But such a cannon could be fired only six or seven times a day. Lances and arrows flew thick from both lines; and heavy stones from the ballists filled up the pauses of the cannonade.

The sultan, feeling that his attack by land must be seconded by sea,

MOSQUE.

formed a bold plan. It was to convey a part of his fleet overland from the Propontis, and launch them in the upper end of the harbor. The distance was six miles; but, by means of rollers running on a tramway of greased planks, eighty of the Turkish war vessels were carried over the rugged ground in one night. A floating battery was then made, from which the Turkish cannon began to play with fearful effect on the weakest side of the city.

When the attack had lasted for seven weeks, a broad gap was to be seen in the central rampart. Many attempts at negotiation had come to nothing, for Constantine refused to give up the city, and nothing else would satisfy the sultan. At last a day was fixed for the grand assault. At daybreak the long lines of Turks made their attack. When the strength of the Christians was almost exhausted in endless strife with the swarms of irregular troops who led the way, the terrible Janizaries advanced. The storm grew louder, the rattle of the Turkish drums mingling with the thunder of the ordnance. Just then the brave Giustiniani, defending the great breach, was wounded; and when, after this loss, the defence grew slacker, a body of Turks, following the Janizary, Hassan, clambered over the ruined wall into the city. Amid the rush Constantine Palæologus, last of the Cæsars, fell dead, sabred by an unknown hand; and with him fell the Eastern Empire.

At noon on the same day Mahomet summoned the Moslems to prayer in the mosque of St. Sophia—thus establishing the rites of Islam where Christian worship had been held ever since the days of Constantine the Great.

The reigns of most of the Turkish sultans have been full of crime and bloodshed. Sultan Selim, who began to reign in 1512, invaded Egypt and conquered it. The Egyptian soldiers were called Mamelukes. Thousands of them were taken prisoners.

After the victory the sultan ordered a splendid throne to be erected on the banks of the river Nile, near the gates of Cairo. Sitting on his throne, he caused all the Mamelukes to be massacred in his sight, and their bodies to be thrown into the river.

Mahomet III., who ascended the throne in 1596, had nineteen brothers. These he caused to be strangled, so that they might not rob him of his power.

Amurath the Fourth became sultan in 1621. This monster caused 14,000 men to be murdered. The sport that pleased him best was to run about the streets at night with a drawn sword, cutting and slashing at everybody whom he met. These facts will show the reader what kind of government the Turks have lived under. Mahmoud the Second ascended the throne in 1808. He was more enlightened than his predecessors. But he was compelled to act with great severity. This was particularly the case in regard to the Janizaries. These were a large body of troops, established by Mahomet the Second in 1300, and who continued to be a very powerful body of soldiers for several centuries. Though called the sultan's guards, they became more dangerous than all the other subjects of the empire. Sultan Mahmoud therefore determined to free himself from their power. Accordingly, in the year 1826, he ordered the rest of his troops to surround the Janizaries. This was done, and they were shot down and massacred without mercy. The sultan afterward endeavored to reform the manners of the Turks, and to make them adopt the customs of other European nations. In this he was followed by his successors, Abdul Medjid and Abdul Aziz; but the progress of the Turks in this direction has been very slow.

ALEXANDER I. OF BULGARIA.

In 1854 Russia threatened an attack on Turkey, which resulted in what is called the Eastern war, one of the greatest struggles which the world has witnessed since the fall of Napoleon at Waterloo in, 1815. By the aid of France and England Turkey was preserved from being overwhelmed by Russia. In 1877, Russia again made war on Turkey and took from her a large portion of her territory in Europe and Asia. Alexander I., Prince of Bulgaria, the brother of the late Empress of Russia, was born

DERVISHES.

April 5th, in the year 1857, and served with the Russian army during the war with Turkey.

Constantinople, the capital of the Turkish Empire, contains 1,075,000 inhabitants, and is consequently the third large city in Europe; 330,000 of these are Christians of various denominations.

The city itself is built on hilly ground and, with its numerous gardens, cypresses, mosques, palaces, minarets and towers, presents a very splendid appearance as seen from the side of the Golden Horn, a branch or offset of the river Bosphorus. But a nearer approach reveals the characteristics common to every eastern town: narrow, crooked, filthy streets, and miserable houses of wood and clay; although, since the Crimean war, the city has been greatly improved in this respect. Great fires, which took place in 1865, 1866 and 1870, swept away square miles of old wooden houses on both sides of the Golden Horn, and on these spaces handsome stone buildings have been erected in the modern European style.

Constantinople contains many magnificent buildings, of which the mosque of Santa Sophia, the grandest ecclesiastical building in the Levant, is the most attractive. This was formerly a Christian church, and is built in the form of a Greek cross, 269 feet long by 243 broad, with a flattened dome 180 feet above the ground. Outside, the building is colored with alternate bands of pale red and yellow, and displays little of the magnificence within, where rich, golden mosaics, porphyry columns supporting figures of arabesque patterns, metallic ornaments, richly-carpeted floors and other glittering and showy displays in various materials, present altogether a very sumptuous appearance. The mosque of Sultan Achmet is also one of the attractions of the city. It has six minarets, each with two galleries. It is considered the finest specimen of a purely Turkish building in Constantinople.

One of the peculiar sights of Constantinople is the dancing dervishes. To see thirty-four of these strange fanatics of different sizes, ages and degrees of corpulence whirling about in a sort of waltzing step, which their naked feet perform skilfully to the sound of the music of a reed flute, is certainly a strange exhibition, particularly when one reflects that it is all done in the interests of religion. The howling dervishes have their habitation across the Bosphorus, over in Scutari. Here the process consists of fierce invocations, and heard in the midst of a thick, stifling incense, are the quaint, wilde jaculations of "Oh, Mediator!" "Oh, Beloved!" "Oh, Advocate!" "In the day of judgment," etc., sounds certainly strange enough, and much unlike the performance of human beings; the dervishes at length howling out their "*La illah—illah la!*" as if they were turning into wolves; while the motion of bending and gesticulating, which is performed to music at the same time, becomes mechanical, and sometimes almost epileptic.

The Turkish shopkeepers all sit upon their platform-counters robed and turbaned, looking as if they had been acting stories from "The Arabian Nights" in private theatricals the night before, and had not yet had time to change their clothes. They are always sitting cross-legged, generally smoking and half-dozing. Donkeys pass and bump up against the door-post, thieves run by pursued by angry soldiers with drawn and flashing sabres, the "Sick Man" himself rides past, sad and hopeless, with the ambassador at his elbow; but nothing moves the calm, self-possessed shopkeeper, in his white-and-green turban.

But if the men are dull, what must the women be? Shut up in a harem, never going out of doors unless closely veiled, not allowed to sweep their own floors or cook their own dinners, slaves being kept for all such purposes; having no religious occupations, no books, no drawing, no music, no visiting the poor or teaching in schools; what in the world do they do with themselves?

One of the great hindrances to improvement in the condition of the women was, until quite lately, the constant importation of Circassian slaves. Instead of Turkish gentlemen intermarrying with the daughters of families in their own class, an influx of strange wives perpetually took place, who had no fathers and brothers on the spot to take an interest in their welfare. In Christian civilization the intermarriage of families is the great cement which binds society together, causes men to help one another, and to love and protect not only sons, but nephews, cousins and daughters' children. When a man brings a strange slave-wife, none of this takes place; and, though an imperial firman has abolished slavery throughout the empire, Circassian purchases still take place.

The interior of Turkey comprises a heterogeneous population of different races. Of the Turks there are the Osmanlis and Turkomans. Then there are Sclavs, Romans, Arnauts, Syrians, Greeks, Armenians, Jews, Arabs, Druses, Gipsies, Tartars, Circassians, Kopts, Nubians, Berbers, etc. Of these the Greeks and Armenians are traders. The Turkomans and Kurds are herdsmen and nomads. The Sclavs, Romans and Albanians are the chief agriculturists in Europe, and the Osmanlis, Armenians, Syrians and Druses in Asia.

Scutari, which is across the Bosphorous and in Asia, was the locality of the hospitals during the Crimean war. It is from Scutari that the caravans depart for the desert. Here there is a picturesque object called Leander's Tower, or, by some, the Maiden's Tower, which has a legend attached to it. According to this legend, one of the sultans had a lovely little daughter, of whom he was so fond that he was anxious to know what the Fates had in store for her in the future. Through the intervention of astrology the child's nativity was cast; and the reply was, that, if she survived her sixteenth birthday, her life would be long and happy. But she must beware of all serpents. The sultan, accordingly, caused a tower to be erected, in which was centred everything that could be procured for her accommodation and delight, and she was placed within it, not to leave until the time was fully passed.

The eventful day arrived, the fair princess was dressed handsomely, await-

CIRCASSIAN.

ing her father's coming, who was to release his child from the prison in which paternal love had immured her. She was looking for the sultan when she perceived a small basket, covered over with fresh leaves, standing on a ledge which surrounded a pretty garden that had been contrived for her, such offerings being common among people who felt interested in her fate. With girlish pleasure she ran to fetch the gift and, reaching it, sat down to examine its contents. When the sultan came, he rushed up, surprised at not being met by the princess—and found her evidently arrayed for the occasion, but seemingly asleep. He called to her, "My child!" No answer. An asp that dropped from the basket revealed that hers was the sleep of death. The serpent had been concealed among the flowers.

A SULTANA'S ROOM.

Not to Turkey can the reader look for aught that is great in literature, science, or art. In military courage and capacity she has shown herself never to have been deficient; but when we have said this, we have said all. Whilst the other countries of Europe have been pressing onward in civilization, she has remained stationary, indeed rather retrogressive than otherwise. The barbaric character of the Oriental has been manifest throughout all her history. Well might Byron exclaim:

> "Know ye the land where the cypress and myrtle
>   Are emblems of deeds that are done in their clime?
> Where the rage of the vulture, the love of the turtle,
>   Now melt into sorrow, now madden to crime?
> .   .   .   .
> 'Tis the clime of the East; 'tis the land of the sun—
> Can he smile on such deeds as his children have done?
> Oh! wild as the accents of lovers' farewell
> Are the hearts which they bear, and the tales which they tell."

REMAINS OF A RUINED TEMPLE AT CORINTH.

GREECE.

"The isles of Greece, the isles of Greece,
  Where burning Sappho loved and sung;
 Where grew the arts of war and peace,
  Where Delos rose and Phœbus sprung;
   Eternal summer gilds them yet,
   But all, except their sun, is set."

GREECE, in regard to its situation and physical features, has been marked out from the beginning as a remarkable land. It juts out into the sea, so as to command easy access to the three great continents, Europe, Asia and Africa.

The limits of ancient Greece were much more extensive than that of the modern kingdom. The greatest extent of the Greek mainland from north to south is little more than 200 miles, and from east to west only 165. Including the numerous islands it embraces, the total area of the kingdom is 19,945 square miles. It is divided into four portions, Northern Greece, the Morea, the Grecian islands and the Ionian islands, which latter were incorporated with the Kingdom of Greece in 1864. The first is that portion which lies north of the Gulf of Corinth. The surface of the whole is generally mountainous. The climate is usually warm and delightful; its clear and cloudless sky has been much celebrated, and the perfect transparency of the atmosphere helps to display the natural objects of its scenery in their highest beauty.

GREECE.

On the plains near the coast snow is seldom seen, and the winters are mostly of short duration. In the centre of the Morea snow generally lies on the ground for several weeks. For a few weeks in February the rains fall, after which time spring commences. Early in March the vine and olives bud, and in May the corn is reaped. The olive is distinguished for its superior excellence, and the orange, lemon, citron, fig, banana and water-melon afford the richest fruit.

Bees are abundant in Greece, and the produce of honey is very great.

The Greek nation boasts of the highest antiquity; the cities of Argos, Thebes, Athens, Sparta and Corinth, claim to have been founded nearly 2000 b. c. The first constitution of Greek cities is beyond the reach of exact history, but monarchy seems to have been the earliest form.

The civil polity of Sparta and Athens, whose governing power began to lessen the influence of other states, was most successful in calling forth the public energies, and making small means produce great results. The progress of military knowledge and of the more refined arts was contemporaneous with that of politics. Most departments of science and the fine arts, pursued with impatient zeal by the highly sensitive Greeks, were carried by them to a higher pitch of perfection than elsewhere in ancient and, in some respects, in modern times; and their commerce, conducted by means of their colonies on the Black sea, and on the coasts of Italy, Sicily and Gaul, was extensive and important.

In literature, in science and in art, the Greeks surpassed all other ancient peoples, and the world owes them a debt of everlasting gratitude. All our philosophical and scientific terms are derived from the Greek. In sculpture and in architecture the Greeks are our masters. Homer, the most ancient, as well as the greatest of poets, was a native of Greece. The subject of his great poem, the "Iliad," was the anger of Achilles during a period of the Trojan war. Troy was a large city on the Asiatic side of the Hellespont, which is now called the Dardanelles. Paris, the son of the Trojan king, had stolen away the wife of Menelaus, a Greek prince.

All the Grecian kings combined together to punish this offence. They sailed to Troy in 1,200 vessels, and took the city after a siege of ten years. This event is supposed to have occurred 1,193 years before the Christian era.

The measure in which the "Iliad" is composed is called the hexameter. In order to give the reader an idea of this measure, as it appears in English, we subjoin a translation of the first few lines, in which Homer states his subject—the wrath of his hero, Achilles.

Observe the Homeric idea of man, indicated in the fourth line, where, after the souls of the heroes have departed, their bodies are spoken of as the heroes themselves:

"Wrath of Pelides, O Goddess, sing of the wrath of Achilles;
Wo was the havoc! and griefs unnumbered it heaped on Achaians;
Yea, full many the stalwart spirits of heroes it hurried
Down into Hades, allotting themselves for a prey to the bandogs
And all carrion fowls (but the purpose of Jove was aworking),
E'en from the time when at first these twain contended and quarrelled,
King among men, Atrides, and kin to the Godhead, Achilles."

One of the principal states of Greece was called Sparta or Lacedæmon. It was founded by Lelex, 1516 B. C. It had a code of laws from Lycurgus, who lived nearly nine centuries before Christ. He was strict and severe, but wise and upright.

When Lycurgus had completed his code of laws he left Sparta. Previous to his departure he made the people swear that they would violate none

SITE OF TROY.

of the laws till he should return. But he was resolved never to return. He committed suicide by starving himself to death; and his remains were thrown into the sea by his command, so that the Spartans might not bring back his dead body. Thus, as Lycurgus never could return, the Spartans were bound by their oath to keep his laws forever.

Athens had two celebrated lawgivers, Draco and Solon. The laws of Draco were so extremely severe that they were said to be written with blood, instead of ink. He punished even the smallest offences with death. His code was soon abolished.

About five centuries before the Christian era, Darius, King of Persia, invaded Greece with a fleet of 600 vessels and half a million of men. He was, however, met at Marathon by 10,000 Athenians, under Miltiades, and totally defeated. Upon gaining the victory, a soldier ran to carry the news to his countrymen at Athens, and so exhausted did he become upon his arrival there, that he could only shout "The victory is ours!" when he fell down dead. Subsequently the Persian monarch, Xerxes, invaded Greece with nearly two millions of men on land, and more than half a million on board his fleet.

When Xerxes arrived in Greece, it so happened that a great mountain, called Mount Athos, stood directly in the way that he wished his ships to sail. He therefore wrote a letter to the mountain, commanding it to get out of the way; but Mount Athos would not stir one step.

In order to bring his land forces from Asia into Greece, Xerxes built a bridge of boats across a part of the sea called the Hellespont. But the waves broke the bridge to pieces, and Xerxes commanded the sea to be whipped for its disrespectful conduct.

The greater part of the cities of Greece submitted to Xerxes; but Sparta and Athens made a stubborn resistance. Though they could muster but few soldiers, these were far more valiant than the Persians. One Spartan, who was told that the Persian arrows darkened the sun (in allusion to their vast numbers), replied, "Then we will fight in the shade."

At Thermopylæ, Xerxes wished to lead his army through a narrow passage between a mountain and the sea. Leonidas, King of Sparta, opposed him with 6,000 men. Seventy thousand Persians were slain in the attempt to break through the pass. At last, Leonidas found that the Persians could not be kept back any longer. He therefore sent away all but 300 men, and with these he remained at the pass of Thermopylæ. The immense host of the Persians came onward like a flood; and only one soldier of the 300 Spartans escaped to tell that the rest were slain.

But Xerxes did not long continue to triumph in Greece. His fleet was defeated at Salamis, and his army at Platæa. In escaping, he was forced to cross the Hellespont in a little fishing-vessel; for the sea, in spite of its being whipped, had again broken his bridge of boats.

After the Persian war, Cimon, Aristides and Pericles were the three principal men of Athens. Pericles at length became the chief person in the republic. Athens was never more flourishing than while he was at the head of the government. He adorned the city with magnificent edifices, and rendered it famous for learning, poetry and beautiful works of art, such as temples, statues and paintings. But the Athenians were fickle, and generally ungrateful to their public benefactors; and they sometimes ill treated Pericles.

In the latter part of his administration, a terrible plague broke out in Athens. Many of the citizens fell down and died while passing through the streets. Dead bodies lay in heaps, one upon another.

The illustrious Pericles was one of the victims of this pestilence. When he lay at the point of death, his friends praised him for the glorious deeds which he had achieved. "It is my greatest glory," replied Pericles, "that none of my acts have caused a citizen of Athens to put on mourning

Three years before the death of Pericles, a war had commenced between Athens and Sparta. These were now the two principal states of Greece, and they had become jealous of each other's greatness. A fierce war followed, in which all the states of that part of Greece called Peloponnesus were engaged. This bloody strife lasted twenty-eight years.

In the course of this war, Alcibiades made a conspicuous figure among the Athenians. He was the handsomest and most agreeable man in Athens. At one period he was greatly beloved by the people, and possessed almost unlimited power. But he was ambitious and destitute of principle.

Not long after this Thebes became for a brief period the most distinguished city in Greece. For this it was indebted to its able generals, Pelopidas and Epaminondas. Epaminondas was one of the best men that lived in ancient times. His private virtues were equal to his patriotism and valor. It is said of him that a falsehood was never known to come from his lips—one of the highest praises that can be bestowed on any man.

Shortly after the close of the Theban war Greece was conquered by Philip, King of Macedon. Thenceforward, Philip controlled the affairs of Greece till his death. Perhaps, after all, he was a better ruler than the Greeks could have found among themselves.

But he had many vices, and among the rest that of drinking to excess. One day, just after he had risen from a banquet, he decided a certain law-case unjustly. The losing person cried out, "I appeal from Philip drunk, to Philip sober!" And, sure enough, when Philip got sober, he decided the other way.

A poor woman, who had some business with Philip, tried in vain to obtain an audience. He put her off from one day to another, saying that he had no leisure to attend to her. "If you have no leisure to do justice, you have no right to be king!" said the woman. Philip was struck with the truth of what the woman said, and he became more attentive to the duties of a king.

Philip was succeeded by his son, Alexander the Great, who became king at the age of twenty. Alexander subdued the Grecian states in the course of one campaign. He was then declared generalissimo of the Greeks, and undertook a war against Persia. The army which he led against that country consisted of 35,000 men.

He crossed the Hellespont and marched through Asia Minor toward Persia. Before reaching its borders he was met by the Persian king, Darius, who had collected an immense army. Alexander defeated him, and killed 110,000 of his soldiers.

He then marched to Persepolis, the capital of Persia, and burnt it to the ground. When Persia was completely subdued, Alexander invaded India, now Hindostan. One of the kings of that country was named Porus. He is said to have been seven feet and a half in height. This gigantic king led a great army against Alexander. Porus was well provided with elephants, which had been trained to rush upon the enemy, and trample them down. Alexander had no elephants, but his usual good fortune did not desert him. The army of Porus was routed, and he himself was taken prisoner and loaded with chains.

In this degraded condition the Indian king was brought into the victor's tent. Alexander gazed with wonder at the enormous stature of Porus. Although a great conqueror, he was himself only of middle size. "How shall I treat you?" asked Alexander of his prisoner. "Like a king!" said Porus. The answer led Alexander to reflect how he himself should like to be treated, had he been in a similar situation; and he was induced to behave generously to Porus.

Alexander the Great was destined to owe his destruction to the wine-cup. While drinking at a banquet in Babylon, he was suddenly taken sick, and death soon conquered the conqueror.

The Greeks, when they heard of Alexander's death, had attempted to regain their liberty. But their struggles were unsuccessful, and the country was reduced to subjection by Cassander, who had been general of Alexander's cavalry. Cassander died in a few years. Thenceforward, the history of Greece tells of nothing but crimes and revolutions and misfortunes.

A high place in the annals of the world will always be accorded to the Greek philosophers. Between six and seven hundred years before the Christian era there were seven philosophers, who were called the "Seven Wise Men of Greece;" the philosopher Thales being considered the wisest of them all.

One night, while this great philosopher was taking a walk, he looked upward to contemplate the stars. Being much interested in this occupation, he strayed out of his path and tumbled into a ditch. An old woman who lived in his family ran and helped him out, all covered with mud. "For the future, Thales," said she, "I advise you not to have your head among the stars, while your feet are on the earth!" Some people think that the old woman was the wiser philosopher of the two.

The philosopher Pythagoras believed that, when people died, their souls migrated into the bodies of animals or birds. He affirmed that his own soul had once lived in the body of a peacock.

Socrates was one of the wisest and best philosophers of Greece. Indeed he was so wise and good, that the profligate Athenians could not suffer him to live. They therefore compelled him to drink poison.

Plato was born 429 years B. C., and was for eight years the pupil of Socrates. Indeed he was that great philosopher's constant companion until the day of his death. He had now no ties to bind him to Athens—perhaps, indeed, he did not feel secure there—and he went to live at Megara with his friend Euclid. Then he set out upon those travels of which we hear so much and know so little; "and," says an old historian, "whilst studious youth were crowding to Athens from every quarter in search of Plato for their master,

PLATO.

that philosopher was wandering along the banks of the Nile or the vast plains of a barbarous country, himself a disciple of the old men of Egypt." After storing his mind with the wisdom of the Egyptians, Plato is said to have gone on to Palestine and Phœnicia—to have reached China disguised as an oil merchant—to have had the "Unknown God" revealed to him by Jewish rabbis—and to have learned the secrets of the stars from Chaldean astronomers.

Aristotle was called by Plato "the Mind of the School," in recognition of his quick and powerful intelligence. In order to win time, even from sleep, Aristotle is said to have invented a plan of sleeping with a ball in his hand, so held over a brazen dish that whenever his grasp relaxed the ball would descend with a clang and arouse him to the resumption of his labors.

Diogenes was the queerest philosopher of all. He was called Diogenes the Dog, either because he lived like a dog, or because he had a currish habit of snarling at everybody. His doctrine was, that the fewer enjoyments a man had the happier he was likely to be. This philosopher went about bare-footed, dressed in very shabby clothes, and carrying a bag, a jug, and a staff. He afterward got a great tub, which he used to lug about with him all day long, and sleep in at night.

One day Alexander the Great came to see Diogenes, and found him mending his tub. It happened that Alexander stood in such a manner as to shade Diogenes from the sun, and he felt

ARISTOTLE.

cold. "Diogenes," said Alexander, "you must have a very hard time of it, living in a tub. Can I do anything to better your condition?" "Nothing, except to get out of my sunshine," replied Diogenes, who disdained to accept any other favor from the greatest monarch in the world.

But not alone in epic poetry and philosophy did the Greeks attain greatness. In the drama the names of Æschylus, Sophocles and Euripides are supreme. The Greek orator Demosthenes has never been equalled, and in sculpture and architecture Phidias and Praxiteles are beyond all comparison.

We will now treat of Greece as she exists in our own day. The present government of Greece is a constitutional and hereditary monarchy. The legislative power, since 1864, is in the hands of the king and the chamber of deputies. The person of the king is inviolable; his ministers are responsible. The right to vote begins at the age of twenty-five, and at thirty the electors are eligible for election. The deputies are chosen for four years, but the senators are appointed for life by the king. They must, however, have attained the age of forty. The population of Greece, including the Ionian islands, is 1,457,894. That of Athens, with its harbor, Piræus, is 50,798. The army amounts to 31,300 men, viz., 14,300 regular troops, and 17,000 irregular. Navy: 34 vessels, 164 cannon, and 1,340 men.

KING GEORGE I.

King George I. (Christian William Ferdinand Adolphus George) is the second son of the King of Denmark and brother of the Princess of Wales. He was born December 24th, 1845, and served for some time in the Danish navy. He was married at St. Petersburg to the Princess Olga, daughter of the Grand Duke Constantine, October 27th, 1867. The Princess Olga was born September 3d, 1851.

During the year 1877, when Russia had taken up the cause of Servia and Bulgaria against Turkey, the Greeks also took up arms for the purpose of annexing those territories which contained Greek population, but were governed by Turkey. The European powers urged Greece not to take part in the conflict, and, as a reward of their neutrality, they guaranteed her the possession of those territories which the Greeks coveted; a promise which was not kept. The Greeks otherwise might have been masters of a great part of Epirus, and of Thessaly, and of the island of Crete.

Travellers generally land at Piræus, the port of Athens, which is about six miles distant, and proceed at once to the city. A little west of Piræus, near the sea-shore, the throne of Xerxes was erected, that he might watch the progress of the battle of Salamis. Here he sat and saw the defeat of his fleet. The macadamized road to Athens follows the line of the most eastern of the long walls erected by Themistocles, remains of which are still visible. Since January, 1869, a railroad has been opened from Piræus to Athens, which is the first ever constructed on the soil of Greece.

The city of Athens owes its celebrity entirely to its ancient greatness and the numerous remains of its former works of art. The modern city presents very little of interest. The surrounding scenery is lovely, and the climate delightful, but the streets are narrow and winding, with mean and badly-built houses.

The Acropolis, or citadel, crowns the summit of a rocky hill, which rises abruptly out of the plain in the midst of the city. It has been a fortress from the earliest ages; it rises 150 feet. The walls, which are built on the edge of the perpendicular rock, form a circuit of nearly 7,000 feet. They are of great antiquity, and were built partly by the Pelagians, by Themistocles and Cymon, by Valerian, and latterly by the Turks and Venetians.

A short distance to the west of this is the Areopagus, or Mars' Hill, of still greater interest to the Christian student, as the spot from which the apostle Paul

VIEW OF CRETE.

addressed the assembled multitude of ancient Athens. On the eastern end was situated the celebrated Court of the Areopagas, the highest judicial court of Athens, whose existence is dated from the time of Cecrops, about 1500 B.C.

Corinth was founded 1900 years B.C., and was one of the most opulent cities of ancient Greece. Her peculiar position on the isthmus rendered her the commercial centre between Europe and Asia, and the sources of her wealth and power were increased by the Isthmian games, which took place in the neighborhood every three years. In 224 B.C. she joined the Achæan League, and became the seat of the assemblies of that confederation.

It is now a miserable and thinly-populated village. The only ruins of antiquity are those of the temple, situated west of the modern village. Seven columns still remain, five looking west, and three toward the south (the column forming the angle being twice counted). Five have their entablature still resting upon them, forming the angle of the building. The columns are of the Doric order, but heavy and ill-proportioned; they are five feet ten inches in diameter at the base, and are formed of limestone covered with stucco. Their appearance proves them to be anterior to the temple of Egina, or to the temple of Theseus, at Athens. It is uncertain to what divinity this building was consecrated; some think to Fortune, others to Minerva. Our artist has given a faithful representation of this temple on page 396.

Missolonghi has been immortalized by events which occurred during the War of Independence. Here, in 1822, Mavrocordato, with 500 men, sustained a siege of two months against a Turkish force of 14,000, commanded by Omar ben Vrioni. In 1825 it was again besieged by the Ottoman army, and held out for a year against the repeated assaults of an immensely superior force. In April, 1826, the besieged determined to cut their way through the ranks

ACROPOLIS AT ATHENS.

of their opponents and escape. Placing the women in their centre, dressed as men, they sallied forth, but the enemy had become aware of their intention, and but 2,000 escaped. The remainder determined to sell their lives as dearly as possible, and allured the Turks into the neighborhood of the powder magazine, when the whole exploded, burying conqueror and conquered in a common tomb. Lord Byron died at Missolonghi in 1824.

The Greek, after having been for centuries governed and oppressed by the Turk, has now an independent country of his own, and it rests with himself to prove whether he is worth all the passionate sympathy which has been expended upon him by many of his English friends, of whom the most celebrated has been Lord Byron. The population of his small country is partly

Albanian, partly Hellenic. The Albanians come from the north, and are of Sclave race; the Hellenes are the real descendants of the ancient Greeks, and may be divided into two bodies—the Pallicares, or people of the mountains, and the Phanariotes, or commercial Greeks, who flocked home from Constantinople as soon as their country was independent.

The Greek people are exceedingly pious; they are not Roman Catholics, but belong to the Greek Church, of which there are four patriarchs, namely: of Constantinople, Jerusalem, Antioch and Alexandria. The inhabitants of the Kingdom of Greece are under the patriarch of Constantinople, who has, however, accorded them a certain local independence in the management of their church affairs. The archbishops and bishops are paid by the state, and by certain dues; but the lower clergy are exclusively supported by the fees paid for baptisms, marriages, burials, etc., and if this is not enough they farm land and even keep shops. They are married men for the most part, and with families, and as their churches are not endowed, like those of the English clergy, they are obliged to provide for their own livelihood as best they can. The number of small churches is immense. It is considered an act of piety to build one, and of sacrilege to cause one to be taken down. In Athens and its neighborhood there are more than three hundred, of which only five or six are really in good working order. The rest are small chapels, only used for service at rare intervals, but none of them are wholly shut up.

An odd relic of paganism exists at Athens. There is one column standing of an ancient temple of Æsculapius. When a friend or child is sick, the people sometimes take a hair from his head, or a thread from one of his garters, and attach the two ends with wax to this pillar, expecting that the invalid will derive benefit from this extraordinary operation.

THE PYRAMIDS.

EGYPT.

OUT of the mists that surround the earliest ages the civilization of Egypt looms, like its mighty pyramids, that look down upon the people of to-day. Go back as far as you will, you cannot find a time when the Egyptians were not civilized.

This most interesting of lands occupies the north-eastern corner of the African continent. The waters of the Mediterranean form the northern limit of its soil. Upon the south it is bounded by Nubia, upon the east and west by the Red sea and the Libyan desert. The lowest of the Nile cataracts marks the frontier between Egypt and Nubia, where the modern town of Assouan stands beside the river's bank, and the foaming waters hurry past the temple-covered islands of Elephantine and Philæ. From the shores of the Mediterranean to the first cataract, the valley of the Nile measures, in a direct line from north to south, an extent of 550 miles. The Nile runs through the midst of Egypt, from the south to the north. This river overflows its banks once a year, and thus fertilizes the country, for it very seldom rains in Egypt.

The river begins to rise about the end of June, and continues rising until the first of October, at which time the traveller may have the opportunity of witnessing the singular appearance of the country. It then remains stationary a few days, and afterward gradually retires to its proper bed. At this period of the year the Nile waters are charged with a thick sediment, a portion of which is left as a deposit upon the soil, to which it imparts the most fertilizing properties.

The rise of the Nile is due to the periodical rains of Abyssinia and the countries farther south, whence the river derives its waters, and upon the greater or lesser quantity of which the height of the inundation depends. The changes in its color are in the highest degree curious during the inundation. The waters are of a greenish hue; they afterward change to a deep brownish-red, closely resembling the appearance of blood, and again become clear after subsiding into their ordinary channel.

According to Josephus, Menes was the first king of Egypt. He ascended the throne 2,320 years before Christ, or 4,207 years ago. The origin, however, of the Egyptian nation, and the history of their kings, are involved in the greatest obscurity and uncertainty. About 200 years later Saophis built the Great Pyramid, and forty years after Sen-Saophis built the Second Pyramid.

The pyramids seem equally large at a distance of six miles as at one. Arrived at the base of the great Pyramid of Cheops, and seeing the enormous size of the masses of stone of which it is composed, the sense of awe produced by these edifices is still further increased.

Cheops, or the Great Pyramid, stands farthest north, and is the one usually ascended and entered by travellers. It is 780 feet high, rising from a base which measures 764 feet each way, and which covers eleven acres of ground! It is estimated that Cheops had employed 100,000 men for ten years to make the causeway from the Nile to the pyramid for the purpose of conveying the stone, and 360,000 men twenty years to build the monument!

The Second Pyramid was built by Sen-Saophis, son of Cheops or Saophis, 2,083 years B. C. Its base is 690 feet square and 447 high. It was first opened, in the year 1200, by the Sultan El-Aziz Othman, son of Saladin.

The Third Pyramid, built by Mencheres, B. C. 2040, is 333 feet square at the base, and 203 feet high.

A short distance from the pyramids is the Sphinx—as much greater than all other sphinxes as the pyramids are greater than all other tombs. It is now so covered with sand that only the human part—the head and body—is visible. The whole figure is cut out of the solid rock with the exception of the fore-paws, and worked smooth. The cap, or royal helmet of Egypt, has been removed, but the shape of the top of the head explains how it was arranged. The Sphinx was a local deity of the Egyptians, and was treated by all in former times with divine honors. Immediately under his breast an altar stood, and the smoke of the sacrifice went up into the gigantic nostrils, now vanished from his face. The size of the Sphinx, as given by Pliny, is, height, 143 feet; circumference round the forehead, 102 feet. The paws of the leonine part extended 50 feet in front.

It is generally understood that sphinxes were the giant representatives and guards of royalty. How appropriate a guard this Sphinx of sphinxes is to these tombs of tombs! Though mutilated and defaced, the lonely Sphinx still possesses a strange and weird beauty.

"Comely the creature is, but the comeliness is not of this world. The beast once worshipped is a deformity and a monster to this generation; and yet you can see that those lips, so thick and heavy, were fashioned according to some ancient mode of beauty, some mode of beauty now forgotten—forgotten because Greece drew forth Cytherea from the flashing foam of the Ægean, and in her image created new forms of beauty, and made it a law among men that the short and proudly-wreathed lip should stand for the sign and main condition of loveliness through all generations to come. Yet still there lives on the race of those who were beautiful in the fashion of the elder world, and Christian girls of Coptic blood will look on you with the sad, serious gaze, and kiss your charitable hand with the big pouting lips of the very Sphinx.

"Laugh and mock if you will at the worship of stone idols, but mark ye this, ye breakers of images, that in one regard the stone idol bears awful semblance of Deity—unchangefulness in the midst of change—the same seeing, will, and intent, forever and ever inexorable! Upon ancient dynasties of Ethiopian and Egyptian kings; upon Greek and Roman, upon Arab and Ottoman conquerors; upon Napoleon, dreaming of an Eastern empire; upon battle and pestilence; upon the ceaseless misery of the Egyptian race; upon keen-eyed travellers, Herodotus yesterday and Warburton to-day; upon all and more, this unworldly Sphinx has watched and watched, like a providence, with the same earnest eyes and the same sad, tranquil mien; and we shall die, and Islam shall wither away, and still that sleepless rock will lie watching and watching the works of a new, busy race with those same, sad, earnest eyes, and the same tranquil mien everlasting. You dare not mock at the Sphinx."

At the time when they constructed these marvellous works, the ancient Egyptians possessed more learning and science than any other people. Their superior knowledge caused them to be looked upon as magicians by the people of other countries.

The Egyptians had, indeed, many absurd superstitions. Their chief goddess was Isis, and another deity was Osiris. Of these they made strange images, and worshipped them. Isis was greatly reverenced, and the people dedicated many splendid temples to her worship.

An Ethiopian woman, named Nitocris, became Queen of Egypt in the year 1678 before the Christian era. Her brother had been murdered by the Egyptians, and she resolved to avenge him. For this purpose Queen Nitocris built a palace underground, and invited the murderers of her brother to a banquet. The subterranean hall, where the banquet was prepared, was brilliantly illuminated with torches. The guests were the principal men in the kingdom. The scene was magnificent, as they sat feasting along the table. But suddenly a rushing and roaring sound was heard overhead, and a deluge of water burst into the hall. Queen Nitocris had caused a river to flow through a secret passage, and it extinguished the torches and drowned all the company at the banquet.

EXTERIOR OF TEMPLE OF ISIS.

The most renowned monarch that reigned over Egypt was Sesostris, who is also called Rameses. The date of his reign is not precisely known, but there are carvings in stone, lately found in Egypt, which are more than three thousand years old, and supposed to present portraits of him. They are, doubtless, the oldest portraits in existence. This king formed the design of conquering the world, and set out from Egypt with more than half a million of foot-soldiers, twenty-four thousand horsemen, and twenty-seven thousand armed chariots. His ambitious projects were partially successful. He made great conquests, and wherever he went he caused marble pillars to be erected with inscriptions on them, so that future ages might not forget his renown.

When Sesostris went to worship in the temple, he rode in a chariot which was drawn by captive kings. They were harnessed like horses, four abreast; and their royal robes trailed in the dust as they tugged the heavy chariot along. But at length the proud Sesostris grew old and blind. He could no longer look around him and see captive kings drawing his chariot, or kneeling at his footstool. He then became utterly miserable, and committed suicide.

A very famous king of Egypt was named Amenophis. He is supposed to be the same with Memnon, in honor of whom a temple with a gigantic statue was erected, of which some remains are still to be seen at Thebes. This statue was said to utter a joyful sound at sunrise, and a mournful sound when the sun set. Some modern travellers imagine that they have heard it.

In the year 525 before the Christian era, Egypt was conquered by Cambyses, King of Persia. He compelled Psammenitus, who was then king of Egypt, to drink bull's blood. It operated as a poison, and caused his death.

Three hundred and thirty-two years before the Christian era, Egypt was conquered by Alexander the Great, King of Macedon. Here he built a famous city, called Alexandria, which was for many centuries one of the most splendid places in the world. But the ancient city is in ruins, and modern Alexandria is far inferior to it.

Alexander appointed Ptolemy, one of his generals, to be ruler of the country. From Ptolemy were descended a race of kings, all of whom were likewise called Ptolemy. They reigned over Egypt 294 years. The last of these kings was Ptolemy Dionysius, whose own wife made war against him. A battle was fought, in which Ptolemy Dionysius was defeated. He attempted to escape, but was drowned in the Nile. His wife, whose name was Cleopatra, then became sole ruler of Egypt. She was one of the most beautiful women that ever lived, and her talents and accomplishments were equal to her personal beauty. But she was very wicked. Among other horrid crimes, Cleopatra poisoned her brother, who was only eleven years old. Yet, though all the world knew what an abandoned woman she was, the greatest heroes could not or would not resist the enticements of her beauty.

When Mark Antony, a Roman general, had defeated Brutus and Cassius at Philippi, in Greece, he summoned Cleopatra to come to Cilicia, on the north-eastern coast of the Mediterranean. He intended to punish her for having assisted Brutus.

As soon as Cleopatra received the summons, she hastened to obey. She went on board a splendid vessel, which was richly adorned with gold. The sails were made of the costliest silk. Instead of rough, sunburnt sailors, the crew consisted of lovely girls, who rowed with silver oars; and their strokes kept time to melodious music. Queen Cleopatra reclined on the deck, beneath a silken awning. In this manner she went sailing along the river Cydnus. Her vessel was so magnificent, and she herself so lovely, that the whole spectacle appeared like a vision. Mark Antony was first warned of her approach by the smell of delicious perfumes, which the wind wafted from the silken sails of the vessel. He next heard the distant strains of music, and saw the gleaming of the silver oars. But when he beheld the beauty of the Egyptian queen, he thought of nothing else. Till Mark Antony met Cleopatra he had been an ambitious man and a valiant warrior. But from that day forward he was nothing but her slave.

Owing to Cleopatra's misconduct and his own, Antony was defeated by Octavius, another Roman general, at Actium, in Greece. He then killed himself by falling on his sword. Cleopatra knew that if Octavius took her alive, he would carry her to Rome and expose her to the derision of the populace. She resolved not to endure this ignominy. Now, in Egypt there is a venomous reptile, called an asp, the bite of which is mortal, but not very painful. Cleopatra applied one of these reptiles to her bosom. In a little while her body grew benumbed, and her heart ceased to beat; and thus died the beautiful and wicked Queen of Egypt. This event occurred thirty years before Christ.

After the death of Cleopatra Egypt became a province of the Roman Empire. It continued to belong to that power, and to the portion of it called the Eastern Empire, till the year 640 after the Christian era. It was then conquered by the Saracens. It remained under their government upward of six centuries. The Saracen sovereigns were dethroned by the Mamelukes, whom they had trained up to be their guards. The Mamelukes ruled Egypt till the year 1517, when they were conquered by the Turks. They kept possession of Egypt till the year 1798. It was then invaded by Napoleon Bonaparte with an army of 40,000 Frenchmen. The Turks, ever since their con-

CAIRO.

quest of Egypt, had kept a body of Mamelukes in their service; these made a desperate resistance. A battle was fought near the pyramids, in which many of them were slain, and others were drowned in the Nile. Not long after this victory Bonaparte went back to France, and left General Kleber in command of the French army.

General Kleber was a brave man, but a severe one, and his severity cost him his life. He had ordered an old Mussulman, named the Sheik Sada, to be bastinadoed on the soles of his feet. Shortly afterward, when the general was in a mosque, a fierce Arab rushed upon him and killed him with a dagger.

In 1801, the English sent Sir Ralph Abercrombie with an army to drive the French out of Egypt. General Menou was then the French commander.

Sir Ralph Abercrombie beat him at the battle of Aboukir, but was himself mortally wounded.

In the course of the same year the French army sailed from Egypt back to France. The inhabitants lamented their departure, for the French generals had ruled them with more justice and moderation than their old masters, the Turks. Egypt is now governed by a successor of Mehemet Ali, who bears the title of pasha, but the country is tributary to the Turkish Empire.

Cairo, the capital of Egypt, was founded by the Arab conquerors of Egypt in the year 970 A. D. The name *El-Kahireh* signifies "The Victorious."

From the citadel of Cairo is displayed a magnificent panorama. To the east are seen the obelisk of Heliopolis and the tombs of the Mamelukes; to the south the lofty quarries of Mount Mokattem, with ruined castles, mouldering domes and the remains of other edifices; south-west and west are the grand aqueduct, mosques and minarets, the Nile, the ruins of old Cairo and the island and groves of Rhoda; beyond the river, on the south-west, the town Ghizeh, amid groves of sycamore, fig and palm trees; still more remote, the pyramids of Ghizeh and Sakkara, and beyond these the great Libyan desert. In the northern direction may be seen the green plains of the delta, sprinkled with white edifices; and to the north and north-east of the spectator is the city of Cairo, with her 400 mosques, whose sunlit domes are glistening in the sun. It is a never-to-be-forgotten sight.

To those who are fond of fun and amusement, the excitement going on in Cairo from morning till night is immense. Dragomans—black, yellow and white—splendidly dressed in flowing trowsers, silk and satin vests, embroidered jackets and immense turbans, quarrelling with the donkey-owners, who are quarrelling and finding fault with the donkey-drivers, who are doing the same with the donkeys. The traveller threatens to belabor the dragoman, the dragoman does belabor the owner, the owner belabors the boy and the boy the donkey, and none of them seem to care much for it. Add to this half a dozen mountebanks; a dozen dealers in relics, turbans and handkerchiefs; fifty dogs, one of whom is playing circus with a monkey on his back; a snake-charmer, with a bagful of immense snakes, all standing erect (if a snake can be said to *stand*), with fangs protruding, ready to make a plunge at their conqueror, who offers to swallow any one of them for a shilling, and you have a faint idea of what is daily going on.

Besides the Mahometans, who of course constitute the bulk of the inhabitants of Cairo, and who number nearly 250,000, there are some 30,000 or 40,000 of other sects and countries: such as Copts (native Egyptian Christians), Jews, Greeks, Armenians and Franks. These are generally to be distinguished from the Mahometans by their dress and their complexion, though of the latter there are many shades among all classes.

Alexandria, the seaport and commercial capital of Egypt, contains nearly three hundred thousand inhabitants. The main objects of interest here are Pompey's Pillar, which is of red polished granite, and 100 feet in height; and Cleopatra's Needles, which were quarried in the reign of Thothmes III., 1495 B. C., and are consequently now 3,382 years old.

The Egyptian native is gentle, and travellers who always go armed to the teeth take a great deal of unnecessary trouble. They will meet with plenty of cheating and lying; but that is generally the worst. Instances of robbery and murder are comparatively rare. The people are now commonly called Arabs, but the rulers are Turks; and in the seaport towns on the delta of the Nile is a great population of Christians, merchants from all the Mediterranean ports, and also Copts and Armenians.

In Egypt, Arabia and Persia, the fruit of the date palm and doum palm trees forms the principal food of the people, and a man's wealth is computed by the number of such palms he possesses. Both the date and the doum palm are found in Egypt, but the former disappears as the traveller descends the Nile and enters Nubia.

Abydos, alluded to in Byron's celebrated poem, "The Bride of Abydos," owes its importance to the fact that the god Osiris was buried here, and rich Egyptians from all parts wished to have their bodies lie in the sacred dust which their god had hallowed. The tombs are very old, and date back to the sixteenth and seventeenth dynasties.

The principal ruins, which cover a great extent, are the Memnonium, or palace of Memnon, the Temple of Osiris, and the Necropolis.

The Temple of Osiris lies north of the Memnonium: this was one of the temples the most revered in Egypt. It was here that, in 1808, the famous inscription, now in the British Museum, known under the name of the Table of Abydos, was found. It contained originally the names of all the ancestors of Rameses the Great, which agree with the names of the oldest of the Pharaohs, which were found at the Memnonium at Thebes. Part of the tablet was unfortunately destroyed, and some of the names lost.

North of the Temple of Osiris lies the Necropolis, or burial-ground, where may be seen numerous tombstones of the time of Osirtasen; here was also a colossal statue of that Pharaoh, now in the museum of Cairo.

Let us now take a glance at Thebes, the most celebrated and magnificent of the ancient capitals of Egypt: the capital of the kingdom of the Pharaohs when in the zenith of their power, and whose remains exceed in extent and grandeur all the most lively imagination can depict. No written account can ever give an adequate impression of the effect, past and present, of its temples, palaces, obelisks, colossal statues, sphinxes and sculptures of various kinds. They continue from age to age to excite the awe and admiration of the spectator. To have seen the monuments of Thebes is to have seen the Egyptians as they lived and moved before the eyes of Moses. To have seen

DOUM PALMS OF UPPER EGYPT.

the tombs of Thebes is to have seen the whole religion of the Egyptians at the most solemn moments of their lives. Nothing that can be said about them will prepare the traveller for their extraordinary grandeur.

> "Not all proud Thebes' unrivalled walls contain,
> The world's great empress on the Egyptian plain,
> That spreads her conquest o'er a thousand states,
> And pours her heroes through a hundred gates,
> Two hundred horsemen and two hundred cars
> From each wide portal issuing to the wars."

The most striking of the ruins are those of Karnak and Luxor, on the eastern bank of the river, with the Memnonium, Medinet Haboo, Koornah, Tombs of the Priests, Tombs of the Kings and the Vocal Memnon, on the western side. The sanctuary of Ammon, a small granite edifice founded by Osirtasen, with the vestiges of the earliest temples around, is the centre of the vast collection of palaces and temples which is called Karnak.

Among the ruins of the Memnonium are the fragments of the stupendous colossal statue of Rameses the Great. It has been broken off at the waist, and the upper part now lies prostrate on the ground. This enormous statue measures sixty-three feet round the shoulders, and thirteen feet from the crown of the head to the top of the shoulders. The Arabs have scooped millstones out of his face, but you can still see what he was—the largest statue in the world. Rameses rested here in awful majesty, after the conquest of the whole of the then known world. Next to the wonder excited by the boldness of this sculpture, is the labor that must have been exerted to destroy it—to destroy these countless statues that strew the plains of Thebes. This wholesale destruction was by the orders of Cambyses, the conquering king of Persia, about 2,400 years ago.

The two immense colossi—one of them commonly known as the Vocal Memnon (the statue that, according to ancient tradition, uttered musical sounds when the rays of the morning sun first glowed above the eastern mountains)—stand, like lonely landmarks, hoary, blackened, time-worn and defaced, in the midst of the Theban plain.

To any one who will take a glance at any map of Egypt, the importance of connecting the Red sea with the Mediterranean at the Gulf of Suez will be at once evident. The town of Suez is situated at the head of the gulf of the same name; the Red sea dividing at its northern extremity into the gulfs of Akaba and Suez. The peninsular region inclosed between these two gulfs is a rugged mountainous wilderness, and the scene of the journey of the hosts of Israel; and Suez, from the nature of the mountains on the Egyptian side, must have been the spot where they crossed. Not far away are the springs known as "Moses' Well," situated in the desert in an oasis, where, under the

MOSES' WELL.

grateful shade of the tamarind and palm, the air laden with the perfume of flowers, the Arab of Suez delights to come and forget the noisome odors of his city abode.

The connection of the Red sea with the Mediterranean by a canal was considered a desirable object at a very early period in the history of the world. It is even asserted that, as early as the time of the Pharaohs, such a canal was actually constructed, extending from the Nile to the Gulf of Suez. In more recent times Napoleon I. projected a canal across the isthmus. Its value lies in the importance of the commerce of India to the rest of the world.

The construction of the Suez canal was carried to a successful issue by the French savant, Ferdinand de Lesseps, in 1869. Subsequently, by a master-

FERRY OF KANTARA.

piece of diplomacy, the British government purchased the khedive's shares in the canal; and extreme bitterness was aroused both in France and in Russia by the preponderance gained by England, both commercially and politically, by this remarkable transaction.

At the east side of the Suez canal lies the plain of Pelusus. The highway from Palestine, Syria and Persia came by this plain; a road still exists, and a ferry had to be established at Kantara, which word expresses "ferry" and tells of the former existence of the means of crossing the waters of the lake Menzaleh at this place; a lake which now exists only on the western side of the canal, the portion on the eastern side having dried up.

Among the many triumphs which have been achieved by scholars in the nineteenth century, the decipherment of the Egyptian hieroglyphics takes a very high place. By this the history of Egypt has been unfolded, and its learning and wisdom made available for the people of to-day. This great achievement resulted from the discovery of the famous Rosetta Stone, by a French artillery officer, in 1799, during the expedition to Egypt under Napoleon I. The stone, which is now in the British Museum, is two feet five inches wide, and contains inscriptions in three kinds of writing, one in hieroglyphics, another in what is called demotic, or the language of the people, and the third in Greek. This last being known, furnished the key to the others, because all the inscriptions were found to be texts of the same decree, being a decree drawn up by the priests of Memphis in honor of their king, Ptolemy Epiphanes, B. C. 198.

A large portion of the literature of Egypt comes down to us in the shape of historical inscriptions graven upon pyramids, obelisks and walls of temples. The sentences are sometimes short and abrupt; but frequently they have a kind of music which is exceedingly fine. They have also what is now called by Egyptologists "The Book of the Dead," but which the Egyptians themselves called "Coming Forth by Day." This book exhibits their religious belief, their views of the judgment after death, and the transformations of the blessed dead before they attained final rest.

The ancient Egyptians are the only people known who have succeeded in bringing the art of embalming or mummifying to perfection. They believed that the soul would revisit the body after a number of years, and therefore it was absolutely necessary that the body should be preserved if its owner wished to live forever with the gods.

In 1881 were discovered the mummies of Sethi I., Thothmes II., Thothmes III., and Rameses II., surnamed the Great; heroes whose exploits and fame filled the ancient world with awe more than three thousand years ago.

The mummy of Thothmes III. was unrolled to make certain that the monogram of his name outside indicated that the remains within were really those of that monarch. The inscriptions on the bandages established the fact beyond all doubt. Once more human eyes gazed on the features of the man who had conquered Syria, and Cyprus, and Ethiopia, and raised Egypt to the highest pinnacle of her power. The spectacle was of brief duration; the remains proved to be in so fragile a state that there was only time to take a hasty photograph, and then the features crumbled to pieces and vanished like an apparition, and so passed away from human view forever. The director of the Boolak Museum, to which the mummies had been taken, felt such remorse at the result that he refused to allow the unrolling of Rameses the Great, for fear of a similar catastrophe.

Besides men and women, the Egyptians also mummified cats, crocodiles, snakes, birds, such as the ibis and hawk, and many other creatures.

A region of territory in Eastern Africa, called Soudan, in itself most insignificant, has, by reason of recent developments, been suddenly brought to the notice of the civilized world, and has engaged public attention in no small degree.

Soudan is the name given to that vast extent of territory in Upper Egypt that stretches from Nubia to the confines of Abyssinia, and from the Red sea to the Libyan desert. The great river Nile, composed of Bah-rel-Abiad, the White, Bah-rel-Azrek, the Blue Nile, and the Atbara, together with the other tributaries, traverses its whole length from south to north. The land, as it recedes from the Red sea westward, assumes an elevation of 1,800 feet. Its surface is rugged, rocky and mainly barren.

This vast territory is peopled by hordes of Arabs of various tribes, whose number is computed to be between 30,000,000 and 40,000,000.

EGYPTIAN FAMILY.

The Arab—and in this nomenclature, besides the natives of Arabia proper, all the inhabitants of northern and half of the eastern portion of Africa are to be comprehended—is a singular race. Wild and ferocious, like the savages of the Far West, the Arabs are endowed with a keener intellect and a highly nervous temperament; a characteristic which has impressed itself upon the Spanish nation by reason of contact. Unlike, however, the aborigines of America, who are stolid, content with hunting and the gratification of their natural wants, the Arabs are ever restless and aggressive, and prey upon their fellow-beings. Although very dark in complexion, they are not negroes; their hair is coarse, but smooth.

Slaves being a staple commodity among the Mussulmans, Mahometanism greatly tended to stimulate the ardor of the Arabs of Soudan to extra exertion, and the consequence has been that the negroes of Central Africa have been the sufferers. Frequent incursions are made into their territories and hordes are captured, who are either employed to till the ground for the benefit of their captors, or sold into slavery, both men and women; the former, if young, being first denaturalized, so as to be marketable for harem service.

The British government endeavored to put a stop to the traffic in slavery, and for that purpose sent out Sir Samuel Baker. But his efforts were futile, for he could find no sympathy or support from any one, not even from the officials themselves; on the contrary, everybody was against him, either from principle or from interested motives. It is a wonder that he was permitted to return alive. In his report he says: "In ordinary times many a government official, if he meets with a gang of slaves driven by a party of marauders to some distant market, with their hands bound to a log of wood behind their backs, will content himself with a friendly 'parley' and a handsome bribe."

Sir Samuel discovered one case in which the Egyptian deputy-governor knowingly allowed a boat to pass which seemed to be laden with grain, but which contained more than 400 men, women and children, packed like herrings below the deck where the supposed cargo was laid.

Gordon Pasha, the celebrated "Chinese Gordon," succeeded Sir Samuel, with no better result. Gordon is supposed to have been killed at Khartoum, a city which was captured by a false prophet called the "Mahdi."

Suakin, an important port on the Red sea, is famed as being the hottest place on the Red sea, if not on the globe. A conversation overheard one day in front of the governor's house will illustrate this. Two sentries were pacing to and fro, when one of them said:

"Abdallah! you knew Suleiman, our brother, who died from the effects of the heat?"

"I knew him," replied Abdallah.

"Listen, O my brother," continued Mustapha. "Last night Suleiman appeared to me whilst I slept, and said: 'Mustapha, Suakin is indeed hotter than hell—for I am in hell, as you may suppose. Hell is a cold place compared to Suakin; so much so, that the night of my arrival there, feeling cold, I woke up the devil to ask him for a blanket.' Surprised, he asked me: 'Soldier, whence came you?' When I told him Suakin, he replied, 'I understand;' and thereupon he cried out: 'Give the man from Suakin a blanket.'"

THE BARBARY STATES.

ALGIERS, Morocco, Tunis and Tripoli are known as the Barbary States. They are bounded north by the Mediterranean sea, east and south by the desert, and west by the Atlantic ocean. These countries of North Africa were inhabited in the time of the Romans. Morocco was called Mauritania; and Algiers, Numidia. These regions were first settled by colonies from Phœnicia, Greece and other countries.

In this region stood the celebrated city of Carthage in ancient times. Its site was about ten miles north-east of the present city of Tunis. France had long been casting covetous eyes upon the little state of Tunis, which nominally was under Turkish rule, but really was independent. It possessed the best, virtually the only harbors of the northern coast of Africa. Lying immediately east of Algeria, it was an asylum for Algerian malcontents and the refuge of insurrectionary tribes. Algeria, since its first occupation by the French, has been a dangerous possession, and even at present it cannot be regarded as thoroughly conquered, especially in the southern districts bordering on the desert. At the Berlin congress, when it was arranged that England, Austria and Russia should each receive a part of the Ottoman Empire, Count St. Vallier, the French delegate, hinted the desire of his government to have a share of the spoils, by opposing the dismemberment of Turkey. One day, while he was expressing his views to Bismarck, the chancellor shrugged his shoulders and said:

"Why not take Tunis for your share? No one will oppose you."

From that moment Count St. Vallier withdrew his opposition. A few months later preparations for the French expedition were being carried forward with energy and secrecy. On the pretext of chastising the Bedouins that had invaded Algiers, the French entered Tunisian territory. Then followed a series of so-called victories over the beggarly, unarmed and half-starved Bedouin Arabs, the bombardment of the defenceless town of Tabarca, expeditions against an imaginary enemy, and finally the parade march toward the capital.

The country now called Morocco was conquered by the Saracens about the same time with the other Barbary states. So also was Tripoli. All these states, except Morocco, afterward fell into the hands of the Turks.

Three distinct races are usually included under the name of Moors, namely, the Arabs, the true Moors, and the Berbers.

The Arabs came originally from the Sahara, over whose boundless wastes a large proportion of their race still wander. The Moors are essentially townsmen. They are the degenerate descendants of that section of the Arab race, who, in the eighth century, after establishing the powerful kingdom of Fez, overran a large portion of Spain.

The Moors fill the chief places under the government; and, notwithstanding a great inferiority in numbers, possess more power than any of the other races.

A STREET IN TUNIS.

During a long period, the Barbary States were in the habit of fitting out vessels to cruise against the ships of other nations. Their prisoners were sold as slaves, and never returned to their own country, unless a high ransom was paid for them. The Americans were the first who made any considerable resistance to these outrages. In the year 1803, Commodore Preble sailed to the Mediterranean sea with a small American fleet. He intended to attack

Tripoli; but one of his frigates, the Philadelphia, got aground in the harbor. The Turks took possession of the Philadelphia. But one night Lieutenant Decatur entered the harbor of Tripoli, and rowed toward the captured vessel with only twenty men. He leaped on board, followed by his crew, and killed all the Turks or drove them overboard; the Philadelphia was then set on fire. After this exploit, Commodore Preble obtained some gunboats from the king of Naples, and with these and the American vessels he made an attack on the fortifications of Tripoli. The Pasha of Tripoli was forced to give up his prisoners.

In the year 1815, Commodore Decatur—the same who had burnt the Philadelphia—was sent with a fleet against Algiers. He captured their largest vessels, and compelled the Algerines, and the Tripolitans also, to agree never more to make slaves of Americans.

In 1816, Algiers was battered by an English fleet under the command of Lord Exmouth. This was the severest chastisement that the Algerines had ever received at that period. But in 1830 the French sent a large naval and military force against Algiers, commanded by Marshal Beaumont. The war continued for seventeen years, an Arab leader, by the name of Abdel Kader, making a powerful resistance to the French. At length Abdel Kader was defeated and taken prisoner; so the country was conquered, and Algiers, under the name of Algeria, is now a province of France.

CENTRAL AND SOUTH AFRICA.

AFRICA is less known than any other grand division of the globe. Many portions of the interior have never been visited by Europeans. The greater part of the inhabitants are negroes, of which there are many tribes. Some of these are intelligent, and live tolerably well, but the greater part are either in a savage or barbarous state. The climate being warm, they need little shelter or clothing. Their houses are therefore poor mud huts, or slight tenements, made of leaves or branches of trees. Their dress is often but a single piece of cloth tied around the waist. They are, however, a cheerful race, and spend much of their time in various amusements.

Besides the negroes, there are several other races of Africans. The inhabitants, from Egypt to Abyssinia, appear to consist of the original Egyptian people, mixed with Turks, Arabs and others. The people of the Barbary States are the descendants of the ancient Carthaginians, mingled with the Saracens who conquered the country, together with Turks and Arabs.

The immense Desert of Sahara—which is almost as extensive as the whole United States—with part of the adjacent regions, appears to be occupied by wandering tribes of Arabs, who move from place to place with their horses and camels, like the people of Arabia, for pasturage or plunder.

Africa may be considered as, on the whole, the least civilized division of the earth. The people are mostly Mahometans, and one-half of them are nearly in a savage state. The rest are in a barbarous condition.

The central parts of Africa abound in wild animals, such as lions, panthers, leopards, elephants, rhinoceroses, zebras and quaggas. The woods are filled with chattering monkeys, the thickets are infested with monstrous serpents, ostriches roam over the deserts, various kinds of antelopes and deer, in vast herds, graze upon the plains, hippopotami are seen in the lakes and rivers, and crocodiles abound in the stagnant waters. Wild birds of every hue meet the eye of the traveller in nearly all parts of the country.

Central and Southern Africa can hardly be said to have any history. The inhabitants possess no written records, and cannot tell what events have happened to their forefathers.

The ancients had very curious notions about Africa, for they had visited only the northern parts, and contented themselves with telling incredible stories about the remainder. They supposed that toward the eastern shore of the continent there were people without noses, and others who had three or four eyes apiece.

In other parts of Africa there were said to be men without heads, but who had eyes in their breasts. Old writers speak also of a nation whose king had a head like a dog. There was likewise said to be a race of giants, twice as tall as common men and women.

But the prettiest of all these fables is the story of the Pigmies. These little people were said to be about a foot high, and were believed to dwell near the source of the river Nile. Their houses were built something like birds' nests, and their building materials were clay, feathers, and egg-shells. These Pigmies used to wage terrible wars with the cranes. An immense army of them would set out on an expedition, some mounted on rams and goats, and others on foot. When an army of the Pigmies encountered an army of the cranes, great valor was displayed on both sides. The cranes would rush forward to the charge flapping their wings, and sometimes one of them would snatch up a Pigmy in his beak, and carry him away captive. But the Pigmies brandished their little swords and spears, and generally succeeded in putting the enemy to flight. Whenever they had a chance, they would break the eggs of the cranes and kill the unfledged young ones without mercy.

It was long supposed that the story of Herodotus about the Pigmies of Africa was altogether mythical, but within the past twenty years abundant evidence has accumulated of the existence of a number of tribes of curious little folks in equatorial Africa. The chief among these tribes are the Akka, whom Schweinfurth found north-west of Albert Nyassa; the Obongo, discovered by Du Chaillu in west Africa, south-east of the Gaboon, and the Batwa, south of the Congo.

These little people range in height from four feet two inches to about four

SCENES IN THE LIFE OF DR. LIVINGSTONE.

feet eight inches. They are intellectually as well as physically inferior to the other tribes of Africa. They are perhaps nearer the brute kingdom than any other human beings. The Obongo, for instance, wear no semblance of clothing; make no huts except to bend over and fasten to the ground the tops of three or four young trees, which they cover with leaves; possess no arts except the

CHRISTMAS AT AN AFRICAN MISSIONARY STATION.

making of bows and arrows, and do not till the soil. They live on the smaller game of the forest, and on nuts and berries.

For many centuries the mystery of the Nile had been a wonder to all who dwelt upon its banks, and to travellers who came there to learn the wisdom of the Egyptians. It flowed from unknown regions, and for the last thousand miles of its course did not receive a rivulet from either side, and only at rare and uncertain intervals a drop of water from the clouds. For nine months of the year its uniform and majestic flood rolled within its steep banks. Then, almost at a given day, from year to year, the river, with no apparent cause, began to rise, overflowing its banks and transforming the narrow valley into a lake. In a few weeks the flood subsided, leaving behind a thin layer of mud, the source of all the fertility of Egypt.

In general terms, tropical Africa consists of an elevated central plateau, separated from low tracts along the coast by lines of hills and mountains, running at various distances from the coast. There are thus three well-marked divisions: the low, unhealthy coast region, the mountain ranges, and the central plateau. Of this plateau the chief water-basins, beginning from the south, are those of the Zambesi, whose waters are discharged eastward into the Indian ocean; the Congo, whose waters flow westward into the Atlantic; and the Nile, whose waters flow northward into the Mediterranean.

The Congo is in volume of water second only to the Amazon. There is a remarkable feature connected with the Congo and the Zambesi. Both rivers flow three-quarters of the way across the continent, and for a considerable space parallel to, and at no very great distance from each other, but in opposite directions; the Zambesi from west to east, the Congo from east to west. The head waters of some of these affluents indeed interlock on an almost level table-land, which was crossed by both Livingstone and Cameron.

David Livingstone was born near Glasgow, Scotland, in 1813. In 1840 he went as a missionary to South Africa, where he showed a decided tendency for scientific and geographical investigations. He died on the 1st of May, 1873, on the shores of Lake Bangweolo. From the death of Livingstone the interest of African discovery centres mainly upon the long journeys of Cameron and of Stanley. The names of Barth, Baker and Speke stand high in the list of African explorers.

Livingstone thought that "we ought to encourage the Africans to cultivate for our markets, as the most effectual means, next to the gospel, of their elevation." He therefore proposed the formation of stations on the Zambesi, beyond the Portuguese territories, but having communication through them with the coast. This a number of religious bodies agreed to do. Livingstone said that "the country is so extensive that there was no need of clashing. All classes of Christians find that sectarian rancor soon dies out when they are working together among and for the heathen."

One of the most remarkable expeditions that ever entered Africa was that which was undertaken by Stanley for the rescue of Emin Pasha in 1887. Emin Pasha, originally a German physician who had been in the Turkish service, entered the service of the Khedive of Egypt in 1876 as surgeon and naturalist on the staff of General Gordon, who had just been appointed Governor-General of the Soudan. Two years after Emin was made Governor of the Equatorial Province, as he had shown great talents for administration. In a very short time he had swept the province clear of the slave traders, and reorganized the affairs of the province. After the success of the Mahdi in the upper part of the province, and the capture of Khartoum, in spite of the near vicinity of the English relief expedition, Emin was put in great danger, but he refused to evacuate the region, and thus remit it to the renewed domination of barbarism and the slave trade. The European world began to be appreciative of the heroic and noble stand made by Emin in the very heart of savage Africa, and the final outcome of this sentiment was the relief expedition which Stanley gallantly offered to lead as a matter of love, not of reward.

HENRY M. STANLEY.

The enterprise was one of stupendous danger and obstacles. Stanley made for the Lake Albert Nyanza, where Emin was known to have had two steamers, and it was supposed that upon reaching the lake there would be little difficulty in communicating with the Pasha himself. Stanley, however, reached the lake with only 173 men out of 341 with which he started out. Sickness, starvation and the poisoned arrows of the fierce dwarfs of the Congo forest accounted for the rest. Stanley at length, after considerable time and difficulty, met Emin; but the Pasha could not be induced to leave equatorial Africa, and so render his past work useless. Stanley then returned to bring up his rear-guard, about whom he began to be alarmed. He met the forlorn remains of it—one white officer and seventy-two men out of 257.

Again, Stanley, with the reunited party, started to traverse the savage and hostile region which he had crossed twice before, but so terrible had been the punishment which he had inflicted on his assailants that his last march was not seriously hampered by foes, though imminently threatened by starvation. But the leader's heroic energy and endurance vanquished everything, and he finally reached the lake for the third time, eight months after he had left it. Fortune was again on the side of his failure. Strange things had happened during eight months. Emin's Egyptian officers had revolted against him, and placed him and Mountenay Jephson, Stanley's assistant, who had left with the Pasha, in confinement. At this time there appeared a fresh irruption of the Mahdists. The ultimate result was to so terrify Emin's rebellious people that the Pasha and his companion were released, and all were willing to accept Stanley's escort to the sea-coast.

Emin Pasha did not, however, stay long with his rescuer. He seemed apparently to have enjoyed his life in the Soudan, and he longed to return. He had ruled there over a large extent of territory, and a submissive, if not attached, population. He had a small standing army, plenty of ivory, and although in the desert, he reigned like a prince. After his rescue, therefore, he made up his mind to return. Although England had furnished the expedition which went to his relief, he preferred to take service under Germany, and go back under its auspices to the province over which he had ruled.

Emin Pasha was born of Jewish parents in Prussian Silesia, March 24th, 1840. He was left an orphan at an early age, was adopted by a Protestant family and baptized in the Christian faith. In 1869 he entered the service of the Turkish government. He subsequently went with Chinese Gordon to the Soudan as medical officer; and when Gordon left the Soudan in 1879 he placed Emin in charge of the Egyptian Equatorial Provinces as their Governor, a position which he retained until his rescue out of the Mahdi's clutches by Stanley.

ASIA.

"Now upon Syria's land of roses
Softly the light of eve reposes,
And like a glory the broad sun
Hangs over sainted Lebanon;
Whose head in misty grandeur towers,
And whitens with eternal sleet,
While summer, in a vale of flowers,
Is sleeping rosy at his feet."

WE will now turn to Asia, the cradle of the human race.

The most important event in all history was the birth of Christ, and the country hallowed by his footsteps has received, and always will retain, the name of the Holy Land.

From the earliest ages of authentic history, Palestine (with whose ancient and sacred history every reader is familiar) has been the object of curiosity at once ardent and enlightened. Since the time that Abraham crossed the Euphrates (3,780 years ago), a solitary traveller, down to the recent massacres in that unhappy country, Syria has been looked upon with greater attention, and described with greater accuracy and minuteness, than any other portion of the ancient world.

Syria is at the present day governed by the Turks, and, like every other country under their sway, is stamped with an aspect of desolation and decay. The term Syria is now applied, not only to what anciently bore that name, but to Palestine also.

The holy places of Palestine are eleven in number, the possession of which by the different sects of Christians and Mussulmans has been the cause of many deplorable catastrophes, and will be of many more. It overthrew the Byzantine empire, rent Christendom asunder, and was the origin of the Crimean war. The jealousy is carried to such an extent in the church of the Holy Sepulchre to-day that they bribe the Turks to oppress each other; and were it not that a Turkish guard is always present in the church, which is common to all Christians, they would tear one another to pieces!

The holy places are: 1. The Church of the Holy Sepulchre, which covers some twelve or thirteen places consecrated to more than ordinary veneration by being in some way connected with the death and resurrection of the Saviour: this is common to all Christians. 2. The Church of the Nativity at Bethlehem, which is likewise common. 3. The Church of the Presentation at Jerusalem—Mahometan. 4. The Church of the Annunciation at Nazareth —Latin Christians. 5. The Church of St. Peter at Tiberias—Latin. 6. Church at Cana in Galilee—Greek Christians. 7. Church of the Flagellation at Jerusalem—Latin. 8. Church of the Ascension, Mount Olivet—Mahometan. 9. Tomb of the Virgin, valley of Jehoshaphat—common. 10. Grotto of Gethsemane—Latin. 11. Church of the Apostles—Mahometan.

Stanley, an Eastern traveller, writes that "there is one approach to Jerusalem which is really grand, namely, from Jericho and Bethany. It is the approach by which the army of Pompey advanced—the first European army that ever confronted it—and it is the approach of the triumphal entry of the Gospels. Probably the first impression of every one coming from the north, west and the south may be summed up in the expression used by one of the modern travellers, 'I am strangely affected, but greatly disappointed.' But no human being could be disappointed who first saw Jerusalem from the east. The beauty consists in this, that you then burst at once on the two great ravines which cut the city off from the surrounding table-land, and that then, and then only, you have a complete view of the Mosque of Omar."

The only Christian monument in Jerusalem of any importance is the church of the Holy Sepulchre.

This church is surmounted by two domes of different dimensions, the larger surmounting the chapel of the Holy Sepulchre, the smaller the Greek church, on the site of the basilica erected by the Emperor Constantine in the fourth century.

Close beside the dome stands the Minaret of Omar, which that magnanimous caliph erected that he might have the privilege of praying as nearly as possible to the church without interfering with the rights of the Christians. As you enter the door of these sacred walls, the first object that strikes your attention is a large, flat stone, over which several lamps are suspended, and numerous pilgrims approaching on their knees to kiss it. This is called the Stone of Unction, where the Lord's body was anointed before burial by the

BIRTH OF CHRIST.

holy women. A few yards off is a circular stone, marking the spot where the Virgin Mary stood during the anointment.

Immediately under the dome stands the Holy Sepulchre, surrounded by sixteen large columns, which support the gallery above. The sepulchre is a small building containing two chambers, built or incased with fine marble; you are expected to remove your shoes previous to entering: the outer chamber is about six feet by ten, in the middle of which stands a block of polished stone, about a foot and a half square, where the angel sat who announced the glad tidings of the resurrection. Through another passage you enter the tomb itself. Whether this be or be not the genuine tomb—and we see no reason to doubt it, answering as it does in every particular the description given it in holy writ—it is impossible to enter it without a feeling of holy awe and reverence, remembering that for 1,500 years kings and queens, knights and holy pilgrims, here have knelt and prayed, believing it to be the identical spot " where Christ triumphed over the grave, and disarmed death of his terrors." This is the spot pointed out to the mother of Constantine by the persecuted Christians, and here she erected a church; here the Latin kings, Godfrey and Baldwin, with countless numbers of knights who have died for the Holy Cross, have knelt and prayed. Who would not reverence the spot! The tomb is about six feet square; one-half of it is occupied by the sarcophagus, which rises about two feet from the floor; this is of white marble, slightly tinged with blue; that is, this slab covers the elevation left in the hewing of the rock, which was the custom in those days. The marble is now cracked through about the centre. On this stone the body of Christ was laid; on this stone the young man was found sitting; and here Mary saw the two angels. There are forty-two lamps, gold and silver, presented by sovereigns of Europe, suspended above it, and continually burning. At the head of the tomb stands a Greek monk, reading prayers. Here continually may be seen poor pilgrims crawling in upon their bended knees, bathing the cold marble with their tears, and sobbing as if their hearts would break.

According to a letter from Jerusalem, printed in a recent periodical, there are many persons in the city who hold extreme or fanciful views on religious topics. Eighteen Americans, it is said, arrived there recently to await the second coming of the Lord. They are respectable, educated and apparently wealthy persons, and are to be followed by others. For many years a half-crazy Englishman, dressed in grave-clothes, and carrying a wooden cross on his shoulders, was wont to address crowds of people in the market-places of the city. He recently died of fever. A German woman, who regarded herself as "the bride of Christ," and who had prepared costly dresses in which to receive her Lord, went away to the Jordan recently and never returned. She died, and was buried by the natives. A young man is now in Jerusalem to whom it has been revealed that the Ark of the Covenant is buried in what is known as the Potter's Field. He is searching for it assiduously. Another, who is described as "a rather gentlemanlike young Jew," has arrived at Jerusalem, and claims to be the Messiah.

Syria is frequently mentioned in the Bible. About the time of Christ it became a Roman province. At this period its capital was Antioch, which was one of the most splendid cities in the world. Damascus, another city of Syria, 136 miles northward of Jerusalem, appears to have been known ever since the time of Abraham. This city was famous in later times for making

CHURCH OF THE HOLY SEPULCHRE.

the best swords, sabres and other cutlery; but the art which the people once possessed is now lost. The inhabitants of this city were also celebrated for manufacturing beautiful silks, to which the name of damask was given, from the place where they were made. Another place in Syria mentioned in the Bible was Tadmor, sometimes called "Tadmor in the Desert;" this was built by Solomon for the convenience of his traders; it was ten miles in extent, but it is now in ruins. The splendid remains of this place, consisting of columns and other things beautifully sculptured in stone, show that it must have been a rich and powerful city. In modern times it is called Palmyra.

At the distance of thirty-seven miles north-west of Damascus are the remains of Baalbec, a very splendid city in the time of the apostles, and then called Heliopolis. It is now in ruins, and contains scarcely more than a thousand inhabitants.

It has been said, that "if all the ruins of ancient Rome that are in and around the modern city were gathered together in one group, they would not equal in extent the ruins of Baalbec.

> "No, not in Egypt's ruined land,
> Nor 'mid the Grecian isles,
> Tower monuments so vast, so grand,
> As Baalbec's early piles;
> Baalbec, thou City of the Sun,
> Why art thou silent, mighty one?"

Along the border of the Mediterranean sea lay what was known in ancient times as Phœnicia. It contained the cities of Tyre, Sidon, Ptolemais and other celebrated places. Tyre is probably one of the most ancient cities of the world, having been founded 2,700 years before the Christian era. It contains a population of 4,000 inhabitants, half Christians and half Mahometans. The present town of Sidon consists of a few narrow and dirty streets, and presents nothing of interest to the traveller. Ptolemais is now called Acre. It was besieged by Bonaparte in 1799, and he would have carried it but for the arrival of Sir Sydney Smith, the British general.

Arabia consists of several separate states or nations. The whole country is bounded on the north by Palestine, Mesopotamia, etc.; on the east by the Persian gulf and the Gulf of Ormuz; on the south by the Indian ocean, and west by the Red sea. The Arabs have always been wandering tribes, and have dwelt in tents, amid the trackless deserts which cover a large portion of their country. Their early history is very imperfectly known.

To the east of Syria lie the rivers Euphrates and Tigris, and about this region was Assyria, the first of the great empires of the earth. Ashur, the grandson of Noah, was the first ruler of Assyria. In the year 2221 B. C., that is, before Christ, he built the city of Nineveh, and surrounded it with walls a hundred feet high. It was likewise defended by fifteen hundred towers, each two hundred feet in height. The city was so large that a person would have travelled sixty miles merely in walking round it. In the year 606 B. C., the King of the Medes and the King of Babylon united their forces and made war on Assyria. They captured Nineveh and overturned the empire, which from this time became extinct. The conquerors completely destroyed Nineveh, and in a few centuries it was almost forgotten. Its site became a mere heap of ruins, and these were at last so covered with soil that the place where Nineveh was built became a matter of doubt. But a few years since, an Englishman by the name of Layard caused excavations to be made on the east bank of the Tigris, near the present town of Mosul, and here he found the ruins of a superb palace, supposed to be that of Sennacherib. This spot is now known to be the site of the ancient Nineveh. Many curious things have been found here, which show how the ancient Assyrians worshipped, and how they made war, and how they dressed themselves, and many other interesting things.

The city of Babylon, two hundred and fifty miles south of Nineveh, and which was founded about the same time as that city, was superior to it, both

HILLAH, ON THE EUPHRATES.

in size and beauty. It was situated on the river Euphrates. The walls were so thick that six chariots drawn by horses could be driven abreast upon the top, without danger of falling off on either side.

In the city of Babylon there were magnificent gardens, belonging to the royal palace. They were constructed in such a manner that they appeared to be hanging in the air without resting on the earth. They contained large trees and all kinds of fruits and flowers. There was also a splendid temple dedicated to Belus, or Baal, who was the chief idol of the Babylonians. This temple was six hundred and sixty feet high, and it contained a golden image of Belus, forty feet in height. A modern town called Hillah has been built upon the place where Babylon stood.

Babylon fell before the conquering arms of Cyrus, the King of Persia. Persia itself was conquered by the Saracens A. D. 632. Persia then became a part of the Saracen Empire. It was ruled by the caliphs, who resided at Bagdad, a splendid city which they built on the river Tigris. This celebrated place was founded A. D. 673, and once contained two millions of inhabitants. It was then filled with costly buildings, but these are now mostly in ruins. The modern city is poorly built, and comparatively insignificant.

Bordering upon Persia and Hindostan lies the far-famed valley of Cashmere.

> "Who has not heard of the vale of Cashmere,
> With its roses, the brightest that earth ever gave,
> Its temples and grottos, and fountains as clear
> As the love-lighted eyes that hang over the wave?
> Oh! to see it at sunset, when warm o'er the lake
> Its splendor at parting a summer eve throws,
> Like a bride full of blushes when lingering to take
> A last look in her mirror at night ere she goes!"—*Lalla Rookh.*

Thus sang the bard as his imagination wandered along the banks of the Indus, among Persian bowers and through the delightful valley of Cashmere. Who can wonder that his soul went out in rapture over the scenes that met his bewildered gaze within this mountain-walled region? Its history goes back, through colossal monuments, chiefly of marble, beyond the dawn of authentic annals. Still its beauty has caused it to be the scene of many a struggle.

The climate of Persia is mild, and the country abounds in beautiful and fragrant trees, shrubs and flowers. The people are less warlike than in former times. The rich live in splendid palaces, and the poor in mud huts. The kingdom is small compared with the vast empire of Xerxes. Persepolis, the ancient capital, is now a heap of ruins. Teheran and Ispahan, the two principal cities, are of comparatively modern date. The king generally resides in the city of Teheran. But he has a beautiful palace at Ispahan, called the Palace of Forty Pillars. Each of the forty pillars is supported by four lions of white marble. The whole edifice looks as if it were built of pearl and silver and gold and precious stones

AVENUE OF TEMPLES.

INDIA.

OF the earliest period of the history of India little is known with certainty. The sacred writings of the Hindoos give to their ancient history an incredible chronology, extending over millions of years, and treat of heroes, kings and dignitaries, in most instances probably merely mythical or fabulous. It is the general opinion of the best authorities that the Hindoos were not the first inhabitants of the country, but were an invading race, who subdued and enslaved the aborigines, who are still represented by rude tribes in the central and southern parts of India.

It is not known at what period this invasion took place, but it was undoubtedly prior to the fourteenth century B. C. The language of the conquerors was probably the Sanskrit, in which their sacred books were written. The Vedas, supposed to have been compiled about the fourteenth century B. C., are esteemed the holiest.

Two great dynasties—the kings of the race of the sun, and the race of the moon—figure in the legends of their early history, and their contests are recorded in the poem known as the "Mahabharata." The most celebrated of these sovereigns was Rama, or Ramchunder, who is supposed to have lived in the twelfth or thirteenth century B.C. His deeds are the subject of the great epic poem, the "Ramayana." The "Ramayana" is the oldest of all epic poems. The "Mahabharata" contains two hundred thousand sixteen-syllable lines, and fills four thick quarto volumes.

The first event in the history of India of which we have an authentic account was the invasion by the Persians, under King Darius, about 518–521 B.C. Long before the invasion of India by Alexander the Great, the Greeks travelled there in search of knowledge; for there, more than two thousand four hundred years ago, says Voltaire, "the celebrated Pilpay wrote his moral fables, that have since been translated into all languages. All subjects whatever have been treated, by way of fable or allegory, by the Orientals, and particularly the Indians." Hence it is that Pythagoras, who studied among them, and Pachymeres, a Greek of the thirteenth century, expressed themselves in the spirit of Indian parables.

India had long been subject to the Persians, and Alexander, the avenger of Greece and the conqueror of Darius, led his army into that part of India which had been tributary to his enemy. Though his soldiers were averse to penetrating into a region so remote and unknown, Alexander had read in the ancient fables of Macedonia that Bacchus and Hercules, each a son of Jupiter, as he believed himself to be, had marched as far, so he determined not to be outdone by them; and thus the year 327 B.C. saw his legions entering India by what is now called the Candahar route, the common track of the ancient caravans from northern India to Agra and Ispahan, after encountering incredible difficulties, and surmounting innumerable dangers.

"Few great things have had a smaller beginning than that stupendous anomaly," the British Empire in India. It was in the course of 1612, in the reign of James, that the agents of the company timidly established their first little factory at Surat. At this period, the nominal sovereigns of the whole of India, and the real masters and tyrants of a good part of it, were the Mahometanized Mogul Tartars—a people widely different in origin, manners, law and religion from the Hindoos, the aboriginal or ancient inhabitants of the country.

In 1744, France and England being at war in Europe, hostilities broke out between the English and French in India. Clive came to the front on the part of the former, while Bussy displayed admirable generalship on the part of the latter. In the year 1756 Surajah Dowlah seized upon Calcutta, and clapped 146 of the English into the "Black Hole," where all but twenty-three persons perished in a single night by suffocation.

The student of the modern history of India is familiar with the names of Warren Hastings, who was elected governor-general of India, Hyder Ali, and his son, Tippoo Saib. Lord Cornwallis, who figured so prominently during our War of Independence, conducted a war against Tippoo Saib with such energy that he compelled the latter to cede about one-half of his dominion and to pay in money $16,000,000. In the war which broke out in 1803 between the English and the Mahrattas, Sir Arthur Wellesley, the Duke of Wellington of the future and hero of Waterloo, did signal service, making a name that was afterward to be emblazoned on the bead-roll of illustrious warriors.

The annexation of Sinde, in 1843, was followed by the wars with the Sikhs, who had been organized into a powerful military state by their great sovereign, Runjeet Singh. These hostilities led to the annexation by the English of the Punjaub.

The next important event in the history of India was one which attracted the attention of mankind in all quarters of the globe, and forms, unquestionably, the most impressive incident in the annals of British India. This was the great Sepoy revolt.

The year 1857-8 was the Hindoo sumbut 1914, in which fell the centenary of Plassy, and Hindoo astrologers had long predicted that in this year the power of the East India Company would terminate for ever. In the early part of 1857 it became apparent that a mutinous spirit had crept into the Bengal army. The military authorities had resolved to arm the Sepoys with Enfield rifles, and a new kind of cartridge, greased, in order to adapt it to the rifle-bore, was introduced into many of the schools of musketry instruction. A report spread among the native troops that, as the cartridges in loading had to be torn with the teeth, the government was about to compel them to bite the fat of pigs and of cows, the former of which would be a defilement to a Mussulman, and the latter would be a sacrilege in the eyes of a Hindoo. The wildest excitement prevailed for a time, but the substitution of the old for the new cartridges temporarily prevented an outbreak. Meanwhile, though the greased cartridges had not been used elsewhere, the cry of danger to caste and creed was raised in many other stations. Disturbances occurred on February 19th at Burrampoor, on March 29th at Barrachpoor, where the first blood of the revolt was shed—the leader in the revolt being a private Sepoy in the Thirty-fourth Regiment, named Mungal Pandy—and April 24th at Meerut.

On May 10th a formidable rising took place at the latter station. The Europeans were massacred, and the mutineers marched to Delhi, where the garrison fraternized with them, and a second butchery was committed. In the north-west provinces simultaneous risings took place, and Benares, the sacred city on the Ganges, was in revolt on June 4th. On June 27th took place the horrible massacre at Cawnpore, under Nana Sahib, Rajah of Bithoor. Lucknow, the capital of Oude, mutinied. The Punjaub was saved by the administrative capacity of Sir John Laurence. The Presidency of Bombay was but little disturbed, and that of Madras was tranquil with scarcely an exception. Delhi was stormed September 14th, after a siege of three months. Two sons and two grandsons of the king were made prisoners by Captain Hodson, who shot them with his own hand. Cawnpore and Lucknow were taken from the rebels, and Gwalior was the last great battle of the campaign. The whole population was disarmed in the course of the spring and summer. One thousand three hundred and twenty-seven forts were destroyed, and 1,367,406 stand of arms captured. Of the number of Europeans killed and wounded during this mutiny no accurate estimate can be procured. Hundreds of English women and children were put to death after the most horrible outrages.

During the mutiny of 1857, the British garrison in Lucknow, numbering about 1,700 men, was besieged by about 10,000 mutineers. After twelve weeks' defence, during which the British lost Sir Henry Laurence, their commander, and suffered from the ravages of cholera, small-pox and fevers scarcely less than from fire and assaults of the enemy, Generals Havelock and Outram fought their way in with a relieving force, September 25th. The defence was now resumed with fresh vigor, Sir James Outram, as senior officer, taking the command. On November 17th, Sir Colin Campbell reached the city with reinforcements. A few days later the residency was evacuated, the British withdrawing by night to the Dilkoosha, where, on the 25th, Sir Henry Havelock died of dysentery. General Outram was left with a division at Alumbagh—the king's summer palace, about four miles from the residency—to watch the enemy, and the rest retired in safety to Cawnpore. In January, 1858, Outram was subjected to desperate attacks at the Alumbagh by 30,000 rebels, whom he defeated with about one-tenth that number of troops; and on February 21st, with six guns, and not quite 400 men, he routed another force of 20,000 troops.

LUCKNOW.

In the meantime the insurgents had fortified Lucknow, and occupied it with a large force. Early in March they were besieged by Sir Colin Campbell, who effected a partial entrance on the 4th; but the capture was not complete until the 21st, when the city was abandoned by the enemy.

One of the most striking events of this struggle was the ending of the great Mogul Empire in India.

The first of the Moguls who figures in Indian history was the great Tamerlane, who, in 1398, overran Bengal, captured Delhi and fixed upon it as his seat of government. But he never completed the subjugation of the country; other conquests and designs called him away, and it was reserved for his descendant, Zahir Eddin Mahomet Baber, to complete what Timour had begun, and to be the founder of the Mogul dynasty in India in the year 1519.

In the seventeenth century the power and prosperity of the Moguls attained their height; but toward its end the tide of the Mogul power began to

BOMBAY.

ebb. In the eighteenth century rebellion broke out in different portions of India, and the inhabitants obtained their independence. The Persians also invaded Bengal, captured Delhi, massacred the inhabitants and bore away plunder to the amount of $600,000,000. Meanwhile, the English, who had outstripped all their European competitors in India, were rapidly increasing in power; and the result of the now inevitable struggle between the Mogul Empire, under a succession of effete and incapable monarchs, and the East India Company, represented by such men as Clive, Hastings, Coote, Wellesley and Lake, could not be long doubtful.

At length, in 1803, the Mogul emperors became simply pensioners of the British East India Company. The last emperor, Abul Muguffer, became monarch in 1837, but was then past his sixtieth year, and he held his empty title merely by British sufferance.

But when the terrible mutiny of 1857 broke out, the revolted Sepoys flocked into Delhi from the adjacent stations, and proclaimed his restoration to the throne of his fathers.

Accordingly, when Delhi was stormed on the 14th of September, the first care of the British was to possess themselves of the person of the aged monarch, who, with a crowd of terror-stricken followers, had taken refuge in the tomb of his ancestor, Humayun. Never was the capture of an emperor effected under such extraordinary circumstances. No successful rival, surrounded by his adherents; no victorious general at the head of his troops, was there to demand his sword. The handful of conquerors were scattered far and wide over the vast city they had just captured; and a single British subaltern rode to the entrance of the tomb, and dragged forth the last of the Moguls from among the cowering multitude that dared not lift a hand in his defence.

Let the historian of the Sepoy war describe the scene: "So Hodson went forth and stood before all, in the open space near the beautiful gateway of the tomb, a solitary white man among so many, awaiting the surrender of a king, and the total extinction of a dynasty the most magnificent that the world had ever seen. It was then but a title, a tradition; but still the monarch of the Moguls was a living influence in the hearts of the Mahometans of India. And truly a grander historical picture was rarely seen than that of the single British subaltern receiving the sword of the last of the Mogul emperors in the midst of a multitude of followers and retainers, grieving for the downfall of the house of Tamerlane and the ruin of their own fortunes."

After his capture he was tried by a court-martial, and sentenced to transportation for life, Rangoon being chosen as his place of exile. He died there on November 11th, 1862, and beneath the shadow of the golden pagoda lie the remains of the last of the Great Moguls.

The extreme length of India, from north to south, is 1,900 miles, and its extreme breadth from east to west, exclusive of British Burmah, about 1,700 miles. The Empire of India, with its feudatory states, embraces a territory of 1,556,836 square miles, with a population of not less than two hundred millions. The climate varies from that of the temperate zone in the Himalayas to the tropical heat of the lowlands; on the central and southern tablelands the climate is comparatively mild, the thermometer falling as low as the freezing point in winter. During the rainy season the fall of rain in Bengal is from fifty to eighty inches. The north-east monsoon begins about the middle of October, and brings rain from the Bay of Bengal, which falls in torrents on the Coromandel coast until the middle or end of December, during which period the opposite coast of the peninsula enjoys fair weather and northerly breezes. From December to June is the dry season, during which little rain falls.

In many districts of India splendid monuments of architecture abound, mostly the work of past ages, and many of remote antiquity, such as the temples of Jain and Ajmeer, and elsewhere, some of which were built long before the Christian era, and are distinguished not only for size and splendor of ornamentation, but for symmetry, beauty of proportion and refinement of taste. The mosques, palaces and tents erected by the Mahometan emperors are the finests pecimens of the Saracenic style of architecture in the world. Those at Agra, Delhi and Lucknow are especially remarkable for their delicacy, beauty and taste. The most wonderful structures in the country are probably the great rock temples in the western part of Deccan and those near Bombay.

A bishop, whose exquisite taste enabled him to appreciate the beauties of Hindoo architecture, has remarked: "These pagans build like giants, and finish off their work like jewellers."

HINDOO GODS.

Benares is celebrated as being the ecclesiastical capital of the Hindoos. It has been appropriately termed the Mecca of the Hindoos. A true Brahmin regards it as the holiest spot on earth, and believes that future blessedness is secure to the worst of men who are fortunate enough to die within its precincts. Hundreds of invalids are brought to Benares to be sanctified by so enviable a death. Even the water of the sacred Ganges is holier here than elsewhere, and quantities of it are taken from the ghauts and conveyed by pious pilgrims to every part of India.

Calcutta is the principal city in India, and has been termed, on account of its magnificent buildings, "The City of Palaces." The two other great cities of India are Madras and Bombay.

The religion of the Hindoos is Brahminism, which teaches them that there is one principal deity, called Brahma, and several other inferior deities, called Vishnu, Siva, etc. They make strange images of these, and worship them. The priests are called Brahmins, and instruct the people in many vain ceremonies and cruel superstitions.

Vishnu, however, is by many looked upon as the greatest of all gods, and many remarkable stories are told of him, and of his coming into this world, which shows the stupendous character of the Hindoo mythology. Once, when a child, under the name of Krishna, he is said to have swallowed some dirt, and his brothers ran and told their mother. She commanded him to open his mouth, so that she could see if they were telling the truth. He opened it, and she saw there THE THREE WORLDS!

At another time a wicked and cruel giant had obtained supreme control from heaven down to hell. Vishnu came to him as a dwarf, begging alms. Bali, the giant, contemptuously asked the shrinking beggar what he wanted. Only three steps of the great giant's dominions were timidly asked.

> "The blinded Bali, mocking, gave assent,
>   And looked upon him with contemptuous eye.
> Swift grew the dwarf through such immense extent,
>   That *one* step spanned the earth, one *more*, the sky!
>
> "Then, looking round, with haughty voice he said,
>   'The *third* where shall I take? O, Bali, tell!'
> At Vishnu's feet the tyrant placed his head,
>   And instantaneously was thrust to hell."

It is also said that once Brahma, Vishnu and Siva had a dispute as to which was the greatest. Vishnu said that he would yield the palm of greatness to whoever would reach to the crown of his head or down to the soles of his feet. For fifty million years Brahma soared like lightning upwards, and Siva like lightning dived downwards for the same length of time; but the one could not reach the head, nor the other the foot. As a consequence, when they returned, they both paid due allegiance to Vishnu.

The "Car of Juggernaut," or (more properly) Jagannatha, and the supposed enormous loss of life by devotees allowing its wheels to run over them, is familiar to all readers of the life and religion of Hindostan; but the stories of it have no real foundation in fact. These misrepresentations have been repeated until they have received implicit credence over the whole globe, and the name of "Juggernaut" is associated only with what is cruel and sanguinary. Whenever there is a sympathetic murderous destruction of human life to be denounced, "Juggernaut" becomes the type of such acts, and is called upon to do duty by all writers and public speakers. It is scarcely possible to conceive a more complete perversion of the truth; and it may be stated that Jagannatha would to a certainty get heavy damages in any court, were he to prosecute his defamers.

Jagannatha's relation to the Hindoo mythology will partly explain his true nature. He is one of the manifestations of Vishnu, and is supposed to be the same as Krishna. The forms under which Vishnu is worshipped are more or less connected with love, while the manifestations of Siva are, on the contrary, of a fierce and terrible kind. Had the character given to Jagannatha been attributed to Siva, something like justification might be found for it.

There is a well-known legend which illustrates the character of these deities. Among the innumerable gods of the Hindoo Pantheon a discussion had arisen as to the reputation of the principal personages. One of the Devas at last proposed to try a practical test by which the matter might be settled. So he went up and kicked Siva. The result was terrible; that god burst into a wild passion and destroyed millions of worlds before he calmed down again. The Deva then kicked Brahma. This deity became angry; he grumbled and growled a little, but did nothing in particular. The Deva then approached Vishnu, who was asleep, but awoke instantly on being kicked. He caught the foot that had given the blow and, stroking it with his hand, said he hoped it was not hurt, at the same time manifesting a warm anxiety, as if he had been the cause of pain to the Deva, or as if he had done him an injury.

HINDOO MUSICIAN.

During the Car Festival self-immolation takes place. This, also, has been very much exaggerated. Hamilton, in his "Gazetteer," states, "that during the four years prior to 1820 only three cases occurred, one said to be accidental, and the other two to get rid of excruciating diseases with which the victims were tormented." If this is anything like a fair estimate of the death-rate, there need be no hesitation in asserting, on the basis of statistics, that the railroad car is a much more bloodthirsty institution than the car of Jagannatha.

The Thugs derive their nomenclature from the Hindoo word *thugna*, which means "to deceive," and were a sect of assassins, now happily exterminated by the British government. They roamed about the country in bands of from thirty to 300, and strangled to death such persons as they could decoy into their company. Their atrocious practices were not followed so much from impulses of plunder or malice, as from religious motives. They were worshippers of the goddess Kali, who presided over sensual indulgence and death.

The movements of the professional dancing-women of India are as graceful as they are wonderful. Their agility is something marvellous, and their "*chic*," if occasionally a little too expressive, is decidedly fetching. The nautch or dancing-girls of Calcutta are a separate and distinct corps of dancers. They dress in massive folds of silk down to the ground, and are decorated with a profusion of jewelry—bracelets, bangles and other ornaments. Their movements are wild and voluptuous, but seldom pass the bounds of modesty, as some writers have stated.

Another class of dancers are the egg-dancers—girls who, dressed in scanty but gorgeous attire, place eggs, on the ends of sugar-canes radiating from a circular frame adjusted to a pad on the head, dancing the while to the music of the tom-tom, and whirling round and round till the eyes of the on-lookers become giddy in the gazing. The egg-dance is a very quaint and curious performance, and one which no visitor to India should fail to see.

The Vale of Cashmere is undoubtedly the most beautiful and picturesque landscape in the world—a vast park, some ninety miles long by from thirty to forty wide. Everything appears arranged by a superhuman hand to delight the eye; fair fields and habitations; rivers and lakes interspersed with verdant and flowery isles; "the low whispering in boats" of all shapes and sizes, plied by Hanjis with intelligent countenances, shapely forms and costumes harmonizing most beautifully with that enchanting prospect; countless streams and canals winding along through waving rice-fields and green banks, whose limpid and rippling waters glisten in the sun like bands of silver. Hence it is that Mogul despots, so fierce elsewhere, seem to melt into human beings during their sojourn in Cashmere. These tyrants, like Nero, had artistic aspirations. Enchanted with the beautiful land, they took pride in embellishing it still more by erecting palaces and mosques, arranging terraces and laying out parks in the most picturesque sites, and by liberally rewarding poets for singing the delights of that enchanting abode. No wonder the Moguls called it the earthly paradise of the Indies, and that Akbar strove so hard to wrest it from its lawful kings. It is related that Jehan-Guir, his son and successor, took such a fancy to this beautiful region that he could never leave it, and that he declared that the loss of his crown would affect him less than that of Cashmere.

Through the influence of the British government young married ladies have no longer before them the horrible prospect of being burned to death upon the funeral piles of their husbands. This inhuman custom, so long prevalent in this region, only began to disappear quite recently, for in 1843, on the death of Soonchet-Sing, uncle of the Maharajah, the *five hundred wives* which constituted his principal harem were burned alive with his body at Ramnagar, and twenty-five others, that he had at Jummoo, shared the same fate. In 1863 another similar immolation took place at the violent and mysterious death of Jowahir-Singh, the Maharajah's cousin. Thirty-two of his widows were consumed with the remains of their late husband. On another occasion a solitary widow is described by an English tourist as sitting on a funeral pile with her husband's head upon her lap. Seized with terror at the approach of the hissing flames, she sprang from the pile and sought to escape, but the attending priests, horrified at her scandalous conduct, caught her and threw her back upon the burning pile, where she perished, uttering screams that would have moved the hardest hearts.

HINDOO PRINCESS.

The Cashmerians are a stout, well-formed people, of Hindoo stock. Their complexion is brunette, and the women are very handsome. The Mahometan women are seldom seen abroad, and then so closely veiled are they that it is almost impossible to get even the slightest glimpse of their hidden beauties. The Hanji women, on the contrary, never cover their faces, and are remarkably handsome in childhood; but as they soon share their husband's occupation (that of boatmen), and live mostly in the open air, their beauty fades very rapidly, but their features never cease to be attractive. The Cashmerians, as a rule, are brave, active and industrious, and fond of music, literature and art. Their language offers many curious analogies with the Sanscrit, but their songs are in Persian.

The Hanji class is that with which tourists are brought most in contact. They are, perhaps, the best of the Cashmerians, and their disposition is not unlike that of the Venetian gondoliers. There is the same charm about them, the same vivacity, the same wealth of imagination. The Cashmerian nobles find much pleasure in their boats, and on pleasant evenings may be heard

> "Sounds from the lake, the low whispering in boats
> As they shoot through the moonlight, the dipping of oars,
> And the wild, airy warbling that everywhere floats
> Through the groves, round the islands, as if the shores,
> Like those of Kathay, uttered music, and gave
> An answer in song to the kiss of each wave.
> But the gentlest of all are those sounds full of feeling
> That soft from the lute of some lover are stealing—
> Some lover who knows all the heart-touching power
> Of a lute and a sigh in this magical hour."

An enthusiastic author thus writes concerning India, and there is little doubt but that he has simply given utterance to what many have felt who have studied the literature and meditated upon the history of its remarkable people:

"Weary of the misery songs of the Western World, weary of its air and steam and pain, weary of polemics and wire-drawn romance and faded sentiment! Art thou weary of all this? When that hour comes take refuge in India of the olden time, where the gazelle starts in the quiet noontide at the footstep of the solemn-eyed Brahmin. In the infinitely deep, solemnly joyful India, where man for the first and last time declared and determined to himself what was eternal truth, and in that faith lived and died. In that glorious India which gave to the world a glorious drama, like that of Shakespeare, and the most perfect, sublime poem ever written, in the Mahabahrata —a poem before which the highest flight of Milton is trifling and the genius of the whole West feeble."

THE SACRED ALTAR OF HEAVEN, PEKIN.

CHINA.

THE territory of the Chinese Empire is nearly the same at the present day that it has been for several centuries. It is bounded on the north by Asiatic Russia, on the east by the Pacific ocean, and on the south by the Chinese sea and Farther India. On the west there are many mountains and sandy deserts, which divide it from Thibet and Tartary.

This empire is very ancient, and has continued longer than any other that has ever existed. It is the most populous empire in the world, containing about three hundred and fifty millions of people. Its history goes back four thousand years from the present time. The name of its founder was Fohi, whom some writers suppose to have been the same as Noah.

There have been twenty-two dynasties, or separate families of emperors, who have successively ruled over China. Yet few of the emperors did anything worthy of remembrance.

The Emperor Ching, who reigned about two thousand years ago, built a great wall in order to protect his dominions against the Tartars. It was forty-five feet high, and eighteen feet thick, and it extended over mountains and valleys, a distance of fifteen hundred miles. This wall still remains, though in a ruinous state. When Ching had completed the wall, he thought himself so very great an emperor that none of his predecessors were worth remembering. He therefore ordered all the historical writings and public records to be burnt. He also caused four hundred learned men, who were addicted to writing histories, to be buried alive. Ching survived this wholesale destruction but a short time, dying after an illness of only three days, in the year 210 B. C.

From this time the empire was devastated by civil wars, and dynasties succeeded each other with great rapidity. There were fourteen between the years 207 B. C. and A. D. 1279. At this time Kubla Khan invaded China with an immense army of Tartars. He and his descendants conquered the whole empire, and the latter governed it for many years.

The Emperor Ching-tsa ascended thet hrone three or four centuries ago. A mine was discovered during his reign, and precious stones of great value were dug out of it. Some of them were brought to the emperor, but he looked scornfully at them. "Do you call these precious stones?" cried he. "What are they good for? They can neither clothe the people, nor satisfy their hunger." So saying, he ordered the mine to be closed up, and the miners to be employed in some more useful kind of labor.

About a hundred years ago, in the reign of Yong-tching, there was the most terrible earthquake that had ever been known. It shook down nearly all the houses in the city of Pekin, and buried one hundred thousand people. A still greater number perished in the surrounding country.

In 1840 a war between Great Britain and China broke out, which continued for two years. The British government sent an expedition against the Chinese, which took Canton and several other places. The war continued till 1842, when peace was made. Soon after a treaty of commerce was made between China and the United States. Mr. Cushing went to China and negotiated this treaty on the part of our country. It is said that he was one day invited by a mandarin to dinner. Mr. Cushing was curious to know what a particular dish was, and not speaking Chinese, inquired: "Quack?—quack, quack?" The mandarin understood him, and, shaking his head solemnly, replied: "Bow-wow!"

In 1852 a great insurrection began in China, headed by a native Chinese, Tae-ping-wang. This man had acquired some notion of the Bible, and in his proclamations he set forth some doctrines similar to those of Christianity. This rebellion was not suppressed until July, 1864, when Nankin, which had been made the rebel capital, was taken, and Tae-ping-wing committed suicide. During the progress of this rebellion, China was for a short time engaged in wars with England and France.

The most famous man China has ever produced was Confucius, who was born about five hundred years before Christ. He was a learned man, and had many disciples or scholars, who attended his lectures and travelled about with him. He composed several books, which are held in great reverence, even to this day, by the learned Chinese.

Pekin, the capital of the Chinese Empire, was built many centuries before the Christian era, though the exact date of its foundation is unknown. Its name signifies the "Court of the North." It consists of four distinct divisions, which are distinguished by the following names: First, Kin-ching, or the prohibited city, containing only the palaces of the emperor and the dwellings of his immediate retainers; second, Hwang-ching, or the imperial city; third, Nin-ching, surrounded by a wall sixty feet high and forty feet broad at the top; fourth, Wai-ching, the Chinese city, with a wall thirty feet high and twelve feet in breadth. In the prohibited city are many artificial lakes, fountains, hanging gardens, pavilions and flower-beds.

CHINESE HANGING GARDEN

Weird legends connected with the city of Foo-chow are numerous. It is said that a king of Foo-chow was once on his way up the mountain-side, attended by some of his soldiers. A very holy priest was sitting with his legs crossed, in devout meditation, directly in the king's path. A soldier commanded him to get out of the way; but he remained imperturbably in his place. At a second, and more vehement command, he got out of the way, but in such a manner as to astonish the whole company. He rose directly up into the air for a considerable distance. The king begged him to descend, and promised to give him whatever he might ask. The modest priest responded with a simple request for as much ground as he could cover

INTERIOR OF A CHINESE TEMPLE.

with his robe. This was readily granted, and the priest began to spread out his robe, when, lo! it expanded as he spread, until it covered the whole mountain-side, and the fields below, clear to the river. Thus it was that Koo-shan became consecrated ground.

In a shady dell, not far from the monastery, is a trickling rill, with high sides of precipitous rock. The appearance of the bed of the rill impresses one with the idea that it must some time have been a stream of considerable size. The legend is, that a devout priest was once seated in meditation near the stream, and being disturbed by the noise of its waters, called out, "*Hak!*" (Stop!) Immediately the rush of waters ceased, and ever since the stream has been only an insignificant rill.

Another legend tells how a pious priest died, and after his death his hair continued to grow. Barber after barber was summoned to shave it, but could not succeed. At last a sister of his, living many miles away, heard of the trouble, and made a pilgrimage to Koo-shan. When she arrived the dead man opened his eyes. She announced her purpose of shaving his head, which she did with entire success. She promised to return periodically and perform this kind office, which promise she faithfully kept until she was sixty years old, when she asked him what he would do when she died. The old man made no answer, but wept; and from that period his hair ceased to grow.

On leaving the foreign settlement for the city, which is three miles away, we enter upon a granite bridge, with forty solid buttresses placed at irregular distances, and connected by stones three feet square, and varying in length from twenty-five to forty-five feet. On these, as sleepers, are laid the stones which constitute the platform of the bridge. It has granite railings, mortised into granite posts. For nearly a thousand years has this bridge resounded to the steady tramp of the multitudes, crossing and recrossing; and it seems ready for another thousand years of service. So dense is the throng that we sometimes find it difficult to keep our footing. Here is a peddler of wonderful salve, cutting his own flesh to show the marvellous curative properties of his salve. Here is a dentist, with a string of hundreds of teeth, the evidence of his skill. He pulls no teeth with cruel forceps, however, but puts a corroding powder about the tooth, which loosens it from the gum, until it can be taken out with the fingers. Here, too, are men with eyes and noses eaten away by disease, piteous applicants for charity. But the bridge is passed, and we plunge into the main street leading to the city. It is only about ten feet wide. There are no wagons or carriages. All the carrying of persons or goods is done by men. The coolies carrying the sedan-chairs, and moving at a rapid pace, call out to the burden-bearers who are in the way, according to the burdens carried, either "Slop-buckets, out of the way!" or, "Turnips, to one side!" or, "Opium, give us the road!"

Generally the crowd is good-natured, but once in a while there will occur a brisk fisticuff battle between coolies who have come into collision. On either side the street are stores and shops, some common enough, and others handsome and elegant. Swinging signs in front bear such high-sounding titles as "Perpetual Longevity," "Myriad Profits," "Flourishing Prosperity." Here is the "Eternal Happiness Oil-store," and there is the "Celestial Fragrance Drug-store,"

In time of a lunar eclipse, the people turn out with gongs, drums, old tin pans, and anything else that will make a noise, and beat away with great vigor. If the eclipse is total, as the darkness increases, the pounding becomes more vehement and excited; and when the whole surface is obscured the din is perfectly terrific. Men shout, "Drum away! Pound away! The dragon has the moon all inside his mouth now. If we don't make him give it up, it will be gone forever!" Then, as more and more of the moon's surface comes out clear, they encourage each other to keep on until the dreaded dragon is compelled to yield it up entirely. When finally the moon sails off fair and clear through the heavens, they go off home with gongs and drums under

CHINESE LOCOMOTION.

their arms, in the happy consciousness of duty discharged, and congratulating one another that the moon is saved for future usefulness.

A curious wheelbarrow used by the Chinese is worth noting. The vehicle is weighted upon each side, and requires nice adjustment and skill in its use. Two persons, one on each side, balancing the other, may thus travel. Sometimes an improvised sail is added for the purpose of assisting the driver in propelling it.

Of the moral character of the Chinese it may be said that they are a very industrious people, and habitually gentle in their manners and behavior; but that, with a curious inconsistency often seen in heathen nations, their punishments are of incredible barbarity. The most shocking pictures of Chinese tortures are to be met with, such indeed as are enough to give us the nightmare. What, then, must be the strange state of mind of those who inflict them.

But if the Chinaman is indifferent to torture inflicted on criminals, he is equally so to physical pain inflicted on those he may be supposed to love—his female children, whose little feet he confines, in accordance with a preposterous notion of beauty, until the members are permanently dwarfed. Little feet are considered a distinguishing beauty of Chinese women, and a walk like that which may be supposed to belong to the "swaying willow," is their ideal of a graceful deportment.

One notable event of 1868 was the arrival of an embassy from China, the

CHINESE FAMILY.

first ever sent by that exclusive empire to any foreign power. Its head was Honorable Anson Burlingame, an American citizen, and lately his country's representative in China. He had so commanded the confidence of the Chinese government that the emperor had induced him to undertake this important mission, not only to the United States, but to several European courts. The Chinese had begun to cross the Pacific in great numbers, to find employment in California and the inland mining States. A treaty, now concluded between the Asiatic Empire and the American Republic, guaranteed security of life, liberty and property to the people of either nation while in the territory of the other.

Formerly Mongolia, the Corea, Cochin China, Siam, Burmah and Thibet were all tributary to China, and sent ambassadors to Pekin to acknowledge their dependence. Thus China was completely surrounded by a chain of smaller tributary states, and this fact helped to establish the belief that the Emperor of China was emperor of the whole world, as even now represented in popular editions of Chinese maps, on which China occupies nearly the whole sheet, leaving Japan, the Philippines and Europe to be represented by small dots. These maps are accepted and thoroughly believed in by the people in the interior of China. The belief that the Emperor of China rules the world, so earnestly propagated by the Chinese officials, found additional support from the fact of European ambassadors being sent to Pekin; these being understood by the people to be sent like the ambassadors of these tributary states to pay respect and do homage to the Chinese emperor.

As a matter of fact the Chinese government does not derive much pecuniary gain from Thibet, chiefly in duties levied at Ta tsien lu; still it is a mine to the Chinese officials, even though it may be actually a burden pecuniarily to the Chinese government. The burden, however, is compensated for by having another dominion in the empire for the sake of prestige, and this is really why China is so jealous of European enterprise entering Thibet, the Corea, or Tonquin.

An English official in India, once desiring to see the real color of the Thibetan skin, paid the parents of a child to wash it in hot water, several waters, and with unlimited soap. Every effort was vain, the skin could not be reached through such a plating of dirt. It is said, with every show of truth, that it would be impossible to wash an adult Thibetan down to the skin. The beauty of a woman in Thibet consists in her being stout, broad, thick-set and heavily membered, and the accomplishments to be desired are that she should be above all things audacious, a good hand at a bargain and also an adept at repartee.

In Thibet, if a man of means dies while the crops are standing, it would bring hail were he disposed of at that time, so he is pickled to await the harvest. This is done by tying his head between his knees and putting him, surrounded with salt, into a bag. The bag is put in a basket, and the basket is sewn up well in cloth to prevent unpleasantness, and he is placed in the stable under the first floor to await the suitable day. Then, the day being chosen for his incremation, the ecclesiastics commence their prayers, etc., as many days ahead of the day fixed upon as the wealth of the family will allow. The day having arrived, he is cremated on a pile of wood saturated with melted butter to make it burn quickly. After that, there only remains to give a good dinner to the ecclesiastics and settle their bill satisfactorily.

In Burmah and Siam the complexion is of great importance, as the natives wear nothing else until twelve or fourteen years of age, when, if the father is wealthy, they come out in a gaudy-colored silk skirt, or lungi, with a short jacket, and a bright handkerchief for the head; but if poor, they usually have to be contented with a string of glass beads for another year, when they arrive at the dignity of a few yards of cheap cotton cloth.

The Chinese emigration to California has assumed such great dimensions that it ought to be alluded to.

It is not, however, to be wondered at that John Chinaman is no social favorite in California—he is so very ugly! very black of hair, very low of stature, "not a thing of beauty," and, moreover, when he laughs he shows his gums horribly. But he is most patient and industrious, cooks like a Frenchman, does up shirts in the laundry like an artist, and "never forgets to sew on the buttons." His first employment in California was as a house-servant, and he still continues to be largely employed in that capacity.

CHINESE CHILDREN.

He has a passion for learning, and seizes every opportunity of acquiring English. A lady, living in Sacramento, was obliged successively to discharge two young Chinese servants, because they would, the moment her back was turned, mind the spelling-book instead of the wash-tub; and "John" keeps to his high-flown poetical language. "In San Francisco his sign-board literature is a study—Virtue and Felicity, Sincerity and Faith, are common inscriptions over his shop doors." A *restaurateur* styles his place of business the "Garden of the Golden Valley," and a drug store receives the appellation of "Benevolence and Longevity." In short, "John" is to be seen in California keeping intact all the well-known peculiarities of his race—a "silent man in his basket-hat, blue tunic and cloth shoes with wooden soles—this man of the long pigtail and bare neck, the restrained, eager eyes and the yellow, serene, impassive face."

But the worst of him as an emigrant is, that he does not come to stay, and so cannot be educated into a responsible citizen. His whole aim is to accumulate two or three hundred dollars—wealth to him—and then recross the Pacific. He holds the worship of his dead ancestors to be a fundamental part of his religion, and every particle of their dust is sacred. This is the reason of his insuperable objection to the introduction of railways into China; he is afraid they will plough up this sacred dust. So he cannot himself endure the thought of resting elsewhere; and when he dies in California, he leaves strict orders that his "remains," sometimes his embalmed body, but usually his bones (boiled and stripped of flesh, that they may be packed compactly in boxes, to reduce the cost of transportation), shall be sent home, 5,000 miles, for burial, by the company to which he belonged.

JAPAN.

JAPANESE LADY.

JAPAN is an extensive empire, containing 26,000,000 of inhabitants. These live to the east of China, upon several islands, of which Niphon is the largest. The people live crowded together in large cities, and resemble the Chinese in their religion, manners and customs.

It is uncertain whether the ancient nations knew anything of this empire, and its early history is almost unknown. It is probable it has remained with little change for thousands of years. Its existence was first ascertained by the Europeans about the year 1400; but as strangers are not permitted to travel in the country, very little is found out concerning it. A treaty of peace and commerce was made between this country and the United States in 1854.

Japan has a temporal and a spiritual emperor. The first is called the Tycoon; the latter, the Mikado, and he lives in complete seclusion in the little principality of Kioto, where he is venerated as a god and surrounded by a strict ceremonial. The political organization is complicated, the Tycoon having thirteen councillors, five of whom are chosen from vassal princes, thirty-eight from among the hereditary nobility. It is these councillors who really govern, the Tycoon being understood to assent to their propositions; and if he cannot or will not do so, then he is expected to resign in favor of his next heir. In fact, the government is a sort of constitutional monarchy.

The population is divided into castes, which are hereditary, as in ancient Egypt. The vassal princes, the hereditary nobility, the priests, soldiers, doctors, civil functionaries, etc., all following their callings, from father to son. The first four castes only have the right to wear swords and wide trousers. The peasants belong to the soil.

The singular charms of their land have developed an æsthetic side to the character of the people that is discoverable not only in their intense love of flowers, but, indeed, as well in the passionate admiration of attractive views of land and sea. As landscape gardeners they are artists, creating marvels of picturesque beauty on an area of ground that others would think it hopeless to attempt improving. On all the roads and pathways throughout the country, wherever there is an especially fine view to be obtained, a resting-place is to be found, and rustic seats provided for the convenience of the wayfarer; and wherever there is travel sufficient to warrant it, there will be found tea-houses, located at every point of more than ordinary attraction as regards scenery.

The Japanese are lovers of nature in all its phases. Their life may be said to be in full communion with the natural. All their temple grounds, and places devoted to wayside shrines, are indicative of their appreciation of the beautiful. Groves of trees encompass these places. No one is found without its surroundings of forest growth, and in most cases high elevations are selected, from which the view is fine and extended, on which to build their temples. It is the same with the burial-places of the dead. Under the sighing branches of the cedars and pines the dead are placed, to await the final destiny of all things, and their tombs are decorated with garlands and wreaths of fresh flowers, placed by loving and reverent hands.

The religion of the people brings them into unison with nature, because they see their gods in all that surrounds them. Their legends tell of strange manifestations of power in the creation of their land, and the production of what they eat and what their eyes look upon. Gods of the hills and mountains, gods of the sea and gods of the flowers, are to them verities and not conceptions, tangible forms and not myths. In worshipping at nature's shrine they honor the gods. They may be said to be highly civilized, and there is a vigor and originality about their mechanical and artistic work which surpasses that of the kindred Chinese; but they have always raised such obstinate objections to communication with other nations, that it is only of late years we have been able to penetrate the mystery of their political and social condition.

The best idea of the people is to be got from their own artistic productions. Engravings, sketches in Chinese ink and colored prints, are to be bought in the shops of the principal towns; and though the perspective, light, and shade is of a peculiar sort, these works of art are very graphic, and represent all sorts of scenes and ceremonies to which a foreigner could with difficulty get access, if at all.

The Japanese are a somewhat diminutive race, the men being rather over five feet tall, and the women between four and five; showing a considerable disproportion between the two sexes. They have large heads, prominent cheek bones and features of a more regular and intelligent type than that of the Chinese. Their skin is also of different shades of brown, varying from dark to nearly fair; but it is never yellow. The young people and children have a good deal of color. The women of the upper classes are very fair, and esteem a delicate complexion as an evidence of rank; but they never come up to our notions of beauty, on account of their eyes being set too obliquely in the head. This marked peculiarity is observable in all the Japanese

JAPANESE FAMILY.

paintings, of which numerous examples are to be seen in the United States now. The faces of both sexes are, however, mobile, and exhibit great variety in expression; they are therefore more attractive than those of other Asiatic nations.

The Japanese only marries one wife, and the women enter very young upon household cares. These, however, are not so heavy as with us, for the houses contain little or no furniture—unless matting be considered as such—for on matting the Japanese family sits, eats and sleeps. In the morning the citizen puts away his pillows and coverlids, sweeps out his room and all is done. In the evening he shuts up his shutters and pulls out his bedding, and sub-divides his house ingeniously with screens, and all his preparations are made.

The Japanese women wear their hair elaborately dressed, their lips painted, and their necks and faces artistically powdered and painted. A Japanese woman is considered very dowdy-looking, indeed, if her hair is not elaborately arranged; and no matter to what social rank you turn, it is rare, indeed, to find one who does not follow the fashion. A very peculiar custom among them is to shave their eyebrows off. Another custom, but one which the people are gradually dropping, is the blacking of the teeth of married women.

It is very disappointing, at times, to be riding down the street and meet a handsome Japanese woman—and there are many of them—and see her friendly smile suddenly disclose teeth as black as coal. Their walk is very peculiar. They all turn their toes in to such an extent that their walk becomes a perfect waddle—the more exaggerated because of the high clogs they wear. They cling to this style of walking with the greatest tenacity. A few years since a foreigner started a dancing-school in Tokio. He had many pupils, and for a time things went on quite merrily, but a cloud soon arose. The girls' habits of walking prevented them from dancing well, and the teacher commenced teaching them to turn their toes out. They obeyed without a murmur; but the next day the teacher was informed that he might teach the girls to dance, but he must let their walking alone; that it was a national custom to walk in their manner, and it must be followed, and any interference with it would lose him his pupils.

Generally gay and lively, often light and frivolous, the Japanese is disposed to turn everything into pleasantry. He skims over the surface, and rarely goes to the bottom of things. He excels in light criticism, caricatures and humorous conceptions. In politics he makes a clever opposition journalist and a dangerous writer of epigrammatic political pamphlets.

A few years ago the stranger on landing in Japan might have imagined himself transported back to feudal times. Soldiers dressed in coats of mail, and armed with the lance, citizens clothed in long, loose vestments, princely processions, a feudal organization permeating the whole social fabric, and controlling all interests and classes, met him at every turn. The outward signs of this primitive civilization are gradually fading away. The mighty influences of steam and electricity are making themselves everywhere felt; railways are being built, canals dug, telegraphs erected, mines opened and worked on the newest and most improved systems. The civilization of the West is pouring into the land through a thousand different channels.

BOTANICAL GARDEN, ADELAIDE.

AUSTRALIA.

AUSTRALIA is an immense island, containing three millions of square miles, and is about as extensive as all the United States. It is yet in its infancy, and may hereafter, from its great resources and its geographical position, become the greatest country on the globe. This great island was discovered by the Dutch in 1610, but the whole of it is now claimed as a territory of Great Britain. Captain James Cook, the celebrated navigator, took possession of it in 1770. It is divided into North Australia, West Australia, South Australia, Victoria, Queensland and New South Wales. Of all the Australian colonies the oldest is New South Wales, it having been settled in 1788; and till West Australia was established, in 1829, it included all the English settlements in the country. It was originally much more extensive than it is now, including much of Victoria and Queensland, which were separated from it in 1851. Its area in acres is about five times that of England and Wales, and more than half as large again as France.

Sydney, the capital of New South Wales, is the oldest city of Australia. It is well built, with fine, broad streets and imposing public buildings, which, combined with its commanding situation on a splendid harbor, has gained for it the appellation of "The Queen of the South." Port Jackson, the harbor of Sydney, for variety, extent, and picturesque combinations, rivals, if it does not surpass, the celebrated harbor of Rio de Janiero. Mr. Anthony Trollope speaks of it as "so inexpressibly lovely that it makes a man ask himself whether it would not be worth his while to move his household gods to the eastern coast of Australia, in order that he might look on it as long as he can look at anything."

Victoria, once called Australia Felix from its beauty and fertility, though the smallest of the Australian colonies, is the most populous and the most wealthy. Melbourne, capital of the colony, has, in the course of forty years, become a city of 200,000 inhabitants, or, with the suburbs within a ten-mile radius, 250,000, thus already taking rank in the ninth place amongst the cities of the British empire, while in other respects unquestionably one of the best-built and finest in the world. As this city is but little known to the world at large, it seems desirable that we should give a brief statement of its wonderful history, and description of its present characteristics.

John Pasco Fawkner died at Melbourne on September 4th, 1869, the undisputed oldest inhabitant in a vast city that had no existence when he sailed up the Yarra-yarra in the schooner Enterprise in the summer of 1835. Where in the midst of a wilderness he had plowed his land and grown his first crop of wheat a city had arisen which, with its suburban townships, numbered nearly 170,000 souls. Long lines of carriages followed the pioneer to his grave, and the people in their thousands lined the spacious streets as the procession passed.

Cook, Flinders and Grant did little more than name the prominent headlands along the southern shores of Australia. Lieutenant Murray, R. N., 1802, discovered Port Philip bay, and in the following year Colonel Collins, with soldiers and convicts to the number of 402, attempted to form a settlement on its shores. A bad site was chosen; the expedition was a failure, and in 1804 the settlement was transferred to Van Diemen's Land. One man named Buckley ran away into the bush and lived for thirty years among the natives. In 1824 two cattle-owners in New South Wales came in search of new pasture-grounds along the Murray river and across the Australian Alps to the present site of Geelong, but returned without accomplishing any result beyond exploring the district. The first attempt to colonize the territory now known as Victoria was in 1834, when Mr. Thomas Henty, with a few free settlers, located themselves at Portland bay, 234 miles from where Melbourne now stands. In the following year John Batman led a party to Port Philip bay and made a remarkable treaty with the blacks, by which they ceded to him 600,000 acres for a quantity of blankets and tomahawks, or, as one account states, for "three sacks of glass beads, ten pounds of nails, and five pounds of flour." The English government subsequently annulled this contract, but the representatives of Batman received £7,000 in compensation. Three months after Batman and his helpers had got to work John Fawkner's schooner sailed past their settlement and up the Yarra-yarra, and was made fast to a eucalyptus tree on the bank, opposite to where the Melbourne Custom House, an ornament to the city, now stands.

The news of the discovery of rich pastures in the neighborhood of Port Philip bay soon spread far and wide. In spite of some opposition from the British government, emigrants flocked thither from New South Wales and Tasmania, taking with them their sheep and cattle. At the end of a few months the settlement contained a population of 224, of whom 38 were women. The possessions of the colonists included 75 horses, 555 head of cattle, and 41,332 sheep. It was at this period that William Buckley, the convict, who had escaped from the disastrous expedition of Collins in 1803, returned to his compatriots. He had been thirty-three years among the blacks and quite forgotten his own language.

There was little in "The Settlement," as infant Melbourne was for some time called, to suggest its future wealth and vastness. In January, 1838, there were a couple of wooden houses serving as hotels for the country settlers when they brought up their wool to send off by ship, or for new arrivals on their way to the "bush." "A small square wooden building" (says Mr. George Arden, an eye-witness), "with an old ship's bell suspended from a most defamatory-looking, gallows-like structure, fulfilled the duty of church or chapel to the various religious denominations, whence, however, the solemn voice of prayer and praise, sounding over the yet wild country, had an effect the most interesting and impressive." There were two or three shops, each selling anything useful, and a branch of a Tasmanian bank. Six months later numerous brick houses of two or three stories had risen; the inns had become handsome and convenient; streets were marked out and macadamized; the population had quadrupled, and a multitude of dealers had opened various kinds of shops.

Fawkner opened the first inn, and on January 1st, 1838, started the first newspaper, *The Melbourne Advertiser*. The first nine numbers were in manuscript, and limited to a circulation of one copy, which was kept at Fawkner's bar for public use.

With the exception of a disastrous financial crash in 1842, the result of over-speculation and land-jobbing, the history of Melbourne till the gold discoveries in 1851 was a history of steady progress and success. Scarcely was the Port Philip settlement five years old when it began to clamor for separation from New South Wales. In 1842 its local institutions were improved, and it was allowed to send six delegates to the Legislative Council at Sydney. But Melbourne continued agitating till, in 1850, its prayer was granted, and the British Parliament passed an act by which, on July 1st, 1851, Port Philip became a separate colony, under the new name of Victoria, said to have been chosen by the queen herself.

But it was in this year, ever memorable in the history of Melbourne, that a rich gold-field was discovered within a hundred miles of the city, at Ballarat. The discovery of gold changed, as by the wave of the magician's wand, the entire future of life in Australia. The pulse of the community, which erewhile beat quietly and steadily, at once mounted to fever-heat. There was but one theme on every lip, and that theme was "gold." It intoxicated the whole body of the people. They rushed pell-mell to the various spots where the dazzling metal was supposed to be obtainable. The laborer left his implements of toil and ran. The mechanic quitted his bench. The clerk abruptly threw up his situation. The merchant left his counting-room. The barrister left his case unfinished. Melbourne was all but deserted. In the course of a few months about one-half of the entire male population of the colony had left their wonted avocations and gone on the popular adventure. Then, too, the people came "in hot haste" from the neighboring colonies, crowd following crowd as fast as ships by sea and conveyances by land would bring them—men of every shade of character, and thousands with no character at all, each and every one attracted by the bewildering glare of virgin gold. Little wonder that business came to a stand-still; that the old landmarks were torn up; that the foundations of society were out of course, and that social disorganization, rapine, dissipation, and even murder, speedily prevailed.

Not less than 10,000 persons landed at Melbourne in one week in 1851. Successful diggers came down to the city, squandered their gold like madmen, and went to search for more. It became possible to realize vast fortunes by supplying the wants of the gold-seekers, when men were willing to give an ounce of gold for a bottle of champagne. Lodgings of any kind were at a high premium; to be allowed to stretch on the floor of a hotel coffee-room was the utmost favor many could obtain. The boilers of a steamer lying on the wharf were used as a sleeping-place by people who would have paid well for beds if money could have obtained them. To meet the exigencies of the case a town of tents, known as Canvas Town, rose on the St. Kilda road. Several thousand inhabitants lived in this temporary settlement, which was regularly laid out in streets, and existed for several months.

The government service had a great difficulty in keeping up its staff of officials. An eminent lawyer from Sydney, appointed to a seat on the bench of the Supreme Court of Victoria, could find nowhere to lay his head, and after spending one night in an arm-chair at the Melbourne Club, resigned the appointment and went back. At one period the police force sank far below the required strength. A mounted force, known as the Cadets, was enrolled, in which many young men who found the labor of gold-digging did not suit them were glad to earn good wages. These guardians of the peace had for a time a prospect of plenty of work before them. The convicts from Tasmania had rushed over in swarms. But, notwithstanding the disorganization produced by the gold-fever, order was on the whole remarkably well maintained. For a while bushrangers made the roads to the diggings unsafe. During 1852-3-4 there were frequent robberies, but with the excitement of those years all disorderly symptoms passed away, and the colony of Victoria settled down into a law-abiding community. With the exception of the Ballarat riots in December, 1854, no serious disturbance is recorded in its history. Gold brought together a teeming population, developed all the resources of the country, constructed railways, and made Melbourne.

Several expeditions have been undertaken by the Australians for the purpose of unveiling the secrets hidden in the interior of their great continent.

In 1859 twenty-four fleet camels were procured from India for an expedition. The command was given to Robert O'Hara Burke, a superintendent of Victoria police, and previously connected with the Irish constabulary and Australian cavalry. One of his colleagues was William John Wills, of the Melbourne Observatory, a young hero with a passionate love for exploration. In August, 1860, the party, consisting of fifteen men with their camels and provisions for twelve months, set forth amidst the acclamations of the Melbourne citizens. A depot was established at the Barcoo river, and on December 16th Burke and Wills, with two men named Gray and King, pushed forward with a horse and six camels northward, and at length reached the Flinders river, where they met the tidal waters of the Gulf of Carpentaria.

On February 23d, 1861, they commenced the return journey, having accomplished the feat of crossing the Australian continent. On April 21st Burke, Wills and King reached the Barcoo rendezvous to find it deserted. The expedition had abandoned the depot that day, giving their companions up for lost. The three adventurers wandered about in the wilderness till near the end of June, subsisting miserably on the bounty of the natives, and partly by feeding on the seeds of the nardoo plant. At length both Burke and Wills died of starvation.

Melbourne abounds in edifices as substantial and enduring as are those of any place in the world; the material, bluestone, of which most of the warehouses and many of the public buildings are in whole or in part constructed, being, so to speak, of an imperishable nature. The House of Parliament, situated on an elevated site at the top of Bourke street, with its grand façade and tower, 270 feet in height, is a magnificent structure. The richly decorated halls in which the two chambers meet have each a measurement of 76 feet by 40 feet, and 36 feet in height. There are splendidly-appointed reading and other rooms for senatorial comfort and convenience and a well-stocked library.

Melbourne has a university which is endowed by government, the professors having liberal salaries and residences. In connection with the university there is a museum—a large hall with galleries running round it—in which are displayed stuffed specimens of Australian birds, beasts and reptiles. The immense variety of Marsupialia, for which Australia is so remarkable, is here fully exemplified. Upon the walls are displayed the bones of the diprotodon—an awful kangaroo of the tertiary epoch, whose pouch rivalled the capacity of a modern omnibus.

There are several markets in Melbourne. One of the principal, and perhaps the most interesting, is the Eastern, familiarly known as "Paddy's Market." Early in the morning on Wednesdays and Saturdays this market presents an animated scene. The abundant stores of potatoes, cabbages, pineapples, peaches, apricots, plums, and a variety of other fruits and vegetables, attract a goodly concourse of buyers. But it is on Saturday night that this market bursts forth in its full glory, when the stalls are lit up with gaslight.

Along the passages an immense crowd of men and women and boys and girls passes continu-

ORNITHORHYNCHUS.

ously, gazing, buying, talking, laughing, whilst the dealers shout the merits of their wares. Everything that can be eaten or drunk, or worn, or worked with or played with, seems on sale here. Oysters, stockings, crockery, chisels, Bibles, song-books, old clothes, opossums, tin-ware, black swans, and innumerable other things are all near at hand; fish, flesh, fowl, and vegetables of every sort are cheap and plentiful. "Cheap Jack" shouts his bargains, and Punch and Judy and Dog Toby attract their crowd as in the old country.

Mutton is a very abundant article. "I was attracted by a loud voice," says an eye-witness, "calling out, 'This way for cheap mutton!' A red-faced man in butcher's garb was standing on a barrow in the midst of the crowd. Around him were piled a number of half-carcasses of sheep, ready-dressed for cooking. The mutton was sweet and of fair average quality. The salesman was holding up his half-sheep (cut lengthways through the middle), while he waved the other hand with animated gestures toward his audience. 'Cheap mutton here! Come along! Now's your time! Who'll buy cheap mutton?' A pause ensues; the mutton is lowered for a moment to ease the arm; up it goes once more, and then I hear him sing out, 'Sold again and got the sugar' (colonial slang for ready money). 'Half a sheep for a shilling!' The purchaser was a little girl, who tottered along with her load as if she held a little brother upsidedown. A young man took another at the same price. But there were few bidders; the supply was evidently greater than the demand; and it was certain that the salesman would have several half-carcasses unsold.... What, I thought, would the starving poor, the employed and unemployed classes of other great towns and cities think of this—half a sheep for a shilling, and scarcely any bidders!"

In Little Bourke street there is a Chinese quarter. In the dull, dark, and not very clean shops, tea, rice, opium, and various articles specially required by the Chinese are the chief commodities sold. The adjacent houses are tenanted by swarms of Celestials. Of these Chinese immigrants numbers are hawkers in the streets of Melbourne, carrying about various fancy wares in baskets suspended from the ends of stout bamboo-canes laid across their shoulders. At Emerald Hill there is a Chinese joss-house, or place of worship, with all the appurtenances for the due celebration of religious rites.

AUSTRALIAN.

The old colony of South Australia is generally flat, as compared with Victoria or New South Wales. Although so far south, and therefore farther from the tropics, and geographically more temperate, yet South Australia is very hot, and perhaps suffers more during the summer months of December, January and February than any of the other colonies, the thermometer often rising at Adelaide, the capital, to 110° or 115° in the shade; but the rest of the year is pleasant.

The climate of West Australia is generally admitted to be one of the finest known. The mortality of the whole colony is said to have averaged only one per cent. since its formation, that of Great Britain being about two and a half per cent. Snow is unknown, and ice is only seen in the morning and in the depth of winter. For men able to work, who possess a very small capital, and have some knowledge of agriculture, there is probably no country in the world where a comfortable and even a luxurious existence may be attained as easily as in West Australia.

Queensland possesses a more uniformly hot climate than the more southern settlements. Over by far the larger part of the colony frost and ice are unknown; while at Brisbane, the capital, the winter—June, July and August—is a most delightful season, with cool mornings and evenings, bright and warm days, the sky always blue, and the air wonderfully transparent. The colony is almost entirely free from epidemic diseases, and is very favorable to those with a tendency to consumption.

The great agricultural specialty of Australia is its wool, the produce of about fifty millions of sheep. Mining forms one of the most remunerative branches of industry. South Australia contains productive copper mines; New South Wales extensive coal measures, and especially gold. The richest gold-fields, however, are those of Victoria. In New South Wales a considerable number of diamonds have been discovered; and these valuable gems have also been found in Victoria and Queensland.

The natives of Australia are described as the most degraded people in the world. They are black, and have frizzled hair like negroes; and they have very lean arms and legs. Their features have a resemblance to the monkey tribe, and they are said to be not much handsomer or more intelligent than the orang-outangs found in the Malaysian islands.

When Captain Cook, about one hundred years ago, was describing the naked savages of the east coast of Australia, he said: "Their principal ornament is the bone which they thrust through the cartilage which divides the nostrils from each other. Our seamen, with some humor, called it their sprit-sail-yard; and, indeed, it had so ludicrous an appearance that, till we were used to it, we found it difficult to refrain from laughter."

The exceedingly wide-spread custom of tattooing the skin may also be alluded to here, as the result of the same propensity as that which produces the more serious deformations. The rudest form of the art was practised by the now extinct Tasmanians and some tribes of Australians, whose naked bodies showed linear or oval raised scars, arranged in a definite manner on the shoulders and breast, and produced by gashes inflicted with sharp stones, into which wood-ashes were rubbed, so as to allow of healing only under unfavorable conditions, leaving permanent large and elevated cicatrices, conspicuous from being of a lighter color than the rest of the skin.

LAKE ROTHE-MAHANA.

NEW ZEALAND.

IN the centre of the South Pacific, and far removed from the shores of Australia, rises the island group bearing the name of New Zealand. It consists of two large and several smaller islands, with a total area estimated at 101,000 square miles. The two large islands are marked by striking physical differences. North Island, with its varied outlines, consists of two sections—the northwestern peninsula, abounding in fertile and well-watered valleys, and the main body of the island, characterized by gently sloping hilly ranges and low-lying table-lands, varied here and there by volcanic peaks. The country is everywhere covered with a luxuriant growth of timber, except in the heart of the island, which is full of lakes, hot springs and geysers, depositing silica and sulphur, like those of the Yellowstone Park in the United States.

South Island, which is the longer and more extensive of the two, presents a very different physical aspect. Its western side is traversed in its entire length by the so-called Southern Alps, a massive range from 10,000 to 13,000 feet high, whose slopes, up to the snow-line, are densely wooded. Towards the west they contain vast snow-fields and glaciers, extensive tracts filled with stony detritus, clefts and fissures of enormous depth, whence flow icy streams to the lakes of the table-land.

The lakes of New Zealand deserve especial notice, as they present many interesting features. They may be generally classed as due either to volcanic or glacial action, the former being the case in the North, the latter in the South Island. In the lake region of North Island there are remarkable groups of hot springs of various degrees of temperature.

But the most wonderful part of the lake region is the small Rothe-Mahana, or Warm lake, with its boiling springs and silicious terraces. Almost everywhere around the lake there is a seething, hissing and boiling sound from the numerous escapes of steam, boiling water, or hot mud; while in the lake itself hot springs are so numerous that the whole body of water is kept at a temperature of 90° or upwards.

The aborigines of New Zealand are called Maoris. These Maoris (which in their language means simply "men") are dying out quite as rapidly as are the Hawaiians, to whom they are akin. In 1842 their numbers were estimated at 114,000; in 1850 at 70,000; now 40,000. According to their own tradition their ancestors came hither some 400 years ago, in canoes, from an island which they called Hawaiki, supposed by some to be Hawaii; by others, who think it unlikely that canoes could make that long voyage of 4,000 miles, one of the nearer Navigator group. The first supposition finds some support from the fact that when Cook was there, in 1766, his Hawaiian interpreter found no difficulty in conversing with the Maoris. Whether there were any human dwellers on the island before the Maoris arrived there is very uncertain. The only quadruped they found was a kind of rat; but birds were plentiful, and the waters abounded in fish, which, with the

NEW ZEALANDER.

roots of a kind of flag, and sweet potatoes, which they apparently brought with them, constituted their chief food when the whites first came in contact with them.

Physically, the Maoris are a fine people. In stature and physical strength they will compare favorably with Europeans. Mentally and morally, in most respects, they rank far above the majority of uncivilized people. Generally they are of a light-brown color, with straight, black hair and prominent features.

New Zealand is most favorably situated for the growth of all the fruits and vegetables of the temperate zone. In minerals, though late in the field, it now almost rivals the richest colonies of Australia. Large amounts of silver have also been exported.

The Maoris are fully conscious of their approaching fate, a fate in which not only the people themselves, but also the native vegetable and animal life seem involved. The Maoris rightly say: "As the white man's rat has extirpated our rat, so the European fly is driving out our fly. The foreign clover is killing our ferns, and so the Maori himself will disappear before the white man."

POLYNESIA.

POLYNESIA consists of many groups of small islands, which are scattered over a large extent of the Pacific ocean. None of them are wholly occupied by civilized people.

The Sandwich islands are among the most important in Polynesia. The islands were discovered by Captain Cook, in 1777, and named in honor of the Earl of Sandwich. In February, 1779, the famous navigator was killed by the natives on the shore of Kaawaloa bay, Hawaii. The spot where he fell is now marked by a stone shaft, erected by England in 1874.

"As these islands are not united under one government," says an early account of their discovery, "wars are frequent among them. The inhabitants are undoubtedly of the same race as those that possess the islands south of the equator; and in their persons and manner approach nearer to the New Zealanders than to their less distant neighbors either of the Society or Friendly islands. Tattooing is practised by the whole of them." Some ten or twelve years after their discovery a Napoleonic king of Hawaii invaded successfully the several islands of the group, conquered and placed them under his own rule, and founded a dynasty that lasted until February, 1874.

From their conquest until the present day the population of the island has steadily and rapidly decreased. Out of an estimated total of 400,000 natives in 1779, only 58,765 remained in 1866, and this latter number was still further diminished between the years 1866 and 1872 to 51,531. The causes of this decrease are said to be "wars, drunkenness and human sacrifices;" but, according to native traditions, vast numbers of the people were swept away during the first part of the present century by periodical epidemics of small-pox and measles. Whatever the cause, the ominous fact remains.

The natives are simple, honest, and obviously cheerful and contented; but, like all residents of the tropics, they are wanting in physical energy. "The people," says a recent writer, "are surprisingly hospitable, and know how to make a stranger at home; they have leisure and know how to use it pleasantly; the climate controls their customs in many respects, and nothing is pursued at fever-heat, as with us."

A great drawback to the progress of the islands was, until late years, the lack of steam communication with the United States; but this has been removed by the Pacific Mail Company, whose steamers now touch at Honolulu once a month, on their voyages between San Francisco and Australia.

The Society islands likewise belong to Polynesia. They are situated about a thousand miles south of the equator, which is nearly the same distance that the Sandwich islands are north of it.

The largest of the Society islands is called Tahiti, or Otaheite. It is a hundred miles in circumference, and is inhabited by about ten thousand people. Like the natives of the Sandwich islands, they are generally handsome and of agreeable manners.

The Otaheitan men are a fine, tall set; the women very handsome and graceful, but somewhat small. They are very fond of dress, and attend the missionary chapels in wonderful costumes formed of portions of a European toilette. They have been brought under the influence of Christianity by Methodist pastors.

Byron, in his poem, "The Island," has written a beautiful description of Otaheite:

> "The chase, the race, the liberty to roam,
> The soil where every cottage showed a home;
> The sea-spread net, the lightly-launched canoe,
> Which stemmed the studded archipelago
> O'er whose blue bosom rose the starry isles;
> The healthy slumber caused by sportive toils;
> The palm, the loftiest dryad of the woods,
> Within whose bosom infant Bacchus broods.
>   .   .   .   .   .   .
> "The cava-feast, the yam, the cocoa's root,
> Which bears at once the cup, and milk, and fruit;
> The bread-tree, which, without the ploughshare, yields
> The unreaped harvest of unfurrowed fields."

DYAKS OF BORNEO.

THE MALAYSIAN ISLANDS.

AMERICA ought no longer to be called the New World; for one composed of the islands which lie in the Pacific and Indian oceans is newer, and to this region the name of Oceania, or Oceanica, has been given. If all the islands were put together, they would cover a space of at least four millions of square miles; that is a space larger than the whole of Europe. Those islands which lie in the Indian ocean, near the continent of Asia, are called Malaysia. The largest of them are Borneo, Sumatra, and Java. Scarcely anything has been written about the history of Malaysia, for the islands are chiefly inhabited by the natives, who keep no record of passing events, and have no desire to know the deeds of their forefathers.

The history of Java is best known, but it is not very important or interesting. It was discovered by the Portuguese in the year 1510. They found it an exceedingly fertile island, producing abundance of sugar, coffee, rice, pepper, spices, and delicious fruits. There were also mines of gold, silver, diamonds, rubies and emeralds. The island is six hundred and fifty miles in length. Soon after its discovery, the Dutch got possession of a large portion of it. They built the city of Batavia, on the north-western coast of the island.

The city is situated on a low, marshy plain, and canals of stagnant water are seen in many of the streets. But the edifices were so splendid that Batavia was called the Queen of the East. Its beauty was much increased by the trees that overshadowed the streets and canals. In the year 1780 the population amounted to a hundred and sixty thousand. People from all the different parts of the world were among them. But the Europeans were the fewest in number, although the government was in their hands. For a time Batavia rapidly declined; the climate was so unhealthy that strangers were attacked by dreadful fevers. Of late years the city has been rendered more healthy by drainage. In the year 1811 the English took possession of the island of Java. They kept it till 1816, and then restored it to its former owners. The Dutch are said to exercise great tyranny over the natives.

A VOLCANIC CONE.

The great mountains of Java are all volcanic cones, situated for the most part near the central line of the island. Eight of these exceed 10,000 feet; seven more exceed 9,000, and eight are between 7,000 and 9,000 feet high, and there are many others of less elevation. The total number of volcanic peaks in Java is said to be forty-six, of which twenty are more or less in a state of activity.

The celebrated Valley of Poison is an extinct crater about half a mile in circumference, which is an object of terror to the inhabitants of the country. Every living thing which penetrates into this valley falls down dead, and the bottom is covered with bones and carcasses of tigers, deer, birds, and even of men, all killed by the copious emanations of carbonic acid gas. In another crater there are sulphurous exhalations which have killed tigers, birds, and innumerable insects. The tales of the deadly "upas tree," which was said to destroy all creatures which slept beneath its shade, or any birds which flew over it, have originated in the word "upas" (poison) being applied to these places and also to a poisonous tree charged with the gases from them.

Of the two aboriginal races of Malaysia, the Malays and the Papuans, the Malays are decidedly the more populous and important. They have spread their language, their domestic animals, and some of their customs widely throughout the Pacific and Indian oceans. They are held to belong to the so-called Mongolian division of mankind. They may be divided into two great groups—the savage and the semi-civilized peoples. The Dyaks of Borneo are the best example of the former. They have no writing or literature; no regular government or religion, and they wear only the scantiest clothing of the usual savage type. But they are by no means a low class of savages, for they build good houses, they cultivate the ground, they make pottery and canoes, they work in iron, and they even construct roads and bridges. At home they are ingenious in their use of wood, bamboo, and a sort of felt cloth with which they roof their houses. We have seen a set of tiny models of Malay workmanship, all executed in these materials, including little houses, household utensils, a yoke for carrying weights across the shoulders, and a bridge fit to span a torrent or narrow river, with a host of other articles.

The Malays excel as seamen, and Malay sailors are in the Eastern seas what the Maltese are in the Mediterranean ports. But it must be confessed that they bear a worse character. The "treacherous Malay" comes up again and again in all tales of Eastern mutinies or piracies; and his dark skin and lithe form have frequently earned him, from rough English captains, the name of a "Malay Devil."

> "He is as treacherous as his coral reef,
> As supple as his palm, and though he loves
> The colors of his bird of paradise,
> His heart is as his skin—and both are dark."

INDEX.

A

Agriculture and commerce of England, 18.
Army and navy of England, 22.
Alfred the Great, 30.
Assassination of William Rufus, 42.
Attempt of England to subjugate Scotland, 58.
Agincourt, Battle of, 73.
Armada, Destruction of the Spanish, 86.
Art, literature and science in England, 125.
Agriculture and manufactures in Ireland, 131.
Agriculture and manufactures in Scotland, 148.
All climates within the United States territory, 161.
Americus Vespucius, 168.
American Independence, 171.
Argentine Confederation, 179.
Aboriginal inhabitants of Canada, 190.
America, Discovery of, by John Cabot, 190.
Arnold and Major Andre, 217.
America, First book printed in, 221.
Adams' administration, 225.
Assassination of Abraham Lincoln, 245.
    of President Garfield, 252.
American painters and sculptors, 271.
    inventive talent, 272.
Assassination of Julius Cæsar, 282.
Augustan age of Roman literature, 282.
Attempted assassination of King Humbert, 298.
Assassination of Marat by Charlotte Corday, 305.
Architecture in Paris, 312.
Art and literature in Spain, 317.
Alhambra, Palace of the, 316.
Anecdote of Murillo, 318.
    of Marshal Soult, 318.
Alfonso, King of Spain, 322.
Amusements and recreations of Scandinavia, 330.
Arnold von Winkelried, 334.
Alpine ascents, 336.
Art, science and literature of Germany, 348.
Austria, its government and population, 357.
Assassination of Alexander II. of Russia, 373.
Alexander III. of Russia, 373.
Algiers, 422.
Abdel Kader defeated by the French, 424.
African wild animals, 425.
    Pigmies, 425.
    explorers, 428.
Arabia and the Arabs, 434.
Australian colonization, 462.
    gold-diggings, 465.
Aboriginal inhabitants of Australia, 469.

B

British tribes and races, 11.
Boadicea, Queen, 26.
Battle of Hastings, 37.
Bacon, Roger, 56.
Bards, the Welsh, 56.
Battle of Crecy, 62.
    of Poictiers, 63.
    of Agincourt, 73.
    of Bosworth, 80.
Bloody Mary, 84.
Bacon, Francis, Lord, 89.
Bunyan, John, 103.
Battle of the Boyne, 105.
Boyne, Battle of the, 105.
Beaconsfield, Lord, 122.
Blarney Stone, in Ireland, 134.
Bruce, King Robert, 157.
Battle of Bannockburn, 158.
Balboa's discovery of the Pacific, 169.
Benito Juarez, 173.
Bolivar, Simon, 178.
Brazil, the country and people, 181.
British Columbia, 199.
Boston Harbor, Destruction of tea in, 210.
Battle of Lexington, 212.
    of Bunker Hill, 213.
    of Trenton, 214.
Bennington, Battle of, 214.
Burgoyne, Surrender of, 216.
Burr, Aaron, 227.
Battle of Buena Vista, 237.
Bryant, William Cullen, 263.
Book-illustration in the United States, 271.
Beauty of Florence, 288.
Bridge of Sighs, Venice, 290.
Bayard, The Chevalier, 302.
Bastile, Storming of the, 304.
Bonaparte, Napoleon, 306.
Boulanger, General, 313.
Bull-fighting in Spain, 322.
Battle of Lutzen, 328.
    of Morgarten, 333.
    of Sempach, 333.
    of Nefels, 334.
Belgium, 337.
Berlin, Life in, 343.
Bavaria, 360.
Bohemia, 361.
Bajazet, Defeat of, 388.
Battle of Marathon, 398.
    of Thermopylæ, 399.
    of Aboukir, 413.
Barbary States, 422.
Baalbec, Ruins of, 434.
Babylon, Fall of, 436.
British Empire in India, 438.
Burke and Wills, 466.

C

Cædmon, the story of, 28.
Cnute, King, 34.
Crecy, Battle of, 62.
Chaucer, the Father of English poetry, 66.
Chevychase, 69.
Cromwell, Oliver, 94.
Culloden, Battle of, 110.
Canada, Conquest of, 110.
Catholic emancipation in England, 116.
Crystal Palace, 118.
Crimean War, 120.
Columbus, Voyages of Christopher, 164.
Cortez and the conquest of Mexico, 170.
Chili, its prosperous condition, 179.

(477)

Central America, 180.
Cabot, Discoveries by John and Sebastian, 190.
Canada, Constitution of, 197.
    its greatness and vast resources, 197.
Canadian fisheries, 198.
Colonization of New England, 204.
Cornwallis, Surrender of General, 218.
Clay, Henry, 230.
Calhoun, John Caldwell, 231.
Chicago, Great fire in, 249.
Custer, Death of General, 250.
Cleveland, Stephen Grover, 255.
California, Giant trees of, 256.
Chautauqua Lake, 259.
Chromolithography in the United States, 271.
Climate of Italy, 273.
Carthage, Destruction of, 279.
Caius Julius Cæsar, 280.
Catacombs of Rome, 283.
Cathedral of Milan, 292.
Charlemagne, Reign of, 300.
Charlotte Corday, 305.
"Cid," Chronicle of the, 315.
Cervantes, Don Miguel de, 317.
Camoens and his poem of the Lusiad, 323.
Charles XII. of Sweden, 329.
Chamouni, Valley of, 336.
Cologne Cathedral, 349.
Catherine the Great of Russia, 367.
Constantinople, Siege of, 388.
Cleopatra, Death of, 411.
Cairo, Life in, 413.
Cambyses' conquest of Egypt, 416.
Calcutta, "Black Hole" of, 438.
Clive, Robert, 438.
Cashmere, Valley of, 446.
China, Great wall of, 450.
Chinese advertisements, 453.
Chinese in California, 457.
Chinese in Australia, 468.

D

Druidical Sacrifices, 24.
Dunstan, St., and the Devil, 32.
Douglas and Harry Hotspur, 72.
Destruction of the Spanish Armada, 86.
Drake, Sir Francis, 87.
Daniel O'Connell, 137.
Dublin, 140.
Discoveries of Cabot, 190.
Duel between Hamilton and Aaron Burr, 223.
Death of Washington, 225.
Douglas, Stephen A., 240.
Death of Lincoln, 245.
    of Custer, 250.
    of Garfield, 252.
Drake, Joseph Rodman, 262.
Dante and his Divine Comedy, 288.
Death of Napoleon Bonaparte, 308.
"Don Quixote," circumstances under which it was written, 317.
Death of Gustavus Adolphus, 329.
Danish literature, art and science, 330.
Death of Arnold Von Winkelried, 334.
Dutch, Character of the, 339.
Dresden, 346.
Dervishes, Dancing, 392.
Desert of Sahara, 424.
Damascus, Ruins of, 433.
Delhi, Storming of, 440.
Dancing-girls of India, 446.

E

Extent and physical aspect of England, 12.
Early British tribes and races, 23.
England, Norman conquest of, 37.
Eleanor of Castile, 55.
England and Scottish border warfare, 69.
English Revolution, 96.
    statesmanship and oratory, 122.
    literature, science and philosophy, 125.
    rule in Ireland, 130.
Edwards, Jonathan, 221.
Ericsson, Inventions of John, 246.
Earliest inhabitants of Spain, 314.
Elizabeth, St., 345.
Empire, Proclamation of the German, 354.
Early history of Russia, 364.
Epaminondas, 400.
Egypt, Ancient civilization of, 407.
Egyptians, Superstitions of the, 409.
    Invasion of, by Napoleon, 412.
Egyptian temples, 414.
Egypt, Conquest of, by Cambyses, 416.
Egyptian mummies, 419.
Egyptians, Religion of the Ancient, 419.
Empire in India, British, 438.

F

Flodden, Battle of, 82.
Fire of London, 102.
Father Matthew and his temperance campaign, 134.
Fisheries, Scottish, 149.
"Fountain of Youth," 168.
Fisheries, Newfoundland, 198.
Franklin, Benjamin, and his discoveries, 221.
Florence, City of, 288.
    Great men born in, 288.
France, Primitive inhabitants of, 299.
French monarchy under Clovis, 299.
France, Wits and literary men of, 303.
French Revolution, 304.
    Consulate and Empire under Napoleon, 306.
    Republic and Empire under Napoleon III., 308.
Franco-German war, 308.
French greatness in literature, science and art, 313.
Frederick the Great, 342.
French retreat from Moscow, 370.
French defeated at Aboukir, 413.
French, Defeat of Abdel Kader by the, 424.
Female dwarfing of the feet in China, 455.
    fashions in Japan, 461.

G

Godwin and his singular death, 36.
Gaveston, Beheading of, 59.
Glendower, Owen, 71.
Garnet Wolseley, Sir, 122.
Gordon, "Chinese," 122.
Gladstone, William Ewart, 124.
"Giant's Causeway" in Ireland, 139.
Georgia, Settlement of, 207.
Grant, General Ulysses S., 247.
Garfield, Assassination of President, 252.
Giant trees of California, 256.
Garibaldi, his life in New York, 296.
Geographical aspect of Spain, 314.
Granada, Splendor of, 316.
Gustavus Adolphus, his victories, 328.
Gessler, Death of, by William Tell, 332.
Germany, Empire of, 340.
    Art, literature and science of, 348.
Greece, its climate and history, 396.

INDEX.

Greece, Philosophers of, 401.
    Orators and Dramatists of, 402.
Greeks, Religion of the, 406.
Ganges, The, 443.

H

Hastings, Battle of, 37.
Harry Hotspur, 72.
Hampden, John, 94.
Hogarth and his pictures, 111.
Highland and Lowland races in Scotland, 146.
Hamilton, Alexander, 222.
Hayne, Robert, 234.
Hayes, Rutherford B., 250.
Hancock, General Winfield Scott, 254.
Halleck, J. Fitz-greene, 262.
Holmes, Oliver Wendell, 264.
Hannibal and his war with Rome, 278.
Herculaneum, Destruction of, 294.
Humbert, King of Italy, 298.
Holland, Scenery of, 339.
Hohenzollern, House of, 341.
Hanging gardens of Babylon, 435.
Hindoo chronology, 437.
    mythology and literature, 438.
Hastings, Warren, 439.
Havelock, General, 440.

I

Indian mutiny, 121.
Ireland, Character of the country and people, 129.
    English rule in, 130.
    Agriculture and manufactures in, 132.
Irish statesmen, patriots and orators, 138.
    Early civilization and scholarship of the, 141.
Ireland, literature, science and art in, 142.
Indians, Penn's treaty with the, 205.
Italy, Climate and physical features of, 271.
Italian people; their great achievements, 274.
India, invaded by Alexander the Great, 438.
    Dancing-girls of, 446.

J

Japanese, Manners and customs of, 458.
    love of nature, 459.
    religion and mythology, 459.
Japan, Female fashions in, 461.

K

Killarney, Lakes of, 135.
Knox, John, 160.
Kosciusko, Fall of, 367.
Kremlin at Moscow, 378.

L

Literature, Golden age of English, 88.
    of England at the present day, 125.
Legends of lakes in Ireland, 136.
Literature of Ireland, 142.
Lowland races of Scotland, 146.
Literature of Scotland, 150.
Lexington, Battle of, 213.
Literature of the American colonial period, 221.
Lafayette's visit to the United States, 229.
Lee, Surrender of General, 244.
Lincoln, Assassination of Abraham, 245.
Literature of the present day in America, 262.
Longfellow, Henry Wadsworth, 263.

Literature and art in Italy, 274.
Lucretia, Rape of, 276.
Louis XVI., Execution of, 305.
Literature of France, 313.
Literature of the Spanish people, 317.
    of Portugal, 323.
"Lusiad, The," 323.
Lutzen, Battle of, 328.
Luther and the Reformation, 344.
Literature, science and art of Germany, 348.
Lycurgus, Draco and Solon, 398.
Literature of Ancient Greece, 402.

M

Magna Charta, 52.
Margaret of Anjou and the robber, 76.
Mary, Queen of Scots, 86.
Milton and his poetry, 100.
Methodism, Rise and development of, 109.
Moore, Poetry of Thomas, 139.
Mexico, Conquest of by Cortez, 171.
Maximilian shot, 174.
Montcalm, Death of, 194.
Maryland, Settlement of, 201.
Mayflower, Pilgrims voyage in the, 202.
"Monroe Doctrine," 229.
Morse invents the telegraph, 236.
Monitor and Merrimac, 245.
Michael Angelo and Raphael, 286.
Milan Cathedral, 292.
Mirabeau, 305.
Marseillaise hymn, 305.
Murillo, Anecdote of, 318.
Madrid, 318.
Maid of Saragossa, 320.
Mythology of the Norsemen, 326.
Margaret, "the Semiramis of the North," 328.
Morgarten, Battle of, 333.
Moltke, Generalship of Von, 353.
Music and musicians in Austria, 360.
Moscow, 377.
Mahometanism, 386.
Marathon, Battle of, 398.
Memnon, Statue of, 416.
Moses' Well, 416.
Mummies, Egyptian, 419.
Mikado of Japan, 458.
Melbourne, 463.
Maoris, The, 471.
Malaysian Islands, 474.

N

Norman conquest of England, 37.
Newton and his discoveries, 106.
Napoleon Bonaparte, 306.
Nihilists, The, 373.
Novgorod, 379.
Nineveh, Ruins of, 434.
Nautch or dancing-girls of India, 446.
New South Wales, 462.

O

Owen Glendower, 71.
Oglethorpe, James, 207.

P

Poictiers, Battle of, 63.
Poets, Homes of the English, 17.
Plague of London, 102.

Parnell, Charles Stewart, 137.
Pizarro and the conquest of Peru, 176.
Penn's treaty with the Indians, 204.
Poe, Edgar Allan, 266.
Payne, John Howard, 266.
Padua, 291.
Pompeii, Destruction of, 294.
Pius IX., 295.
Peter the Hermit, 300.
Paris, Magnificence of, 312.
Prim, Assassination of General, 321.
Peter the Great, 365.
Plague at Athens, 399.
Philip of Macedon, 400.
Porus, Defeat of, 401.
Philosophers of Greece, 401.
Palestine and Syria, 429.
Persia, Climate of, 436.

Q

Quebec, Founding of, 110.
    Capture of, 110.

R

Robin Hood, Little John and Friar Tuck, 44.
Richard Cœur-de-Lion, 50.
Rob Roy, 148.
Riel's rebellion, 195.
Romulus and Remus, 274.
Roman Catacombs, 283.
Rienzi, Nicoli de, 284.
Rabelais, 303.
Russia, History of, 364.
Russian superstition, 382.
Rameses the Great, 416.
Religion of ancient Egypt, 419.
    of the Japanese, 459.
Rothe-Mahana, Lake, 471.

S

Scandinavian invasion of Great Britain, 30.
Spanish armada, 87.
Shakespeare, 88.
Science and art in England, 125.
Science, art and literature in Ireland, 142.
Scotland, its freedom and independence, 144.
Science, art and literature in Scotland, 150.
Scotland's union with England, 160.
Scott, General Winfield, 238.
Signal Service, United States, 260.
Science, art and literature in the United States, 262.
    in Italy, 274.
    in France, 313.
    in Spain, 317.
Soult, Anecdote of Marshal, 318.
Saragossa and its sieges, 319.
Science, art and literature in Portugal, 323.
Sea-Kings, 326.
Swedes and Norwegians, 330.
Switzerland, early races of, 331.
Sempach, Battle of, 333.
Science, art and literature in Germany, 348.
Siberia, 383.
Science, art and literature in Greece, 402.
Suez Canal, 418.
Science, art and literature in Japan, 459.

T

Tournaments, 58.
Translation of the Scriptures, 92.
Trenton, Battle of, 214.
Taylor and Scott invade Mexico, 237.
Tilden, Samuel J., 251.
Tell, William, 332.
Tyrol and the Tyrolese, 362.
Turkey, Geographical position and population of, 385.
Turkish History, 387.
    Shopkeepers, 392.
Turkey, Women of, 393.
Thermopylæ, Pass of, 399.
Tadmor, Ruins of, 433.
Thugs, The, 445.
Tycoon of Japan, 458.
Ta-mania, 464.

U

Union of Scotland and England, 160.
United States, Remarkable rate of progress of the, 161.
    Settlement of the, 201.
    Treaty of peace between England and the, 218.
    Signal Service, 260.

V

Voyages of Columbus, 164.
Venezuela, 178.
Vatican and St. Peter's, 286.
Venice, Grand Canal of, 291.
Valencia, 315.
Victories of Gustavus Adolphus, 328.
Vienna, Siege of, 358.
Van Diemen's Land, 463.

W

William the Conqueror, 37.
Wat Tyler, Insurrection of, 68.
Wickliffe and the Reformation in England, 73.
"Wars of the Roses," 75.
Warwick the "King-maker," 76.
Witchcraft and astrology, 78.
Wolsey, Fall of Cardinal, 82.
Wallace and Bruce, 157.
Wolfe, Death of General, 194.
Washington, George, 219.
Webster, Daniel, 233.
Whittier, J. G., 265.
Westphalia, Peace of, 341.
William, Emperor of Germany, 351.
Wall, The great Chinese, 450.

Y

Yosemite Falls, 257.
Yarra-yarra, 463.

Zulu war and death of Prince Napoleon, 121.
Zambesi and the Congo, 428.
Zealand, New, 470.

www.ingramcontent.com/pod-product-compliance
Lightning Source LLC
Chambersburg PA
CBHW021425300426
44114CB00010B/657